Goodwill's

DICTIONARY OF
IDIOMS AND PHRASES

By
Anand Sagar

GOODWILL PUBLISHING HOUSE®
B-3 RATTAN JYOTI, 18 RAJENDRA PLACE
NEW DELHI -110008 (INDIA)

Published by
GOODWILL PUBLISHING HOUSE®
B-3 Rattan Jyoti, 18 Rajendra Place
New Delhi-110008 (INDIA)
Tel. : 25750801, 25820556
Fax : 91-11-25764396
E-mail : goodwillpub@vsnl.net
website : www.goodwillpublishinghouse.com

Printed at : Kumar Offset Printers, Delhi-92

A-1

A-1—*the symbol of highest quality*; *first-rate*. The planning of New Delhi is A-1 even today.

Macbeth is A-1 in Shakespeare's plays.

You will find this article A-1 in the market.

ABACK

Taken aback—*taken by surprise*. He was taken aback when he found his friend in the brothel.

ABANDON

Abandon oneself—*to yield without restraint*. It is unfortunate that more and more modern youth are abandoning themselves to liquor.

ABC

ABC—*elementary knowledge.*
I am still learning the ABC of higher life.

He does not know even ABC of politics.

ABIDE

Abide by—*conform; adhere.*
You must abide by the rules of the school.

1

ABLE

Able bodied—*strong; robust.* There is need for able bodied persons in the defence services.

ABLOOM

Abloom—*in flowering state.* Nature is abloom in spring.

ABORTIVE

Abortive effort—*labour without success.* Better be successful in one game than make abortive efforts in all games.

2

ABOUND

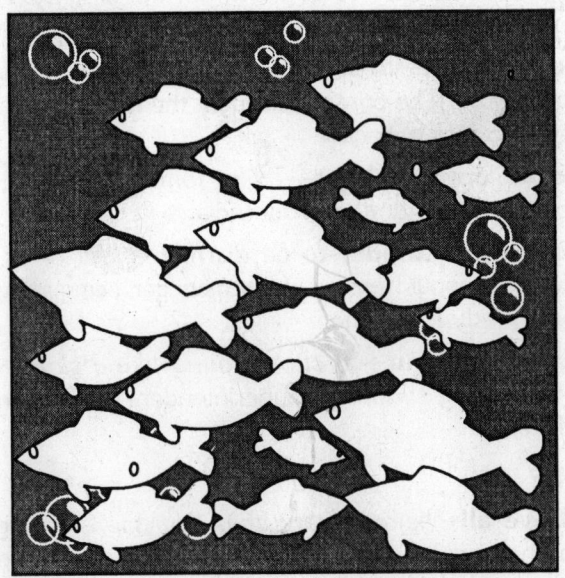

Abound—*to be in plenty*. The sea abounds in fish. Forests abound with wild beasts.

ABOUT

1. **About ship**—*to put the ship on the opposite track; to reverse the course of action, life, history etc.* Mahatma Gandhi about shipped the British Empire.

2. **Bring about**—*to cause to take place.* Quit India Movement brought about the independence of India.

3. **Come about**—*happen : to take place.* Whatever may come about, I must get this contract.

4. **Go about**—*prepare to do.* Please go about your business instead of wasting your time.

5. **Out and about**—*resorted to normal activity.* After a long illness, my father is at last out and about.

6. **To be about**—*to be stir : to be on the point of doing something.* The constable caught the man when he was about to pick a pocket.

7. **To be dotted about**—*To be found anywhere.* Fifth columnists are dotted about India.

8. **To be put about**—*to be distracted.* All of us were much put about because of our manager, being indisposed for a pretty long time.

9. **To hang about**—*to stick around like a slave.* Many a man hang about the Superintendent in Government Offices.

ABOVE

1. **Above all**—*before everything else.* He is very gentle and honest, but above all, he is very hard working.

2. **Above board**—*honourably open; frank and fair.* Your actions should be above board.

3. **Above criticism**—*out of reach.* No human being is above criticism.

4. **Above ground**—*alive; not buried.* Everybody needs something to live by while he is above ground.

5. **Above mentioned**—*stated above.* Please reply to the above mentioned questions immediately.

6. **Above one's *station***—*beyond one's position.* He may try his best but the post is definitely above his station.

7. **Above one's understanding**—*that which is not easily understandable.* His talk is always above one's understanding.

4

8. **Above oneself**—*elated; conceited.* He was above himself when he got the news that he topped the list in the IAS competition.

9. **Over and above**—*in addition to.* Over and above this problem, I want to discuss some other problems too.

10. **To live above one's means**—to *spend more than one's income.* Only the foolish live above their means.

ABRACADABRA

Abracadabra—*gibberish; meaningless; beyond one's understanding.* The talk between two scientific experts was all abracadabra to me.

ABREAST

Abreast—*with fronts in line; side by side.* The youth must march abreast with ideas.

ABRIM

Abrim—*full.* The glass was abrim with liquor.
The child was abrim with joy.

ABROACH

Abroach—*in a condition to let something run out.*
Don't leave the bottle abroach.
His breast was abroach with secrets.

ABROAD

Abroad—*out of doors; spread over a wide area.*
Murder is soon abroad.
He often goes abroad.

ABSENCE

Absence of mind—*obstruction of thought.* He could not do well in history paper on account of absence of mind.

ABSENT

1. **Absent-minded**—*inattentive.* An absent-minded student is never successful in his life.

2. **Absenteeism**—*the habit of absenting oneself from duty, station etc.* Absenteeism is a common feature in government service.

3. **Out of sight, out of mind**—*to forget those who are not present.* Please write me as soon as you reach Mumbai, do not be out of sight, out of mind.

ABSEY

Absey book—*elementary knowledge.* The CBI is still in the absey book about D'Souza's murder.

ABSOLUTE

1. **Absolute alcohol**—*water free alcohol.* Absolute alcohol is very dangerous for your health.

2. **Absolute zero**—*the zero of absolute scale.* For millions of people in the world success is an absolute zero.

6

3. **A captain absolute**—*a self-willed person*. In a democratic government, a leader cannot afford to become a captain absolute, he has also to look the other man's point of view.

ABSORB

Absorb—*very busy*. When I reached home, I found my brother absorbed in studies.

ABSTAIN

Abstain from—*avoid*. You should abstain from drinking.

ABSTRACT

1. **Abstract of title**—*summary of facts concerning ownership*. Please let me have the abstract of title before I buy this property.
2. **To abstract a thing from**—*to withdraw; to take out*. I have abstracted every penny from my bank account.

ABUNDANCE

Abundance of the heart—*overflowing emotion*. Mahatma Gandhi supported the cause of Harijans with abundance of the heart.

ABUZZ

Abuzz—*in motion; merriment; action, etc*. The house was abuzz with marriage celebrations.

ACCEDE

Accede to—*agree to; accept*. After much persuasion he acceded to my request.

ACCEPT

1. **Acceptable to**—*agreeable*. The terms quoted by you are acceptable to me.

2. **Accept one's hand of friendship**—*to be friendly with*. India has always accepted the hand of friendship from every country.

ACCEPTANCE

Acceptance—*confirmation*. The acceptance of our proposals from Messrs Parry & Co. has duly been received.

ACCESS

Access to—*approach; influence*. Do you have any access to the honourable minister?

Accommodating—*ready to make adjustments; obliging; easily corrupted*. Bribe-seekers are very accommodating.

ACCOMPLISH

Accomplished in—*skilled in*. Stanley is accomplished in singing.

Accomplished—*highly skilled; graceful; polished*. Our professor is an accomplished scholar.

ACCORD

1. **Of one's own accord**—*Without any pressure; willingly*. He did everything of his own accord.

2. **With one accord**—*with full agreement*. Election of Shri Lal Bahadur Shastri as India's second Prime Minister was with one accord of the Congress Party.

ACCORDANCE

In accordance with—*in a manner consistent with.* To do things in accordance with law is always a safe thing.

ACCORDING

1. **According as**—*according to the manner in which.* The success in the examination depends according as the student prepares for the same.

2. **According to**—*in accordance with; agreeable to.* I completed the job according to your instructions.

ACCOUNT

1. **Account for**—*explain.* You will have to account for your negligence.

2. **Account of, on**—*because of.* He was fined on account of his absence from the University.

3. **Account with, in**—*having business relations.* Goodwill Publishing House is are in account with most of the booksellers in the country.

4. **Call to/bring to account**—*demand an explanation; clear up a responsibility.* The Lok Sabha called Mr. Jones to account for the import licences scandal.

5. **Go to one's long account**—*die.* Mr. Brown has gone to his long account.

6. **Hold to account**—*hold responsible.* Opposition is held to account for all the troubles in the country.

7. **Make account of**—*set value upon.* A saint does not make account of wordly possessions.

8. **On account**—*in part payment.* A cheque for Rs. 2000 from Messrs Johnson & Co. is received on account, the balance will be received in due course.

9. **On no account**—*for any reason or consideration*. A teacher should on no account beat the student.

10. **On one's account**—*on one's own risk, responsibility*. I may remind you once again that everything you are doing is entirely on your own account.

11. **Take into account**—*consider*. The judge must take into account the nature of the crime before awarding punishment.

12. **Take no account of**—*ignore; overlook*. A modern teacher takes no account of boyish pranks in the class.

13. **The great account**—*the day of judgment*. Only to the great account, the world can save it from a war.

14. **To be accounted**—*to be esteemed*. Chanakya was accounted highly in the court of Ashoka.

15. **To close one's account with**—*to close financial dealings*. We have closed our account with the Punjab National Bank.

16. **To find one's account**—*to derive advantage*. An officer finds his account in whatever he does for you in his routine.

17. **To open an account with**—*to start financial dealings*. We have opened an account with the Syndicate Bank.

18. **To turn to account**—use *for the best*. Wise men turn to account even their misfortunes.

19. **To turn to good account**—*make use of*. You must turn to good account any opportunity that comes your way.

20. **To square on account**—*to clear the accounts*. By paying rupees three hundred only (Rs. 300/-) to us, your accounts will be squared up fully.

ACE

1. **Ace**—*top most or someone of distinguished achievement*. Many ace pilots die in war.
2. **With an ace of**—*narrowly*. After the motor accident he escaped with an ace of death.

ACID

Acid—*biting; ill-natured; critical*. He made an acidic remark.

He is a man of acid nature.

Acid test—*a searching test*. This is the acid test of your character.

ACOCK

Acock—*in a defiant manner*. The Prime Minister finds the opposition acock in the Parliament.

ACQUAINT

To be acquainted with—*to be familiar*. He is acquainted with all the details of problem.

ACQUIRE

1. **Acquired character**—*a character originating in actual life; not inherited*. True greatness is an acquired character.
2. **Acquired taste**—*a liking that comes after some experience*. Love of luxury is an acquired taste.

ACQUIT

1. **Acquit oneself**—*Prove*. The soldier acquitted himself in the battle.
2. **Acquit oneself of**—*to discharge a duty*. He acquitted himself of marrying his daughter.

ACROSS

1. **Come across**—*meet.* I came across an old friend in the bazar.
2. **Get across**—*take effect on the audience.* His speech did not get across in the Parliament.
3. **Put it or get it across**—*to make acceptable; to bring to a successful end.* The bridegroom was unwilling to marry, but his uncle got it across to him.

ACT

1. **Act of God**—*result of natural forces.* An earthquake is an act of God.
2. **Act of grace**—*flavour; pardon.* He was saved from death by an act of grace.
3. **Act on**—*to act in accordance with; to exert influence.* I have acted on your advice.
4. **Act upto**—*come in practice; up to the standard of; to fulfil.* The soldiers die acting upto high sense of patriotism.
5. **To act**—*to behave.* Students are taught to act properly in schools.
6. **To act upon**—*to obey.* Always act upon the advice of elders.

ACTION

1. **Action taking**—*resorting to law instead of fighting.* Action taking is common in urban areas of India.
2. **Man of action**—Sardar Patel was a man of action.
3. **To put in action**—*to practise.* If the Indian Plans were put in action to the extent they are on paper, the economy of India would have improved to a great extent.

ACTIVE

1. **Active life** –*life devoted to good works as opposed to contemplation.* Sikhism is the religion of active life.
2. **Active list**—*a list of full-pay officers engaged in or available for active service.* A Field Marshal, even after retirement, is on active list.
3. **Active service**—*service in the battle area.* Many soldiers die on active service.

ADAM

1. **Adam's ale**—*water.* Please get me a glass of Adam's ale.
2. **Not known from Adam**—*have no knowledge of; have never heard of.* I have not known from Adam your friend Mr. Kapoor.
3. **Old as Adam**—*known from the earliest time.* There are a large number of historical places in India which are as old as Adam.

ADAMANTINE

Adamantine lustre—*distinction.* He is a general of adamantine lustre.

ADD

1. **To add fuel to the fire**—*incite; to worsen matters.* Samuel's way of speech always adds fuel to the fire.
2. **To add insult to injury**—*to harm as well as insult.* An abuse always adds insult to injury.

ADDICT

Addicted to—*enslaved to a habit.* My friend is addicted to liquor.

ADDLE

1. **Addle brained, addle-headed, addle-pated—** *barren; empty; muddled; confused.* Many addle headed people manage to get into the Parliament.

2. **Addle egg—***proud.* My father-in-law is an addle-egg.

ADHERE

Adhere to—*to stick to.* One should adhere to one's principles.

AD HOC

Ad hoc—*formed for one subject only.* From time to time ad hoc committees are formed to examine the cost of living in the country.

ADIEU

To bid adieu—*to take leave.* As the train whistled out, I bade him adieu.

ADO

Ado about nothing—make *much; to exaggerate a trifling matter.* It is a systematic policy of the opposition in Parliament everywhere in the world to make much ado about nothing to pull a feather or two from the cap of the party in power.

ADONAIS

Adonais—*a youth beloved of aphrodite; a beautiful youth; a beau or dandy.* Many an adonais glitters on the campus.

ADVANCE

1. **Advance copy—***one sent in advance.* This is an advance copy of our Dictionary of Idioms and Phrases.

2. **Advance, in**—*beforehand; in front.* Please let me have a copy of your speech in advance.

   The soldiers fought in advance.

3. **Advance in life**—*growing old.* As a man advances in life, he becomes more serious and conscious.

ADVANTAGE

1. **Advantage ground**—*superiority in place of position.* Once a man gets popular, he is at advantage ground to go ahead with his schemes at a quick pace.

2. **To have advantage over**—*to be in a better position.* An employer has always many advantages over his employees.

3. **To take advantage of**—*to avail oneself of.* You can take advantage of my influence for getting a job in Hindustan Machine Tools.

4. **To take a person at an advantage**—*to catch one by surprise.* The girls' team took the boys' team at an advantage in the hockey match.

AD VERBUM

Ad verbum—*word for word.* The school girl crammed the poem, ad verbum.

ADVISE

Advise—*inform.* I have advised him telegraphically that I am leaving by Superfast train.

AEGIS

Under the aegis of—*under the patronage of.* A great function was held under the aegis of the Government of India to honour Khan Abdul Ghaffar Khan.

AFFAIR

Affair of honour—*duel*. The Frenchman died in an affair of honour with an English gentleman to contest the hand of a young beauty in Paris.

AFFETTUOSO

Affettuoso—*tenderly*. As he parted from his beloved friend, he kissed her affettuoso.

AFFILIATE

1. **Affiliate with**—*attached with*. K.M. College is affiliated with Delhi University.
2. **Affiliate to**—*to be a member of*. I am affiliated to the Congress Party.

AFFRONT

To offer an affront to—*to insult*. Mohan offered an affront to his father.

AFIELD

Far afield—*at a distance*. The economic regeneration of our society is still far afield.

AFOREHAND

Aforehand—*beforehand*; *before time*. One often knows of one's death aforehand.

AFTER

1. **After all**—*everything being taken into account*. After all he is your brother, you must not behave like that.
2. **Hanker after**—*to go about desperately*. An intelligent person should not hanker after a clerical job.
3. **Look before and after**—*to think*. A wise man always looks before and after while doing anything.

16

4. **To look after**—*to take care of.* The women should always look after the house and men should work in offices.

AFTERMATH

Aftermath—*later consequences, especially if bad.* Japan is still suffering from the aftermath of atom bomb.

AGAIN

1. **As much again**—*twice as much; double.* I cannot sell this book for hundred rupees; even if you pay as much again, it will still be below my cost price.

2. **Now and again**—*occasionally.* I visit Ireland now and again.

3. **Time and again; over and over again; again and again**—*often; repeatedly.* The teacher explained the problem again and again till every student understood it.

AGAPE

Agape—*with gaping mouth; shocked.* Yahya Khan's action in Bangladesh left the people agape.

AGAINST

1. **Against a rainy day**—*in preparation for hard days.* It is wise to keep some money against a rainy day.

2. **To run against**—*to meet by chance.* I ran against Jennifer in Mumbai during my last visit.

3. **To work against time**—*to work with a view to finishing it within a given time.* We are asking all the labourers of our factory to work against time for completing the Government contract before the end of this month.

AGE

1. **A golden age**—*a prosperous period.* Years 1972 and 1973 were a golden age for my brother's business.
2. **For ages**—*for a long time.* My brother has not written to me for ages.
3. **Over-age**—*too old.* This man is over-age for government employment.
4. **To come of age**—*to become major; to attain the age of 21.* Suresh got married when he came of age.
5. **Under-age**—*too young.* This boy is under-age for military service.

AGENCY

By the agency of—*through the help of.* By the agency of God, we completed our expedition to the Himalayas.

AGITATO

Agitato—*excitedly.* You cannot win a point by speaking agitato.

AGNUS

Agnus dei—*lamb of God.* A politician is no agnus dei.

AGO

Long, long ago—*many, many years back.* Long, long ago, there was a king named Shiraz, who sacrificed everything for the well being of his nation.

AGONY

Agony column—*the part of a newspaper dealing with deaths, missing persons etc.* One day I found the name of my friend in the agony column.

AGREE

1. **Agree on.** At last the family agreed on to carry on the business jointly.
2. **Agree to.** The whole family agreed to the suggestion of Naresh.
3. **Agree with.** I fully agree with you.

AGREEABLE

Agreeable to—*suitable.* This climate is agreeable to me.

AGOG

To be all agog—*to be eager.* The whole nation was all agog to have the last glimpse of Pandit Nehru.

AHEAD

To go ahead—*to advance*. Go ahead with your plans.

AHORSE BACK

Ahorse back—*on the back of the horse*. Napoleon often slept ahorse back.

AIDE-DE-CAMP

Aide-de-camp—*an assistant*. Mr. Tom Walter was an aide-de-camp to the General Manager.

AIL

Ail at—*objection*. What ails him at ?

AIM

1. **Aim at**—*to make up mind for a definite purpose*. He aims at becoming a pilot one day.
2. **Cry aim**—*to encourage by calling out "aim"; to applaud*.
3. **Take aim**—*aim deliberately*. She took aim at her boy friend.

AIR

1. **Air-worthy**—fit *to be flown*. This helicopter is air-worthy.
2. **Airy**—*light of heart*. Many women are airy and hence cannot be depended upon.
3. **An air of absurdity**—*an appearance of foolishness*. He is always having an air of absurdity.
4. **In the air**—*unformed*. Many schemes are in the air.
5. **On the air**—*broadcasting by wireless*. The morning news is now on the air.

6. **Take air**—*become known*. Let your secrets not take air.
7. **Take the air**—*have an airing*. Let us go out and take the air.
8. **To give a person the air**—*to dismiss him*. A dishonest person is given the air in no time.

AJAR

To be ajar—*half open*. When we reached home, we found the door ajar.

ALARM

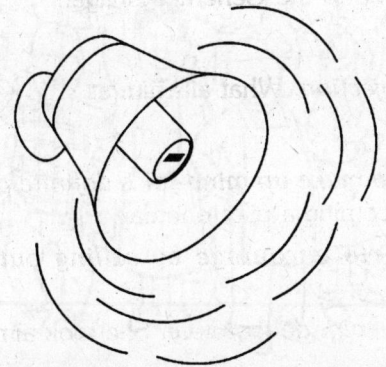

1. **To raise an alarm**—*to give notice of danger*. When the fire broke out in Super Market, the people of the locality raised an alarm.
2. **To take alarm**—*to be frightened*. A person who always takes alarm cannot prosper in life.

ALAS

Alas the day—*unhappy day*. Alas the day when Pandit Nehru lost his life.

ALERT

On the alert—*on the watch*. A constable should be always on the alert.

ALIVE

1. **Alive with**—*swarming with*. The room is alive with mosquitoes.

2. **Be alive**—*be brisk; hurry up*. Be alive to catch the train.

ALL

1. **Alla breve**—*in quick common time*. You must achieve your goal alla breve.

2. **All at once**—*suddenly*. All at once, a robber attacked me.

3. **All and some**—*one and all*. All and some attended the meeting.

4. **All and sundry**—*individually and collectively; everyone*. The law applies to all and sundry.

5. **All cheering**—*giving cheerfulness to all*. It was an all cheering function.

6. **All-fired**—*infernal*. It was an all-fired battle.

7. **All in**—*everything included*. All in, we were five people against fifty.

8. **All in all**—*having full control*. The Principal is all in all in the college.

9. **All of a sudden**—*suddenly*. His mother expired all of a sudden.

10. **All out**—*at full power or speed*. I rode all out to catch the train in time.

11. **All over**—*everywhere; over the whole place*. When I entered the valley, I found water all over.

12. **All over with**—*finished; done with; completely at an end with*. In five minutes it was all over with him.

13. **All-rounder**—*able in various walks of life*. He is an all-rounder, well up both in studies and in games.

14. **All's one**—*it is just the same*. It's all one, whether you go or stay.

15. **All there**—*completely sane; alert*. Till the end he was all there.

16. **All the same**—*nevertheless*. The doctor did his best for the patient; all the same he died.

17. **All to one**—*altogether*. All to one, there were a hundred souls.

18. **All through**—*every part*. The mechanic has looked all through his scooter.

19. **All up with**—*at an end with; beyond any hope for*. The patient was sinking every minute. So it was all up with him.

20. **At all**—*in the least degree or to the least extent possible*. He did not make any effort at all to help himself.

23

21. **For all**—*notwithstanding*. He failed for all the effort he made and money he spent.

22. **For good and all**—*finally*. I intend leaving Delhi for good and all.

23. **Once for all**—*once and once only; finally*. Once for all, I request you to leave this place.

24. **When all is said and done**—*after all*. When all is said and done, life is very difficult for the common man now-a-days.

ALLOT

Allot—*to give ownership*. This house is allotted to me.

ALLOW

Allow for—*to take into consideration*. While marking the papers an examiner always allows for cleanliness.

ALLOWANCE

To make allowance for—*to take into consideration*. In offering this job, we should make allowance for family background.

ALMIGHTY

Almighty dollar—*money*. The almighty dollar rules the world today.

ALONG

1. **All along**—*constantly*. All along you had been saying that you want to go to Kolkata and now when the opportunity has arisen, you decline to do so.

2. **Along with**—*in the company of*. Next time when I go abroad I shall take my wife along with me.

ALOOF

Keep aloof—*stay away*. Keep aloof from all selfish friends.

ALPHA

Alpha and omega—*beginning and end*. Money is alpha and omega of modern man.

Truth is alpha and omega of education.

ALTAR

To lead to altar—*marry*. Jackie led Mary to altar.

AMAZON

Amazon—*a manlike; warlike; strong and vigorous woman*. She was an Amazon in police and cowed down criminals.

AMBROSIA

Ambrosia—*food of the gods that conferred everlasting youth and beauty*. Modern food is no ambrosia.

AMEND

To make amends—*to compensate*. The teacher advised Alan to make amends for his conduct

AMISS

1. **To take amiss**—*to take offence at*. You may tell me whatever you want, I will not take amiss.
2. **Not amiss**—*nothing wrong about it*. To reprimand an erring child sometimes is not amiss.

AMUCK

Run amuck—*become mad*. The constable ran amuck and shot down two fellow policemen.

ANCHOR

1. **At anchor**—*anchored*. The ship is at anchor in the harbour.
   The wife is anchor at home.
2. **To cast anchor**—*to let down the anchor; to come to a halt*. The ship cast the anchor in the port.
   The bride cast the anchor in marriage.
3. **To come to anchor**—*to halt the ship*. After fifteen hours' sailing the ship came to anchor.
4. **Weigh anchor**—*to take up the anchor*. The ship weighed anchor and sailed away.

ANCIENT

The ancient of days—*God*. A man who trusts in the ancient of days, generally succeeds in life.

ANGEL

1. **Angel of death**—*messenger of death*. AIDS is the angel of death.
2. **Visits like angels**—*rare visits*. Now-a-days your visits are like angels.

ANIMAL

Animal spirits—*cheerful and full of life*. This young boy is full of animal spirits.

ANON

Ever and anon—*every now and then*. He comes to my place ever and anon.

ANSWER

1. **Answer back**—*to answer one who expects silent submission.* Few students can answer back the teacher.

2. **Answer the call of nature**—*to defecate.* Everyday we have to answer the call of nature.

3. **Answer to**—*to show signs of accepting as one's name.* Our parrot answers to Timmy.

4. **To answer**—*succeed.* I am afraid his efforts will not answer.

ANT

Ant-hill—*the earth.* We are denizens of the ant-hill.

ANTE

Ante bellum—*before the war.* Bangladesh was a Pakistani colony ante bellum.

ANTIDOTE

To act as antidote—*to neutralize.* Truth acts as an antidote to falsehood.

ANY

1. **Anyone**—*anybody.* The question is so simple that anyone can solve it.

2. **At any rate**—*whatever may happen.* At any rate, I must get first class in the examination.

ANYTHINGARIAN

Anythingarian—*one with no beliefs in particular.* Modern man is an anythingarian.

Anythingarianism is a modern cult.

APART

To set apart—*to devote*. Some time must be set apart daily for prayers.

APE

1. **Apes in hell, leads**—*feigned to be the lot of old maids in after life*. The old maid will lead apes in hell.
2. **God's ape**—*a born fool*. He is a God's ape.
3. **To put an ape in one's hood**—*to make a fool of*. Don't put an ape in your hood.

A-PER-SE

A-per-se—*anything unique in excellence*. Taj Mahal is a-per-se.

APEX

On the apex—*culminating point*. During his last years of life, Jawahar Lal Nehru stood on the apex.

APOGEE

Apogee—*culmination*. This leader has reached the apogee of his career.

A POSTERIORI

A posteriori—*applied to reasoning from experience, from effect to cause*. Life is a battle a posteriori.

APOSTLE

1. **Apostle of**—*advocate of*. He is an apostle of sex.
2. **Apostle of peace**—*one who preaches peace*. Mahatma Gandhi was an apostle of peace.

APPEAL

1. **Appeal**—*influencing power*. Beauty has its own appeal.

2. **Appeal to the country**—*seek approval by a general election*. A democratic government appeals to the country for the confirmation of its policies.

3. **To appeal**—*fascinate*. A beautiful girl always appeals to the eye.

APPEARANCE

1. **Keep up appearances**—*to keep up an outward show, often with intent to conceal, absence of the inward reality*. Everybody is trying to keep up appearances these days.

2. **Put in an appearance**—*to appear in person*. He put in an appearance at the marriage.

3. **To all appearances**—*outwardly*. To all appearances, she was a brave lady.

APPLE

1. **Apple of discord**—*any cause of envy and contention*. Money is the greatest apple of discord in families.

2. **Apple of sodom or dead sea apple**—*a fruit described by the ancients as fair to look upon but turning to ashes when touched*. Politics is an apple of sodom.

   Fame is a dead sea apple.

3. **Apple of the eye**—*something especially dear*. Peter is an apple of his mother's eye.

   Rosy is an apple of her father's eye.

4. **Apple-pie order**—*perfect order*. You will find everything in our house in an apple-pie order.

5. **Upset the apple cart**—*to throw all plans into confusion*. Elections may upset the apple-cart of ruling party.

APPLY

1. **Apply for.** He has applied for a clerical post.
2. **To apply oneself to**—*to devote*. The teacher advised the students to apply themselves to studies.

APPOINTMENT

1. **To fix up an appointment**—*to fix up an engagement with a person at a particular time*. Please fix up an appointment with the manager, before you can see him.
2. **To keep an appointment**—*to appear in time at a fixed place*. He always keeps his appointment.

APPRENTICESHIP

To serve apprenticeship—*to undergo the training of an apprentice*. You must serve apprenticeship with a guru to learn yoga.

APPROACH

Approach stroke or approach shot—*means of approach to highly influential people*. Bribe is an approach shot anywhere.
He enjoys an approach stroke to the minister.

A PRIORI

A priori—*reasoning from cause to effect*. Good ends must be achieved by good means, a priori.

APRON

Apron-strings, tied to a woman's—*bound as a child to its mother*. A minister is tied to the apron-strings of the Prime Minister.

ARAB

Street-Arab—*homeless boy or girl*. Modern world is full of street-Arabs.

ARBOR

Arbor day—*a day set apart for the planting of trees.* India celebrate its Arbor Day in the monsoons.

ARCHITECT

To be the architect of—*maker.* A truly great man is the architect of his destiny.

ARGUE

1. **To argue into**—*to persuade towards a course of action.* Whatever arguments you may give him, he is not going to be argued into your sentiments.

2. **To argue it away**—*to get rid of by reasoning.* Unemployment in the country cannot be argued away.

3. **To argue one out of**—*to satisfy by reasoning against.* One cannot argue a drunkard out of his cup.

ARM

1. **Armed eye**—*the aided eye; opposed to the naked eye.* You can see more stars with armed eye than with the naked eye.

2. **Arm in arm**—*with arms interlocked.* The friends walked arm in arm.

3. **Arms race**—*competition among nations in building armaments.* There is an arms race between the U.S.A. and Russia.

4. **At arm's length**—*away from familiarity.* Keep your enemies at arm's length.

5. **Bear arms**—*serve as a soldier.* When war is on, all patriots bear arms.

6. **In arms**—*carried as a child.* The mother carried the child in arms.

7. **In arms**—*armed.* Police is in arms against dacoits.

8. **King of arms**—*chief herald.* Jawaharlal was the king of arms in politics.

9. **Lay down one's arm**—*surrender.* Japan and Germany laid down arms in the Second World War.

10. **Right arm**—*main support or assistant.* He was the right arm of his father.

11. **Secular arms**—*civil authority.* The secular arm of India is gangrened.

12. **To take up arms**—*to resort to fighting.* They took up arms against the king.

13. **Under arms**—*armed.* Vietnamese are under arms.

14. **Up in arms**—*in readiness to resist.* Israelis are always up in arms.

15. **With open arms**—*hearty welcome.* They received us with open arms.

ARMOUR

Armour-clad—*clad in armour.* They fought each other, armour-clad.

ARSY-VERSY

Arsy-versy—*backside foremost; contrary.* Congress and BJP are arsy-versy.

ART

1. **A fine art**—*to be an operation or practice requiring craftsmanship*. Diplomacy is a fine art.

2. **Art and part**—*sharing; participating*. The student community is art and part of the political movement.

3. **Black art**—*magic*. Sankalp earns his living through black art.

ARTICLE

1. **Articles of faith**—*binding points*. What are your articles of faith in this war of burning buses ?

2. **In the articles of death**—*at the point of death*. He found his beloved friend in the articles of death.

3. **Of great article**—*of great importance*. This is a book of great article.

   This is a man of great article.

ARTISTIC

Artistic temperament— *the emotional and capricious temperament ascribed to artists*. You cannot depend on a man of artistic temperament to keep his promises.

ARTY-CRAFTY

Arty-crafty—*self-consciously artistic*. Modern painters are arty-crafty.

AS

1. **As it were**—*so to speak*. He was a great man; as it were, a lord of the assembly.

2. **As yet**—*up to the moment*. He has not arrived home as yet.

ASHES

1. **Sackcloth and ashes**—*symbol of repentance.* The defeated nations do not wear sackcloth and ashes.

2. **To bring back the ashes**—*to wipe out defeat*. England cricketers did their best to bring back the Ashes from Australia.

3. **To lay in ashes**—*to burn to the ground*. The whole factory lay in ashes.

ASIDE

1. **Aside from**—*apart from*. He has a big bank balance, aside from his landed properties.

2. **Aside to set**—*to quash*. The Supreme Court set aside the Presidential Ordinance.

AT

1. **At a loss**—*to be puzzled*. I am at a loss to understand what made you to go to David's house.

2. **At a standstill**—*without any further movement*. The talks of professors of G.K. College are again at a standstill.

3. **At daggers drawn**—*extremely bitter enmity*. Susan and Jane are at daggers drawn now-a-days.

4. **At fault**—*in the wrong*. When you say you are not familiar with the problem, you are at fault.

5. **At home in**—*fully acquainted*. He is at home in English.

6. **At large**—*unrestrained*. The thief was at large when the police made vain efforts to catch him.

7. **At liberty**—*free to do anything*. He is at liberty now-a-days.

8. **At the bottom of**—*the source of*. David was at the bottom of the conspiracy against the Manager.

9. **At the top of**—*with maximum force*. He shouted at the top of his voice.

ATOMIC

Atomic warfare—*war using atomic weapons*. There is always a danger of atomic warfare while the atomic pile rises in the world.

ATTEND

1. **Attend to**—*pay attention to*. You must attend to your duties.

2. **Attend on**—*to serve*. A hundred ministers attended on the King.

ATTENDANCE

To dance attendance on—*to attend to the convenience of*. The clerks dance attendance on the Superintendent.

AVAIL

To avail oneself of—*to have it or to benefit therefrom*. I will avail myself of this golden chance.

AVANT

Avant-garde—*vanguard; poineers.* Today we do not have any avant-garde in arts, letters or politics.

AWAKE

To be awake to—*to be fully aware of.* The leaders of the country are awake to all the dangers that the nation is facing today.

AWAY

1. **Do away with**—*abolish; kill.* The Parliament did away with the British laws.

   The king did away with his enemies.

2. **Explain away**—*explain so as to make the thing as not to exist.* The Government is trying to explain away the assassination of Mr. Brown.

3. **Fall away**—*dwindle ; waste away; lose zeal and drop off as followers.* When Buddha gave up austerities, many of his followers fell away.

4. **Fire away**—*go on; proceed without further delay.* Please fire away the work assigned to you.

5. **Make away with**—*kill; destroy.* The police made away with the criminal.

6. **Once in a way**—*now and then; occasionally.* He comes to see me once in a way.

AWE

Awe-inspiring—*fearsome.* The personality of this King is awe-inspiring.

AWRY

1. **Look awry**—*to look askance at anything.* When I asked for his help, he looked awry.

2. **To go awry**—*to go astray*. Many a young man goes awry.

3. **Walk awry**—*to go wrong*. Many things are likely to walk awry in life.

AXE

Axe to grind—to *serve a private purpose*. I do not like Stanley, he is always in the habit of grinding his own axe.

A to Z

From A to Z—*completely, thoroughly*. The department store sells A to Z consumer goods.

BABY

1. **Baby-sitting**—*looking after children.* Our teachers and professors do no more than baby-sitting.

2. **Hold the baby**—*to be left in the lurch with a responsibility.* When Prime Minister Jawaharlal Nehru died, Shri Lal Bahadur Shastri held the baby.

BACK

1. **Back and belly**—*clothing and food.* It is very hard to earn back and belly now-a-days.

2. **Back and forth**—*to and fro.* She was walking back and forth in the corridor.

3. **Back down**—*abandon one's opinion of position.* When the public wind blows against them, strong men do not back down.

4. **Back friend**—*a friend who stands at one's back.* There are few back friends left now-a-days.

5. **Back handed**—*indirect; insincere; deceitful.* Beware of the back-handed friend.

6. **Backing down**—*shirking.* Once you have made a commitment, let there be no backing down.

7. **Back-number**—*a person or thing out of date; past the stage of usefulness.* An aged man is a back-number. A dismissed minister is a back-number.

8. **Back of**—*behind*. China is back of Pakistan.

9. **Back out**—*to evade a commitment*. Dishonest business people back out of their deals when the market goes up.

10. **Back out**—*to evade an undertaking*. It is no heroism to back out of your commitments.

11. **Backstair influence**—*secret and illegitimate influence*. Come what may, I will get a job without backstair influence.

12. **Back water**—*to ply oars backwards*. We had to back water *to reach the shore*.

13. **Behind one's back**—*during one's absence*. Behind my back at the office, my assistant puts everything in disorder.

14. **Break the back of**—*to overburden; to accomplish the hardest part of work*. Governance of a big country can break the back of the strongest Prime Minister.
    I have not yet broken the back of writing this book.

15. **On the back of**—*close behind*. Russia is on the back of India.

16. **Put one's back into**—*to do with might and main*. You must put your back into the preparation for examination.

17. **Take a back seat**—*sink into; obscurity*. Mr. Peter now takes a back seat.

18. **Talk through the back of one's neck**—*to talk utter nonsense*. Stop talking through the back of your neck.

19. **To back up**—*to support*. For a good cause one must always back up.

20. **To save one's back**—*to come off scathless with difficulty*. Somehow he did manage to save his back.

21. **To set one's back**—*to make one angry*. I do not think it is advisable to set anybody's back.

22. **To turn one's back upon**—*to turn away*. It is shame on you to turn your back upon your friends in trouble.

BACKBITE

Backbite—*Speak evil in absence*. It is not good to backbite your friends.

BACKBONE

1. **Backbone**—*main support*. A Prime Minister is the backbone of a democratic government.

2. **Backboneless**—*without firmness*. A weak democratic government suffers from backbonelessness.

3. **To the backbone**—*thoroughly*. All our staff are honest to the backbone.

BACKWARD

Backward and forward—*to and fro*. One's luck goes backward and forward.

BACON

1. **To bring one the bacon**—*to succeed in one's purpose*. I had to work hard before I brought him the bacon.

2. **To save one's bacon**—*to save oneself with great difficulty*. Thank God, I have saved my bacon.

BAD

1. **Bad blood**—*ill feeling*. Do not have bad blood with anyone.

2. **Bad debt**—*a debt which cannot be recovered*. Sooner or later you have to write off a bad debt.

3. **Bad form**—*ill manners*. A person with bad form does not succeed in life.

4. **Bad man**—*a ruffian*. Every town today is full of bad men.

5. **Bad shot**—*wrong guess*. His examination was a bad shot.

6. **Bad time**—*unfavourable time*. During the bad time many close relatives and friends do not stand by.

7. **Go to the bad**—*to go to the moral ruin*. The whole nation is going to the bad.

8. **In bad books**—*in disfavour*. Tony is in bad books of the principal.

9. **With a bad grace**—*ungraciously*. He received the guests with a bad grace.

BAG

1. **Bag and baggage**—*with all belongings*. I left Pakistan in 1947 bag and baggage.

2. **Bag of bones**—*an emaciated living being*. When my father died in 1966, he was a bag of bones.

3. **In the bag**—*secured or as good as secured*. Russia has India in the bag.

4. **In the bottom of the bag**—*as a last resort*. He had his gun in the bottom of his bag to help his brother in the fight.

5. **Let the cat out of the bag**—*to disclose secrets*. The women quite often let the cat out of the bag.

BAIL

1. **Accept, Admit to, Allow bail**—*to set the prisoner free on security*. The magistrate accepted the bail of the rich man to set the prisoner free.

41

Mr. Robert was admitted to the bail.

Dr. Andrews who murdered his wife, was not allowed bail.

2. **Bail up**—*to secure in a bail; to stop and disarm in order to rob; to put up one's hands in surrender.* The debtor was bailed up.

The thief bailed up the passerby.

When he showed his pistol, the man bailed up.

3. **Give leg bail**—*to be beholden to one's legs for escape.* The thief gave leg bail to the constable.

BALANCE

1. **Balanced personality**—*a steady mind.* Mahatma Gandhi had a balanced personality.

2. **Balance of advantage**—*great influence.* He has balance of advantage in getting the job of an overseer.

3. **To hang in balance**—*to be uncertain.* The future of a young man hangs in the balance.

4. **To lose one's balance**—*to fall physically.* While getting down from the car, my wife lost her balance.

BALL

1. **Ball at one's feet**—*success in one's grasp*. In the next General Elections, no party will find the ball at its feet.

2. **Keep the ball rolling**—*keep things going*. When a man dies, his family has to keep the ball rolling.

BAND

Band of hope—*an association of young persons pledged to life-long abstinence from alcoholic drinks. First instituted in 1847.* There is no band of hope in the world today.

BANDY

Bandy words—*to discuss; to exchange reprimands.* When you have lost a case, bandying words will not save the situation.

BANG

Bang-up—*in the height of excellence of fashion.* Every university boy is in the bang-up.

43

BANK

1. **Break the bank**—*in gambling, to win from the management the sum fixed upon as the limit it is losing on any day.* He broke the bank and won a large sum of money.

2. **From bank to bank**—*from the time a collier begins to descend to his work till he reaches the top again.* From bank to bank a collier works in artificial light and knows not whether it is day or night.

3. **To bank upon**—*to depend.* Even at the age of thirty he banks upon his parents.

BANKRUPT

Go bankrupt—*lose all the money.* Many traders go bankrupt because of their dishonesty.

BANNER

Keep the banner flying—*keep fighting; doing work.* While I am away from the office, please keep the banner flying.

BANNS

To forbid the banns—*make formal objection to a projected marriage.* When the boy wanted to marry, the girl's mother forbade the banns.

BAPTISM

1. **Baptism of blood**—*martyrdom.* Maharani of Jhansi accepted the baptism of blood at the altar of the freedom of India.

2. **Baptism of fire**—*martyrdom by fire*—Guru Arjan Dev, the fifth Guru of the Sikhs, suffered baptism by fire.

BAR

1. **At the bar**—*to practise as a barrister or advocate.* For many years Abraham Lincoln was at the bar.
2. **Call to the bar**—*become a barrister.* Many Indian leaders, including Nehru and Gandhi, were called to the bar.
3. **Cross the bar**—*die.* Mr. Tom crossed the bar on January 2, 1975.

BARGAIN

1. **Dutch bargain**—*a bargain ending with drink.* In all bargains, the drunkards always prefer Dutch bargains,
2. **Into the bargain**—*over and above.* He bought a house and got furniture into the bargain.
3. **Sell one a bargain**—*to befool him; to trap him into saving something ridiculous.* The lawyer sold the litigant a bargain.
4. **Strike a bargain**—*to come to terms.* The man struck a good bargain with the shopkeeper.

BARK

1. **Bark is worse than the bite**—*angry words are worse than actual* deeds. The bark of Principal, Mr. Walter was worse than his bite.
2. **Bark up the wrong tree**—*to follow the wrong scent.* In investigating the murder of Mr. David, the police was barking up the wrong tree.

BASKING

Basking shark—*a dangerous but harmless person.* A police officer is a basking shark.

BASKET

To have too many eggs in one basket—*to have too many works to do.* A modern businessman has always too many eggs in one basket.

BAT

1. **Bated breath**—*restrained breathing.* The people heard the tidings with bated breath.

2. **Bats in the belfry**—*crazy notions.* Every youngster has bats in the belfry.

3. **Off one's own bat**—*by one's own activity.* One rises or falls off one's own bat.

4. **Off one's own bat**—*by one's own efforts.* I have made all money entirely off my own bat

5. **To carry out one's bat**—*not to be out; to keep working triumphantly till the end.* Mr. Andrews hopes to carry out his bat.

BATTERY

1. **Masked battery**—*a battery out of the enemy's view.* All India Radio is a kind of masked battery.

2. **To turn a man's battery against himself**—*to defeat a person with his own arguments.* I turned his battery against himself while discussing politics with him.

BATTLE

1. **Battle royal**—*a general melee.* It was a battle royal on the campus during elections.

2. **Half the battle**—*anything that brings one well on road to success.* Passing a university examination is half the battle to getting employment.

3. **Not to know from battledore**—*to be thoroughly ignorant.* So far as chess is concerned, I do not know ABC from battledore.

BAY

1. **Hold at, keep at, bay**—*show the defiance*. The criminal kept the constables at bay.
2. **Stand at bay**—*face the enemy*. When the enemy attacked, the patriots stood at bay.
3. **To bay at the moon**—*thinking of something impossible to be achieved*. Your efforts are all baying at the moon.

BAYONET

At the point of bayonet—*under threat of force*. The soldiers robbed the civilians at the point of bayonet.

BE

Be-all and end-all—*the final result*. One should never be too proud, death is the be-all and end-all of all human beings.

BEAD

1. **Draw a bead on**—*to take aim*. The dacoit drew a bead on the policeman.
2. **To tell one's beads**—*to say prayers*. An aged man should retire from politics and tell his beads.

BEAM

1. **On one's beam-ends**—*in acute distress*. You have to offer help when you find someone on beam-ends.
2. **On the beam**—*at right angles to the course*. Don't disturb a youngster whom you find on the beam.

BEAN

1. **Full beans**—*in high spirits*. After the college exams the students are full of beans.
2. **Give one beans**—*to treat one severely*. When a child does something wrong, do not give him beans.

BEAR

1. **Bear a hand**—*give assistance.* Kindly bear me a hand in lifting this burden.
2. **Bear away**—*sail away.* The ship bore away with the tide.
3. **Bear down**—*sail with the tide.* The boat bore down at sunset.
4. **Bear hard**—*have ill-will to.* Do not bear hard on the child.
5. **Bear in hand**—*to make out; to maintain; to keep in expectation; to flatter one's hopes.* Please bear the youth in hand.
6. **Bear out**—*to corroborate; to confirm.* Please bear out that I have done no harm to you.
7. **Bear up**—*to keep up one's spirits.* You must bear up until the trouble is over.
8. **Bear up for**—*sail towards.* Please bear up for a great position in life.
9. **Bear with**—*make allowance for.* You should bear with your friend's weakness.
10. **Borne in upon**—*forcibly impressed upon.* It must be borne in upon you that I am not going to take lies.
11. **Bring to bear**—to *bring into operation.* Great influence was brought to bear upon the minister for getting quotas of steel.

BEARD

Beard a lion in its den—*to challenge a greater power on its own soil.* Challenging the might of the Mughals, the Sikhs bearded the lion in its own den.

BEAT

1. **Beat about the bush**—*approach a subject in an indirect manner.* There is no use always beating about the bush.

2. **Beat a retreat**—*to retreat*. Before the advancing forces of the enemy, the patriots beat a hasty retreat.

3. **Beat down**—*of a buyer, trying to reduce prices of goods*. The Indian ladies are often competent in beating down the prices.

4. **Beat it**—*make off hastily or furtively*. When the dog appeared, the cat beat it.

5. **Beat off**—*drive back*. The elephants beat off the lion.

6. **Beat one's brains**—*to puzzle one's brains about something*. Do not beat your brains about the illness of your father.

7. **Beat out**—*to flattern or reduce in thickness by beating*. Iron is beaten out into sheets.

8. **Beat the air**—*to fight to no purpose*. In fighting against the people, a government can only beat the air.

9. **Beat the bounds**—*to trace out boundaries in a perambulation, certain objects in the line of the journey being formally struck, and sometimes boys also whipped to make them remember*. The boys were beat the bounds.

10. **Beat up**—*to beat or whip into froth, paste, etc.* Beat up the milk to get the cream.

11. **To beat upon**—*to strike upon again and again*. When an earthquake beats upon the houses, they fall down.

BEATIFIC

Beatific vision—*a glimpse of the glory of heaven*. The picture of Lord Krishna is a beatific vision.

BEAU

Beau ideal—*ideal beauty; a type of embodiment highest in excellence*. Truth should be the beau ideal of life and not money which is the beau ideal now-a-days.

BEAUTY

1. **Beauty queen**—*the most beautiful lady in a region.* Miss Jane is the beauty queen of I.P. College.

2. **Beauty sleep**—*the sleep before midnight, considered the most refreshing.* Let us have some beauty sleep before the clock strikes twelve.

BECOME

To become of—*to happen; the end of.* What will become of his sons after his death ?

BED

1. **A bed of roses**—*a condition of comfort or luxury.* Life is not a bed of roses.

2. **Bed-fellow**—*a close friend*. David and Danny are bed-fellows.

3. **To take to bed**—*to get sick*. He has been taken to bed for the last ten days.

BEFORE

1. **Be beforehand with**—*to forestall; in advance or in anticipation; by way of one's preparation; in advance of one's needs*. He was beforehand with stocking large quantities of flour.

2. **Beforehand with the world**—*comfortably provided for*. The prince was beforehand with the world.

   Every minister wants his son to be beforehand with the world.

3. **Before the wind**—*in the direction in which wind is blowing*. The ship went gaily before the wind.

BEG

1. **Beg for a fool**—*to sue for the guardianship of, and administration of the estate of, on grounds of mental deficiency*. The widow of Mathew is begging for a fool.

2. **Begging letter**—*a letter soliciting alms or some subscription*. The mail of begging letters is heavy but it is seldom replied.

3. **Beggar-my-neighbour**—*a game that goes on till one has gained all the other cards*. In the modern cut-throat world everyone is playing the game of beggar-my-neighbour.

4. **Go a-begging**—*to be in want of a purchaser, occupant, etc.* Because of a ceiling on properties, huge buildings go a-begging for customers.

5. **To beggar the description**—*to assume truth of the matter of dispute*. The beauty of Kashmir beggars description.

BEGIN

1. **Beginning of the end**—*closing chapter or chapters*. It is beginning of the end for the Indian National Congress which Mahatma Gandhi had rightly advised that it should be dissolved.
2. **To begin the world**—*to start in life*. It is very difficult to begin the world now-a-days.
3. **To begin with**—*in the first place*. To begin with I am not acquainted with Indian History.

BEHAVIOUR

To be at one's best behaviour—so *placed that watchfulness on one's behaviour is called for*. The business executives should be always on their best behaviour.

BEHIND

1. **Behind door**—*surreptitious; clandestine*. Mr. Stanley had been guilty of many behind the door transactions.

2. **Behind hand**—*being behind; tardy; ill-provided; in arrears*. Our commitments for June will be behind hand in July. Let us complete them in time.

3. **Behind one's back**—*in somebody's absence*. I do not like your habit of criticising a man behind his back.

4. **Behind the scenes**—*in private*. The Principal and the lecturers are having their discussions behind the scenes.

5. **Behind the time**—*lazy*. The main reason for his dismissal from service was his being behind the time.

6. **Fall behind**—*not keep up with*. He has fallen behind in English studies.

BELL

1. **Bear off or carry off bell**—*to have or gain the first place*. In the last General Elections, Mr. Jackson bore off the bell.

2. **Bell book and candle**—*excommunication ending "Do to (shut) the book, quench the candle, ring the bell."* It is too early to hope that the party in power will bear the bell book and candle.

3. **Bell-bottomed**—*widening towards the other end*. Modern boys and girls wear bell-bottomed pants as the latest thing in fashion.

4. **Bell the cat**—*take the leading part in any hazardous job.* The Opposition wants to oust the Prime Minister from power but nobody is ready to bell the cat.

5. **To sound clear as a bell**—*to sound quite clear or distinct.* His love for you sounds clear as a bell.

BELOW

1. **Below one's breath**—*silently.* We are talking below our breath.

2. **Below the mark**—*not up to the standard.* His work is below the mark.

BELLY

Belly god—*one who makes a god of his belly; a glutton.* Brown is a belly god.

BELT

1. **Hitting below the belt**—*to hit an opponent's body lower than the waist (forbidden in some sports); hence*

to deliver a mean blow; attack unfairly. It was a moral code with our Aryan forefathers never to hit a man below the belt.

2. **Hold the belt**—*to hold the championship in wrestling, boxing, etc.* My friend held the belt in the last boxing championship.

BEMOCK

Bemock the moon—*do a foolish thing.* If you have lost game, don't bemock the moon.

The Opposition cannot win the war against the Prime Minister bemocking the moon.

BENCH

1. **Bench hole**—*a latrine.* Go, ease yourself on the bench-hole.

2. **On the bench**—*holding the office of a judge.* Mr. John Walter is on the bench of the Delhi Court.

3. **Raise to bench**—*to become a judge.* My friend, Mr. Brown has been raised to the bench.

BEND

Bend one's knee—*to be humble before.* Never bend your knees before anybody except God.

BENEATH

Beneath contempt—*not worthy of contempt.* The Minister thought him beneath contempt.

BENEFIT

Benefit of doubt—*favourable judgment when culpability is uncertain.* Many criminals are set free because of the benefit of doubt.

BENGAL

Bengal light—*a brilliant light, sulfide of antimony, used a shipwreck signal and to illuminate country at night.* When a minister dies, there is no Bengal light for him.

BENT

1. **Take to the bent**—*to take flight.* When we came, they took to the bent.
2. **To the top of one's bent**—*to the full measure of one's inclination.* He enjoyed liquor to the top of his bent.

BERSERK

To run berserk—*to become frenzied, mad.* Many men in Mumbai run berserk on account of hot and damp weather.

BERTH

To give a wide berth to—*to keep well away from generally.* It is best to give a wide berth to insincere friends and acquaintances.

BESIDE

1. **Beside oneself**—*having lost self-possession.* When the boy returned home, the mother was beside herself with joy.
2. **Beside the mark, point, question**—*irrelevant.* Your discussion is beside the mark.
   Your argument is beside the point.
   Your answer is beside the question.

BEST

1. **At one's best**—*on the most favourable supposition.* The cricketer was at his best yesterday.

2. **Best boy, girl**—*favourite associate.* Ram was the best boy in the party.

Jennifer was the best girl in the college.

3. **Best maid**—*bridesmaid at a wedding.* Mary was the best maid at Elizabeth's wedding.

4. **Best man**—*bridegroom's man at a wedding.* Who will be the best man at your wedding ?

5. **Best part**—*greater part.* I had little money for the best part of my life.

6. **Best-seller**—*a book that has had very good sales.* Train to Pakistan was a best-seller novel.

7. **For the best**—*with the best intentions.* I helped her with the best intentions.

8. **Give one the best**—*concede victory.* In this game of cards, I give you the best.

9. **Had, were best**—I had best. I were best. Me were best. It were best for me.

10. **Have the best of it**—*gain advantage in a contest.* Bangladesh had the best of it in war with Pakistan.

11. **Make the best of one's way**—*to go as well as one can.* Let us make the best of our way in life.

12. **Put one's best foot forward**—*to make best beginning.* In whatever work we are called upon to do, let us put our best foot forward.

13. **To the best of my belief**—*so far as I know.* To the best of my belief, he is a reasonable man.

BETTER

1. **Be better than one's word**—*do more than one has promised.* Let us be better than our word.

2. **Better late than never**—*something which is necessary should be done even after some delay.* Even if you start with your studies now it will be better late than never.

3. **Better off**—*in superior circumstances.* People today are better off than before independence.

4. **Get the better of**—*to gain the advantage over; to over-come.* By and by you will get the better of any trial or trouble.

5. **One's betters**—*one's superiors.* One should always respect one's betters.

6. **Think better of**—*revise one's opinion about.* I have learnt to think better of you.

BETWEEN

1. **Between ourselves**—Between ourselves, I am leaving tomorrow.

2. **Between the cup and lip**—*between hope and reality.* There is many a slip between the cup and lip.

3. **Between the devil and deep sea**—*in a desperate dilemma.* As an author, I am between the devil and deep sea.

4. **Between two fires**—*to earn displeasure of both the parties.* A wise arbitrator always avoids to be between two fires.

5. **Between you and me**—Between you and me, I am running away from here.

6. **Between whiles**—*at intervals.* I hope to write to you between whiles.

7. **Between you, me and the bedpost**—Between you, me and the bedpost, I need your help.

8. **Between you me and the cat**—Between you me and the cat, I am quite bankrupt.

9. **Between you, me and the post**—Between you, me and the post, I have lost my money.

10. **Go-between**—*act as a mediator.* There is no go-between for Peter and Robert.

BEYOND

1. **Beyond measure**—*unmeasurable.* The success achieved by Tony is beyond measure.

2. **To go beyond**—*to surpass.* Never go beyond reality.

BID

1. **Bid good-bye**—*to take leave of the departing person.* As soon as the train whistled he bade good-bye to his friends.

2. **To bid welcome**—*to receive cordially.* When we reached the party, we were bid welcome by Alan's uncle.

3. **Bid fair**—*to seem likely.* He bids fair to become a minister.

BIG

1. **Big bellied**—*having a big belly; pregnant.* The big-bellied lady is about to bear a child.

2. **Big business**—*large enterprises and business houses.* Big business runs the government in many countries of the world.

3. **Big with a young**—*pregnant.* She is big with a young now-a-days.

4. **To look big**—*to impress one by prosperity.* Reality is reality, looking big will not convince me.

5. **To talk big**—*to talk pompously.* He is in the habit of talking big.

BILL

Bill of fare—*menu card; list of food, dishes, etc.* He told the bearer to bring the bill of fare before ordering his dinner.

BIND

1. **Be bound up in**—*to be wholly devoted to*. He was bound up in his work.
2. **Bind/dare**—*responsible*. I dare or I will be bound.
3. **Bind over**—*subject to legal obligation*. He was bound over for the security of the child.

BIRD

1. **A bird's eye-view**—*a general view*. We could hardly have a bird's eye-view at the time of White's cremation.
2. **Bird-eyed**—*quick sighted*. He is a bird-eyed man.
3. **Bird in hand**—*certainty*. A bird in hand is worth two in the bush.
4. **Bird's eye-view**—*a general view from above*. You can have a bird's eye-view of Delhi from the top of Qutab Minar.
5. **Birds of same feather**—*persons of similar habits*. Birds of the same feather flock together.

60

6. **Bird-witted**—*incapable of sustained attention*. My friend, Sunil is bird-witted.
7. **Like bird**—*with quickness*. He did everything like a bird.
8. **To kill two birds with one stone**—*to gain two ends with one attempt*. Every politician tries to kill two birds with one stone.

BIRSE

Set up one's birse—*to rouse the wrath of*. George has set up William's birse.

BIT

1. **Bit and sop**—*something to eat and drink*. Let me have bit and sop.
2. **Bit by bit**—*piecemeal*. I will manage to write the book bit by bit.
3. **Do one's bit**—*do one's due share*. I will gladly do my bit for you.
4. **Take the bit in one's teeth**—*throw off control*. The child has taken the bit in his teeth.
5. **To give a bit of one's mind**—*to speak frankly*. When I asked him for some money, he gave a bit of his mind and said no.

BITE

1. **Bite the dust**—*to fall; to die*. The greatest conquerors have at last bitten the dust.
2. **Bite the thumb**—*to express defiance*. When the king ordered him to go, he bit his thumb.

BITTER

1. **Bitter end**—*to the last*. The Indian Army fought to the bitter end.

2. **Bitter sweet**—*mixture of sweet and bitter.* Life is bitter sweet.

BLACK

1. **Black and blue**—*severely.* The teacher beat the boy black and blue.

2. **Black leg**—*a worker continuing to work during a strike or one taking on a striker's job.* In every trade union there are black legs.

3. **Black out**—*to obliterate with black.* Real news are blacked out.

4. **Black sheep**—*a disreputable member of a community.* There are black sheep everywhere in social organizations.

5. **Blackhole**—*military lock-up.* During every war many soldiers are blackholed by opposite groups.

6. **Blackmail**—*to take undue advantage.* You can no longer blackmail him, as full details have been published in the papers.

7. **In black and white**—*in writing.* Please submit your demands in black and white.

8. **In one's black books**—having *incurred someone's displeasure.* He is in the black books of his teacher.

BLANKET

1. **On the wrong side of blanket**—*illegitimately.* He was born on the wrong side of the blanket

2. **Wet blanket**—*a damper of spirit; kill-joy.* A selfish man is a wet blanket.

BLIND

1. **Blindfold**—*reckless*. Your blindfold habits will ruin you one day.
2. **Blind man's holiday**—*time before lighting a candle*. Susan and Walter enjoy a blind man's holiday.
3. **Turn a blind eye**—*ignore*. It is best to turn a blind eye to other people's doings instead of coming into conflict with them.

BLOCK

1. **Block up**—*to obstruct*. Rains have blocked up the Garden road.
2. **Chip of the old block**—*just like the father*. His child is a chip of the old block..

BLOOD

1. **Blood and iron**—*relentless use of force.* Hitler mastered Germany through blood and iron.

2. **Blood hound**—*a detective.* I hope you are not a blood hound.

3. **Blood sucker**—*an extortioner.* Most of the shopkeepers are blood suckers.

4. **Flesh and blood**—*human being.* A flesh and blood is never happy in life.

5. **In cold blood**—*after due thinking.* The man was killed in cold blood.

6. **In hot blood**—*under excitement.* He killed the man in hot blood.

BLOW

1. **Blow hot and cold**—*to be irresolute.* If you want to win the war, you must not blow hot and cold.

2. **Blow one's own trumpet**—*to praise oneself.* It is not good to blow one's own trumpet.

3. **Blow over**—*to pass away as a danger or scandal.* Every unpleasant happening blows over in the course of time.

4. **Blow up**—*to bring into discredit.* The people blew up the leader.

5. **Blow upon**—*come into being; to shatter by explosion, to inflate; to scold.* The earthquake blew up.

The minister blew up with anger.

6. **To come to blows**—*to come to fight.* After their heated discussion both the groups came to blows.

BLUE

Once in a blue moon—*rarely; very seldom.* He comes to see me once in a blue moon.

BLUNT

To blunt the edge of—*to weaken force.* Time blunts the edge of anger.

BOARD

To sweep the board—*to be all successful.* David has always been sweeping the board in his life.

BOAT

1. **To have an oar to another's boat**—*interfering in another's affairs.* It is unwise to have an oar in another's boat.

2. **To sail in the same boat**—*having the same fate.* Both husband and wife are sailing in the same boat.

BODY

1. **Body and soul**—*wholly; completely.* He devoted his body and soul for getting first class in the entrance examination.

2. **Body politic**—*collective body of the people.* The leaders must serve the body politic.

BOLT

1. **Bolt from the blue**—*an unexpected attack*. Her sudden illness was a bolt from the blue.

2. **Have shot one's bolt**—*to be unable to do more than one has done*. The Congressmen have shot their bolt.

BONE

1. **Bone of contention**—*something that causes strife*. Money is always a bone of contention in the family.

2. **Make no bones of**—*have no scruples about*. Many men do not make bones of their morals.

3. **To pick a bone with someone**—*to dispute*. I do not want to pick a bone with anyone.

4. **To the bone**—*to the inmost part; upto the core*. He is a Communist to the bone.

BOOK

1. **Bring to book**—*call to account*. You will be brought to book for all your misdeeds.

2. **Take a leaf out of another's book**—*to profit by another's example*. It is time for young men to take a leaf out of their elders' books.

3. **Talk like a book**—*to talk bookishly*. Do not talk like a book before me, let me know your mind.

4. **To be in one's good books**—*to be one's favourite*. He is in the good books of the manager.

5. **To be in one's bad books**—*commanding a bad opinion*. He is in the bad books of his manager.

6. **Without book**—*from memory; unauthorisedly*. The judge talked without book.

BOOT

1. **Boot is on the other leg**—*the tables are turned; the responsibility is now the other way; the reverse is the truth.* He cannot be blamed, the boot is on the other leg now.

2. **Die in one's boots**—*die in action.* My brother died with his boots on.

3. **Get the boot**—*get dismissed.* The dishonest employees got the boot.

4. **Have one's heart on one's boot**—*to have lost courage.* The constable had his heart in his boots.

5. **Like old boots**—*vigorously.* He worked like the old boots.

6. **To be given the boot**—*to be dismissed.* He has been given the boot from the service.

7. **To make boot of**—*to profit.* The new policy of the Government is going to punish those who are making boots by charging higher prices.

BORN

1. **To be born under a lucky star**—*to be lucky by birth.* He is born under a lucky star.

2. **To be born with a silver spoon in one's mouth**—*to be a rich man's child*. Liza was born with a silver spoon in her mouth.

BOSOM

Bosom friend—*best friend*. You are my bosom friend.

BOTTLE

1. **Bottle up**—*to enclose as in a bottle*. We were bottled up in the house.

2. **Pass the bottle of smoke**—*to acquiesce in some false-hood; to make pretence*. The men in power are forced to pass the bottle of smoke.

BOTTOM

1. **Bet one's bottom dollar**—*to bet all one has*. In excitement, he betted his bottom dollar.

2. **Bottomless pit**—*hell*. Let the wicked go to the bottomless pit.

3. **From the bottom of the heart**—*with heartfelt sincerity*. We thank you from the bottom of our heart for what you have done for us.

4. **Get to the bottom**—*investigate the truth*. Let us get to the bottom of the story.

5. **Stand on one's own bottom**—*independent*. You must learn to stand on your own bottom.

6. **Touch bottom**—*reach the lowest point*. Goodwill of the ruling party has touched the bottom.

BOUND

1. **By leaps and bounds**—*by startlingly rapid stages*. With the help of a guru you can make progress by leaps and bounds in the spiritual world.

2. **Out of bounds**—*not within limits of movements.*
Soldiers are out of bounds after 10 p.m. in many civil
areas.

BOUNTIFUL

Lady Bountiful—*a great charitable lady.* Dolly is the
Lady Bountiful in our town.

BOW

1. **Bowing acquaintance**—*a slight acquaintance.*
Although I have a bowing acquaintance with him, I feel
I shall be able to convince him to offer you a suitable job.

2. **On the bow hand**—*wide of the mark.* He did his
best but his efforts were on the bow hand.

3. **To draw the long bow**—*to make extravagant
statement.* Do not draw the long bow in the court
because you will never be able to prove your statement

4. **To make one's bow**—*to retire gracefully.* The
common fault of many leaders is that they never want
to make their bow once they become ministers.

5. **Two strings to one's bow**—*an alternative in reserve.*
In dealing with your enemy you should have at least two
strings to your bow.

BOWWOW

Bowwow—*a threatening pose; a full-mouthed literary
style.* In dealing with a strong opponent, a mere
bowwow will not help you.

Carlyle wrote in bowwow.

BOX

1. **In the wrong box**—*in a false position; in a scrap.*
In a crowd of scientists I find myself in the wrong box.

2. **To be in the box**—*to be in a fix*. He is in the box now-a-days.

BOY

Boy friend—*a girl's favourite male companion for the time being*. Every nice girl should have a nice boy friend.

BRAIN

1. **Brain fag**—*a tired condition of the brain or nerve*. Everyone suffers from brain fag after a hard day's work.
2. **Brain wave**—*sudden bright idea*. A brain wave can often carry you through an emergency.
3. **Brains trust**—*a committee of experts*. All India Radio has a brains trust to speak on the national problems.
4. **To blow out one's brain**—*to shoot to kill*. During the war the soldiers are ordered to blow out one's brain.

BRANCH

Root and branch—*thorough; thoroughly*. He uprooted the cause of distress root and branch.

BRAND

Brand from the burning—*one snatched out of a pressing danger.* His life was brand from the burning when his friend came to his help.

BRASS

1. **Brass farthing**—*a whit.* The father refused to give a brass farthing to his son.
2. **Brass tacks**—*details of practical business.* You must understand the brass tacks before you can be promoted to a higher job.

BRAZEN

Brazen-faced—*shameless.* There are more and more brazen-faced boys in schools and offices.

BREACH

1. **Breach of promise**—*often used for the breach of the promise of marriage.* The boy's father is responsible for the breach of promise.
2. **Breach of the peace**—*a violation of the public peace by riot, etc.* Bad characters are responsible for the breach of the peace in the street.

BREAD

1. **Bread and butter**—*livelihood.* Everybody works hard for his bread and butter.
2. **Bread buttered on both sides**—*very fortunate circumstances.* The sons of millionaires find bread buttered on both sides.
3. **Bread study**—*any branch of study taken up as a means of earning one's livelihood.* Most of the education today is mere bread study.

4. **Know which side one's bread is buttered on**—*to know how to act in self interest.* Every modern youth knows which side his bread is buttered on.

5. **Take the bread out of one's mouth**—*to deprive one of one's means of living.* If you dismiss a man from job, you take the bread out of his mouth.

BREAK

1. **Break a jest**—*to utter a jest; cut a joke.* Mahatma Gandhi quite often broke a jest

2. **Break away**—*revolt.* Bangladesh broke away from Pakistan.

3. **Break cover**—*to break away from concealment.* At an opportune moment the soldier break cover and attack their foe.

4. **Break down**—*to demolish; collapse; fail completely.* In times of emergency all controls tend to break down.

5. **Break even**—*to avoid loss but fail to gain.* The parties have broken even in the bargain.

6. **Break forth**—*burst forth.* Nature breaks forth in Spring.

7. **Break ground**—*to lead in something.* The labourers have broken the ground for new work.

8. **Break in, upon or into**—*to enter violently.* The intruder broke in upon our meeting with a pistol.

9. **Break loose**—*to extricate oneself forcibly.* The boy has broken loose from the family.

10. **Break no squares**—*make no difference to; do no harm; matter little.* Your speech breaks no squares in the government policy.

11. **Break off**—*to detach by breaking; to put an abrupt end to; to leave off abruptly.* The boy has broken off with the family.

12. **Break one's mind**—*to communicate one's idea to some one.* At last the mother broke her mind to the son.

13. **Break out**—*appear suddenly.* Plague has broken out in the city.

14. **Break the heart**—*to crush with defeat.* The death of my brother has broken my heart.

15. **Break the ice**—*to get through with first difficulties.* Our Tenth Five-Year Plan has not broken the ice.

16. **Break upon the wheel**—*to punish severely.* The rebels were broken upon the wheel.

BREAST

Make a clean breast—*to make a full confession.* The murderers of John Mathew have not yet made a clean breast.

BREATH

1. **Above one's breath**—*aloud.* Please speak above your breath.

2. **Below or under one's breath**—*in a low voice.* Some people are in the habit of speaking under their breath.

3. **Catch the breath**—*stop breathing for a moment.* Yogis can catch the breath.

4. **Out of breath**—*tried after running.* I was out of breath after catching the bus.

5. **Take breath**—*rest.* Please take your breath before you talk.

6. **Spend one's breath**—*talk profitlessly*. Why are you spending your breath ?
7. **With bated breath**—*with wonder*. The boys listened to the teacher with bated breath.

BREATHE

1. **Breathe again**—*to be relieved from anxiety*. After the result, Mohan is breathing again.
2. **Breathe freely**—*to be at ease*. In my house you can breathe freely.
3. **Breathe upon**—*to tarnish the name of*. Your action breathes upon your father.
4. **To breathe one's last**—*to die*. My friend breathed his last on 27th May, 1975.

BREACH

Wear the breaches—*said of a wife; to be master*. My wife does indeed wear the breaches in the house.

BREED

Breeding-in-and-in—*breeding from near relatives*. There is no breeding in-and-in among the Hindus.

BREEZE

Breeze up—*to freshen*. Let us breeze up in the garden.

BRIBERY

Bribery oath—*an oath taken by an elector that he has not voted for bribe*. Nobody is asked to take bribery oath because everybody is taking bribes.

BRIC

Bric-a-brac—*old curiosities*. The almirah of Rosy is full of bric-a-brac.

BRICK

1. **Like a ton of bricks**—*heavily and promptly*. The death of my brother fell on me like a ton of bricks.

2. **To drop a brick**—*to make a horrifying blunder in speech or action*. The speaker dropped a brick when he addressed the chairman as "Honourable Minister"

BRIEF

1. **In brief**—*in short*. Please describe the matter in brief.

2. **Take a brief**—*to accept a case*. The lawyer has accepted my brief.

3. **The brief and long**—*total story*. The brief and long is that the doctor killed my brother.

4. **To be brief**—*in a few words*. To be brief, I am too busy to meet Dr. Paul.

BRING

1. **Bring about**—*cause to happen*. Mr. Nehru brought about great changes in the country.

2. **Bring down**—*to humble; to shout; to overthrow; to lower*. Do not bring down your friends.

3. **Bring down the house**—*to call forth a general burst of applause*. Madona brought down the house.

4. **Bring forth**—*to produce*. Evil brings forth evil.

5. **Bring forward**—*to advance in accounting*. I have brought forward the sum due to you.

6. **Bring home**—*prove*. The teacher brought home the point to the students.

7. **Bring in**—*to introduce*. I was brought in to the grand assembly.

8. **Bring out**—*to make clear*. Please bring out the meaning of your poem.

9. **Bring over**—*convert*. You cannot bring me over to communism by violence.

10. **Bring round**—*to win over; to bring to consciousness.* Sprinkling of water on his face brought him round.

11. **Bring under**—*subdue*. The chairperson failed to bring the members under.

12. **Bring up**—*to educate*. Teacher said, "Children should be brought up as simply as possible".

13. **Bring up the rear**—*to come last*. I bring up the rear in the procession.

14. **To bring about**—*to cause to happen.* His negligence brought his failure.

15. **To bring to mind**—*to recall*. Please bring to mind, I paid you rupees ten last Sunday.

16. **To bring to light**—*to make known.* The Commission has brought to light all the facts.

BROKEN

Broken man—*ill; bankrupt.* It is not good to be a broken man.

BROOM

1. **New brooms keep clean**—*people newly appointed to a position work conscientiously.* Many new brooms sweep clean.

2. **To marry over the broomstick**—*to go through an irregular form of marriage.* The boy and the girl married over the broomstick.

BROTH

Broth of a boy—*the quintessence of a good fellow.* Michael has the broth of a boy.

BROTHER

Brother-german—*one having both parents in common.* Tara Singh is my brother-german.

BROWBEAT

Browbeat—*to bear down with stern looks.* The boss quite often browbeats the employees.

BROWN

Brown study—*gloom; sadness.* Keats was often found in brown study.

BRUSH

1. **Brush away**—*to put aside.* Unless you brush away his weaknesses, you cannot make him change.

2. **Brush up**—*revive, freshen.* Please read the book "Brush Up Your English" by Mr. Brown.

BUBBLE

1. **Bubble over**—*to be angry*. My child bubbled over her pocket money.
2. **To prick the bubble**—*to destroy an illusion*. Defeat and death prick the bubble of life.

BUCK

1. **Buck up**—*cheer up*. Buck up, you are winning the game.
2. **Pass the buck**—*to shift the responsibility to someone else*. The ruling party tries to pass the buck to the Opposition for inflation and rising prices.

BUCKET

1. **Give the bucket**—*to dismiss*. The dishonest employee was given the bucket.
2. **Kick the bucket**—*die*. Many soldiers kicked the bucket in Kargil war.

BUD

Nip in the bud—*to destroy in its very beginning*. It is always desirable to nip the evil in the bud.

BUILD

1. **Build up**—*to cover with buildings*. Queens Town has now been built up.
2. **To build castles in the air**—*to plan visionary and impossible schemes*. It is no use building castles in the air; do something solid.

BULGE

To get the bulge on one—*to get a decided advantage over another*. It is not easy to get the bulge on the ruling party.

BULL

1. **A bull in the China shop**—*one who lacks the delicacy which the situation calls for.* In high society, a villager is like a bull in the China shop.
2. **Bull into**—*plunge hastily.* Do not bull into high places.
3. **Take the bull by the horns**—*grapple firmly with a danger or difficulty.* If you are in trouble, always take the bull by the horn.

BURN

1. **Burn a hole in one's pocket**—*to be anxious to spend money quickly.* A hundred-rupee note burns a hole in the pocket of a youngster.
2. **Burn daylight**—*to waste time.* I don't like people burning daylight .
3. **Burn one's boats**—*to stake everything on success.* If you want to win a victory against heavy odds, burn your boats behind you.
4. **Burn out**—*destroy or drive by burning.* The soldiers burnt out the whole town.

5. **Burn the candle at both ends**—*to waste quickly.*
The boy burnt the candle at both ends by gambling and
bad investment.

Save your money and health. Don't burn the candle at
both ends.

6. **Burn the midnight oil**—*to work hard at studies.*
Many students burn the midnight oil near the
examinations.

7. **To burn one's fingers**—*to suffer from interfering
in other's affairs.* Confine to your work and do not
burn your fingers.

BURST

To burst into tears—*to fall crying.* On seeing her
son injured Veronica burst into tears.

BURY

Bury the hatchet—*to renounce enmity.* India and
Pakistan have buried the hatchet.

BUSH

Beat about the bush—*to go round about anything.*
If you need money ask for it. There is no use beating
about the bush.

BUSINESS

1. **Make it one's business**—*to make or do something
or see it done.* He has made pulling down his
competitors his business, these days.

2. **Mind your own business**—*do your work and do
not meddle with others.* Will you please mind your
own business ?

3. **Send about one's business**—*dismiss*. If you misbehave, I will send you about your business.

BUT

1. **But and a ben**—*a two-roomed house.* He lived in a but and a ben.
2. **Live but and ben**—*live respectively in those rooms; in close neighbourhood with anyone.* For many years she lived but and ben in her village.

BUTT

Butt in—*interpose.* When I am speaking, don't butt in.

BUTTER

Butter one's words—*speak with flattery.* Please don't butter your words when you speak to me.

BUY

1. **Buy and sell**—*to traffic in.* Dr. Paul is buying and selling politics.
2. **Buy in**—*collar a stock.* Big business people buy in and create shortages.
3. **Buy off**—*to get rid of by bribery.* The prisoner bought off his release.
4. **Buy off, out**—*to dispossess entirely by payment.* He bought off the hotel he went to dine in.
   He bought out the rented house.
5. **Buy up**—*to buy the entire stock.* He bought up the entire company.

BY

1. **By and by**—*step by step; before long.* By and by he became a minister.

2. **By and large**—*generally speaking.* By and large, mothers control the house.

3. **By dint of**—*by virtue of.* By dint of hard work, he secured first position in the university.

4. **By the by**—*by the way.* By the by, what is your name ?

5. **By the way**—*in passing.* By the way, how much money have you in your pocket ?

6. **Let bygones be bygones**—*let the past be forgotten.* I would very much appreciate if you will please let bygones be bygones and talk about the present only.

CA'CANNY

Ca'canny—*to get easy; deliberately to restrict output or effort.* More and more trade unionists are going ca'canny now-a-days.

CAESARIAN

Caesarian operation—*the delivery of a child by cutting through the abdomen.* Julius Caesar was born through a caesarian operation.

CAKE

1. **A piece of cake**—*something easy and pleasant.* Life these days is not a piece of cake.

2. **Cakes and ale**—*all the good things of life*. Some men have cakes and ale in the world while many do not have even dry bread and water.

3. **Eat one's cake and have it too**—*have the advantage of both the alternatives*. Many rich people eat the cake and have it too.

4. **Take the cake**—*carry off honours*. Mr. Andrews has taken the cake.

CALF

Golden calf—*wealth as an object of worship*. Many people today worship the golden calf.

CALL

1. **At call**—*readily available*. For some fortunate people money is at call.

2. **Call attention to**—*to point out; to recall.* Let me call attention to your childhood days when your condition was miserable.

3. **Call cousins**—*claim kindred.* Let us call cousins.

4. **Call down**—*to invoke; to rebuke.* Do not call down a friend.

5. **Call for**—*to call loudly; to claim.* He called for his old debts.

6. **Call forth**—*evoke.* Let us call forth the help of gods.

7. **Call in**—*to call somebody or something for assistance.* Let us call in the CBI report.

8. **Call in question**—*challenge; throw doubts on.* People have called in question the murder of Mr. M.N. Dey if it was by his enemies or by his friends.

9. **Call off**—*to withdraw.* The strike was hastily called off by the port labour unions.

10. **Call on**—*to appeal; to make a short visit.* Let us call on the Prime Minister for help. I will call on Mr. Chopra tomorrow.

11. **Call out**—*to challenge to a duel; to summon.* The Frenchman called out the English cavalier.

12. **Call over**—*to read aloud.* He called over the register of rolls.

13. **Call to mind**—*recollect.* Let us call to mind the olden and golden days.

14. **Call to order**—*to call upon; to observe the rules of debate.* The Speaker called the Lok Sabha to order.

15. **Call up**—*summon.* All retired soldiers were called up because of war.

16. **To call away**—*to divert*. His attention was called away by the appearance of a young girl.

17. **To call bad names**—*abuse*. It is not good to call him bad names.

18. **To call into being**—*to create*. God has called the whole world into being.

19. **Within call**—*within calling distance*. If you are sincere, you will always find me within call wherever I am.

CANDLE

1. **Burn the candle at both ends**—*to waste or use up in two ways at once*. Please don't burn the candle at both ends.

2. **Candle power**—*unit for the measurement of light*. This is a 20-candle power lamp.

3. **Not fit to hold a candle**—*not fit to be compared to*. Ram is not fit to hold a candle to his father although he bears his name.

4. **Sell by the candle**—*to offer for sale as long as a small piece of candle burns itself out*. The old car was sold by the candle.

5. **The game is not worth the candle**—*the thing is not worth the expense of labour for it*. The picnic was not worth the candle.

CANINE

Canine appetite—*a huge hunger*. The have-nots suffer from canine appetite.

CANVAS

Under canvas—*living in tents*. For years the refugees lived under canvas.

86

CAP

1. **Cap and bells**—*marks of a professional jester.* He bears cap and bells.

2. **Cap-a-pie**—*from head to foot.* He was a gentleman, cap-a-pie.

3. **Cap in hand**—*submissively.* She has set her cap in hand.

4. **Feather in one's cap**—*something to be proud of.* The book "My Love" is a feather in the cap of the author.

5. **Set one's cap at**—*to captivate.* She has set her cap at him.

6. **The cap fits**—*the allusion is said to apply; the quotation is fit.* When Professor Williams talks of dictatorship, the cap fits him.

7. **Throw up one's cap**—*a sign of joy.* When they won the match, the children threw up their caps.

CAPER

Cut a caper—*execute a frisk.* When the madam entered the room, the children cut a caper.

CAPITAL

1. **A capital sentence**—*death as punishment.* At last the court decided to award a capital sentence to Peter for the murder of his wife.

2. **Capital error**—*blunder.* By giving employment to that bad fellow you have made a capital error.

3. **Make capital out of**—*to turn to one's advantage.* A shrewd beggar makes capital out of his misfortunes.

CAPTAIN

Captain of industry—*great industrial employer.* Don't expect a job from me, because I am no captain of industry.

CARD

1. **Cards in one's hands**—*everything under control.* Shrewd business folk keep the cards in their hands.

2. **Cards on the table**—*one's resources and moves fully open.* Mahatma Gandhi kept his cards on the table.

3. **House of cards**—*a weak scheme.* If you work on a house of cards, you will never be successful.

4. **Knowing card**—*one who is fully awake.* A successful business man is a knowing card.

5. **On the cards**—*not improbable*. Revolution is on the cards everywhere.

6. **Play one's cards well**—*make the best of chances*. You must play your cards well to win success.

7. **Show one's cards**—*to show one's secrets*. Never show your cards to your competitors.

8. **Speak by the card**—*to speak with precision and to the point*. A great leader speaks by the card.

9. **Sure card**—*sure means to succeed*. Money is a sure card in the world now-a-days.

10. **Throw up the cards**—*to accept defeat*. You have no way out now except to throw up your cards.

CARE

1. **Take care**—*to be careful*. Take care lest you fall.

2. **Take care of**—*to look after*. Please take care of the baby.

CARPET

On the carpet—*under discussion*. Many national problems are on the carpet in the Parliament.

CARRY

1. **Carry all before one**—*to bear down all obstacles*. He carries all before him.

2. **Carry away**—*deprive of self-control by exciting the feelings*. Mr. Jinnah carried away the Muslims.

3. **Carry off**—*to cause the death of*. Heart trouble carried off my brother.

4. **Carry on**—*manage; continue*. Who is carrying on your business? How do you carry on these days?

5. **Carry one's point**—*to overrule objections*. The minister knows how to carry his point.

6. **Carry out**—*accomplish*. He carried out the plan of his life.

7. **Carry the day**—*to be successful*. It is not easy to carry the day in elections.

8. **Carry too far**—*to continue beyond reasonable limits*. Don't carry quarrels too far.

9. **Carry through**—*to support through difficulties*. Stamina will carry you through all obstacles.

10. **Carry up**—*to continue building upwards*. They intend to carry up skyscrapers in Delhi.

11. **Carry weight**—*to have weight; to have influence or authority*. My advice carries no weight with the chairman.

CART

Put the cart before the horse—*to reverse the natural order of things.* Don't try to teach your father, son; it is like putting the cart before the horse.

CARTE

1. **Carte blanche**—*freedom of action.* Do not give too much carte blanche to your subordinates.

2. **Carte de visite**—*a small photographic portrait pasted on the card.* Carte de visite is not common now-a-days.

CARVE

1. **Carve out**—*to gain* by *one's exertions.* You must carve out a nice career.

2. **Cut and carve**—*refine.* You must cut and carve your style.

CASANOVA

Casanova—*a person conspicuous for amorous adventures.* Ahluwalia is a small Casanova.

CASE

1. **In any case**—*in all events.* I will meet you tomorrow in any case.

2. **In case**—*in the event of; lest.* Call me in case you need my help.
Go slow, in case you fall.

3. **In case to**—*in fit condition for.* He is in case to go home.

4. **Make out one's case**—*give good reason for one's position.* The lawyer made out a good case for the client.

5. **Take the case of**—*take for example.* How revolutions are born ? Let us take the case of Quit India Movement.

Gandhiji never wanted violence yet took the case of Quit India Movement.

CASH

1. **Hard cash**—*ready money.* How much hard cash do you have ?
2. **In cash**—*with money.* I am in cash now-a-days.
3. **Out of cash**—*without money.* I was out of cash yesterday.

CASSANDRA

Cassandra—*one who expresses gloomy views of the social and political future but is not listened to.* Don't mistake Robert for a Cassandra.

CAST

1. **Cast about**—*to look about.* I am casting about for some money to tide over the emergency.
2. **Cast a horoscope**—*to make an astrological calculation.* The pundits have cast my horoscope in vain.
3. **Cast anchor**—*anchor a ship.* The ship cast anchor in Mumbai.
4. **Cast an eye**—*look.* Don't cast an eye on beauties.
5. **Cast a spell on**—*to enchant.* Mahatma Gandhi cast a spell on the listeners.
6. **Cast a vote**—*record one's vote.* To whom are you casting your vote ?
7. **Cast away**—*to waste.* I cannot afford to cast away any more money.
8. **Cast back**—*revert.* A second revolution will cast back our history since 1947.

9. **Cast down**—*deject or depress*. Why are you feeling cast down ?

10. **Cast in one's teeth**—*to bring up as a reproach*. Corruption was cast in the teeth of the minister.

11. **Cast lots**—*draw lottery*. Lots are cast by our office for allotment of houses to employees.

12. **Cast-off**—*reject*. He is wearing cast-off clothes. I wear clothes cast-off by my son.

13. **The last cast**—*in extremities*. The Janta Party is now in the last cast.

14. **To cast a glance at**—*to see*. The whole college casts a glance at Dolly.

CASTE

To lose caste—*to descend in social status*. A poor man quite often loses his caste among his rich friends.

CAT

1. **Bell the cat**—*do a difficult task*. Everybody wants to remove a tyrant but nobody is willing to bell the cat.

2. **Cat and dog life**—*full of quarrels*. All these four years I had been living a cat and dog life with my wife.

3. **Cat's paw**—*tool of another person*. One cannot be successful for long working on cat's paw.

4. **Catted and fished**—*secured* and *controlled*. After marriage a girl is catted and fished.

5. **Enough to make a cat laugh**—*comic; unbelievable.* Your statement is enough to make a cat laugh.

6. **Rain cats and dogs**—*rain very heavily.* It is raining cats and dogs outside.

7. **Room to swing a cat**—*minimum of space.* There is not room enough to swing a cat in my house.

8. **See which way the cat jumps**—*see which way the wind blows before committing yourself.* Let us see which way the cat jumps in this matter.

9. **To let the cat out of the bag**—*to reveal a secret.* Women generally let the cat out of the bag.

10. **Turn cat in the pan**—*to turn sides with dexterity.* Politicians always continue to turn the cat in the pan.

CATCH

1. **Catch-as-catch-can**—*free style of wrestling.* Life today is catch-as-catch-can.

2. **Catch at**—*snatch at*. The cat caught at the rat.

3. **Catch fire**—*become ignited*. Petrol soon catches fire.

4. **Catch bold of**—*seize*. The constable caught hold of the thief.

5. **Catch on**—*to comprehend; to catch the popular fancy*. I cannot catch on your speech.

   Jeans have caught on.

6. **Catch out**—*to detect an error*. The accountant was caught out.

7. **Catch sight of**—*see*. I could not catch sight of my friend in the crowd.

8. **Catch up**—*to overtake*. The car will catch up the cart.

9. **To catch a Tartar**—*to fight with a stranger enemy*. In Vietnam the Americans have caught a Tartar.

10. **To catch one's breath**—*to check suddenly*. When the candidate was copying, the examiner caught his breath.

CAUSE

1. **First cause**—*the original cause; creator of all*. I spend most of my time in contemplating on the first cause of the universe.

2. **Formal cause**—*the essence or idea of a thing*. What is the formal cause of your invitation ?

3. **Hour of cause**—*time of trial*. Death is the highest hour of cause.

4. **Make common cause with**—*unite for a common object*. The BSP had made a common cause with the Congress.

5. **Material cause**—*that which frames an event*. What is the material cause of White's murder ? Nobody yet knows.

6. **Show cause**—*give reason for a certain kind of action.* When he filed a case, he was asked to show cause.

7. **The final cause**—*the end or object of the universe.* Nobody knows the first or the final cause of why we are born and why we die.

CAVE

Cave in—*to slip.* When the mine caved in many labourers died.

CELESTIAL

The Celestial empire—*China.* This country is not the celestial empire.

CERTAIN

1. **A certain person**—*implying some degree of contempt.* You met my friend. Don't tell me that you met a certain person.

2. **A lady of a certain age**—*of an age but not stated accurately.* A lady of a certain age dined with me last night.

3. **For certain**—*assuredly.* I will meet you for certain.

4. **In a certain condition**—*pregnant.* When I met her, she was in a certain condition.

CESTUI

Cestui que trust—*a person entitled to the benefit of trust.* Mr. Mathew is cestui que trust.

CHALK

1. **By a long chalk**—*by a considerable distance.* You cannot catch me by a long chalk.

2. **Chalk out**—*trace.* I will chalk out your program.

3. **Not to know chalk from cheese**—*to know nothing about the matter.* So far as science is concerned, I do not know chalk from cheese.

CHANCE

1. **An *eye* to the main chance**—*thought for self-enrichment.* A modern man never forgets to keep an eye to the main chance.
2. **By chance**—*incidentally.* I met him by chance on the road.
3. **Chance upon**—*find out by chance.* How did you chance upon my address?
4. **Even chance**—*equal probability for and against.* You have even chance of getting into IAS.
5. **Stand a good chance**—*have a reasonable expectation.* You stand a good chance of winning the prize.
6. **Take one's chance**—*risk an undertaking.* When you are in trouble, you have to take a chance to get out of it.
7. **The main chance**—*the great object.* Election is the main chance of a politician.

CHANGE

1. **Change colour**—*blush or turn pale.* When you talk of marriage, the girl changes colour.
2. **Change oneself**—*change clothes.* Change yourself quickly for marriage.
3. **Change one's mind**—*to form a different opinion.* Strong men do not change their mind easily.
4. **Change one's tune**—*to change from joy to sorrow.* When there is a death in the family, you have to change your tune.

5. **Put the change on**—*delude; trick.* Please do not try to put the change on me.

6. **Small change**—*coin.* Can you give me small change for a rupee?

CHAPTER

To the end of the chapter—*throughout.* I will be true to my principles to the end of the chapter.

CHARGE

1. **Give in charge**—*hand over to the police.* He wants to give the culprit in charge.

2. **Take charge of**—*to assume charge of.* Please take charge of my desk in my office.

CHASE

Wild goose chase—*futile search.* Life today is a wild goose chase.

CHATTEL

Goods and chattel—*all moveable things.* I feel I will have to move out of my rented house one day goods and chattel.

CHEAP

1. **Cheap and nasty**—*offensively inferior and of low vaiue.* The New Year card he sent me was cheap and nasty.

2. **Cheap jack**—*a travelling hawker who professes to give cheap bargains.* The days of cheap jacks are over. Now everyone intends to fleece you everywhere.

3. **Dirt cheap**—*ridiculously cheap.* Nothing is dirt cheap now-a-days.

4. **Feel cheap**—*to have a sense of inferiority and humiliation.* I feed cheap in this matter.

5. **On the cheap**—*cheaply.* If you are in police, you can get everything on the cheap.

CHEAT

To pat a cheat upon—*to deceive.* You cannot put a cheat upon a man of God.

CHECK

To keep in check—*to keep under control.* Keep your children in check.

CHEEK

Cheek by jowl—*side by side.* The lovers walked cheek by jowl.

CHEER

Cheer up—*to become cheerful.* Cheer up! for your life is not long.

CHEESE

Make cheese—*to whirl round and then sink down suddenly so as to make the skirt stand out like cheese.* Merry are the maids that make cheeses.

CHEF

Chef d' Oeuvre—*a masterpiece.* This book is going to be my Chef d' Oeuvre.

CHEW

1. **Chew the cud**—*to ruminate in thought.* On Republic Day I will chew the cud in a village far off from any highway to find what has become of our freedom.

2. **Chew the rag, the fat**—*to keep on arguing the point.* Please stop chewing the rag. Let us take dinner and go to bed now.

CHICK

Chick-a-diddle, Chick-a-biddy—*terms of endearment.* Come, my chick-a-diddle, let us go home.

CHICKEN

Chicken-hearted—*a coward.* Tom is a chicken-hearted fellow.

CHILD

1. **Child's play**—*easy.* IAS examination is not a child's play.

2. **From a child**—*since the days of childhood.* I know you from a child.

3. **Second childhood**—*childishness of old age.* Don't forget that we, in old age, pass through second childhood.

4. **With child**—*pregnant.* The woman is with child.

5. **Child wife**—*very young wife.* My friend Walter was married to a child wife.

CHILL

Take the chill of—*to warm slightly.* Take the chill of the water, please.

CHIP

1. **Chip on one's shoulders**—defiant; *challenging manner.* Ministership is a chip on your shoulders.

2. **Chip of the old block**—*one with the characteristics of his father.* Your son is a chip of the old block.

CHITTY

Chitty-faced—*looking like a child.* Remember that chitty-faced girl !

CHOICE

1. **For choice**—*by preference.* I am an author for choice.

2. **Make choice of**—*to select.* Make choice of the book you want.

3. **Take one's choice**—*take what one wishes.* You can take your choice here.

CHOKE

1. **Choke down**—*repress.* You cannot choke down people's difficulties.

2. **Choke off**—*get rid of.* You cannot choke off rising prices through punitive action.

3. **Choke up**—*fill completely.* Her heart was choked up with sorrow.

CHOOSE

1. **Cannot choose**—*can have no alternative.* Beggars cannot choose.

2. **Not much to choose between**—*each about equally good or bad.* There is not much to choose between unemployment and cheap employment.

3. **Pick and choose**—*select with care and at leisure.* You cannot pick and choose your destiny.

4. **The chosen people**—*Israelites.* Israelis are no longer the chosen people.

CHOP

1. **Chop and change**—*buy and sell; to change about; vicissitude.* Every successful man passes through chop and change before he comes to his own.

2. **Chop in**—*to break in; to interrupt.* Please don't chop in when I am talking.

3. **Chop up**—*to cut into small pieces.* Please chop up these vegetables.

CHUCK

1. **Chuck it**—*stop; give over.* Please chuck talking and do something worthwhile.

2. **Chuck up**—*to give in; to give up.* When you face a stronger foe, chuck up.

3. **To give one the chuck**—*to dismiss.* The manager gave the peon the chuck.

CINDERELLA

Cinderella dance—*a dancing party ending at midnight.* Let us have Cinderella dance in the moonlight.

CIRCLE

1. **Reasoning in a circle**—*assuming what is to be proved as the basis for argument.* There is no use reasoning in a circle.
2. **Vicious circle**—*wicked life.* Money is an evil and yet one cannot live without money. It is all a vicious circle.

CITY

Eternal city—*Rome.* Benaras is as well an eternal city as Rome.

CLAP

1. **Clap eyes on**—*to catch sight of.* He clapped his eyes on the girls.
2. **Clap hands**—*to make an agreement.* Vajpayee and Bush have clapped hands.

3. **Clap hold on**—*seize roughly.* The constable clapped hold on the ruffians.
4. **Clap on the back**—*encouragement.* When John passed his college examination, his father clapped him on the back.

5. **Clap-trap**—*a trick to gain applause.* Politics is a clap-trap.

6. **Clap up**—*conclude suddenly.* The secretary clapped up his speech.

7. **Classy**—*of high class or society.* He moves in a classy circle.

CLEAN

1. **Clean hands**—*freedom from guilt of corruption.* No rich man has clean hands these days.

2. **Clean slate**—*a fresh start.* Write your life on a clean slate from tomorrow.

3. **Come clean**—*to confess; to divulge everything.* He came clean in court and was acquitted.

4. **To make a clean breast of**—*to admit frankly.* I am ready to make a clean breast of my mistakes.

CLEAR

1. **Clear off**—*get rid of; dispose of; to go away.* Clear off stolen property.

Clear off old clothes.

Clear off from here.

2. **Clear out**—*to get rid of; to empty.* Clear out bad characters.

Clear out state water.

Clear out of here at once.

3. **Clear the air**—*simplify the situation and relieve tension.* The CBI must clear the air about the Tehelka incident.

4. **Clear the way**—*make the way open.* Clear the way for the royal procession.

5. **Clear up**—*to make or become clear.* Please clear up the mystery of the murder.

CLIP

Clip the wings—*restrain ambition.* Sonia knows how to clip the wings of her party men.

CLISH

Clish-clash—*gossip.* Please stop this clish-clash and let us talk factually.

CLOCK

1. **Clock in**—*to register time of coming.* The employees are expected to clock in.

2. **Clock out**—*to register time of going.* Please clock out when you leave office.

3. **Know what o'clock it is**—*be wide awake.* Every politician must know what o'clock it is.

4. **Like clock work**—*regularly.* He takes his exercise like clock work.

CLOSE

1. **Close a bargain**—*to make an arrangement*. He closed a bargain on this matter.

2. **Close call**—*narrow escape*. The brother of George had a close call.

3. **Close down**—*to come to a standstill*. The trade unions closed down the factories.

4. **Close in upon**—*surround and draw in*. The policemen closed in upon the gang of shoplifters.

5. **Close shop**—*a place where members of a particular community or trade union are employed*. Many Marwari business houses are a closed shop.
   All Parsi institutions are a closed shop.

6. **Close with**—*accede to; to grapple with*. I will close with you for the sale of your goods.

7. **Closet strategist**—*a mere theorist in strategy*. Mao Tsetung was no closet strategist.

8. **With closed doors**—*when private people are not allowed to enter*. David was holding a meeting with closed doors.

CLOTH

1. **Cloth in words**—*to express in words*. I cannot clothe my gratitude in words.

2. **To cut one's coat according to one's cloth**—*to adjust expenditure according to measure*. Wise is one who cuts his coat according to his cloth.

CLOUD

1. **Cloud castle**—*daydream*. Liza passes her time in building cloud castles.

2. **Cloud on one's brow**—*depressed look*. He could not easily see a cloud on Mathew's brow.

3. **In the clouds**—*in the world of imagination*. He lost his career in the clouds.

4. **Under a cloud**—*in trouble; in disgrace or disfavour.* Mr. Stephen was under a cloud.

CLOVER

Live in clover—*live luxuriously*. The rich live in clover.

COAL

1. **Blow the coals**—*to excite passions*. Please do not blow the coals in the meeting.

2. **Carry coal to Newcastle**—*take a thing where it is in abundance*. To bring Yoga from the West to the East is like carrying coal to Newcastle.

3. **Heap coals of fire on the head**—*to excite remorse by returning good for evil*. Mahatma Gandhi heaped coals of fire on the head of the Pathan who came to murder him.

COAST

The coast is clear—*there is no obstacle or danger in the way*. The army was ordered to proceed as the coast was clear.

COAT

Turn coat—*one who changes his principles*. A person in the habit of turning coat never succeeds in life.

COCK

1. **A cock and bull story**—*an unbelievable story*. We are not going to work on your cock and bull story.

2. **Cocky cow**—*a dairy farmer.* Delhi Milk Scheme is our cocky cow.

3. **Knock into a cocked hat**—*to give profound beating.* The thief was knocked into a cocked hat.

4. **That cock won't fight**—*that scheme will not work.* That cock of yours will not fight.

5. **To live like a fighting cock**—*to live on the best of food.* The whole family is living like a fighting cock now-a-days.

COFFIN

Drive a nail in one's coffin—*to do something tending to hasten death.* Doctor's injection drove a nail in the patient's coffin.

COIN

1. **Coin money**—*to make money rapidly.* A trader is always coining money.

2. **Pay a man in his own coin**—*tit for tat.* While I wait and see, I let God pay my enemies in their own coin.

COLD

1. **Cold-blooded**—*without feeling.* It was a cold-blooded murder at Dublin.

Frogs and fish are cold-blooded animals.

2. **Cold comfort**—*uninteresting.* The whole party was a cold comfort.

3. **In cold blood**—*deliberately*. The man was murdered in cold blood.
4. **Leave one cold**—*fail to impress*. The actor's performance left us cold.
5. **Leave out in the cold**—*neglect*. Don't leave your parents out in the cold.
6. **Throw cold water on**—*discourage*. Do not throw cold water on youthful ambitions.
7. **To catch cold**—*to get influenza*. Everybody is likely to catch cold in winter.
8. **To give cold shoulder to**—*to disgrace*. The boss gave cold shoulder to his employees.
9. **To have cold feet**—*not ready to fight*. The general had cold feet in the last war.

COLOUR

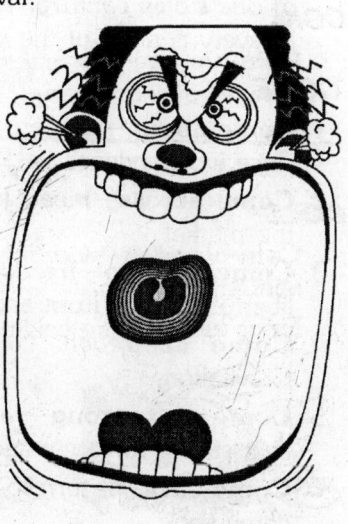

1. **Come off with flying colours**—*to win meritoriously*. Our class team came off with flying colours.
2. **Come out in one's true colours**—*to show one's true character*. When a man loses temper, he comes out in his true colours.
3. **Fear no colours**—*fear no one*. I fear no colours except God.
4. **Give colour**—*to give plausibility*. You must give colour to your story.

5. **High colour**—*rudeness of complexion.* She bears high colour.

6. **Join the colours**—*enlist.* Major Jackson joined the colours in 1939.

7. **Lose colour**—*lose one's good looks.* I wish you will never lose your colour.

8. **Nail one's colours to the mast**—*to commit oneself to some party or plan of action.* Michael has nailed his colours to the mast of youth power.

9. **Off colour**—*disposed; faded.* The boss is quite often off colour.

COLUMN

Fifth columnist—*one who works against the interests of one's own country.* There are many fifth columnists in every country of the world.

COME

1. **Come about**—*happen.* Great things have come about since independence.

2. **Come across**—*meet.* I came across an old friend in the market.

3. **Come and go**—*freedom of action.* Everybody is at liberty to come from and go in our house.

4. **Come at**—*reach.* Newton came at the Law of Gravitation.

5. **Come at it strong**—*to go to great length.* He came at it strong for becoming a minister.

6. **Come back**—*return to popularity.* Samuel has indeed come back.

7. **Come by**—*obtain.* He came by a big job through his friend.

8. **Come down**—*descend.* When are you coming down the ivory tower into the rose garden?

9. **Come down upon**—*to be severe upon.* Don't come down upon little children.

10. **Come down with**—*to pay down.* He came down with full payment.

11. **Come high**—*cost much.* Food comes high now-a-days.

12. **Come in**—*enter.* Please come in.

13. **Come in for**—*receive as one's share.* He came in for large property.

14. **Come into**—*to fall heir to.* He came into a large estate.

15. **Come low**—*to cost less.* Even death is not coming low these days.

16. **Come·of**—*to descend from.* He comes of a respectable family.

17. **Come of age**—*reach full legal age.* The youth has come of age and demands voting rights.

18. **Come off**—*escape.* He could not come off the death trap.

19. **Come out**—*to be published.* No newspaper came out today.

20. **Come out with**—*utter.* The murderer came out with truth.

21. **Come round**—*to happen in due course.* Great events come round in the year.

22. **Come short**—*fail.* He came short of success.

23. **Come short of**—*fail to attain.* He came short of his mission.

111

24. **Come to**—*amount to.* Your debt comes to one hundred rupees.

25. **Come to grief**—*meet with disaster.* Men driven by curiosity often come to grief.

26. **Come to oneself**—*to return to normal state of mind.* A drunkard takes time to come to himself.

27. **Come to pass**—*happen.* Great things have come to pass since 1974.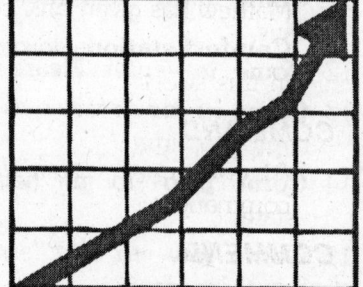

28. **Come to stay**—*become permanent.* Inflation has come to stay.

29. **Come true**—*to be filled.* May your mother's prayer come true.

30. **Come under**—*included under.* Roses come under flowers.

    Cauliflower does not come under flowers.

31. **Come upon**—*to attack; to affect; to hold answerable; to meet.* Hitler came upon the enemy with full force.

32. **Come up with**—*to overtake.* The police came up with the robbers.

33. **To come down with**—*to pay money.* Wait, I will come down with ten rupees.

34. **To come to a standstill**—*to come to a stop.* The train has come to a standstill.

35. **To come to blows**—*to fight.* After the heated discussion, leaders of both the groups came to blows.

36. **To come to light**—*to reveal*. Many things have come to light now.
37. **To come up to**—*to reach*. The train has come up to the outer signal.

COMFORT
1. **Cold comfort**—*little, if any comfort*. The death of Mathew has given only cold comfort to the Opposition.
2. **Comfort station**—*lavatory*. There is no comfort station in this street.

COMMAND
At command—*available for use*. My house is at your command.

COMMEND
Commend me to—*kindly remember me to*. Please commend me to the president.

COMMIT
Commit to memory—*learn by heart*. In ancient times all knowledge was committed to memory.

COMMON
1. **Common good**—*the interest of the community at large*. Learn to do everything you can for the common good.
2. **Common people**—*people at large*. Abraham Lincoln said, "God must have loved the common people because He made so many of them."

COMPANY
1. **Keep company**—*associate*. Keep company with the good only.

2. **Know a man by his company**—*determine the character of a man from the quality of his friends.* You can know Dr. Dube from his company.

COMPARE

Beyond compare—*without rival.* Mrs. Brown is beyond compare today; she has pulled down all the giants around her.

COMPASS

Fetch a compass—*go round in a circuit.* Please stay still and do not fetch a compass.

COMPLIMENT

1. **Compliments of the season**—*compliments appropriate to times.* Please do not send me your compliments of the season. I take them granted.

2. **Left-handed compliment**—*taunting remark*. Thanks even for your left-handed compliment.
3. **Pay or present compliments**—*pay respects*. Pay my compliments to your friend.

CON

Pros and cons—*points in favour and against*. You must study the pros and cons of the whole situation.

CONSCIENCE

In all conscience—*certainly*. In all conscience I will get first class in the examination.

CONSENT

Age of consent—*age at which a girl can be married without consulting her parents*. Lucy has reached the age of consent.

CONSEQUENCE

In consequence—*as a result of*. He died in consequence of a car accident.

CONTACT

To be in contact with—*to be in touch with*. We were in contact with Miss Maria till we were at Mumbai.

CONTEMPT

1. **Contempt of court**—*interference with the administration of justice*. Tony was found guilty of the contempt of court.
2. **To hold in contempt**—*to hate*. He is held in contempt by his colleagues.

CONTEND

Contend against—*dispute.* You cannot contend against destiny.

CONTRARY

1. **In contrary to**—*against.* He spoke in contrary to the ruling party.
2. **On the contrary**—*on the other hand.* Danny is not a rich man. On the contrary, he is a poor fellow.
3. **To the contrary**—*to the opposite effect.* The result was to the contrary.

COOK

Cook one's goose—*finish off; kill; to ruin.* Don't cook your friend's goose.

COOL

Cool one's heels—*to be kept waiting.* He has to cool his heels in the ministerial office.

COPY

Copy-cat—*slavish imitator.* It is the age of copy-cats.

CORNER

1. **All the corners of the earth**—*everywhere.* We have searched all the corners of the earth but have not been able to find David anywhere.
2. **To cut off the corner**—*to take a short cut.* By cutting off a corner, we reached Eastern Market in fifteen minutes.
3. **To drive one into the corner**—*to put in a fix.* Do not depend on Mohan; he will always drive you into the corner.

4. **To put in the corner**—*to punish*. The child was put in the corner by his teacher.

5. **Turn the corner**—*to get past a difficulty or danger*. India has yet to turn the corner.

6. **Within the four corners of**—*contained*. Women should live within the four corners of the house.

COST

1. **At the cost of**—*at the expense of*. You cannot succeed at the cost of others.

2. **To count the cost**—*to consider the risk*. Please count the cost of working on this plan.

COUNT

To count upon—*to depend*. How long can one count upon one's parents?

COUNTRY

Go to the country—*to appeal to the nation during election*. Ministers might go to the country.

COURAGE

1. **Pluck up courage**—*to nerve oneself*. You must pluck up courage to face dangers.

2. **Dutch courage**—*fictitious courage induced by drinking*. Mr. Brown showed Dutch courage by pulling out a knife unnecessarily.

COURT

Out of court—*without claim to be considered*. They decided the matter out of court.

COVER

1. **Cover shorts**—*to buy such stocks as have been sold short in order to meet one's engagements.* Every shopkeeper is forced to cover shorts.

2. **Cover the buckle**—*to execute a certain difficult step in dancing.* You cannot cover the buckle.

CRACK

1. **Crack a bottle**—*drink a bottle.* Mr. White can crack a bottle of beer.

2. **Crack a crib**—*break into a building.* The rioters cracked a crib.

3. **Crack a joke**—*jest.* Please do not crack a joke with me.

4. **Crack credit**—*Destroy one's credit.* Mohan Singh has cracked his credit.

5. **Crack up**—*to fail suddenly; to go to pieces.* The whole plan cracked up for want of money.

6. **In a crack**—*in a moment.* I shall be there in a crack.

CRADLE

From the cradle—*from birth.* He is good from the cradle.

CRAVEN

Craven—*surrender.* They cried craven and went down.

CREAM

Cream of the society—*best people in town.* The cream of the society was present at the marriage of Dolly.

CREATURE

Creature comforts—*material luxuries, wine, etc.* Men are dying for creature comforts.

CRISS

Criss-cross—*to cross repeatedly.* Dame Fortune has criss-crossed me.

CROP

To crop up—*happen unexpectedly.* Since he has declined to study further, the problem of finding a job for him has cropped up now.

CROPPER

Come a cropper—*have a fall.* Looking to her behaviour, she will one day come a cropper.

CROSS

1. **Cross as two sticks**—*particularly perverse and disagreeable.* Liquor and love are cross as two sticks.
2. **Cross one's mind**—*occur.* It crossed my mind to see you.
3. **Cross one's palm**—*put a coin in the hand.* If you want anything done, you must cross the authority's palm.
4. **Cross one's path**—*come in one's way.* As she crossed my path, I won her.

CROW

1. **As the crow flies**—*in a straight line.* My house is four kilometres from here as the crow flies.
2. **Eat crow**—*to be forced to do something very disagreeable; humiliate himself.* The Principal has forced many students to eat the crow.

3. **Have a crow to pluck with**—*have something to settle with*. I do not have a crow to pluck with you.

CROWN

Crown of the causeway—*middle of the street*. My shop is crown of the causeway.

CRY

1. **A far cry**—*a great distance*. Truth in India is a far cry.

2. **Cry against**—*protest*. You must cry against corruption.

3. **Cry down**—*condemn*. You must not cry down what you cannot live without.

4. **Cry off**—*to withdraw from agreement*. The NCP will cry off from the Congress.

5. **Cry out**—*to be in childbirth*. The lady is crying out.

6. **Cry over spilt milk**—*bemoaning what cannot be undone*. There is no use crying over spilt milk.

7. **Cry quits**—*declare a thing even*. Let us cry quits.

8. **Cry up**—*praise*. People cry up the rising sun.

9. **Cry your mercy**—*beg pardon*. You must cry mercy for this lapse.

10. **Great cry and little wool**—*much ado about nothing*. In politics there is much cry and little wool.

11. **Hue and cry**—*noise*. There is much hue and cry in the market.

12. **Within cry of**—*within the hearing distance*. He lives within cry of my house.

CRYSTAL

Crystal clear—*quite clear*. Chairman's remarks were crystal clear to everybody.

CUCUMBER

Cool as cucumber—*undisturbed*. It is best to be cucumber at the time of trouble.

CRUSH

Crush a cup—*empty a cup*. Come, crush a cup.

CRUTCHES

To walk upon crutches—*to depend on others*. You cannot walk always on crutches.

CUP

1. **Cry cupboard**—*cry for food*. The children cry cupboard.
2. **In one's cups**—*under the influence of liquor*. I found him in his cups.
3. **There is many a slip between the cup and lip**—*failure is possible at the last moment*. Don't be very sure about his success, there is many a slip between the cup and lip.

CURLIE

Curlie-wurlie—*any fantastic round ornament*. Some ladies are fond of curlie-wurlie.

CURRY

To curry favour—*flatter*. Clerks generally try to curry favour of their officers.

CURTAIN

1. **Behind the curtain**—*away from public view*. Most of the leaders live behind the curtain.
2. **Iron curtain**—*incommunicable barrier*. There used to prevail an iron curtain in communist countries.

CUT

1. **Cut above**—*something distinctly better*. Milk is a cut above any other drink.

2. **Cut and come again**—*abundant supply*. There is no cut and come again of water in our city.

3. **Cut and dried**—*readymade*. She offered cut and dried food.

4. **Cut and run**—*to be off quickly*. Please cut and run to your office.

5. **Cut dead**—*refuse to recognise*. When she talked to him, he cut dead.

6. **Cut in**—*interpose*. Please don't cut in when I am talking.

7. **Cut it fine**—*to take risks by calculating too narrowly*. The diplomats always cut it fine.

8. **Cut it out**—*leave off*. If you have no time to attend a party, cut it out.

9. **Cut it too fat**—*overdo a thing*. When you have to flatter somebody, don't cut it too fat.

10. **Cut off with a shilling**—*to bequeathe nothing*. His father cut him off with a shilling.

11. **Cut one's coat according to one's cloth**—*to adapt oneself to circumstances*. You must cut your coat according to your cloth.

12. **Cut one's losses**—*to reduce losses*. A good trader must cut his losses.

13. **Cut one's stick**—one's *departure*. It is time to cut our stick.

14. **Cut out for**—*fit for.* He is cut out for a minister.

15. **Cut short**—*abridge.* You must cut short your speech.

16. **To cut both ways**—to be *equally applicable for and against.* His arguments cut both ways.

17. **To cut down**—*to reduce.* In the interest of the country, the Government must cut down its expenditure on defence.

18. **To cut to the heart**—*to wound one's feelings.* By saying that he is a thief, he has cut him to the heart.

CYCLOPS

Cyclops—*one-eyed monster.* Every materialist is a kind of Cyclops.

CYNIC

Play the cynic—*criticize everything.* For God's sake don't play the cynic.

123

DAGGER

1. **At daggers drawn**—*in a state of hostility.* America and Cuba are at daggers drawn.

2. **Look daggers**—*look in a hostile manner.* She looked daggers at her step son.

DAMOCLES

Sword of Damocles—*a big danger.* The Pakistan-China alliance is a sword of Damocles hanging over India.

DAMP

1. **To damp the enthusiasm**—*to discourage.* Your working has damped the enthusiasm of the whole society.

2. **To strike a damp into**—*to discourage.* I don't know why some parents strike a damp into the heart of their children in doing some work.

DANCE

1. **Dance a bear**—*exhibit a dancing bear.* The circus master danced a bear.

2. **Dance attendance on**—*flatter.* Most people dance attendance on ministers.

3. **Dance upon nothing**—*to be hanged.* King Charles danced upon nothing.

4. **Lead one to a dance**—*to put one on a wrong track*. He led the detective to a dance.

DANDY

Handy Pandy Jack-a-Dandy—*a foolish fellow*. Every university student is a Handy Pandy Jack-a-Dandy.

DANGER

Danger line—*the boundary between danger and safety*. The more ambitious a person is the quicker he reaches the danger line.

DARE

Dare say—*suppose*. I dare say he is a good boy.

DARK

1. **A leap in the dark**—*unknown danger*. China's attack on India was a leap in the dark.

2. **Dark continent**—*Africa*. There is much light in the dark continent.

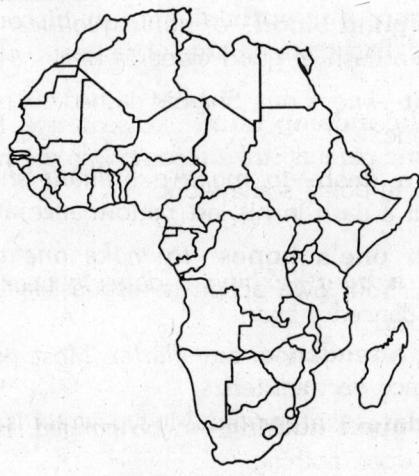

3. **Dark horse**—*a horse whose capabilities are not known*. There are many a dark horse in the ruling party.

4. **Darken one's door**—*visit*. Please do darken my door.

5. **Keep dark**—*to be silent*. It is best to keep dark about political conspiracies.

6. **Keep it dark**—*conceal it*. Please keep it dark.

7. **Prince of darkness**—*devil*. Let not the prince of darkness take you.

8. **The dark ages**—*earlier periods of history*. During the dark ages, a man had very limited wants.

9. **To be in the dark about**—*possessing no knowledge*. Do not pose to be in the dark about the matter.

DASH

1. **Dash off**—*produce hastily*. I can dash off a sonnet.

2. **Dash of good blood**—*of noble qualities*. Peter does not have a dash of good blood in him.

3. **Dash out**—*knock out*. She has dashed out her enemies one by one.

4. **To cut a dash**—*to make a brilliant show*. Gogia Pasha cut a dash in his last performance at Delhi.

5. **To dash one's hopes**—*to make one completely hopeless*. Your own action is responsible for dashing your hopes.

DATE

1. **Out of date**—*antiquated*. My typewriter is out of date now.

2. **Up to date**—*abreast of times.* Newspapers keep your knowledge up to date.

DAY

1. **Call it a day**—*leave off.* Let us call it a day and go home now.

2. **Day by day**—*daily.* Prices are rising day by day.

3. **Day in and day out**—*for a long time.* I have been writing books day in and day out.

4. **Day of doom**—*judgement day.* A thief should never forget the day of doom.

5. **Day off**—*a day's holiday.* Please take a day off and have some rest.

6. **Days of grace**—*extra days allowed for payment of bills.* Do pay your bills within the days of grace.

7. **Day out**—*servant's free day.* It is a day out for our cook.

8. **D-day**—*dooms day.* July 4th is a D-day for Englishmen in America.

9. **Every dog has his day**—*no one is always unlucky.*

10. **One of these days**—*some time in the near future.* We are going to meet one of these days.

11. **See daylight**—*understand a difficult problem.* I have just begun to see daylight about India's problems.

12. **To lose the day**—*to lose war.* At last China lost the day to India.

13. **Win the day**—win *victory.* Napoleon won the day.

DEAD

1. **A dead-letter**—*a law which is no longer in operation; unclaimed letter.* Why do you rely on what is a dead letter now ?

2. **At dead of night**—*at midnight.* The thieves stole away the whole cash at dead of night.

3. **Dead as a door-nail**—*completely dead.* I found him dead as a door-nail.

4. **Dead drunk**—*completely drunk.* He came dead drunk before his wife.

5. **Dead language**—*language no longer spoken.* Sanskrit is not a dead language.

6. **Dead loss**—*a complete loss.* The books soiled in rain are a dead loss to us.

7. **Dead set against**—*utterly opposed to.* Robert is dead set against Tony.

8. **Deadly sin**—*mortal sin*. There is no deadly sin now-a-days.

9. **Dead stock**—*unsaleable stock*. A part of the stock is always a dead stock in every business.

10. **Put the dead wood on**—*gain a great advantage over*. He put the dead wood on his closest friends.

DEAF

1. **Deaf-nut**—*a nut without a kernel*. I can assure you, the business you have started is going to be a deaf-nut.

2. **To be deaf to**—*to be indifferent*. He is deaf to my suggestions.

3. **To give a deaf ear to**—*to disregard*. He gave a deaf ear to the professor's lecture.

DEAL

1. **A good deal**—*a lot*. There is a good deal of money in it.

2. **Deal in**—*trade in*. He deals in cloth.

3. **Deal out**—*to distribute*. Please deal out the cards properly.

DEATH

1. **At death's door**—*very near death*. I found him at death's door.

2. **Death on**—*to be fatal to; fond of; good at*. Liquor was death on him.

He was death on his friend.

He was death on kissing.

3. **Jaws of death**—*point of death*. I found her in the jaws of death.

4. **Put to death**—*kill*. The minister put his King to death.

5. **To be sick unto death**—*tired*. I am quite sick unto death for any more service.

6. **To death**—*to the uttermost*. They duelled to death.

DEBT

1. **Debt of honour**—*debt not recognised by law but binding in honour*. Every debt of honour must be paid.

2. **Debt of nature**—*death*. Everybody has to pay the debt of nature.

3. **Floating debt**—*public debt*. India is under heavy floating debt.

4. **In one's debt**—*under one's obligation*. It is best not to be in anyone's debt.

DECLARE

Declare off—*to renounce or withdraw*. He declared off early in the game.

DECOY

Decoy duck—*one employed to trap others*. Police employ decoy ducks to entice criminals.

DEEP

In deep waters—*in difficulties*. Good men are in deep waters but all men in deep waters are not good.

DEFAULT

Judgment by default—*judgment given against a person because he fails to plead his case*. It was a judgment by default that ruined him.

DEFECT

Defects of one's qualities—*virtues carried to excess; faults apt to accompany or flow from good qualities.* Only morally strong men can be non-violent and cowardice is certainly not a defect of their quality.

DEFENCE

1. **In defence of**—*in support of.* We are in defence of Tom to select him as our leader.
2. **Stand on the defensive**—*to be in an attitude of self-defence.* In arguing the import licence scandal the Prime Minister stood on the defensive in the House of Common.
3. **The best defence is offence**—*one who strikes first, achieves superior position.*

DEFICIENCY

Deficiency disease—*a disease due to lack of necessary substances.* Absence or shortage of vitamins causes various deficiency diseases like Ber-Beri, rickets etc.

DEGREE

1. **By degrees**—*by little and little; gradually.* You can reach the top of the ladder in your career by degrees.
2. **Forbidden degrees**—*the degrees of blood relationship within which marriage is not allowed.* The marriage of brother's son and sister's daughter is forbidden degrees.
3. **Third degree**—*a police method of extracting a confession by bullying or torture.* Third degree methods are customary rather than exceptional with police all over the world.

4. **To a degree**—*to a great degree; to an extreme.* The BJP led government has failed to deliver the goods to a degree; and hence frustration rules supreme in the nation.

DELIVER

Deliver the goods—*to carry out what is required or promised.* John Mathew the author of "Original Jokes" could not succeed in delivering the goods.

DEMAND

In great demand—*much sought after.* Wherever a minister or a billionaire goes, he is in great demand.

DEMARCATION

Line of demarcation—*boundary.* Durand line is a line of demarcation between Pakistan and Afghanistan.

DEMOCRAT

Democrat wagon—*popular support.* Every leader fights for a seat in the democrat wagon.

DENY

Deny oneself—*to refuse to allow oneself gratification; to exercise self-denial.* Great leaders must deny themselves comforts and luxuries to set a right example before the masses.

DEPART

The departed—*dead.* May God rest in peace the departed soul.

132

DEPTH

1. **Out of one's depth**—*in water where one cannot touch the bottom; too deep for one's safety; beyond one's understanding.* The minister now finds himself out of his depth in Parliament.

    I am out of my depth in this subject.

2. **The depth bomb**—*a powerful bomb that explodes under water.* The loss of every by-election is a depth bomb for the ruling party, because it makes its position precarious.

3. **The depths**—*the lowest pitch of humiliation and misery.* Millions in India today have reached the depths.

DESCEND

To descend upon—*to attack.* Vulture is on the look-out to descend upon a corpse.

DESIGN

Argument from design—*the argument for the existence of God from evidence of design in creation.* One may be an atheist but argument from design is irrefutable.

DESTINATION

Destination moon—*a very difficult task.* To become a minister or a billionaire is a destination moon for millions of people.

DETAIL

Detail on—*circumstantially; point by point; piecemeal.* The minister discussed the snap poll in detail at Narora with his lieutenants.

DEUCE

Deuce ace—*a throw of two dice turning up deuce and ace; bad luck.* Mr. Mathew's most mysterious murder was a deuce ace.

DEVIL

1. **Between the devil and the deep sea**—*in a desperate dilemma.* Quite often, even a successful politician finds himself between the devil and the deep sea.

2. **Devil a bit, thing**—*not at all; not one, etc.* If you don't come, I care devil a bit.

   An ambitious man does not care devil a thing.

3. **Devil and all**—*much ado.* Politics is the devil and all. To reach in time was the devil and all.

4. **Devil of a mess**—*very bad mess.* World currency today is in devil of a mess.

5. **Devil's advocate**—*pleader of a bad cause.* One who glorifies corruption is a devil's advocate.

6. **Devil's books or cards**—Whenever I go there, I always find them busy in devil's books.

7. **Devil's dozen**—*thirteen.* Give me a devil's dozen of your best books.

8. **Devil to pay**—*serious trouble ahead*. If we do not rectify our economy, we have a devil to pay.

9. **Give the devil his due**—*give everybody his right*.

10. **Printer's devil**—*printing mistake*. There are few books today without the printer's devil.

11. **Talk of the devil**—*There comes the person we were talking about*. It was all talk of the devil when Mr. Andrews appeared.

12. **The devil among**—*disturbance*. I knew there was the devil among the gathering.

13. **The devil of**—*unpleasant person*. He is the devil of a director.

DEW

With the dew on—*quite fresh*. She bought vegetables with the dew on.

DIAMOND

1. **Black diamond**—*coal*. Black diamond is available in abundance in India.

2. **Diamond cut diamond**—*an encounter between two very sharp persons*. The Congress and the BJP are diamond cut diamond in India.

3. **Rough diamond**—*an uncut diamond; a person possible of great worth but of rude exterior and unpolished manners*. The Principal of our college was a rough diamond.

DEVOID

To be devoid of reason—*to be foolish*. Are you devoid of all reason ?

DEVOUR

To devour the way—*to go fast*. The camels devoured the way quickly.

DIE

1. **Die away**—*to disappear by degrees; become gradually inaudible*. The noise died away in the distance.

2. **Die back**—*to die by degrees*. The tree was dying back for a year before falling down.

3. **Die down**—*to subside*. All agitations die down in the course of time.

4. **Die game**—*to keep one's spirit to the last*. All great men die game.

5. **Die hard**—*to struggle hard against death; to be long in dying*. India's economic ills will die hard.

6. **Die off**—*to die quickly or in large numbers*. With large doses of DDT, mosquitoes die off.

7. **Die out**—*to become extinct; to disappear*. Honesty is dying out in the world.

   With large-scale building activities in the cities, vegetation is dying out.

8. **The die is cast**—*an irrevocable step has been taken; there is no turning back now*. Once the snap poll is announced, the die is cast.

9. **To die daily**—*to suffer spiritual death*. He dies daily.

10. **To die hard**—*to die with great struggle*. Old habits die hard.

11. **To die in harness**—*to die while still at work.* Pandit Nehru died in harness.

12. **To die with one**—*to be finished.* Nazi secrets died with Hitler.

13. **Upon the die**—*at stake.* Our soldiers killed many Chinese upon the die of their lives.

DIFFER

To agree to differ—*to give up an attempt to convince each other.* I and my wife agreed to differ.

DIFFERENCE

1. **Make a difference between**—*to treat differently.* Let us not make a difference between the poor and the rich.

2. **To split the difference**—*to come to a compromise.* They came to split the difference after nearly a year.

DIG

1. **Dig in**—*to cover over by digging; to work hard.* The deal was dug in.

   You must dig in to achieve success.

   After a long battle, the army dug in.

2. **Dig oneself in**—*to entrench oneself; to establish oneself in position.* Mr. Jawahar Lal Nehru dug himself in Prime Ministership.

3. **Dig up**—*to remove from the ground by digging.* Let us not dig up old differences.

4. **To dig at**—*to remark against.* It does not pay to dig at your elders.

DILEMMA

On the horns of a dilemma—*in a difficult situation from two alternatives*. Unable to resign or justify his position, the President found himself on the horns of a dilemma.

DILLY

Dilly-dally—*to trifle; to procrastinate*. Nobody can win war through dilly-dally.

If you seek success, don't dilly-dally.

Dilly-dally war is a lost cause.

DIME

Dime museum—a *cheap show*. Marriage dowry is no dime museum.

DINT

By dint of—*through the power of*. Walter was able to get that job by dint of his uncle's influence.

DIP

1. **Dip into**—to *look into it here and there*. Dip into thoroughly and then start a suitable business.
2. **Dip of the horizon**—*the angle of visible horizon below the level of the eye*. Though dead in 1948, Gandhiji has not yet gone down the dip of the horizon.
3. **To dip into the future**—*to think of coming events*. On completing his education, he has to dip into the future for service.

DIRT

1. **To eat dirt**—*to put up with insult*. An honourable man never eats dirt.

2. **To throw dirt at**—*to abuse.* Do not throw dirt at others.

DISCARD

Throw into the discard—*throw on the scrap heap.* Old men with energy, knowledge and experience cannot be easily thrown into the discard.

DISCORD

Apple of discord—*cause of quarrel.* Money was the apple of discord among the brothers.

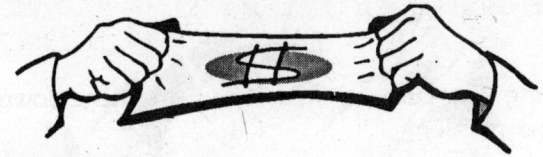

DISCOVERY

A voyage of discovery—*gathering of new ideas.* My visit to America was a voyage of discovery.

DISCRETION

1. **At discretion**—*according to one's judgment.* The magistrate decided the matter at discretion.

2. **At the discretion of**—*by the wish of.* At the discretion of God they have been blessed with a son.

3. **Be at one's discretion**—*to be completely under one's power or control.* The President can declare Emergency in the country at his discretion.

4. **Surrender at discretion**—*surrender unconditionally.* The Pakistani armies in Bangladesh surrendered at discretion.

5. **Years of discretion, age of discretion**—*mature years*. Rosy at fifteen has already reached the age of discretion.

DISGUISE

A blessing in disguise—*a misfortune which produces a good result*. An employer's harsh treatment sometimes proves a blessing in disguise to a lazy employee.

DISH

Dish up—*serve attractively*. Let us sit together and dish up our ideas.

DISMAL

1. **Dismal science**—*political economy*. You find many leaders sunk in the dismal science.
2. **The dismals**—*low spirits*. He is in the dismals now-a-days.

DISMISS

Dismiss from one's mind—*to cease to think about a thing*. When he came to know that his parents will not agree to his marrying Jane, he dismissed her from his mind.

DISPENSE

Dispense with—*terminated.* His services have been dispensed with from Monday.

DISPUTE

Beyond, without, dispute—*indubitably; certainly.* The leadership of the Prime Minister is beyond dispute.

DISSENT

Note of dissent—*note of disagreement.* Many members of the Congress have given notes of dissent on the subject of election of a new Chief Minister for the State of Punjab.

DISSOLVE

Dissolved in tears—*weeping copiously.* The boy was dissolved in tears.

DISTANCE

1. **Keep one at a distance**—*to treat with aloofness.* Mr. Gandhi keeps most of his supporters at a distance.
2. **Keep one's distance**—*to abstain from familiarity; to keep aloof from.* It is best to keep your distance from flatterers.
3. **Within striking distance**—*near enough to hit each other.* Both the armies were standing within striking distance.

DISTINCTION

Distinction without difference—*not much difference.* Hardly a distinction without difference for me whether you stay here in the night or not.

DIVERSITY

Unity in diversity—*to be connected through some inner link.* Almost all nations have some unity in diversity.

DIVINE

1. **Divine right of King**—*right to rule as they like.* The days of divine right of Kings have gone.
2. **Divine service**—*public worship.* My father is devoting his major time in divine service.

DIZZY

To make dizzy—*to bewilder.* Sophia Loren made the whole audience dizzy.

DO

1. **Be done**—*to be at an end; to have done; finished.* The marriage is done.
2. **Do away with**—*abolish; destroy.* Let us do away with dowry.
   Evils must be done away with.
3. **Do brown**—*to cook or roast to brownness; to swindle.* I came to know when the trader tried to do brown.
4. **Do by**—*act towards.* When the trouble comes, will you please do by me?
5. **Do down**—*put down; subdue; to cheat; the better of.* The King did down the rebels.
   When I was away, he did me down.
   You cannot do me down by tall talk.
6. **Do for**—*suit.* This coat will do for me.
7. **Do in**—*to deceive; to get the better of; to exhaust; to ruin; to murder.* You cannot do me in by clever talk.

The man was done in by his friends.

The work has not yet been done in.

8. **Do nothing**—*useless.* Rakesh is a do nothing fellow.

9. **Do one proud**—*to make one feel flattered; to treat one lavishly.* It does me proud to help you.

   Everybody does the minister proud.

10. **Do over**—*to do again; to cover over, as with paint.* The students were told to do over the exercise.

    The painter did over the door.

11. **Do to death**—*to murder.* The doctors did my brother to death.

12. **Do up**—*fasten up; put up; make tidy; arrange; tie up dress.* The doll was done up.

    I am quite done up with today's work.

13. **Do well**—*to be justified; to prosper.* Many villagers do well in the cities.

14. **Do with**—*make use of; to meddle with; to get on with.* Can you do with this pencil ?

    Nothing doing with my business.

    I'll manage to do on with anybody.

15. **Do without**—*not to be dependent on; to dispense with.* I can do without anything in the world.

16. **Have done**—*desist; stop it; have no more dealings.* I have done with gambling at once.

    What have you done with her ?

17. **Have to do with**—*to have any sort of connection.* I have nothing to do with you.

    What have you to do with her ?

18. **To do as the Romans do**—*to adjust according to surroundings*. When in Rome do as the Romans do.

19. **To do in the eye**—*to cheat*. The quality of a thief lies in doing in the eye.

20. **What's to do**—*what is the matter?*

DOE

Doe—John *Doe and Richard Doe; imaginary plaintiff and opponent in the old legal action for ejectment proverbial as a legal action.* Walter City Court is full of John Does and Richard Does.

DOG

1. **Dog cheap**—*very cheap*. Mangoes are dog cheap in India in summer season.

2. **Dog in the manger**—*one who will not let others enjoy what he had himself no use of*. An old man need not be a dog in the manger.

3. **Dog of war**—*havoc*. The plague caused the dog of war.

4. **Dog's age**—*a long time*. We have not met a dog's age.

5. **Dog's chance**—*a bare chance*. You have not a dog's chance to win this job.

6. **Go to the dogs**—*to be ruined*. Due to excessive drinking his health has gone to the dogs.

7. **Throw, give or send, to the dogs**—*to throw away or abandon*. In a losing battle, a great general will not send his soldier to the dogs.

8. **To lead a dog's life**—*to lead a life so wretched that even a dog would not be content with* it. Millions in India today are leading a dog's life.

9. **To throw to dogs**—*to abandon sacrifice*. Mohan threw his whole life to the dogs.

DOLLAR

Almighty dollar—*the power of money*. Almighty dollar rules the world.

DONE

Done for, out, up—*utterly exhausted*. I am completely done up with my routine of writing books.

DONKEY

1. **Donkey work**—*drudgery*. All life is a donkey work.

2. **Donkey's years**—*a long time*. It is strange that we have not met for donkey's years.

3. **To talk the hind-leg off a donkey**—*to do so with invincible pertinacity*. The Opposition in the House of Common quite often talks the hind-leg off a donkey.

DOOMSDAY

Doomsday—*for ever*. His habits are not going to change till doomsday.

DOOR

1. **Next door to**—*in the next house; near; very nearly; bordering upon*. The feverish patient was next door to lunacy.

Mary lives next door to David.

2. **Out of doors**—*in the open air*. Men who work out of doors enjoy good health.

3. **Show one the door**—*turn out of the house*. If the servant does not work faithfully, show him the door.

4. **At death's door**—*about to die*. He is at the death's door now-a-days.

DOUBLE

1. **A double dealer**—*a deceitful person*. He is a double dealer.

2. **Double-edged**—*striking both ways*. I appreciate your double-edged argument.

3. **Double-eyed**—*deeply strained with guilt*. Raja is double-eyed.

4. **Double-faced**—*false*. I am not going to agree to this double-faced argument.

5. **Double-minded**—*undecided*. You are always double-minded in selecting your career.

6. **Double up**—*to fold double; to bend over with laughter, etc*. When he cracked a joke, everybody doubled up.

DOVECOT

Flutter the dovecots—*disturb commonplace*. A topless lady flutters the dovecots.

146

DOWN

1. **Down and out**—*at the end of one's resources*. I was down and out when he came to my help.
2. **Down-hearted**—*dispirited*. He is bound to be down-hearted after losing his job.
3. **Down in the mouth**—*in low spirits*. The Pakistani soldiers in Bangladesh were down in the mouth when General J.S. Aurora conquered them.
4. **Down on one's luck**—*in ill-luck*. Nobody helps when one is down on one's luck.
5. **Down to the ground**—*completely*. The house was burnt down to the ground.

6. **Down under**—*at the antipodes*. Many men are flourishing down under.

7. **Down with**—*put down; swallow*. Down with the bitter pill, quick. I am down with lethargy.

8. **Go down with**—*be acceptable to*. Your goods will go down with the bride.
Honest men will not go down with the corrupt folk.

9. **To grind down**—*to bring peace by force*. The days of grinding down have gone.

10. **To hiss down**—*silence*. I request you to hiss down.

11. **To send down**—*to punish*. The thief has been sent down.

12. **Up and down**—*to and fro*. I walked the whole day up and down.

13. **Ups and downs**—*misfortune*. There are many ups and downs in the life of a man.

DRAG

1. **Drag on**—*to go on as such*. I would advise you to finish the matter as early as you can, there is no use dragging on the same.

2. **Drag up**—*to rear roughly*. Danny was dragged up somehow.

3. **To drag in**—*introduce*. The company is going to drag in a new brand of cigarette in the market next month.

DRAUGHT

To suffer the draught—*to suffer adverse conditions*. His bad behaviour will make him suffer the draught one day.

DRAW

1. **At daggers drawn**—*openly hostile*. India and Pakistan are at daggers drawn with each other.
2. **Draw a blank**—*get no results*. In his struggle for higher life, the modern man quite often draws blank.
3. **Draw back**—*to fall back*. Your sins will draw back on you.
   They drew back their petition.
4. **Draw cuts**—*draw lots*. Let us draw cuts to find the winner.
5. **Draw in**—*to reduce; to contract; to become smaller.* The cotton cloth draws in after washing.
6. **Draw it fine**—*to be too fine; or precise*. Few folk draw it fine now-a-days.
7. **Draw it mild**—*refrain from exaggeration*. When you criticize somebody draw it mild.
8. **Draw near**—*approach*. My birthday is drawing near.
9. **Draw off**—*to cause to flow from a barrel*. They drew off milk from the barrel.
10. **Draw on**—*to approach; to pull on*. They drew on the quilt.
11. **Draw on one's imagination**—*to make imaginative or lying statement*. A good historian does not draw on his imagination.
12. **Draw on one's memory**—*to try to remember; to make use of what one remembers*. Draw upon your memory and let us know where you were born.
13. **Draw the cloth, board, table**—to *clear up after a meal*. When the guests left, the hostess drew the cloth.

14. **Draw the line**—*define a limit.* Before you open a bottle of liquor, please draw the line.

15. **Draw the long bow**—*boast; exaggerate.* In police company, do not draw the long bow.

16. **Draw to a head**—*mature.* No deal of Dr. Brown has yet drawn to a head.

17. **Draw up**—*form in regular order; to cut into shape; to stop.* Please draw up the deed.

    When you have taken two pegs, please draw up.

18. **In drawing**—*correctly drawn.* The contract agreement is in drawing.

19. **Out of drawing**—*inaccurately drawn.* This portrait is out of drawing.

20. **Out of the top drawer**—*of top grade.* This fruit is out of the top drawer.

DREADFUL

Penny dreadful—*cheap sensational fiction.* This is the age of penny dreadful.

DREAMLAND

Dreamland—*the end of one's dreams.* Managership in a big hotel is my dreamland.

DRESS

1. **Dress down**—*to handle with severity.* You cannot dress down even a rat these days.

2. **Dressed day**—*second day of a three-day visit.* He went to see his auntie on the dressed day.

3. **Dress up**—*to dress elaborately; to dress for a part; to masquerade.* The bridegroom was dressed up.

4. **Evening dress, Full dress**—*dress prescribed by custom for evening receptions, dinners, etc.* Posh hotels permit customers only in evening dress.

DRINK

1. **Drink in**—to *absorb rain, etc.* Sand drank in the whole barrel of milk.

   Blotting paper drank in the ink.

2. **Drink off**—to *quaff whole and at a gulp.* That fellow drank off the whole bottle of whiskey.

3. **Drink oneself drunk**—*to drink until one is drunk.* Mr. Fisher drank himself drunk at the house of Mr. Hardy.

4. **Drink the others under the table**—*to continue drinking and remain sober after the others have completely collapsed.* Mr. Mathew drank the others under the table.

5. **Drink to the health of**—*drink wishing someone good.* They drank to the health of the Queen.

6. **Drink up**—*exhaust by drinking.* He drank up his ancestral property.

7. **In drink**—*intoxicated.* I found my friends in drink.

8. **On the drink**—*drunk.* In the evening, John is always on the drink.

9. **Strong drink**—*alcoholic liquor.* Better stay away from strong drink.
10. **The drink**—*the sea.* The ships stay away from strong drink.
11. **To drink hard**—*to be given to excess drinking.* He has been given to drink hard.
12. **To drink up**—*to finish by drinking.* They drank up the party.

DRIPPING

Dripping roast—*a source of easy and continuous profit.* Dreamland Restaurant is a dripping roast.

DROP

1. **A drop in the bucket**—*a very small quantity.* Russian help to India is a drop in the bucket
2. **Drop a curtsy**—*to curtsy.* The village women dropped a curtsy when the Prime Minister arrived.
3. **Drop astern**—*to get more and more left behind.* The ship dropped astern because of its damaged engine.
4. **Drop away, off**—*to depart; disappear.* Famous politicians drop off in their old age.
5. **Drop down**—*to sailor or row away.* The three friends dropped down in a boat.
6. **Drop in**—*to come casually.* Please drop in when you are in the town.
7. **Drop off**—*fall asleep.* Many passengers drop off in the bus.
8. **Drop out**—*to disappear from one's place.* Many students who do not do well in studies drop out.
9. **Dropping fire**—*unremitting; irregular discharge of small arms.* The enemy faced a dropping fire.

The Indian Army faced a dropping fire in Bangladesh.

10. **Get the drop on one**—*to be ready to shoot first.* They got the drop on the lamb rather than on a lion.

11. **To take a drop**—*to drink small quantity of liquor.* Let us take a drop.

12. **To drop a hint**—*to give an indication.* I have dropped a hint that they are going to dismiss you from service.

13. **To drop a remark**—*to speak casually.* They are only dropping a remark now-a-days.

14. **To drop on one's knees**—*humble oneself.* One must drop on one's knees before God.

DROWN

Drown out—*driven out by flood.* The whole village has been drowned out.

DRY

1. **Dry as dust**—*dull.* The picture was absolutely dry as dust.

2. **Dry beat**—*a good beating but not resulting into shedding of blood.* The thief was given a dry beating.

3. **Go dry**—*to adopt liquor prohibition.* Tamil Nadu is the one State that has gone dry again in India.

4. **Dry facts**—*uninteresting ideas.* Please do not bore me with your dry facts.

5. **High and dry**—*isolated.* My wife left for U.S.A. leaving me high and dry.

6. **To dry up**—*to dry completely; to stop talking.* Dry up the fruit before packing.

7. **To go dry**—*to be without liquor.* Many cities have gone dry in world now-a-days.

DUCK

1. **Duck diamond**—*beloved.* I can give up everything for my duck diamond.

2. **Lame duck**—*defaulter; bankrupt; anything disabled.* A dismissed minister is a lame duck.

3. **Like a dying duck**—*languishing.* Indian economy is a dying duck.

4. **Make, play, ducks and drakes with**—*to waste recklessly.* Please do not play ducks and drakes with your parents' hard-earned money.

DUE

1. **Give the devil his due**—*give a fair hearing or fair play to one of the notorious characters.* The Prime Minister of India knows how to give the devil his due.

2. **In due course**—*in the ordinary course of time.* You will meet my friends in due course.

DUEL

Hail the duel—*score a goal.* The Indian team failed to hail the duel.

DULL

Dull-brain—*stupid fellow.* Do not talk to him, he is a dull-brain.

DUST

1. **Bite the dust**—*to be humiliated.* She made him bite the dust.
2. **Dust one's jacket**—*give one a drubbing.* A good teacher quite often dusts the jackets of his pupils.
3. **Kick up a dust**—*raise hue and cry.* Politics is the art of kicking up a dust over nothing.
4. **Throw dust in one's eyes**—*to deceive.* Many children try to throw dust in the eyes of their own parents.

DUTCH

1. **Dutch comfort**—*thank god, it is no worse.* Many men in misery still cling to Dutch comfort.
2. **Dutch lunch, dinner, etc**—*one which everyone brings or pays for himself.* Let us have Dutch lunch if we cannot afford a free-for-all banquet.
3. **Talk like a Dutch uncle**—*to rebuke.* Please don't talk to me like a Dutch uncle.

☆ ☆ ☆

EAGLE

Eagle-eyed—*keen sighted*. Nothing can remain secret before the eagle-eyed Income Tax Officer.

EAR

1. **About one's ears**—*all around*. The houses fell about my ears.

2. **Be all ears**—*give full attention*. When someone speaks to you, please be all ears.

3. **Ear-shot**—*hearing distance*. He stood within ear-shot.

4. **Ear witness**—*a witness that can testify from his own hearing*. There was no eye witness to the murder but

157

there was at least an ear witness, a blind man in the house.

5. **Give ear**—*attend.* When I speak to you, please give ear.

6. **Go in at one ear and out at the other**—make *no permanent impression.* Any advice given to him goes in at one ear and out at the other.

7. **Have a person's ear**—*to be sure of his favourable attention.* Mathew had the M.D.'s ear.

8. **Have itching ears**—*be desirous of hearing.* When Liza sings, I have itching ears.

9. **Lend an ear**—*listen.* When you are free from your work, please lend me an ear.

10. **Over head and ears**—*overwhelmed; completely engrossed.* I found the boy over head and ears in study.

    When her mother died, the boy was over head and ears in sorrow.

11. **Set by the ears**—*to set at strife.* It is not good to set the family members by the ears.

12. **Tickle the ears of**—*to gratify, flatter.* This news will surely tickle the ears of Peter.

13. **To turn a deaf ear**—*to refuse to listen.* She turned a deaf ear to all he said.

14. **Walls have ears**—*there may be listeners around.* Speak gently because the walls have ears.

EARLY

1. **Early and late**—*at all times.* My friends are most welcome to visit me early and late.

2. **Keep early hours**—*to rise and go to bed early.* Old men keep early hours.

3. **The early bird gets the worm**—*one who starts early is more successful.*

4. **To come to an early grave**—*to die untimely.* Raja's father came to an early grave.

EASE/EASY

1. **Easy and free**—*not strict.* Our officer is easy and free.

2. **Easy circumstances**—*affluence.* You are a man of easy circumstances.

3. **Easy come, easy go**—*money acquired without efforts and spent thoughtlessly.*

4. **Easy-going**—*indolent; involved in comforts.* The old princes generally had an easy-going life.

5. **Easy honours**—*honours evenly divided.* The battle was a game of easy honours.

6. **Easy money**—*money made without much labour.* Everybody wants to make easy money now-a-days.

7. **Ease off**—*slacken gradually.* All agitations will ease off in due course of time.

8. **Ease oneself**—*defecate.* Where do you ease yourself in this office ?

9. **Easy street**—*a situation of comfort and affluence.* Everybody want to be in an easy street now-a-days.

10. **Easy virtue**—*loose character.* The girl in question is of easy virtue.

11. **Ill at ease**—*uncomfortable.* In other people's houses, I feel ill at ease.

12. **Take it easy**—*be in no hurry.* There is ample time to catch the train. Please take it easy.

13. **Take one's ease**—*make oneself comfortable.* Take your ease in my house.

EAT

1. **Eat away**—*gnaw gradually; destroy.* Rust eats away iron.

2. **Eat off**—*to clear by setting cattle to it.* Let your cows eat off this meadow.

3. **Eat one's hat**—*an undertaking promised on conditions which one thinks very improbable.* Your assistance will eat my hat.

   I will not eat my hat for you.

4. **Eat one's head off**—*to cost more for food than one is worth.* In these days of high prices, a pet eats off one's head.

5. **Eat one's heart out**—*to pine away brooding.* After her brother's death, she ate her heart out.

6. **Eat one's terms**—*to study for the bar.* Peter ate his terms in the Dublin University.

7. **Eat one's words**—*to retract; recant.* Those who quite often eat their words are not trusted by their friends.

8. **Eat out**—*to finish eatables; to encroach.* Let us eat out the breakfast.

   Let your gossip not eat out my studies.

9. **Eat the air**—*to be deluded with hopes.* For twenty-eight years of my married life, I have been eating the air.

10. **Eat up**—*devour completely; consume; absorb.* They ate up whole dinner.

    Do not be eaten up with your studies.

11. **To eat humble pie**—*to have to apologise; to be humiliate.* Do not be arrogant lest you may have to eat the humble pie.

ECHO

Cheer to the echo—*to applaud most heartily.* When the Prime Minister spoke to the Delhi University students, they cheered to the echo.

ECONOMY

Economy of truth—*falsehood*. Your letter enjoys economy of truth.

EDGE

1. **Edge in a word**—*to get a word in with difficulty.* When the ministers discussed the matter, the secretary tried in vain to edge in a word for his friend.

2. **On edge**—*in a state of expectation*. The nation was on edge when India got her independence on August 15,1947.

3. **Set on edge**—*to excite*. Exotic dances in the movie set the audience on edge.

4. **Set one's teeth on edge**—*to cause discomfort*. The battle of Waterloo set Napoleon's teeth on edge.

5. **To play with edge of tools**—*to deal carelessly with dangerous matters*. Our Principal thinks that Robert is playing with edge of tools.

6. **To take the edge off**—*to make blunt; ineffective.* You are taking the edge off your argument.

EFFACE

Efface oneself—*to avoid notice*. Great men efface themselves in society.

EFFECT

1. **For effect**—*so as to make a telling effect*. She made a thunderous speech for effect.

2. **General effect**—*effect made as a whole*. What is the general effect to your commitments ?

3. **Give effect to**—*to carry out; perform.* The law must be given effect to.

4. **In effect**—*in truth; in reality.* In effect, Gandhiji was the supreme ruler of India.

5. **Leave no effects**—*to die without property; to bequeathe.* I hope to leave no effects.

6. **Take effect**—*to begin to operate; to come into force.* New income tax rules have taken effect last year.

EFFIGY

To burn in effigy—*to burn the figure of a person as an expression of dislike.* Those bad elements who rise to power quite often see themselves burnt in effigy.

EGG

1. **A bad rotten egg**—*a worthless person.* A disobedient student is a bad egg.

2. **A good egg**—*excellent person or scheme.* The Old Age Pension scheme is a good egg.

3. **In the egg**—*in an early stage.* Our social reforms are still in the egg.

4. **Put all eggs in one basket**—*to risk all on one enterprise.* The new actress put all her eggs in her maid in picture and came out with flying colours.

5. **Take eggs for money**—*to be put off with mere promises of payment.* Next time I will not take eggs for money.

6. **To egg on**—*to induce.* He egged on me to insult you.

7. **To have too many eggs in the basket**—*to have too many things to do.* A modern man is worried because he has too many eggs in the basket.

EIGHT

1. **An eight days**—*a week.* I lived with Dr. Paul an eight days.

2. **Figure of eight**—*a figure shaped like 8*. They made a figure of eight in skating.

ELBOW

1. **At one's elbow**—*close at hand*. She kept ample money at her elbow.

2. **Bend, crook, or lift the elbow**—*to drink too much*. Those who lift the elbow come to a trouble.

3. **Out at elbow**—*with coat ragged*. The philosophers are out at elbow.

4. **Up to the elbow**—*completely*. I am down in work up to the elbow.

ELDER

Elder hours—*respectable hours; usually not after 10 p.m.* They played card games in elder hours.

EL DORADO

El Dorado—*the golden land; paradise*. Modern youth try to reach El Dorado without work.

ELECTRIC

Electric blue—*a stately blue colour.* I had the walls of my verandah painted electric blue.

ELEMENTS

1. **In the elements**—*boisterous; very happy.* I found Danny in the elements.

2. **Out of elements**—*minus natural happiness.* He was out of elements during the marriage.

3. **War of elements**—*great storm.* In Fiji Island there has been a war of elements.

ELEPHANT

White elephant—*anything that gives more trouble than it is worth.* To keep a big house these days, is to maintain a white elephant.

ELEVEN

Eleven and twenty long—*exactly right.* Your score in life is eleven and twenty long.

ELEVENTH

Eleventh hour—*nick of time; very last moment.* The police caught the robber red-handed at the eleventh hour.

ELF

1. **Elf lock**—*tangled lock of hair.* My wife has an elegant elf lock.

2. **Elf struck**—*bewitched.* That lady elf struck me completely.

ELFISH

Elfish-selfish—*beautiful but selfish.* Timmy was elfish-selfish.

ELIXIR

Elixir of life—*a liquor once supposed to prolong life indefinitely.* Hope is the only elixir of life in the modern world.

ELL

Give him an inch and he will take an ell—*a concession will encourage the taking of liberties.*

EMBARK

Embark in, on—*get/journey on board a vessel; start a new business.* I hope to embark on S.S. Queen Mary next week.

EMBARGO

Under the embargo—*under the impediment.* Our whole business is under embargo.

EMERALD

Emerald type—*a small size of type.* This book is not intended to be printed in emerald type.

EMPLOY

In the employ of—*in service of.* I am in the employ of A.S. High School, Sydney.

EMPTY

1. **Come away empty**—*to come away without receiving anything.* Gandhiji came away empty handed *from* the

Round Table Conference and straightaway launched the Civil Disobedience Movement.

2. **Empty compliment**—*a hollow compliment; without warmth.* Our political leaders are in the habit of paying empty compliments.

3. **Empty-handed**—*bringing no gift.* He came back from his friend's house empty-handed.

END

1. **At a loose end**—*with nothing to do.* Millions in India are at a loose end.

2. **At an end**—*terminated.* People's unconditional support to the Congress Party is at an end.

3. **At loose ends**—*in disorder.* When the teacher entered the class room, it was at loose ends.

4. **At the end of one's tether**—*without further resource.* Unemployment puts the youth at the end of their tether.

   He was at the end of his tether when his father sent him money.

5. **Be the end of**—*to cause the death of.* Let agriculture be the end of our economic troubles.

6. **Come to an end**—*become exhausted.* My motor engine has come to an end.

7. **End for end**—*with the position of the ends reversed.* Tom and Walter are end for end in hearts of the people.

8. **Get hold of the wrong end of the stick**—*misunderstand blunderingly.* To hold Mohan responsible for the murder of Rosy is to get hold of the wrong end of the stick.

9. **In the end**—*after all*. In the end, the director must be held responsible for the success or failure of a film.

10. **Keep one's end up**—*to maintain one's part*. It is not easy for a common man to keep his end up in the economic strain and stress today.

11. **Make both ends meet**—*to live within one's income*. Happy is the man who can make both ends meet gracefully.

12. **No end**—*very much*. There is no end of trials and troubles today.

13. **Odds and ends**—*miscellaneous things*. He told me about the odds and ends of his business.

14. **On end**—*erect; at a stretch*. I can live without food and water for three days on end.

15. **Place on end**—*upright*. Place the newspaper on end.

16. **To gain ends**—*to find purpose*. You must work hard to gain end.

17. **To gain one's own ends**—*to satisfy one's own selfish purpose.* Some people do help only to gain their own ends.

18. **To put an end to**—*stop.* Lawlessness among students must be put an end to.

19. **World without end**—*for ever.* We want the world without end.

20. **To end in smoke**—*to come to nothing.* All of his efforts ended in smoke.

ENGROSS

1. **Engrossing a deed**—*writing it out in full and regular form.* Engrossing a deed is necessary before you sign it.

2. **Engrossed in**—*completely absorbed.* You are engrossed in her love.

ENOUGH

Enough and to spare—*in sufficient quantity.* I have money enough and to spare.

169

ENTER

1. **Enter a protest**—*write it in books.* The Chairman made a mistake when he did not enter a protest against the misbehaviour of the members of the executive committee.

2. **Enter into**—*to become a party to.* I cannot enter into any agreement without forethought.

3. **Enter on**—*to begin; to engage in.* Let us enter on the publication of Bright Uncle's News.

4. **Enter upon**—*to begin to; to engage in.* When are you entering upon new business?

ENTIRETY

In its entirety—*in its completeness.* The Prime Minister must view the public discontent in its entirety.

EPITOME

In epitome—*on a small scale.* The troubles of India are the troubles of the world in epitome.

EQUATION

Personal equation—*any tendency to error or prejudice due to personal characteristics for which allowance must be made.*

EPOCH

Epoch-making—*a period remarkable for improvement.* We are all living in an epoch-making era.

EQUAL

1. **Equal to the occasion**—*fit for any emergency.* The Indian Army has proved itself equal to the occasion in every Pakistani aggression.

2. **To have no equal**—*to be without rival.* So far as tragic acting is concerned, Meena Kumari had no equal.

ERRAND

1. **A fool's errand**—*a futile journey.* My visit to my friend for money was a fool's errand.

2. **A sleeveless errand**—*a fool's errand.* Your search for name and fame is a sleeveless errand.

3. **Make an errand**—*invent a reason for going.* You can always make an errand for going home.

4. **Once errand**—*for the express purpose and nothing else.* Let help to others be your once errand.

5. **Run errand**—*to be sent to convey messages or perform small pieces of duty.* Children love to run errands.

6. **To go on errand**—*to go with a message.* He went on an errand to the Prime Minister.

ERROR

Writ of error—*reversal of judgment.* We secured a writ of error from the High Court.

ESCAPE

1. **Escape literature**—*light reading.* Fiction is merely an escape literature.

2. **To escape one's notice**—*not to come within observation.* This error escaped my notice.

ESTATE

The fourth estate—*the press.* The fourth estate is the most important institution in democratic countries but of no importance in totalitarian nations.

ETERNITY

The eternities—*the ever lasting reality or truth.* Democracy can be successfully run only by due esteem of the eternities.

EUROPE

European plan—*in hotels, system of charging for lodging and service without including meals.* The European plan is popular in some American hotels as well.

EVE

1. **Born of Eve**—*every human being.* Very few born of Eve can resist the temptation of food.
2. **Daughter of the Eve**—*woman.* The daughter of the Eve is an essential part of the universe.

3. **On the eve of**—*at the time of doing something.* He worked hard on the eve of examination.

EVEN

1. **Be even with**—*be revenged on; be quits with.* Blood for blood is the wrong mode to be even with somebody.

2. **Even date**—*same date.* Thanks for your letter of February 17 and I draw your kind attention to my letter of even date.
3. **Even hand**—*just.* I have distributed the profits even handed.
4. **Even money**—*an equal sum on bet on either side.* Black marketeers are putting even money on both the groups fighting election.
5. **Even now**—*a very little while ago.* I met her even now.
6. **Even on**—*without intermission.* Richard is attacking the corrupt government even on.
7. **Even upon**—*come square with.* Balder is planning to be even upon Peter.

EVENING

1. **The evening of life**—*old age.* My father is now enjoying the evening of life.
2. **The evening star**—*decline.* It is now the evening star of her beauty.

EVER

1. **Ever and anon**—*from time to time; ever so; to an extent; to a very great extent*. He comes to my house ever and anon.

2. **Ever green**—*always green; always fresh*. The recollections of your kindness shall remain ever green in my mind.

3. **Ever so**—*to any extent*. He will do for her anything ever so.

4. **For ever**—*to all eternity*. Truth will triumph for ever.

5. **The Ever-lasting**—*God*. The Ever-lasting knows better.

EVERY

1. **Every bit, whit**—*the whole; quite*. He was every bit a gentleman.
   He worked hard every whit.

2. **Every here and there**—all *over; dispersedly*. You find flowers in Delhi every here and there.

3. **Every man jack**—*everybody*. Every man jack is welcome to the meeting.

4. **Every mother's son**—*everyone without exception*. Every mother's son should fast one day in a week for health.

5. **Every now and again**—*now and then*. We face troubles every now and again.

6. **Every now and then**—*at intervals*. Miss Grace rings me up every now and then.

7. **Every other**—*every second or alternate*. I go to Connaught Place every other day.

8. **Every so often**—*at intervals*. He rings me every so often.

9. **Every which way**—*every way; in disorder.* You come across troubles every which way.

EVIDENCE

1. **In evidence**—*received by the courts as competent evidence.* He made his statement in evidence.

2. **Turn king's evidence**—*give evidence against an accomplice in crime.* One of the accomplices in the murder of Dr. Paul's wife has turned king's evidence.

EVIL

1. **An evil-minded**—*wicked.* Beware of evil-minded persons.

2. **Speak evil of**—*to slander.* Don't speak evil of your friends.

3. **The evil one**—*the devil.* Beware of the evil one in your daily life.

EXAMPLE

1. **To make an example**—*to punish.* The court should make an example of Man Singh.

2. **To set a good example**—*to create a good precedent.* Our leaders should themselves set good examples in serving the people; others will naturally follow.

EXCEPTION

1. **Exception proves the rule**—*the making of an exception proves that the rule holds good in case not*

excepted. One honest man among thousands who are blackmarketeers is an exception that proves the rule.

2. **To take an exception**—*object*. He took exception to my remarks.

3. **With the exception of**—*except*. Every boy with the exception of John will attend the party.

EXCESS

1. **Carry to excess**—*to do too much*. Do not carry even good ideas to excess.

2. **In the excess of**—*more than*. You have money in excess of what you need.

EXCHANGE

In exchange—*in return*. You may take my book in exchange of your pen.

EXHIBITION

Make an exhibition of oneself—*to behave foolishly; excite; ridicule*. Those who wear mini-skirts make an exhibition of themselves.

EX-OFFICIO

Ex-officio—*by virtue of one's office*. The head of the office is ex-officio chairman of the office's Staff Council.

EXPENSE

At the expense of—*to pay the cost of*. Do not earn wealth at the expense of your health.

EXPERIENCE

Experience of meeting—*one for the relating of spiritual experiences*. Experience of meeting is something most desirable for those who seek the truth.

EXPLAIN

Explain away—*to modify the force by explanation; generally in a bad sense.* The murder of Mr. Michael is being explained away but the coming generation will dig out the truth.

EXPLOSION

Explosion shot—*a golf stroke to send a ball forcibly out of a bunker.* 'Garibi Hatao' was an explosion shot in 1971.

EXPLOSIVE

1. **High explosive**—*very irritable man.* Your younger brother is a high explosive.
2. **An explosive situation**—*a situation which may burst out any time.* An explosive situation developed in South East Asia due to the presence of United States warships.

EXPRESS

1. **Express oneself**—*to give expression to one's thoughts.* You must express yourself clearly, calmly and correctly.
2. **An express wish**—*an ardent desire.* It was an express wish of Mr. Nehru that his ashes should be scattered over the fields of India.
3. **Express bullet**—*fast danger.* NATO is an express bullet from imperialist countries.

EXTENT

1. **A vast extent of marsh**—*useless stuff.* The manifesto of the communist parties in India is a vast extent of marsh.

2. **To a great extent**—*for the most part of it.* You are responsible to a great extent for that error.

EXTREME

1. **Go to the extreme**—*to go too far; to use extreme measures.* The government dares not go to the extreme against Danny.

2. **In the extreme**—*in the last; highest degree; extremely.* In Moscow winter is cold in the extreme.

3. **The last extremity**—*the last pitch of misfortune.* Hunger is the last extremity of economic misery.

EYE

1. **All my eye**—*humbug.* Your greatness is all my eye.

2. **Be all eyes**—*give full attention.* Be all eyes to your superiors.

3. **Be a sheet in the wind's eye**—*be intoxicated.* With all your glory do not be a sheet in the wind's eye.

4. **Clap, lay, set, eye on**—*to see.* He clapped his eyes on the girl.

   He laid his eyes on the purse.

5. **Cry one's eyes out**—*weep copiously.* When someone dies, there is no use crying your eyes out.

6. **Cut one's eye-tooth**—*to cease to be a child.* Children cut their eye-teeth early these days.

7. **Eye for eye**—*full revenge.* Eye for eye is an old doctrine of vengeance.

8. **Eye of day**—*sun.* Let us enjoy the beauty of the eye of day.

9. **Give an eye to**—*attend.* Every youth gives an eye to the pretty girls.

178

10. **Have an eye on**—*to contemplate; to have regard to; to incline towards.* You must have an eye on your chosen career in life apart from any romance.

11. **In eye**—*in sight.* Keep the baby in eye.

12. **In one's mind's eye**—*in imagination.* He has risen high in his mind's eye.

13. **In the wind's eye**—*against the wind.* It is hard to drive your scooter in the wind's eye.

14. **Keep one's eye on**—*to observe closely; to watch.* You must keep your eye on the growing child.

15. **Keep one's eye skinned**—*to be extremely watchful.* In the months ahead the Opposition will have to keep its eye skinned against the machinations of the party.

16. **Make a person open his eyes**—*cause him astonishment.* The loss of by-elections must be a lesson to make the ruling party open their eyes.

17. **Make eyes at**—*to look at in an amorous way; to ogle.* The youth enjoy making eyes at each other.

18. **Mind your eye**—*take care.* Mind your eye lest you may cause an accident.

19. **My eye**—*a voice of surprise.*

20. **Open a person's eye**—*to make him see something of which he is ignorant.* Hunger, unemployment and corruption have opened the eyes of the youth today.

21. **Pipe, or put a finger in the eye**—*to weep.* If you have lost your purse, don't pipe your eye.

22. **Put a person's eye out**—*billed him; supplant him in favour.* His fondness for his son put the minister's eye out.

23. **See eye to eye**—*think alike.* David and Danny do not see eye to eye.

24. **See with half an eye**—*see without difficulty.* One can see with half an eye the coming troubles of our country.

25. **Throw sheep's eyes at**—*ogle sheepishly.* She threw sheep's eyes at her lover.

26. **Turn a blind eye on**—*to feign not to see.* The management of the firm came to trouble because they turned a blind eye on the working conditions in the factory.

27. **Under the eye of**—*under the observation of.* The boy was brought up under the eye of his mother.

28. **Up to the eye**—*deeply involved.* Roberts is up to the eye in power politics.

F's

Three F's—*free sale; fixity of tenure; fair rent*. If we enforce the three F's in India, prices will come down immediately.

FACE

1. **Face down**—*to bash by stern looks*. The father faced down the flirt.
2. **Face out**—*to carry off by bold strokes*. She faced out her success in getting a job.
3. **Face the music**—*to accept unpleasant consequences at their worst*. The smugglers must be put before law to face the music.
4. **Face to face**—*opposition; in actual presence*. The two enemies met face to face in the battle-field.
5. **Face value**—*value as stated in paper*. The face value of this coin is one rupee.
6. **Fly in the face of**—*to set oneself directly against*. The smugglers fly in the face of law and order.

7. **Have two faces**—*to be double faced*. Every politician has at least two faces.

8. **In the face of**—*in defiance of*. You must not work in the face of law.

9. **Lose face**—*lose prestige*. Many ministers have lost faces.

10. **On the face of it**—*on its own showing*. The Congress is collapsing on the face of it.

11. **Pull a long face**—*to look dismal*. When a politician loses elections, he pulls a long face.

12. **Put a good face on**—*to assume bold appearance*. Every corrupt man tries to put a good face on his activities.

13. **Run one's face**—*to obtain things on credit by sheer imprudence*. You must not run your face in the grocery shop.

14. **Save one's self**—*to avoid humiliation*. You must pay something to the creditors to save your face.

15. **Set one's face against**—*to oppose strenuously*. A.B. Vajpayee has set his face against corruption.

16. **Show one's face**—*appear*. I will show my face at your marriage, even though I am seriously ill.

17. **To look in the face**—*to be bold*. To look in the face of one's enemy is a reflection of boldness.

18. **To make faces**—*to grimace*. Do not make faces at your elders.

19. **To one's face**—*in his presence*. Nobody dares criticize a minister or a millionaire to his face.

20. **To put a new face on**—*to alter aspect of*. The appointment of new chairman has put a new face on company's policy.

FACT

1. **As a matter of fact**—*in reality.* As a matter of fact, Allan Border was a great cricketer.
2. **In fact**—*indeed.* In fact, we met last year.
3. **In point of fact**—*indeed.* In point of fact, our college team won the match without much effort.
4. **The fact of the matter**—*the plain truth.* The fact of the matter is that the older a man gets, the harder he has to work.

FADE

Fade away—*to disappear gradually.* Evils do not fade away.

FAG

Fag-end—*the refuse or meaner part of a thing.* To serve our guests at the fag-end of table is contrary to good manners.

FAGGOT

Burn one's faggot—*to recant a heresy.* The Pope forced the atheists to burn their faggot.

FAIL

1. **Fail of**—*to come short of accomplishing any purpose.* Sonia has not failed her ambition.
2. **Without fail**—*certainly.* We are meeting tomorrow without fail.

FAIR

1. **A day after the fair**—*too late.* He arrived in the office a day after the fair.

2. **A fair hand**—*writing which can be easily read.* John has a fair hand.

3. **All is fair in love and war**—*all methods used in love or war are justified.*

4. **Behind the fair**—*too late.* In working for success he was behind the fair.

5. **Bid fair**—*promise.* He bids fair to become a minister.

6. **Fair and square**—*honest.* You ought to be fair and square in all your dealings.

7. **Fair means**—*honestly.* He won the game by fair means.

8. **Fair play**—*no cheating.* Let us adopt fair play in everything.

9. **Fair promise**—*good chance.* There appears to be a fair promise in this business.

10. **Fair trade**—*the principle of reciprocity.* The trade today may be free but it certainly is not fair.

11. **Fair-weather friends**—*not good in need.* Keep away from fair-weather friends.

12. **Get one's fairing**—*to get one's deserts.* Everyone gets his fairing in life.

13. **In a fair way to**—*likely to succeed.* She is in a fair way to bear a child.

14. **Keep fair with**—*remain on amiable terms with.* You must keep fair with your friends.

15. **One's fair fame**—*good name.* Nehru would always enjoy fair fame through out the world.

16. **Stand fair with**—*to be in the good books of.* Home Minister stood fair with the Prime Minister.

17. **The fair sex**—*feminine sex*. The fair sex is not fair to the unfair sex.

FAIRY

Fairy tale—*an incredible tale*. His love story is nothing but a fairy tale.

FAITH

1. **In good faith**—*with sincerity*. He told me all this in good faith.

2. **To pin one's faith upon**—*to depend*. I am pinning my faith upon you in this case.

FALL

1. **Fall across**—*to meet by chance*. I fell across an old friend on the road.

2. **Fall among**—*to find oneself in the midst of*. One night I fell among the thieves.

3. **Fall away**—*to decline; to languish; to grow lean; to revolt*. Glory always falls away.

   In the absence of his beloved, he fell away.

   Many Congressmen fell away.

4. **Fall back**—*to retreat*. In these days of high prices, many common folk are falling back on their reserves.

5. **Fall back, fall edge**—*no matter whatever happens*. Fall back, fall edge, the labour party will move heaven and earth to win elections.

6. **Fall behind**—*to lag*. Our Five Years Plans are falling behind.

7. **Fall flat**—*to fail*. All his efforts to succeed fell flat.

8. **Fall for**—*to be enamoured of; to be taken in by*. The boy fell for the first girl he met on the road.

9. **Fall foul**—*to come in conflict*. The boy fell foul of the in-laws.

10. **Fall in**—*to take places in ranks*. The soldiers were ordered to fall in.

11. **Fall in with**—*to agree; to comply with;. to meet by chance*. The ministers had to fall in with the Prime Minister.

    I fell in with an old teacher.

12. **Fall off**—*to deteriorate; to die; to perish; to draw back*. The leaves fall off in autumn.

13. **Fall on**—*to begin eagerly*. The studious students fall on their books near the examination.

14. **Fall on one's feet**—*to come well out of a difficulty to gain unexpected good fortune*. The soldiers fell on their feet in Bangladesh.

15. **Fall over**—*to go over to the enemy; to go to sleep*. Many Pakistani soldiers fell over in Bangladesh.

16. **Fall short**—*to turn out to be short in supply on.* Sugar fell short in the marriage.

17. **Fall through**—*fail; come to nothing.* All plans of men and mice fall through.

18. **Fall upon**—*attack.* The people fell upon the policemen near the holy place.

19. **To fall a prey**—*to become a victim.* You have just fallen a prey to his advice.

20. **To fall in with**—*agree.* I do not fall in with your views.

21. **To fall out**—*give up.* Do not fall out of your hope.

22. **Try a fall**—*take a bout in wrestling.* D'Souza and Braganza are trying a fall in political wrestling.

FALSE

1. **Play one false**—*to act falsely or treacherously to a person.* I hope the party leaders will not play false to Tom.

2. **Put one in a false position**—*to bring anyone into a situation in which he must be misunderstood.* I tried my best but he put me in a false position.

FAMA

Fama clamosa—*any notorious rumour ascribing immoral conduct to a minister.* No minister cares a dime for fama clamosa.

FAME

House of ill fame—*brothel.* Gentlemen should stay away from houses of ill fame.

FAMILY

1. **In a family way**—*in a familiar informal manner*. Let us gossip in a family way.
2. **In the family way**—*pregnant*. I don't think the bride is in the family way.
3. **Official family**—*cabinet*. The official family has lost a top minister.

FANCY

1. **To catch the fancy of**—*to please*. My cycle caught the fancy of my friend.
2. **To take a fancy to**—*to love; to take interest*. The young girl took a fancy to the prince.

FANTI

To go fanti—*to opt the ways of the natives*. Many Americans have gone fanti in India.

FAR

1. **By far**—*to a great degree*. Rajiv Gandhi is by far the most powerful person in the world today.

2. **Far and away**—*by a great deal*. Napoleon won the war by far and away.

3. **Far and near**—*everywhere*. You find Indians far and near in the world.

4. **Far and wide**—*all about*. Roses were far and wide in the garden.

5. **Far be it**—*God forbid*. Far be it that I should think evil of you.

6. **Far between**—*infrequent*. My visits to temples are few and far between.

7. **Far cry**—*a long distance*. Peace was a far cry from the cold war.

8. **Far-fetched**—*having distant meaning*. His words are far-fetched.

9. **Far-reaching**—*widely applicable*. This is my far-reaching plan.

10. **Far-sighted**—*seeing to a great distance*. My father is a far-sighted man.

11. **In so far as**—*to the extent possible*. I will help you in so far as it lies within my power.

FASH

Never fash your thumb—*take no trouble in the matter.* Never fash your thumb in criminal matters.

FAST

1. **Fast by**—*close to.* He lives fast by the railway station.
2. **Fast friend**—*bosom friend.* Both of them are fast friends.
3. **Fast with gout**—*confined.* You are fast with gout.
4. **Hard and fast**—*definite.* There are no hard and fast rules in international politics.
5. **To play fast and loose**—*to be unreliable.* Don't play fast and loose with your parents.

FASTEN

Fasten on—*to direct one's eyes on.* The boy fastened on the girl almost at first sight.

Blame was fastened on the boy.

FAT

1. **A fat lot**—*much.* There is a fat lot in politics.
2. **Fat-brained**—*dull; stupid.* He is a fat-brained man.
3. **Fat-headed**—*dull; stupid.* He is a fat-headed man.
4. **Fat stock**—*livestock fattened for the market.* His fat stock will bring him good money.
5. **Fat-witted**—*dull; stupid.* He is a fat-witted man.
6. **The fat is in the fire**—*a critical act as precipitated the trouble.* Now that you have told her all the facts, the fat is in the fire.

FATAL

1. **Fatal blow**—*a blow which causes death.* He struck his enemy a fatal blow.
2. **Fatal thread**—*allotted length of life.* All of us hang by the fatal thread.

FATHER

1. **Father of the nation**—*greatest leader.* Mahatma Gandhi was the Father of the Nation.
2. **Gathered to one's fathers**—*to die and be buried.* Timmy crushed under a bus and has been gathered to the fathers.

FATUOUS

Fatuous fire—*Will-o'-the-Wisp.* At night in the marshes we often meet fatuous fires.

FAULT

1. **At fault**—*guilty.* For the sad state of our education today our teachers are at fault.
2. **Find fault**—*to censure; to criticize.* It is easier to find fault than to remedy them.

FAUNA

Fauna and flora—*animals and plants.* Fauna and flora are the real wealth of a nation.

FAVOUR

1. **Favours to come**—*favours still expected.* Even after marriage there are favours to come.
2. **In favour of**—*on the side of.* He drew his will and testament in favour of his sister.

FAWN

To fawn on—*to flatter.* The children fawn on their parents.

FEAR

Without fear and favour—*impartially.* We must do our duty without fear and favour.

FEATHER

1. **A feather in one's cap**—*a striking distinction.* Producing such a nice picture is a feather in director's cap.

2. **Feather one's nest**—*to accumulate wealth for oneself while serving others in a position of trust.* He is in the habit of feathering his nest.

3. **In high feather**—*in high spirits.* When a person wins something, he is in high feather.

4. **Make the feathers fly**—*to throw into confusion by a sudden attack.* Napoleon often made the feathers fly.

5. **Show the white feather**—show *signs of cowardice.* When Napoleon attacked, the Austrians showed the white feather.

FEED

1. **Fed up**—*tired; bored.* Students are fed up with this false education that leads them from nowhere to nowhere.

2. **Off one's feed**—*disinclined to eat.* Because of illness the patient is off his feed.

FEEL

1. **To feel at home**—*to at feel ease or make them comfortable.* All of us should try to make the foreign tourists feel at home while they are in India.

2. **To feel the pulse**—*to find out one's secret.* Before taking any decision in respect of my brother's marriage, my daddy would like to feel his pulse.

FELLOWSHIP

Fellowship—*expression of love and mutual regard.* The King gave his minister the right hand of fellowship.

FENCE

To sit on the fence—*avoid committing oneself.* Many politicians are sitting on the fence in India and Pakistan regarding Kashmir problem.

FETCH

1. **Fetch and carry**—*perform humble service for someone.* He fetched and carried for his guru.

2. **Fetch off**—*to bring out of danger or difficulty.* He fetched off his family from Pakistan.

3. **Fetch out**—*to draw forth; to develop.* He fetched out the meaning of the poem.

4. **Fetch up**—*to recover; to come to a stop; to bring up; to fear.* He fetched up the girl into a beautiful maidenhood.

FEW

1. **A good few**—*a considerable number.* A good few attended the mourning meeting.
2. **In few**—*in a few words.* In few, I will do my best to help you.
3. **Quite a few**—*large number.* Quite a few came to meet the minister.
4. **Some few**—*an inconsiderable number.* Some few came to the meeting.

5. **The few**—*the minority.* The few defeated the many.

FIDDLE

1. **Fiddle-faddle**—*to trifle; to dally; trifling talk or behaviour; nonsense.* Please don't fiddle-faddle with my pen.

   If you fiddle-faddle, you lose the game.

   I don't like all this fiddle-faddle.

   He is a fiddle-faddle fellow.

   Fiddle-faddle; shut up.

2. **Face like a fiddle**—*a dismal face*. Our teacher has a fiddle face.
   Our teacher has a face like a fiddle.
3. **As fit as a fiddle**—*in the best condition*. At the time of marriage he was as fit as a fiddle.
4. **To play the first fiddle**—*to take a leading role*. Peter plays the first fiddle in school drama.
5. **To play the second fiddle**—*to play a subordinate role*. Jane plays the second fiddle in our school drama.

FIELD

1. **Fair field and no favour**—*equal conditions to contest*. Let our job be a fair field and no favour.
2. **Field of view**—*what is visible at the moment*. No job is in my field of view.
3. **Keep the field**—*to maintain one's ground*. In these days of soaring prices it is hard to keep the field in daily expenditure.
4. **Take the field**—*to begin war-like operations*. When a child is angry with the parents, he takes the field.

FIERY

1. **Fiery cross**—*a charred cross dipped in blood*. Westernism bears the fiery cross for the cultured nations of the East.
2. **Fiery new**—*hot from newness*. Modern purchasers look for articles fiery new.

FIFTH

Fifth column—*enemy sympathisers in a country at war*. In confrontation of two countries, some people of one country are prone to work as fifth columnist for another country.

FIG

Not to care a fig—*not to care at all.* I do not care a fig for your advice.

FIGHT

1. **Fight it out**—*struggle on until the end.* If we seek to purge the nation of corruption we shall have to fight it out.

2. **Fight shy of**—*to avoid from mistrust.* The virtuous must not fight shy of fighting it out with the wicked in this Kurukshetra of modern civilization.

3. **Live like the fighting cocks**—*to get the best of meat and drink.* It is spiritually degrading for the educated classes to live like the fighting cocks.

4. **Fight to a finish**—*to fight till the end or death*. Our army shall always fight to a finish.

FIGURE

1. **Cut a figure**—*to make a conspicuous appearance*. Robert cuts a figure at every social function.

2. **Figure on**—*count on*. In every emergency I figure on you for help.

3. **Person of figure**—*man of distinction*. In the world of literature Bernard Shaw will always remain a person of figure.

4. **To cut a sorry figure**—*to be ridiculed*. The chairman cut a sorry figure in the meeting.

FILL

Fill in—*to occupy esp. time; to add what is necessary to complete*. Food, sex and greed fill in all spare time of the modern man.

FILMY

Filmy ferns—*ferns with very thin leaves; weak people*. Public School children are filmy ferns.

FIND

1. **Find one in**—*to supply one with*. You will find God in children.

197

2. **Find one's account in**—*to find satisfactory profit in*. Every top government officer finds his account in the firms he deals within his official capacity.

3. **Find one's feet**—*to be able to stand*. A student finds his feet only after quitting the portal of universities.

4. **Find oneself**—*to feel, as regards health, happiness, etc.* After long illness the boy at last has found himself.

5. **Find out**—*discover; detect*. The CBI must find out the truth about the murder of Anil Chopra.

6. **To find one's legs**—*to rise; to stand up*. When the drunkard found his legs he noticed that he was lying on the road.

FINE

1. **In fine**—*in short*. In fine, I cannot meet you today.

2. **Fine gentleman, lady**—*an idle person ostentatiously fashionable; sometimes refined*. Dr. Paul is a fine gentleman.

   You find fine ladies at every social function.

3. **Fine arts**—*painting, sculpture and music*. Fine arts require spare money for their pursuit.

4. **Fine writing**—*literary matter or style pretentiously ornate*. These are not the days of fine writing.

FINGER

1. **A finger in the pie**—*a share in the doing of anything, often of meddling character*. The Opposition in Parliament has its finger in every pie.

2. **To have at one's fingers' ends**—*to be perfect master of a subject*. The students have facts at their fingers' ends.

3. **Have one's fingers all thumbs**—*to be awkward in handling*. The old woman Principal has her fingers all thumbs.

4. **On one's finger-tips**—*to be well-versed in*. He has history at his finger-tips.

5. **To burn one's fingers**—*to get into unexpected trouble*. You have burnt your fingers in that speculative deal and today you are penniless.

6. **To look through one's fingers**—*to pretend not to see*. The teacher has to look through his fingers.

7. **To the finger-nails**—*completely*. He is under debt to the finger-nails.

FINISH

Fight to a finish—*to fight till the end or death*. Our army shall always fight to a finish.

FIRE

1. **Between two fires**—*between two difficulties*. Sometimes circumstances put us between two fires.

2. **Fire and brimstone**—*wrath; extreme irritation*. He was full of fire and brimstone with his corrupt uncle.

3. **Fire and sword**—*devastation*. The Partition brought fire and sword to the people.

4. **Fire away**—*begin*. Fire away with your work immediately.

5. **Fire off**—*to discharge; to ask; utter in rapid succession*. The examiner fired off a hundred questions.

6. **Fire out**—*dismiss*. Fire out this servant, he is a dishonest man.

7. **Fire up**—*to fly into passion*. Hardly had I uttered this word than he fired up and began to beat me.

8. **On fire**—*burning*. India today is a house on fire.

9. **Set on fire, set fire to**—*burn*. They set the house on fire.

   They set fire to this building.

10. **Set the Thames on fire**—*do something remarkable*. It is high time that you should set the Thames on fire.

11. **To pour oil on fire**—*to worsen an already bad situation*. The President's speech poured oil on fire.

12. **Under fire**—*exposed to the enemy's fire*. The ruling party is always under fire in Parliament.

FIRST

1. **First and the foremost**—*the most important*. The first and the foremost thing for you is to learn computers.

2. **First come, first served**—*to be obliged on one's turn*. The allotment of society flats is on the first come, first served basis.

3. **From first to last**—*throughout*. She stood by me from first to last.

4. **First fruit**—*first profit; first result*. Nervousness is the first fruit of affluence.

5. **First-hand information**—*information got through one's own self*. Our newspaper always gives first-hand information to its readers.

6. **First thing**—*before doing anything else*. Yoga should be the first thing in the morning.

7. **First water**—*highest quality*. This is a diamond of the first water.

FISH

1. **A fish out of water**—*a person who feels uncomfortable in his surroundings*. While travelling abroad, I felt like a fish out of water.

2. **Fish in troubled waters**—*to take advantage of disturbed times to further one's own interests*. To fish in troubled waters is the order of the day.

3. **Have other fish to fry**—*have something else to do or attend to*. Besides teaching, every teacher has some other fish to fry.

4. **Make fish of one and flesh of another**—*to make invidious distinction.* Ministers make fish of one and flesh of another in dealing with the public.

5. **Neither fish nor flies nor good red herring; neither fish nor flesh nor fowl**—*to be neither one thing nor another.*

6. **Pretty kettle of fish**—*confusion.* Our office is a pretty kettle of fish.

7. **Queer fish**—*a person of odd habits or of a nature with which one is not in sympathy.* A truly cultured man is a queer fish in modern sophisticated society.

FIT

1. **Fits and starts**—*irregularly.* We should work regularly and not by fits and starts.

2. **Fit of the face**—*a grimace.* To make a fit of the face harms one who makes it mentally and morally.

3. **Fit out**—*equip.* The bus is fitted out for the tour.

FIX

1. **Fix on**—*to single out; decide for.* You must fix on great ambitions in life.
2. **Fix up**—*to arrange or settle.* They have fixed up an interview tomorrow.

FLAG

1. **Dip the flag**—*to lower the flag and then hoist it as a token of respect.* They dipped the flag in honour of the King.
2. **Red flag**—*a flag used as a signal of danger or defiance.* Kashmir under Dr. Abdullah may hoist the red flag.
3. **Strike or lower the flag**—*to pull it down as a token of surrender.* The Pakistanis struck their flag in Bangladesh.
4. **White flag**—*an emblem of truce or surrender.* Since you have lost the battle of life, it is time to show the white flag.

FLAME

1. **An old flame**—*sweetheart.* Liza is an old flame of mine.
2. **To burst into flames**—*to burn with a glow.* The van carrying explosive burst into flames.
3. **To fan the flames**—*to make it more intense.* Your anger would fan the flames of fight.

FLAT

1. **Flat out**—*Full speed.* Near examination the students study their books flat out.
2. **Flat rate**—*a fixed uniform rate.* Sugar is sold at a flat rate in the country, irrespective of transport charges.

3. **That's flat**—*I tell you plainly.* I am leaving this house permanently and that's flat.

FLEE

Flee for one's life—*to run away in order to save another's life.* Many good-hearted persons had to flee for their lives during the riots.

FLESH

1. **All flesh**—*all human beings.* All flesh must die one day.

2. **An arm of flesh**—*human strength or help.* You need an arm of flesh to help you in this war of nerves with your boss.

3. **Flesh and blood**—*human nature; relatives.* No flesh and blood can bear the health torture.

   He worked hard for his own flesh and blood.

4. **Flesh and felt**—*the whole body.* The flesh and felt is subject to decay.

5. **Fleshy-minded**—*given to pleasure of senses only.* The era of fleshy-minded kings is over.

6. **In flesh**—*in good condition.* You will find him in flesh.

7. **In the flesh**—*in bodily life; alive; incarnate.* Gandhiji is no longer there in the flesh.

8. **To put on flesh**—*to become fat.* Happiness is the best thing to put on flesh.

FLIGHT

In the first, top, flight—*in the highest class.* Rosy is now in the top flight in St. Anthony Public School.

FLING

Full fling—*at the utmost speed*. The boy ran at full fling.

FLIP

Flipperty flopperty—*loose; dangling*. He wore flipperty flopperty clothes.

FLOOR

1. **To floor the paper**—*to answer question in it*. The chairman floored the paper.
2. **To take the floor**—*to speak in debate*. The minister took the floor.

FLOW

1. **Flow of soul**—*genial conversation*. I always enjoy the flow of soul.
2. **Flow with milk and honey**—*full of prosperity*. India once flowed with milk and honey.

FLOWERY

1. **A flowery style**—*style of writing in which figures of speech abound*. He prefers writing in a flowery style.
2. **The Flowery Land**—*China*. Is China any longer the Flowery Land?

FLY

1. **A fly in the ointment**—*some slight flaw which corrupts a thing of value*. Your interference in this matter was a fly in the ointment.
2. **A fly on wheel**—*a person who overestimates his powers*. Our next door country is a mere fly on wheel.

3. **Fly a kite**—*to send up and control a kite; to obtain money as by accommodation bills when the endorser himself has no money; to put up a feeler as to how people will take anything.* Police is flying a kite for the arrest of the smugglers.

He flew a kite for Rs. 1,00,000.

4. **Fly at upon**—*to attack suddenly.* The Arabs flew upon the Jews.

5. **Fly in the face of**—*to oppose; to insult.* The disgruntled elements flew in the face of the Prime Minister.

6. **Fly open**—*to open suddenly or violently.* Gas flew open the cork of the bottle.

7. **Fly out**—*to break in a rage.* Don't fly out if something goes wrong.

8. **High flown**—*extravagant; bombastic.* Please do not talk in high flown terms.

9. **Let fly**—*to attack; to throw or send off.* He let fly the gossip against you.

10. **No flies on**—*no want of alertness in; no flaw in.* Let there be no flies on administration.

11. **The bird is flown**—*the wanted man has escaped.* It is no use chasing him now; the bird has flown already.

12. **To fly at**—*to rush upon suddenly; attack.* The dog flew at the lady's throat.

13. **To fly high**—*to be ambitious.* Let us not fly high but proceed according to the facts of life.

14. **To fly to arms**—*to take up arms.* The Indian army flew to arms for the liberation of Bangladesh.

FOCUS

In focus—*placed on, adjusted, so as to secure distant image.* The future of our firm is not yet in focus.

FOG

In fog—*puzzled.* My future is in fog.

FOIL

Put on the foil—*to overcome; to bring to naught.* Police is putting the efforts of dacoits on the foil.

FOLLOW

1. **Follow home, follow out**—*to follow to the end.* You must follow the victory home.

2. **Follow-my-dear**—*a game in which all have to mimic whatever the leader does.* Corruption is the game of follow-my-dear.

3. **Follow on**—*continue endeavours.* If you fail, follow on.

4. **Follow suit**—*to do what another has done.* If I go home, you follow suit.

5. **Follow up**—*to pursue an advantage closely; to pursue a question that has been started.* You must follow up your success in business.

6. **To follow in the footsteps of**—*to follow the example of.* We should try to follow in the footsteps of Mahatma Gandhi.

FOOD

1. **Food for thought**—*something which affords an occasion to think.* The death of my wife has given me food for thought.

2. **Food values**—*the relative nourishing qualities of different foods.* Cultural values spring from food values.

FOOL

1. **Be a fool to**—*nothing in comparison.* I am a fool to Tony.
2. **Fool away**—*to squander to no purpose.* I have fooled away the holidays.
3. **Fool's bolt is soon shot**—*this stock of argument is soon over.*
4. **Fool's paradise**—*a state of false expectations.* For quarter of a century after attaining independence, the people of India lived in fool's paradise.

5. **Fool with**—*meddle with.* The political leaders are fooling with the students.

6. **Go on a fool's errand**—*fruitless work.* In life most of us go on a fool's errand.

7. **Make a fool of**—*bring a person into ridicule.* Don't make a fool of me by holding hopes of becoming a minister.

8. **No fool like an old fool**—*lower are always foolish.*

9. **Play the fool**—*to behave as a fool.* He thinks the President is playing the fool to the members of executive committee.

FOOT

1. **Foot the bill**—*pay expense.* I have to foot the bill of the expenses of my daughter.

2. **Have one foot in the grave**—*to be on the point of death.* Many leaders have one foot in the grave.

3. **Know the length of one's foot**—*to know one's weakness and manage it.* One should know the length of one's foot.

4. **On foot**—*walking or running; in activity or being.* We have many plans on foot in India.

5. **Put one's foot in it**—*to spoil anything by indiscretion.* When we were looking for Indo-Pakistani friendship, foreign powers put their foot in it.

6. **Set on foot**—*originate.* He has set the whole project on foot.

7. **The ball is at your feet**—*you have nothing to do but seize opportunity.* It's time you should realise that the ball is at your feet.

8. **To carry off his feet**—*to make him enthusiastic.* I carried him off his feet.

9. **To have feet of clay**—*liable to be overthrown.* A political party always has feet of clay.

10. **To put one's best foot forward**—*to make one's best effort.* You must put your best foot forward to become a great leader like Lincoln.

FOR

1. **As for**—*so far as concerns.* As for the work, you must depend on yourself.

2. **For all**—*notwithstanding.* He fought and lost for all my advice.

3. **For as much as**—*because.* He pursued the thief for as much as he had a gun.

4. **For that**—*because.* He bought a house for that ready cash.

5. **For the better**—*indicates improvement.* The patient has taken a turn for the better.

6. **For to**—*in order to.* He worked hard for to pay off his debts.

7. **For why**—*why; because.* He did not eat for why he was ill.

8. **Nothing for it but**—*nothing else to be done in that case.* If he does not come, there is nothing for it but go and catch him.

9. **To be in for**—*to have something unpleasant impending.* The child is in for thrashing for disobedience.

10. **To take for better or worse**—*to accept for all circumstances.* I took his advice for better or worse.

11. **What is he for a man ?** —*what kind of man is he ?*
What are you for a man ?

FORBID
Forbidden fruit—*anything tempting but prohibited.*
Job is a forbidden fruit to many of the young graduates today.

FORCE
1. **Force and fear**—*element of compulsion.* Law does not recognise an agreement made under force and fear.
2. **Force the pace**—*to keep the speed high.* You cannot force the pace of economic happiness.

FORE
1. **At the fore**—*displayed on the foremast of a flagship.* Money is at the fore in life.
2. **To the fore**—*on hand.* Keep some cash to the fore always.

FORELOCK
Take time by the forelock—*to seize an opportunity.* If a job comes your way, take time by the forelock.

FORGET
Forget oneself—*to lose one's self-control or dignity; to descend towards or deeds unworthy of oneself.* Don't forget yourself when you mix with the crowd.

FORK
Fork out, over—*to hand or pay over.* When my friend incurred a debt, I had to fork out the payment.

FORM
Form, good or bad—*according to good or bad social custom.* The boys turned out in good form.
The old folks are very often in bad form in society.

FORTUNE

1. **To make a fortune**—*to learn a lot*. He has made a fortune in the business.
2. **To try one's fortune**—*to take a risky step*. Let us try our fortune and join in his business.

FOUL

1. **Claim a foul**—*to assert that a rule has been broken and claim the penalty*. You can claim a foul in sports.
2. **Fall foul of**—*to come into conflict*. The students are falling foul of the authorities everywhere.
3. **Foul play**—*dishonest dealing*. We should not indulge in a foul play with our friends.
4. **Make foul water**—*disturb the atmosphere*. Do not make foul water here.
5. **Through fair and foul weather**—*through good and bad times*. She promised to live by me through fair and foul weather.
6. **Through foul and fair**—*through everything*. You have now passed through foul and fair.

212

FOUNTAIN

1. **A crown is the fountain of honour**—*all the honour belongs to the ruler.* Queen Elizabeth is the fountain of honour.

2. **Fountain of justice**—*full justice.* The Prime Minister of India is a fountain of justice.

FOUR

1. **Four corners of the earth**—*anywhere; everywhere.* Let peace prevail in the four corners of the earth.

2. **On all fours**—*on hands and feet; low down.* His son is still on all fours.

3. **The four sea**—*everywhere.* Wind blows over the four seas.

FOX

Fox and geese—*a game played with pieces on board, where the object is for certain pieces called geese to surround or corner one called the fox or prevent him from passing.* The teacher and the students are playing fox and geese in the class.

FRAME

In proper frame of mind—*in a good mood.* Do not discuss my future at present; I am not in proper frame of mind today.

FREE

1. **A free-lance**—*not directly connected with any organisation.* I am a free-lance journalist.

2. **Be free with**—*to be familiar with; to take liberty with.* Don't be free with other's money.

3. **Free company**—*a band of mercenaries ready for any service.* The Indians abroad are a free company.

4. **Free fight**—*confused fight.* The House of Common is quite often the scene of free fight.

5. **Free hand**—*complete freedom of action.* The President has free hand in the Parliament.

6. **Free kick**—*a kick allowed without interference.* Earning money is by no means a free kick.

7. **Free on board (f.o.b.)**—*delivered by ship free of freight to the purchaser.* Few things now come from abroad f.o.b.

8. **Free verse**—*poetry without metrical laws.* This is the age of free verse.

FRENCH

Take a French leave—*to proceed on leave without permission.* Many government servants are fond of availing French leave.

FRESH

1. **Fresh lease of life**—*new scope for living.* Every newly married couple gets practically a fresh lease of life.

2. **In the fresh of morning**—*in the pleasant.* We will meet in the fresh of morning.

3. **Fresh water college**—*small college.* In Utah I taught in a fresh water college.

FRET

Fret and fume—*to be angry with; to be cross.* There is no use fretting and fuming about a loss in business or in life.

FRIEND

1. **Be friends with**—*be on good terms with.* Let us be friends with each other.

2. **Have a friend at court**—*to have a friend in a position where his influence is likely to be useful.* It is best to have a friend, like Tom, at court.

FROM

1. **From door to door**—*from house to house.* I am selling my wares from door to door.

2. **From hand to mouth**—*to live within a little income.* Most of the working class people of India to-day are living from hand to mouth.

FRONT

1. **Come to the front**—*to become noticeable.* After the death of his father, Walter came to the front and took charge of the entire factory.

2. **In front of**—*before.* Please wait for me in front of the coffee house.

FRY

Out of the frying pan into the fire—*out of one evil into the greater evil.* From education to politics, life is out of the frying pan into the fire.

FULL

1. **Full of years**—*at a good old age.* I haven't seen anyone full of years in my family.

2. **Full up**—*full to the limit*. The cup is full up with tea.
3. **In full**—*without reduction*. You have to pay the price of life in full.
4. **In full cry**—*in chase together; giving tongue*. The people today are in full cry for food.
5. **In full swing**—*at the height of activity*. The school is in full swing this month.
6. **In the fullness of time**—*at the due or destined time*. Rosy will join I.F.S. in the fullness of time.
7. **To the full**—*in full measure; completely*. I have paid off my debts to the full.

FUN

1. **In fun**—*in joke*. Don't take him seriously when he is in fun.
2. **Like fun**—*in a rapid manner*. He delivered his oration like fun.
3. **Make fun of**—*to ridicule*. Don't make fun of your friends.

4. **Poke fun at**—*ridicule*. Don't poke fun at your parents.
5. **To be great fun**—*to be very amusing*. Life is said to be great fun in America.

FURTHER

See one further—*see one hanged*. I don't want to see you further.

FURY

To bear full fury—*to undergo full force*. France bore the full fury of Hitler's blitz invasion.

☆ ☆ ☆

GAB

Gift of the gab—*talent for talking.* You cannot be a great man without the gift of the gab.

GAD

Up on the gad—*upon the spur of the moment.* The great deeds of the world have been performed up on the gad.

GAIN

1. **Gain ground**—*to make progress.* Fashions are gaining ground in society.
2. **Gain on or upon**—*to overtake by degrees.* Virtue gains upon vice in the last run.
3. **To gain one's point**—*to defeat opposition in argument.* It is very difficult to gain his sister's point.
4. **To gain time**—*to get time on some pretext; to make full preparations.* Today's statement of the Police Inspector will enable the criminal to gain time.

GAITER

Ready to the last gaiter button—*completely ready.* Are you ready to the last gaiter button for today's performance ?

GALA

Gala day—*festive day*. Sunday is always a gala day.

GALANTY

Galanty show—*shadow of puppets*. Life is nothing but a galanty show.

GALE

Hanging gale—*arrears of rent*. He has not as yet cleared his hanging gale for the last three months.

GALL

1. **Gall and wormwood**—*anything extremely disagreeable*. Would you please stop your gall and wormwood talk.
2. **In the gall of bitterness**—*in a state of hostility to God*. In the gall of bitterness even some Saints start abusing.

3. **To dip one's pen in gall**—*to write violently*. His dip of pen in gall brought him to task.

GALLANT

To play the gallant with—*to flirt*. David's habit of playing the gallant with college girls has disreputed his whole family.

GALLERY

Play to the gallery—*to play to the applause of the least cultured*. In order to get votes, every politician plays to the gallery.

GALLOP

To gallop through—*to make quick progress*. You cannot get good marks just by galloping through books.

GALLOWS

Cheat the gallows—*to deserve but escape hanging*. Many leaders in India today are cheating the gallows.

GALVANIZE

Galvanize into activity—*show new dynamic energy*. A murder galvanizes police into activity.

GAME

1. **Big-game**—*large animals hunt*. Business today is a big game.

2. **Die game**—*to keep up courage until the last*. Good sportsmen always die game.

3. **Game and game**—*draw; equal victory scored by each side*. The hockey match has ended in game and game.

4. **Make game of**—*make sport of.* Don't make game of great spiritual ideals.
5. **Play the game**—*act in a fair, sportsmanlike, straightforward way.* If you seek lasting success in life, you must play the game.
6. **Red game**—*grouse.* I have no red game for you.
7. **Round game**—*a game, as at cards, in which the number of players is not fixed.* Economic competition is a round game.
8. **The game is not worth the candle**—*the benefits are not worth the labour and expense.* Marriage is a game certainly not worth the candle.
9. **The game is up**—*the scheme has failed.* When the police came, the bank breaker found that the game was up.
10. **To play a double game**—*to manage things cleverly.* If you want me to help you in this matter, please stop playing a double game.

GANDER

Sauce for the goose is sauce for the gander—*what is good for one is also good for another.*

GANG

To gang up—*to join.* The Inspector ordered the police to gang up.

GAP

To stop a gap—*to make up deficiency.* His hard labour enabled him to stop a gap in his studies.

GARB

A wolf in the garb of a lamb—*a scoundrel in the dress of a saint.* Many a modern saints is a wolf in the garb of a lamb.

GARDEN

1. **Philosopher of the garden**—*one who believes in the enjoyment of life*. Epicurs was a philosopher of the garden.
2. **To lead up the garden path**—*to entice; to mislead*. If the leader leads up the garden path, where will the public go ?

GAS

Step on the gas—*to speed up*. The driver stepped on the gas to pursue the thief.

Gas—*to talk the length*. He gassed for five hours but to no avail.

GASTRIC

1. **Gastric fever**—*typhoid*. You are suffering from gastric fever.
2. **Gastric juice**—*the acid liquid secreted by the stomach for digestion*. One may suffer from excess of gastric juice.

GATE

1. **Between you and me and the gatepost**—*in close confidence*. Rest assured the talk we had will remain between you and me and the gatepost.
2. **Gate crasher**—*uninvited intruder*. There were many gate crashers at his wedding party.
3. **Gate of horn**—*by which true dreams come*. I don't know when I will pass through the gates of horn.
4. **Gate of justice**—*where justice is given to the people*. The Supreme Court is the gate of justice.
5. **Stand in the gate**—*to occupy a position of defence*. The girl stood in the gate to face the intruder.

6. **To break gates**—*to enter college hostel after the prescribed hours.* Susan's habit of breaking gates was the cause of her being expelled from the hostel.

GATHER

1. **A rolling stone gathers no moss**—*a person who does not stick to one job never succeeds in life.*
2. **Gather breath**—*to recover wind.* The runner paused to gather breath.
3. **Gather ground**—*make progress.* By and by you will gather a ground.
4. **Gather oneself together**—*to collect all of one's powers like one about to leap.* The President is now busy gathering herself together for the elections.
5. **Gather to a head**—*to ripen; to come into a state of preparation for confrontation.* The grains have gathered to a head.
   The political parties are gathering to a head for the elections.
6. **To gather colour**—*to be browned.* Her face is gathering colour.
7. **To gather strength**—*to become strong.* The patient is gathering strength now.
8. **To gather way**—*to get headway.* The train has gathered way.

GAUNTLET

1. **Take up the gauntlet**—*to accept a challenge.* A politician who does not take up the gauntlet loses the battle without having fought it.
2. **To run the gauntlet**—*to face; criticism, danger, etc.* Every minister runs the gauntlet in Parliament.

3. **To throw down the gauntlet**—*to give up a challenge.* When a pickpocket faces you with a revolver it is better to throw up the gauntlet.

GAZETTE

Have one's name appear in the gazette—*to be mentioned in one of the official newspapers, especially of bankrupts.* Pay all your debts well in time and don't let your name appear in the gazette.

GAZING

Gazing stock—*one who is exposed to public view.* The unnatural beauty of the young girl was the gazing stock of young people.

GEAR

1. **Gear up**—*make the speed higher.* The students gear up for the examination.

2. **Gear down**—*make the speed lower.* The students gear down for the summer vacation.

3. **In gear**—*in working order.* The car is in gear.

4. **Out of gear**—*not working.* The car has gone out of gear.

GEE

Gee up—*proceed faster.* The teacher told the boy to gee up.

GENERAL

1. **In general**—*as a general rule.* Students of rich families do well in general.

2. **Lover-general**—*one who makes love to every woman.* Krishna is a lover-general.

GENTLE

Gentle craft—*shoe-making; angling.* David follows the gentle craft in Super Market.

GENTLEMAN

1. **Gentleman's agreement**—*an agreement resting on honour and not any formal contract.* There is a gentleman's agreement between Dolly and Timmy to help each other.

2. Gentleman's gentleman—*valet.* Even a minister respects his gentleman's gentleman.

GESTURE

A friendly gesture—*an expression of friendship.* In inviting the Prime Minister of Pakistan to visit India, the Indians have made a friendly gesture.

GET

1. **Get ahead**—*make progress.* In modern society everyone tries to get ahead.

225

2. **Get along**—advance. They get along well in a good school.

3. **Get a move on**—*start.* Can we get a move on with this now?

4. **Get away with it**—*pull it off; carry a thing through successfully or with impunity.* In 1971 the ruling party got away with elections.

5. **Get off**—*to escape.* Somehow the thief got off.

6. **Get on**—*proceed.* Get on to your duty at once.

7. **Get out**—*to free oneself.* He is trying to get out of the contract.

8. **Get over**—*to surmount; to recover from.* I must get over all obstacles to reach the goal.

9. **Get round**—*to circumvent; to persuade; to talk over.* The leaders of two parties have got round the constitutional difficulties.

10. **Get there**—*achieve one's object; succeed.* Without study, how do you hope to get there in examination?

11. **Get through**—finish. Please meet me when you get through the work in hand.

12. **Get up**—*to arise; to ascend; to prepare; to learn up for an occasion; to commit to memory.* Please get up.

    They got up the Mount Everest with difficulty.

    Have you got up your lesson for the examination?

    They got up the stage for the inaugural ceremony.

    They got up the whole Bhagavad Gita.

13. **Get-up**—*the style of production.* The get-up of our books has been liked by all our readers.

14. **To get a chance for the better**—*to improve*. The patient has got a chance for the better.

15. **To get along**—*to advance*. The scheme seems sound, we can get along with it.

16. **To get at**—*to reach*. We are trying to get at the peak of this hill.

17. **To get into**—*put on*. Let's get into the bargain.

18. **To get into a scrape**—*to get into an unexpected trouble*. By going abroad my brother got into a scrape.

19. **To get rid of**—*to leave*. I want to get rid of my wife at all cost.

20. **To get through**—*to pass*. I am sure he will get through his final examination.

21. **To have got to**—*to be obliged to*. I have got to go home.

GHOST

1. **A ghost of a chance**—*very little chance*. He has only a ghost of a chance to get a job.

2. **Ghostly enemy**—the *devil*. Beware of the ghostly enemy.

3. **Ghostly weapons**—*religious arguments*. You cannot win her confidence just by ghostly weapons.

4. **To give up the ghost**—*to die*. He gave up the ghost on June 19. The old lady gave up the ghost last night.

GIDDY

Giddy success—*bewildering*. Politics soon brought him giddy success.

GIFT

1. **Gift of the gab**—*power of talking*. Ladies generally have the gift of the gab.
2. **Look a gift horse in the mouth**—*to criticize a gift*. Don't look a gift horse in the mouth.

GILD

1. **Gilded youth**—*rich young people of fashion*. The gilded youth are welcome everywhere.
2. **Gild the pill**—*make a disagreeable thing seem less so*. Political glory gilds the pill.

GILT

Gilt-edged securities—*those stocks whose interest is considered perfectly safe*. Government loans are gilt-edged securities.

GIN

Gin and it—*gin and Italian vermouth*. Mussolini was fond of gin and it.

GINGER

1. **Ginger bread-work**—*cheap and showy ornamental work*. She is wearing ginger-bread work.
2. **Ginger shall not be in the mouth**—*the love of pleasure is immortal*.

GIRD

To gird up one's loins—*to prepare for action*. The General asked the soldiers to gird up their loins.

GIRL

Old girl—*a kindly disrespectable mode of address for a female of any age.* He rode the old girl to the market.

GIVE

1. **A give-and-take policy**—*a fair measure of policy on both sides.* Success in the modern world depends on a give-and-take policy.

2. **Give and take**—*reciprocity in concession; fair exchange of jokes.* Give and take is the basis of all business.

   There was great give and take at the banquet.

3. **Give away**—*to give for nothing; to betray.* He gave away his house.

   He gave away all his secrets.

4. **Give birth to**—*bring forth; originate.* The bar gave birth to a brood.

5. **Give chase**—*pursue.* The police gave the robber a chase.

6. **Give ear**—*listen.* Please give ear for the whole story.

7. **Give forth**—*to emit; to publish.* They gave forth the whole story.

8. **Give ground**—*yield.* Don't give ground to sadness.

9. **Give into**—*yield.* The management gave into the employee's union.

10. **Give it to one**—*to beat or scold severely.* The teacher gave it to the boy.

11. **Give out**—*to report; to emit; to run short*. The Press gave out the scandal.

The chimney gave out smoke.

12. **Give over**—*to cease*. The newspaper has given over.

13. **Give the lie to**—*to charge openly with falsehood*. The secretary of the club gave the lie to the chairman.

14. **Give tongue**—*express; bark*. The dying girl gave tongue to her feelings.

The dog gave tongue.

15. **Give up**—*abandon*. They gave up the whole enterprise.

16. **Give way**—*to fall back; to yield; to withdraw; to break; to collapse; to begin rowing*. The army gave way.

The enemy gave way.

The roof gave way.

17. **To give oneself airs**—*to feel proud*. My father-in-law has given airs to himself for his wealth.

18. **To give the ghost**—*to die*. The old lady gave up the ghost last night.

19. **To give the world**—*punish*. The chairman's statement has given the world.

20. **To give up place to**—*to give one's place to someone else*. We have given that place to his brother.

GLAD

1. **Glad of**—*glad to have*. I am glad of your success.

2. **Glad rags**—*best clothes*. They were dressed in glad rags.

GLAMOUR

To cast a glamour over—*to enchant*. The young actresses cast a glamour over the youth.

GLANCE

To glance at—*to make ironical remarks*. The teacher glanced at the students.

GLASS

To live in a glass house—*to be open to attack or retort*. Those who live in glass houses must not throw stones at others.

GLIMPSE

To get a glimpse of—*to see fleetingly*. The boy managed to get a glimpse of his would-be bride.

GLORY

Glory be—*an exclamation of praise and honour*. Glory be to Mahatma Gandhi for winning the independence of India.

GLOVE

1. **Hand and glove**—*fast friends*. They are hand and glove with each other.
2. **To fit like a glove**—*exactly*. Today's statement of the Prime Minister fits like a glove to our national policy.

GLUT

Glut in the market—*supply in excess of demand*. In the rainy season vegetables glut the market.

GO

1. **At the first go**—*at the start*. Stanley was leading the race at the first go.

2. **Go about one's business**—*to attend to one's affairs.* A businessman goes about his business and lets others to go about their business.

3. **Go abroad**—*go to a foreign country.* When did you go abroad?

   Has the news gone abroad?

4. **Go against**—*turn unfavourably.* To tell a lie goes against my grain.

5. **Go aside**—*to err; to withdraw; to retire.* Many great men go aside under the pernicious influence of materialism.

   Honesty has gone aside from the world.

6. **Go at**—*attack.* Napoleon went at the enemy with full force.

7. **Go back on**—*to betray; to withdraw from.* Don't go back on your commitment.

8. **Go bail**—*give security for.* Will you go bail for me?

9. **Go black**—*to assume the ways of black people.* The Americans are reluctant to go black.

10. **Go down**—*to sink; decline; to be swallowed; believed; accepted.* The reputation of my neighbour has gone down after the raid.

    Your story goes down well.

11. **Go far**—*last long.* Woollen clothes go far.

12. **Go for**—*to set out to secure.* The army went for the enemy.

13. **Go for nothing**—*to have no value.* Truth goes for nothing in the world.

14. **Go halves**—*share equally.* Whatever we earn, we should go halves.

15. **Go hard with**—*to turn out ill for.* Life goes hard with the beggars.

16. **Go in**—*assemble; to admit the audience.* They went in the meeting.

17. **Go in and out**—*to move about freely.* Few people go in and out in the Prime Minster's residence.

18. **Go in for**—*make a practice of; devote oneself to.* Most of the modern youth go in for making money.

19. **Go in unto**—*have sexual intercourse with.* Don't go in unto prostitutes.

20. **Go it**—*act in a striking or dashing manner.* Mr. Paul is losing nerve and verse and can now hardly get it.

21. **Go off**—*to leave; to die; to explode; to fade; to deteriorate.* The workers went off in a hurry.

    My brother went off on June 19, 1974.

    Glory of politics is going off.

    All ties go off by and by.

22. **Go on**—*continue.* Go on with your statement.

23. **Go one better**—*excel.* David cannot go better than Danny.

24. **Go one's way**—*depart.* The old leaders have gone their way.

25. **Go over**—*review; recall.* The judge went over the whole story.

26. **Go-slow policy**—*to restrict production to force the hands of the employers.* When workers demand higher salaries, they follow a go-slow policy.

27. **Go the whole hog**—*go to the full extent:* Political leaders go the whole hog to win elections.

28. **Go through**—*to perform; read.* She went through the marriage ceremony.

Please go through the book.

29. **Go through fire and water**—*to undertake any trouble or risk.* People are going through fire and water to get rich quickly.

30. **Go to**—*come now.* Enough is enough. Go to.

31. **Go to pieces**—*break up entirely.* With the departure of chairman, the firm will go to pieces.

32. **Go to the wall**—*to be pushed aside.* The ruling party does not easily go to the wall.

33. **Go under**—*to die; to be submerged; to be defeated.* My brother has gone under.

The rock went under in the high tide.

34. **Go with**—*accompany; agree with.* I am ready to go with you on this point.

35. **Go without**—*suffer the want of.* Millions in India are going without food.

36. **Go without saying**—*to be plainly self-evident.* It goes without saying that we cannot live without food.

37. **Great go**—*degree examination.* The students are preparing for the great go.

38. **Let go**—*release.* President Bhutto let go Mujibur Rehman.

39. **Little go**—*preliminary examination.* We are having the little go this month.

40. **No go**—*not possible.* There is no go on this point.

41. **To go about**—*from place to place.* For getting orders, he goes about the whole city.

42. **To go hand in hand**—*complete agreement*. On the issue of rice production in the country all the ministers went hand in hand.

43. **To go the way of all earth**—*die*. The old man has gone the way of all earth this morning.

44. **To go through**—*to examine*. The doctor has gone through the patient thoroughly.

45. **To go to great expense**—*to spend a lot*. He is going to great expenses in business now-a-days.

46. **To go the rack and ruin**—*to be completely burnt*. As a result of fire the whole market has gone to rack and ruin.

47. **To go under**—*to be called by some title*. Mr. Fisher goes under the assumed name of 'Walter'.

48. **To go up the line**—*leave the base for the front*. The Indian army has gone up the line in Kargil.

GOAT

Get one's goat—*enrage*. Beware lest you get your boss's goat.

GOD

1. **God-forsaken**—*miserable*. The patient is God-forsaken.

2. **God of this world**—*the devil*. Atom bomb is another god of this world.

3. **God's acre**—*graveyard*. The corpse lies in God's acre.

4. **God's book**—*the Bible.* God's book is being read in every church.

5. **God's truth**—*an absolute truth.* Death is a God's truth.

GOLD

1. **A golden age**—*a prosperous period of history.* The golden age has passed from the modern world now.

2. **Gold digger**—*one who is bent upon making money through all means.* A village money-lender in India is a gold digger.

3. **Golden mean**—*the middle way between extremes.* Buddha preached the path of the golden mean.

4. **Golden opportunity**—*every favourable chance.* We have got a golden opportunity of starting a new business now.

5. **Golden rule**—*do as one would be done by.* It is in the interest of every body to follow the golden rule.

6. **Gold fever**—*desire for money.* Human weakness is gold fever.

7. **Gold standard, on, off**—*using or not using gold as the medium of exchange.* The U.K. and the U.S.A. were once on the gold standard.

Now all countries have given off the gold standard.

GONE

1. **A gone man**—*hopeless.* The new clerk possesses a gone man personality.

2. **Gone under**—*ruined beyond recovery.* No big smuggler had gone under because of MISA.

GOOD

1. **A good hand at**—*clever in doing.* He is a good hand at watch repairing.

2. **Be as good as one's word**—*fulfil one's promise.* Be as good as your word and do the work.

3. **For good**—*permanently.* They left India for good.

4. **For good and all**—*for ever.* The friends decided to part for good and all.

5. **Good for anything**—*good for any enterprise.* An active boy is good for anything.

6. **Good for nothing**—*useless; worthless.* Rich men's children prove good for nothing.

7. **Good money**—*genuine.* You are having a good money note.

8. **Good offices**—*mediation.* I got this job through the good offices of my uncle.

9. **Good people, good folk**—*fairies.* There are no more good folk in the world now-a-days.

10. **Good sailor**—*a person not liable to sea sickness.* One has to be a good sailor for long voyages.

11. **Make good**—*perform; fulfil; come to success; justify.* You must make good this loss.
    She made good her promise.

12. **No good**—*useless; worthless.* Education is no good now-a-days.

13. **Stand good**—*to be lastingly good.* Truth always stands good.

14. **Think good**—*to be disposed; willing.* He thinks good of going home.

GOOSE

1 **All his goose are swans**—*he overestimates.* Richard thinks that all his goose are swans.

2. **To kill the goose that lays golden eggs**—*to sacrifice future profits.* I do not want to kill the goose that lays golden eggs by selling my book at cheap rate.

GORDIAN

To cut the Gordian knot—*to overcome a difficulty by violent measures.* Politicians will have to cut the gordian knot to survive.

GORGE

Heave the gorge—to *stretch.* The woman heaved the gorge in the bus.

GRAB

Have the grab on—*have great advantage of.* He has the grab of Mathew's influence in getting a job.

GRACE

1. **Airs and graces**—*behaviour*. It's high time that you should change your bad airs and graces.

2. **Fall from grace**—*to fall from favour*. Peter has fallen from grace of his boss in the course of time.

3. **Take heart of grace**—*take courage from grace*. My friend took his wife's heart of grace.

4. **To be in one's good graces**—*to be in one's good books*. The clerk is in the good graces of his manager.

GRADE

1. **Grade up**—*improve*. Please grade up the quality of your products.

2. **Make the grade**—*to overcome obstacles; to stand a test; to be up*. The boy has at last made the grade in the school.

3. **On the up-grade**—*progressing*. The patient is on the up-grade now-a-days.

GRAIN

1. **Against the grain**—*against the natural temper*. One cannot succeed if one works against the grain.

2. **With a grain of salt**—*with reservation*. She accepted the proposal of marriage with a grain of salt.

GRAND

1. **Grand style**—*style adopted to lofty subjects*. The President of our college spoke in the grand style.

2. **Grand total**—*the total of subordinate sums*. The grand total of life is zero.

GRANT

Take for granted—*presuppose*. One should take death sooner or later for granted and build his life on that assumption.

GRAPE

Grapes from thorns—*good from bad*. He has the art of getting grapes from thorns.

GRAPPLE

To grapple with—*to tackle*. It is difficult to grapple with the problem arising from high cost of living.

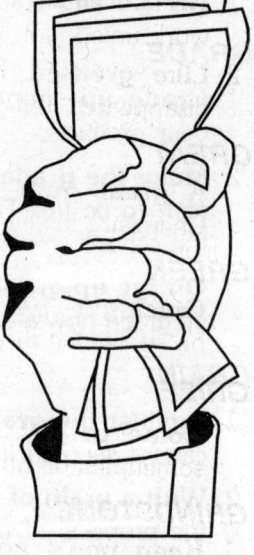

GRASP

1. **Grasp at**—*to catch at*. His efforts to grasp at the running train failed.

2. **Out of one's grasp**—*beyond one's reach*. This sum is out of Manu's grasp.

GRASS

1. **Go to grass**—*to retire*. A writer who earns his living day to day cannot go to grass.

2. **Let the grass grow under one's feet**—*idle away time*. If you let the grass grow under your feet, you will fail in life miserably.

3. **Snake in the grass**—*hidden enemy*. Everywhere you find snakes in the grass.

GRAVE

1. **Dig one's own grave**—*cause one's own death*. Don't dig your grave with your own teeth.
2. **Quiet as the grave**—*quiet*. During curfew a town becomes as quiet as the grave.
3. **With one foot in the grave**—*on the point of death*. People do not give up greed even with one foot in the grave.

GREASE

1. **Grease one's palms**—*bribe*. No one will do your work unless you grease his palm.
2. **Like greased lighting**—*very fast*. The aeroplane disappeared like greased lighting.

GREAT

A great gun—*a man of note*. The professor of Chemistry in our college is a great gun now-a-days.

GREEK

Greek gift—*one given with intent of harming*. At last he succeeded in giving a Greek gift to Dolly.

GRIEF

Come to grief—*meet with misfortune*. Everybody sometimes or other comes to grief.

GRINDSTONE

1. **Keep one's nose to the grindstone**—*to subject one to severe toil or punishment*. Those who are born poor keep their noses to the grindstone.
2. **Take a grinder**—*a gesture of contempt*. In confrontation with the ruling party many Opposition leaders are now taking the grinder.

3. **To grind one's own axe**—*to serve one's self-interest.* Mary is in the habit of grinding her own axe.

GRIP

To lose one's grip—*to lose control.* The grandfather has lost his grip on his youngest grandson.

GROUND

1. **Break ground**—*to take the first step in any project.* For discipline in India we have yet to break the ground.

2. **Fall to the ground**—*come to nothing.* Plans of men and mice fall to the ground.

3. **Gain ground**—*to advance.* Steady work always gains ground.

4. **Give ground**—*to lose advantage.* At Agra Summit we have given ground to Pakistan.

5. **Hold or stand one's ground**—*to stand firm.* You must stand your ground in the face of adversity.

6. **Let in on the ground floor**—*to admit on the terms as the original promoters.* Nobody lets in new investment-seekers on the ground floor.

7. **Lose ground**—*fall back.* In the last twenty-eight years India has lost much ground.

GROW

1. **Grow on, upon**—*to gain a greater hold on.* The secretary grew upon the President.

2. **Grow out of**—*result from.* Your misery grows out of your bad planning.

3. **Grow to**—*to advance to; come to.* Friendship grows to sincerity.

4. **Grow together**—*become united by growth*. Many of our contemporary leaders have grown together.

5. **Grow up**—*mature*. Children grow up silently.

GRUBB

Grubb street—*cheap literary production*. My writings belong to the Grubb street.

GUARD

1. **Guardian angel**—*a person specially devoted to the interest of another*. Nehru was known to be a guardian angel to hundreds of Congressmen.

2. **Mount guard**—*go on guard*. The police have mounted guard round all the places of worship.

3. **On one's guard**—*on the watch*. You have to be always on your guard against enemies.

4. **Off one's guard**—*unwatchful*. You can never afford to be off your guard.

5. **Run past a guard**—*get past a guard*. You cannot run past a guard without permit.

GUINEA

Guinea pig—*a person used as the subject of an experiment*. Patients are quite often used as guinea pigs in hospitals to try new medicines and injections.

GUN

1. **As sure as a gun**—*certainly*. I will meet you tomorrow as sure as a gun.

2. **Blow great guns**—*to blow temptuously; of wind*. The wind is blowing great guns.

3. **Great gun**—*a person of great importance*. Sardar Patel was a great gun.

4. **Kiss the gunner's daughter**—*to be tied to a* gun *for flogging*. Napoleon made many soldiers kiss the gunner's daughter.

5. **Son of a gun**—*a rascal; rogue*. Beware of the son of a gun.

6. **Stick to one's guns**—*maintain one's position*. The Principal is bent upon sticking to his guns.

GUTTER

Gutter-press—*press catering to vulgar tastes*. A gutter-press in any country cannot thrive for long.

HABEAS CORPUS

Habeas corpus petition—*a writ for the production of prisoner in court.* Many political prisoners often invoke habeas corpus petitions.

HABIT

1. **Habit and repute**—*notoriety that affords strong and generally conclusive evidence of fact.* Many criminals are trapped by the police through habit and repute.

2. **Habit of mind**—*mental constitution.* Something or the other is always a habit of mind in every human being.

3. **To get into a habit**—*to become habitual.* His hobby of drinking has resulted in getting into a habit.

HAIL

1. **To hail from**—*to come from.* Our manager hails from Kuala Lumpur.

2. **Within a hail**—*near enough to be called.* He is standing within a hail distance.

245

HAIR

1. **Against the hair**—*against the grain*. Honesty runs against the hair of politicians.

2. **A hair of the dog that bit him**—*a small dose of that which caused the trouble*. Theft was a hair of the dog that bit him.

3. **Hair-breadth escape**—*very narrow escape*. During partition my brother had a hair-breadth escape.

4. **Keep one's hair on**—*keep cool*. Mr. Fisher always kept his hair on.

5. **Lose one's hair**—*to grow angry*. If someone cracks a joke, don't lose your hair.

6. **Make one's hair stand on end**—*to give the greatest surprise or fright*. The murder of his lieutenant made his hair stand on end.

7. **Not to turn a hair**—*not to be disturbed*. He did not turn a hair when his friend died.

8. **Put up the hair**—*dress the hair up*. Maidens put up their hair.

9. **Split hairs**—*make superficial distinctions*. Many men are fond of splitting hairs.

10. **To a hair**—*exactly*. He resembled his father to a hair.

11. **To get a person by the short hair**—*have complete control over him*. Parents should get children by the short hair.

12. **To the turn of a hair**—*with perfect nicety*. She copied her exercises to the turn of a hair.

HALCYON

Halcyon days—*time of peace and happiness*. Halcyon days of India were before the partition.

HALF

1. **Better half**—*wife*. My better-half has gone to Mumbai.
2. **Half-and-half**—*a mixture of two equal things*. This cocktail is beer and brandy half-and-half.
3. **Half backed**—*inexperienced*. The half-backed clerk has been dismissed from service.
4. **Half-hearted**—*lacking courage*. Half-hearted efforts are never successful.
5. **Half-mast**—*half-flown flag*. Due to the death of the Prime Minister, the flags in the country are flying half-mast.
6. **Go halves**—*to share equally*. Let us go halves before we divide the shop.
7. **Not half**—*not moderately; not even half; not at all; very much*. He was not even half a villain.
8. **To do things by halves**—*imperfectly*. Many labourers of our factory are doing things by halves.
9. **To get half a nelson on**—*to hold complete control*. Parents should get half a nelson on their children.
10. **To meet half-way**—*to compromise*. The only solution to their difference is that they should meet half-way.
11. **Too clever by half**—*very clever*. John is too clever by hall in his work.

HALL

1. **Bachelor's hall**—*a place free from the restraining influence of a wife*. He prefers to live in the bachelor's half rather than in his house.
2. **Hallmark**—*important feature*. Today's statement of the Prime Minister is a hallmark of the Government's policy.

3. **Liberty hall**—*a place where everybody may do what he pleases*. Bachelor's hall is a liberty hall.

HALT

Halt between two opinions—*hesitate*. Do not halt between two opinions in telling the truth.

HAMMER

1. **Bring the hammer**—*to sell by auction*. The shop was brought to the hammer.
2. **Hammer home**—*make one thoroughly understand*. He hammered him home to be punctual at the dining table.
3. **Knight of the hammer**—*blacksmith*. The knight of the hammer of our village died this morning.
4. **To hammer an idea into one's head**—*to make one understand*. It is very difficult to hammer an idea into Robert's head.

HAND

1. **A bird in hand**—*any advantage held at present*. A bird in hand is better than two in the bush.
2. **At any hand**—*in any case*. We shall meet tomorrow at any hand.
3. **At first hand**—*directly from the source*. I know the story at first hand.

248

4. **At hand**—near. I keep the bookshelf at hand.

5. **At the hand of**—*by the act of*. My grandfather died at the hand of a dacoit.

6. **Bear a hand**—*to take part; to lend support*. Will you bear me a hand in this enterprise?

7. **By hand**—*by use of the hands*. This painting was made by hand.

8. **By the strong hand**—*by force*. You can get something done only by the strong hand.

9. **Change hands**—*to pass to other ownership*. This shop has changed hands many times.

10. **Come to hand**—*to be received*. A wonderful book has come to my hand.

11. **Come to hand**—*to receive*. All the members of my family came to hand at the railway station this morning.

12. **Come to one's hand**—*to be found easy; to come to close quarters*. Fortune has come to my hand.

13. **For one's own hand**—*on one's own account*. I have bought this cloth for my own hand.

14. **From good hands**—*from reliable source*. We have come to know from good hands that a few posts of clerks are lying vacant under your control.

15. **From hand to mouth**—*poverty*. With this small income we are living from hand to mouth now-a-days.

16. **Good hands**—*trustworthy source; good keeping*. The girl is in good hands.

17. **Hand and foot**—*with assiduous attention*. You can achieve your objective hand and foot.

18. **Hand and glove**—*on intimate terms*. Timmy and Maria are hand and glove.

19. **Hand down or on**—*transmit in succession.* Imamship of Jama Masjid handed down from father to son.

20. **Hand it to one**—*admit one's superiority.* I do really hand it to you.

21. **Hand of God**—*unforeseen event.* There is hand of God everywhere.

22. **Hand over hand**—*by steady and rapid gain.* They climbed the mountain hand over hand.

23. **Hand over head**—*headlong.* She fell down hand over head.

24. **Hands down**—*with utter ease.* They won the match hands down.

25. **Hands up**—*surrender.* They were told "Hands up".

26. **Hand to hand**—*close quarters.* The new military camps are going to be hand to hand.

27. **Handwriting on the wall**—*a foreshadow of disaster.* It is not too late for the ruling party to see the handwriting on the wall.

28. **In any hand**—*in any case.* Prices must not be allowed to rise in any hand.

29. **In hand**—*as present payment; in control.* I have five rupees in hand.

30. **Lay hands on**—*to obtain.* I cannot lay my hands on the book I want.

31. **Lend a hand**—*to give help.* Please lend me a hand in this enterprise.

32. **Off hand**—*immediately.* I cannot give any decision off hand. I must have some time to think over the problem.

33. **Off one's hands**—*no longer under one's responsible control.* When children grow up they are off our hands.

34. **Old hand**—*an experienced man.* There are many old hands in politics.

35. **On all hands**—*on every side.* There is corruption on all hands.

36. **On hand**—*readily available.* The car is on hand.

37. **Out of hand**—*at once; immediately; out of control.* Please pay out of hand.

    The child is getting out of hand.

38. **On one's hand**—*under one's responsibility.* I have too many tasks on my hands.

39. **Pass through many hands**—*share in action*. This book has passed through many hands.

40. **Poor hand**—*unskilled person*. I am a poor hand at mathematics.

41. **Set one's hand to**—*engage*. Do your best whatever you set your hand to.

42. **Show of hands**—*a vote by showing of hands*. The matter was decided by a show of hands.

43. **Stand one's hand**—*pay for one's drink*. I cannot stand your hand for the simple reason that I do not drink myself.

44. **Strike hands**—*to make a contract*. Let us strike hands in this bargain.

45. **Take in hand**—*to undertake*. Please take in hand the education of my boy.

46. **Take off one's hands**—*to relieve one of*. Please take this responsibility off my hands.

47. **To have clean hands**—*to be honest*. You cannot have clean hands in any office.

48. **To one's hand**—*in readiness*. You will find him to your hand for work.

49. **To take in hand**—*to undertake*. It is high time that you should take in hand the responsibility of your parents.

50. **Under one's hand**—*under one's signature*. This deed was signed under my hand.

51. **Upper hand**—*mastery*. Vajpayee has the upper hand in Indian politics.

52. **Wash one's hands off**—*to disclaim responsibility*. We have washed our hands of T.V. trouble shooters.

53. **Young hand**—*an inexperienced youth.* It is not for young hands to meddle in politics.

HANDKERCHIEF

Throw the handkerchief—*to summon; to pursuit; to call upon; to take.* The King threw the handkerchief among the ladies of the harem.

HANDSOME

1. **Know a handsome or two**—*be experienced about.* I know a handsome or two of government jobs.

2. **To feel handsome**—*to feel well.* The patient is feeling handsome.

HANG

1. **Draw, hang, and quarter**—*to drag on a hurdle.* The Opposition will draw, hang and quarter the ruling party.

2. **Hang fire**—*to be slow in effect.* The import licences scandal still hangs fire.

3. **Hang in the balance**—*to be in doubt or suspense.* The promotion of Tom hangs in the balance.

   The fate of examinees hangs in the balance.

4. **Hang off**—*to let go.* The leaders should hang off the scandals.

5. **Hang on**—*to cling; to linger; to wait about; to give.* The boy hung on the girl the whole day.

6. **Hang one's head**—*to feel ashamed.* After a convincing defeat the cricketers hung their heads.

7. **Hang out**—*to display.* They hung out their nameplates.

8. **Hang over**—*to project over or lean from.* She hanged over the window of the attic.

9. **Hang over one's head**—*to be in danger.* The whole country is hanging over head owing to increased cost of living.

10. **Hang together**—*keep united.* I know you two do not hang together.

11. **Hang up**—*to suspend; to delay.* They hanged up the final decision for two months.

12. **Hang up one's hat**—*to take up one's decision.* He hangs up his hat in my house.

13. **To get the hang of a thing**—*to understand* a *thing.* We cannot get the hang of your statement.

14. **To hang heavy**—*become burdensome.* The new job is hanging heavy on my head.

HANKY

Hanky-Panky—*jugglery; underhand trickery.* Democracy itself is becoming hanky-panky.

HAPPY

1. **Happy despatch**—Your resignation will be a happy despatch.

2. **Happy-go-lucky**—*taking things as they come.* Stanley is a happy-go-lucky fellow.

HARA

Hara-kiri—*ceremonious Japanese suicide by ripping belly.* Frustrated Japanese gentlemen commit hara-kiri.

HARBOUR

Harbour refuge—*heaven; place of shelter.* A true Yogi is a harbour of refuge for distressed souls.

HARD

1. **Die hard**—*to serve desperately.* Evils die hard in the world.

2. **Go hard with**—*turn ill for.* Life goes hard with my brother's family.

3. **Hard and fast**—*strict.* There is no hard and fast rule in becoming a member of the I.T. Union.

4. **Hard drinker**—*one who drinks excessively and persistently.* There are many hard drinkers in Delhi University.

5. **Hard facts**—*undeniable facts.* Hard facts about India cannot be ignored.

6. **Hold hard**—*stop.* Please hold hard until I return.

7. **Hard-headed**—*clear.* Our Manager is a hard-headed man.

8. **Hard-hearted**—*cruel.* The army has got to be hard-hearted.

9. **Hard nut to crack**—*difficult problem to solve.* How to increase Good production in our country is a hard nut to crack.

10. **Hard of hearing**—*petty deaf.* Old folks are often hard of hearing.

11. **Hard put to it**—*in great difficulty.* He is hard put to make a living.

12. **Hard up**—*in want.* I am hard up of money now-a-days.

13. **Hard words**—abuse; *difficult words.* Call him no hard words.

HARE

1. **First catch your hare**—*make sure you have a thing first before you think what to do with it.* First catch your hare before you cook it.

2. **Hold with the hare and hunt with the hounds**—*to play a double game; to be with the both sides at once.* It pays some politicians well to hold with the hare and hunt with the hounds.

HARK

Hark back—*revert.* He was harked back to the parent office.

HARNESS

To die in harness—*to die at one's work.* The leaders who die in harness are remembered till ages.

HARUM

Harum-scarum—*flighty; rash; a giddy, rash person.* After the murder of Mr. Kennedy the behaviour of the Prime Minister was harum-scarum.

There is no place for a harum-scarum in modern life.

HASH

1. **Settle a person's hash**—*make an end of.* I can settle a hash of my friend only when he is willing to act on my advice.

2. **Silence one's hash**—*clear the mess.* Silence or settle the hash of once.

3. **To make a hash of**—*to spoil completely.* He has made a hash to this plan.

HAT

1. **A bad hat**—*a rascal.* The naughty child is a bad hat.

2. **Hats off to**—*all honour to.* Hats off to the Prime Minister.

3. **Mad as a hatter**—*quiet mad.* The youngster was mad as a hatter.

4. **My hat**—*an exclamation of surprise.* You want to buy this house ? My hat !

5. **Send (pass) round the hat**—*take up a collection.* The priest passed round the hat.

6. **Talk through the hat**—*to talk wildly or at random.* Please stop talking through your hat.

7. **Under one's hat**—*in confidence.* I can tell you under my hat that I am going abroad next summer.

HATCH

1. **Count your chickens before they are hatched**—*to depend too securely on some uncertain future event.* If you wish to rise, don't count your chickens before they are hatched.

2. **Under hatches**—*below deck; off duty; under arrest; in confinement.* Our luggage was under hatches.

The officer was under hatches.

The thief was under hatches.

HATCHET

1. **To bury the hatchet**—*to end the fight*. Will both of you please bury the hatchet and compromise?

2. **To throw the hatchet**—*exaggerate*. Many women are in the habit of throwing the hatchet.

HAVE

1. **Have away**—*to remove*. Please have away your luggage from here.

2. **Have it**—*attack*. Don't have it at my friend.

3. **Have it out**—*discuss or express quickly*. Let us have it out. Whatever you want to say, have it out

4. **Have on**—*wear*. Why are you not having on a coat today?

5. **Have and have-nots**—*rich and poor*. All haves and have-nots sitting in this gathering are requested to contribute something for the Temple Building Fund.

6. **Have up**—*to call to account in court*. Let us have him up before the judge.

7. **Have with you**—I am ready to have with you.

8. **He's had it**—*there is nothing for him; it's all up with him; He's been killed*.

HAVOC

To play havoc with—*to cause destruction*. A war always plays havoc with human lives.

HAW

Haw-haw—*loud vulgar laughter*. I hate people making haw-haw.

HAWK

1. **Hawk-eyed**—*keen-sighted*. The old man of this village is hawk-eyed.

2. **Know a hawk from a handsaw**—*to be able to judge between things*. Even a child knows a hawk from a handsaw.

HAY

1. **Go hay-wire**—*to become excited*. He goes hay-wire with every young girl.

2. **Make hay while the sun shines**—*seize an opportunity while it lasts*. Wise men make hay while the sun shines.

3. **To make hay of**—*throw into confusion*. The Minister's statement has made hay of Parliament's decision on planning of India.

HAZARD

At all hazards—*at all risks*. I am ready at all hazards to save the life of my wife.

HEAD

1. **At the head of**—*leading*. Who is at the head of this council?

2. **Cannot make a head or tail**—*cannot understand*. It is difficult to make a head or tail of the Prime Minister's speech of today.

3. **Come to a head**—*reach climax*. When matters come to a head, you must take a quick decision.

4. **From head to foot**—*all over the body*. He is having pimples from head to foot.

5. **Give a horse his head**—*let him go as he chooses*. When you cannot feed a horse, at least give him his head.

6. **Go by the head**—*submerge head foremost*. While diving go by the head.

7. **Good-head**—*talent*. He is good-headed man.

8. **Go to one's head**—*to disturb one's good sense*. Money and power go quick to one's head.

9. **Have a head on one's shoulders**—*have ability and balance*. You can face the world while you have a head on your shoulders.

10. **Head and shoulders**—*very much*. He is in debt head and shoulders.

11. **Head off**—*to deflect from the path*. He headed off for his house from his office.

12. **Head or tails**—*guesswork*. A good worker does not depend on head or tails.

13. **Head over heels**—*in a somersault*. He jumped down head over heels.

14. **Hot-head**—*rash person*. A hot-head is always a loser in life.
15. **Keep one's head**—*keep one's self-possession*. You must keep your head at all times.
16. **Lay heads together**—*confer*. Let us lay our heads together for the good of the country.
17. **Lose one's head**—*lose self-control*. You can never afford to lose your head.
18. **Off one's head**—crazy. If you want to get rich quickly, you are off your head.
19. **Out of one's head**—*spontaneously*. He delivered the speech out of his head.
20. **Over head and ears**—*deeply submerged*. You will meet him always over head and ears in the newspaper.
21. **Show one's head**—*appear*. The King must show his head *to* the people.
22. **Take it into one's head**—*to conceive the notion*. He took it into his head to form a society.
23. **To put something into someone's head**—*to suggest*. Many members of the club put something into the head of the leader to make Mr. Robert their new Secretary.
24. **Turn one's head**—*make proud*. Let money and success not turn your head.

HEAP
Knock, strike all *of* **a heap**—*to confound*. The leader struck the enemies all of a heap.

HEAR
Hear, hear—*an exclamation of approval from the listeners of a speech*.

261

HEART

1. **After one's heart**—*exactly to one's liking.* The house was after my heart.

2. **At heart**—*in real character.* At heart everybody is a great man.

3. **Break one's heart**—*cause profound grief* The death of Timmy broke my heart.

4. **Break the heart**—*to die of grief, etc.* The man broke his heart for the misbehaviour of his family.

5. **By heart**—*by rote.* Many students learn their lessons by heart.

6. **Find in one's heart**—*to be able to bring oneself to.* Find in your heart to do the job quickly.

7. **From the bottom of heart**—*most sincerely.* I thank everybody from the bottom of my heart.

8. **Have at heart**—*cherish.* I have at heart the memory of my brother.

9. **Have one's heart in one's boots**—*to have a sinking feeling.* If you are doing well in life, that is not the reason for having your heart in your boots.

10. **Have one's heart in the mouth**—*to be in trepidation.* If you are looking for success, don't have your heart in the mouth.

11. **Heart and hand**—*with great labour.* He devoted himself to his duty heart and hand.

12. **Heart and soul**—*with great devotion.* He served his guru heart and soul.

13. **Heart of hearts**—*dearest affection.* I remember you with the heart of hearts.

14. **Heart of oak**—*brave; resolute heart.* Napoleon had a heart of oak.

15. **Heart-to-heart**—*frank and free.* Let us have a heart-to-heart talk and finish the matter once for all.

16. **In good heart**—*in good spirit.* I confined to you my secrets in good heart.

17. **Nearest one's heart**—*dearest.* Nearest to my heart is my wife.

18. **Out of hearts**—*in low spirits.* It is but natural to be out of hearts when you fail in some examination.

19. **Set the heart at rest**—*render easy in mind.* This letter from your mother will set our heart at rest.

20. **Set the heart upon**—*to desire earnestly.* It is not good to set your heart upon anything in the world.

21. **Speak to the heart**—*comfort.* This song speaks to the heart.

22. **Take heart**—*be brave.* Take heart and do your duty in life.

23. **Take to heart**—*to be deeply moved.* I took his death to heart.

24. **To have no heart**—*to have no feelings.* The old man of our street has no heart for his children.

25. **Wear one's heart on one's**—*to show the feelings openly.* If you are angry with your friend, do not wear your heart upon your sleeves.

26. **With all my heart**—*most willingly.* I apologise for my misbehaviour with all my heart.

HEAT

1. **At a heat**—*in a simple effort*. You cannot succeed by working at a heat, take the help of your friends.

2. **Turn on the heat**—*use brutal treatment, mental and physical*. The police very often turn on the heat to extort confessions from offenders.

HEATHER

1. **Set the heather on fire**—*to create disturbance*. The criminals quite often set the heather on fire to make good their escape.

2. **Take to the heather**—*to become an outlaw*. Mr. Brown took to the heather when the police did him no justice.

HEAVE

1. **Heave in sight**—*come in view*. I will be there to welcome you when you heave in sight.

2. **Heave ho**—*call to have the anchor*. The Captain of the ship called heave ho.

3. **Heave to**—*bring a vessel to a standstill*. The vessel was heaved to.

HEAVEN

1. **In the seventh heaven**—*in a state of exalted happiness*. After marriage a bride is in the seventh heaven.

2. **Heaven of heavens**—*highest heavens*. May God rest in heaven of heavens the soul of Pandit Nehru.

HEEL

1. **At, on, upon a person's heels**—*close behind*. The police are always at the heels of notorious criminals.

2. **Come to heel**—*come in behind; to obey or follow like a dog.* Wherever a minister goes, sycophants come to heel.

3. **Cool or kick one's heels**—*to be kept waiting.* If you want to meet an officer, you should be ready to cool your heels for an hour or so at least.

4. **Down at heels**—*having the heels of one's shoes trodden down; in poor circumstances.* An honest worker is always down at heels.

5. **Heel and toe**—*with strict walking pace, as opposed to running.* You cannot overtake a cycle heel and toe.

6. **Heels over gowdy**—*upside down.* The boy plunged heels over gowdy into the tank.

7. **Heels over head**—*upside down.* Few men can escape death after falling heels over head from heights.

8. **Kick up one's heels**—*to frisk.* While the mother milked the cow the child kicked up its heels.

9. **Lap, set, clap by the heels**—*to fetter; to put in confinement.* The mad man was clapped by the heels.

10. **Out at heels**—*having one's showing through holes in the socks or stockings.* A man in economic difficulties is usually out at heels.

11. **Show a clean pair of heels**—*to run off.* The thief showed a clean pair of heels.

12. **To take to one's heels**—*to flee.* Face your troubles instead of taking to your heels.

13. **Tread on one's heel**—*to come crowding behind.* When you have money, your friends come treading on their heels.

14. **Trip up one's heels**—*to trip up or overthrow.* Don't trip up your friend's heels.

15. **Turn on one's heels**—*to turn sharply round; to turn back or away*. The cat turned on her heels to face the dog.

16. **Under the heels**—*crushed; tyrannized*. Hitler put many people under the heels.

HELL

1. **Hell for leather**—*at a furious pace*. He drove the horse hell for leather, with the bride behind him.

2. **Hell of noise**—*great noise*. The school students are making a hell of noise.

HELM

At the helm of affairs—*those who control or are in authority*. The persons at the helm of affairs must be serious and patient.

HELP

1. **Help off with**—*to aid in taking off; disposing or getting rid of*. He helped him off with the booty.

2. **Help oneself**—*to take to oneself without waiting for offer or authority*. At a social dinner you are expected to help yourself.

   Help yourself to a cup of tea.

3. **Help on with**—*to help to put on*. She helped him on with his coat.

4. **Help out**—*to eke out; to supplement*. You have got to help your living out of this job.

5. **Help over**—*to enable to surmount*. Help over the little boy in his studies.

6. **It cannot be helped**—*nothing can be done in the matter*. Today everybody is in trouble because of the rising prices but it cannot be helped.

7. **More than one can help**—*more than is necessary*. Rising prices are more than the poor can help.

8. **So help me God**—*a form of solemn oath*.

HELTER

Helter-skelter—*in a confused hurry; tumultuously*. When Napoleon attacked, the Italian army ran helter-skelter.

HEN

Hen-hearted—*coward*. Hen-hearted have no place in army.

HERE

1. **Here and there**—*thinly; irregularly; aimlessly*. Good men are found here and there.

   Why are you wandering here and there ?

2. **Here goes**—*an exclamation indicating that the speaker is about to do something.* Here goes the effigy of John to flames!

3. **Here you are**—*this is what you want; this is something for you; this way.*

4. **Neither here nor there**—*of no special importance.* Socialism in India is neither here nor there.

HERMETIC

Hermetically sealed—*closed completely; made airtight by melting the glass.* This bottle is hermetically sealed.

A totalitarian society is hermetically sealed.

HERRING

1. **Dead as a herring**—*quite certainly dead.* Your project is dead as a herring.

2. **Neither fish nor flesh nor good red herring**—*of no real purpose or quality; of no use.* A foolish friend is neither fish nor flesh nor good red herring.

3. **Packed like herring**—*very closely packed.* The passengers were packed in the train like herring.

HEY

1. **Like hey-go-mad**—*helter-skelter.* When the school is over, children run like hey-go-mad.

2. **Hey for**—*now for; off we go for.* After lunch hey for your work.

3. **Heyday**—*period of fullest vigour.* He gained everything during the heyday of his life.

HIDE

1. **To hide one's head**—*to feel ashamed*. He is hiding his head after cheating us.
2. **To hid one's light under a bushel**—*to conceal*. No use hiding your light under a bushel as we know everything.

   He wandered high and low in search of food.
3. **To play hide-and-seek**—*to deceive*. Never encourage the habit of playing hide-and-seek with your friends.

HIGGLEDY

Higgledy-piggledy—*haphazard; in confusion*. The cows are running higgledy-piggledy in the street.

HIGH

1. **High and dry**—*up out of the water; stranded*, The leaders of the old Congress have been left high and dry.

2. **High and low**—*rich and poor; up and down; everywhere.* High and low came to the meeting.

3. **High and might**—*exalted; arrogant.* India is ruled by the high and mighty.

4. **High born**—*of high family.* David is a high born boy.

5. **High feather**—*high spirits; happy trim.* The patriots fought for freedom in high feather.

6. **High hand**—*arbitrary arrogance.* He rules the country with a high hand.

7. **High life**—*the life of fashionable society; the people of fashionable society.* There is high life in South Delhi. Keep away from high life.

8. **High life below the stairs**—*servant's imitation of the life of their employers.* The evil about Indian Socialism is that there is high life below the stairs.

9. **High living**—*luxurious life style.* Middle classes can no longer afford high living.

10. **High seas**—*ocean.* No nation has control over the high seas.

11. **High spot**—*an outstanding feature.* Bhangra is a high spot of Punjabi marriages.

12. **High tea**—*tea with snacks, etc., as opposed to a plain tea.* I cannot offer you dinner but I promise you high tea.

13. **High time**—*happy time; quite time when something was done.* He had high time in marriage. It is high time that you go home now.

14. **High time**—*time for action.* It is high time that you should realise your responsibility towards your parents.

15. **High words**—*angry altercation*. Let us avoid a bargain with high words.

16. **Hit the high spots**—*go to excess*. When you are drinking, please don't hit the high spots.

17. **On high**—*aloft; in heaven*. The aeroplane is on high.

    After drink he was on high.

18. **On one's high horse**—*in an attitude of fancied superiority very much on one's dignity*. In modern society it is best to avoid being always on your high horse.

19. **On the high ropes**—*in an elated or highly excited mood*. When the cricketers came off with flying colours, they were on the high ropes.

HILL

Up hill and down dale—*vigorously and persistently*. You must work up hill and down dale to achieve success in life.

HILT

Up to the hilt—*completely; thoroughly; to the full*. Napoleon was a soldier up to the hilt.

Everyone in this department is sunk in corruption up to the hilt.

HINGES

Off the hinges—*disorganized; out of gear*. An army must never be off the hinges.

HIT

1. **A hit or a miss**—*a case in which either success or complete failure is possible.* A young man's career today is a hit or a miss.

2. **Hard hit**—*gravely affected by some trouble, or by love.* When his mother died, the boy was hard hit.

3. **Hit a blot**—*to find a weak spot.* A politician always hits a blot in the opposition.

4. **Hit at**—*to aim a blow; sarcasm; gibe at.* The Opposition is always hitting at the party in power.

5. **Hit below the belt**—*take undue advantage of.* In the fast-paced life of today nobody thinks much of hitting below the belt.

6. **Hit off**—*to imitate or describe felicitously.* He hit off a speech in the style of late Prime Minister Jawaharlal Nehru.

7. **Hit out**—*strike out with fist*. The ruffians hit out the police.

8. **Hit the nail on the head**—*to achieve the desired objective*. In dealing with employees, Mohan does not know how to hit the nail on the head.

9. **Hit upon**—*to come up; discover; devise*. In the deep and dark loneliness of the night you often hit upon great ideas.

HITCH

1. **Hitch one's wagon to a star**—*have big ambitions*. It is always best for a youth to hitch his wagon to a star.

2. **Hitch up**—*to marry*. Napoleon hitched up Josephine.

HITHER

Hither and thither—*here and there*. When I reached home I found all my things scattered hither and thither.

HOCUS

Hocus pocus—*jugglery; deception*. High life is all hocus pocus now-a-days.

HODGE

Hodge podge—*mess*. India today is a hodge podge of economic and political currents.

HOG

1. **To bring one's hog in a fine market**—*to make a complete mess of something*. Corruption in high places has brought India's hogs to a fine market.

2. **Go the whole hog**—*to do a thing thoroughly or completely; to commit oneself to something unreservedly*. I don't think Prime Minister of Pakistan will go to the whole hog to wage a war against India.

HOLD

1. **Hold forth**—*to put forward; to show; to speak in public; to declaim*. Few politicians can hold forth for truth now-a-days.

2. **Hold hard**—*stop*. He was ordered to hold hard talking nonsense.

3. **Hold in**—*restrain; check*. Hold in your indignation. When somebody loses temper, you must hold in.

4. **Hold of**—*regard*. I hold of my visit with pleasure.

5. **Hold off**—*keep at a distance*. You must hold off evil company.

6. **Hold one in hand**—*amuse in order to gain some advantage*. P.M. of Pakistan can no longer hold Dr. Abdullah in hand.

7. **Hold one's own**—*maintain one's position*. A man without money cannot for long hold his own against a man with money.

8. **Hold one's peace, tongue**—*to keep silence*. If you have nothing worthwhile to say, better hold your tongue.

9. **Hold over**—*postpone*. The meeting has been held over for tomorrow.

10. **Hold together**—*remain united*. We must hold together against the common foe.

11. **Hold up**—*to raise; to keep back; to endure; to bring to standstill; to stop and rob*. He is holding up forces of violence in the country.

    The dacoits held him up on the road.

12. **Hold up one's head**—*to face the world with self respect*. Everybody today is dying to hold up his head.

274

13. **Hold with**—*take sides with.* I do not hold with Russian or American ideologies.

14. **To hold good**—*to apply.* An ordinary vehicle permit does not hold good everywhere in the country.

15. **To hold out**—*to offer.* There is nothing good in our stock which I can hold out to you.

HOLE

1. **A hole in one's coat**—*a stain on one's reputation.* Bad debts are a hole in one's coat.

2. **Hole out**—*to play the ball into the hole.* It is not easy to hole out in politics.

3. **In holes**—*full of holes.* Your shirt is all in holes.

4. **Make holes in**—*use large amount of.* Women are in the habit of making holes in their husband's pockets.

5. **To pick holes in**—*to find fault with*. Will you please stop picking holes in the matter.

6. **Toad in the hole**—*meat baked in butter, etc.* He is fond of toad in the hole.

Politics is for her a toad in the hole.

HOLLOW

Hollow-hearted—*insincere*. Hollow-hearted people are never successful in life.

HOME

1. **At home**—*at ease*. Please be at home.

2. **At home in**—*expert* in. Rajesh is at home in mathematics.

3. **Bring home to**—*to prove.* I will bring this problem home to you.
Bring home to him the importance of doing this work immediately.

4. **Eat out of house and home**—*to live at the expense of another so as to ruin him.* Our in-laws are eating us out of house and home.

5. **Home thrust**—*a pointed remark that goes home.* Ram makes many home thrusts against Sham.

6. **Long home**—*the grave.* My brother has gone to the long home.

7. **Make oneself at a home**—*be comfortable.* Please make yourself at home here.

8. **Pay home**—*to strike to the quick; to retaliate.* If you hit, you will be paid home.

HONEST

To turn an honest penny—*to earn a living honestly.* His father turned an honest penny throughout his life.

HONOURS

1. **Do the honours**—*to render courtesies as a ghost.* Royal Restaurant does the honours to every guest.

2. **Honour bright**—*appeal to honour.* Honour bright goes farther than litigation.

3. **Last honours**—*funeral rites.* We performed the last honours of my brother in June 1979.

4. **Upon my honour**—*an appeal to one's honour in support of a statement.* Upon my honour, I never spoke against you.

5. **Word of honour**—*a promise which cannot be broken without disgrace.* I give you a word of honour to help you in your needs.

HOOK

1. **By hook or by crook**—by fair *or* foul means. People today make money by hook or by crook.

2. **Hook it**—*decamp; make off.* He hooked it with Rs. 5,000.

3. **Off the hooks**—*out of gear; suspended; dead.* Everything is off the hooks in India today.
Prohibition is off the hooks.

4. **On one's own hook**—*on one's own responsibility.* You can do any thing on your own hook.

HOP

1. **Hop it**—*take oneself off.* If you are fed up with society, you cannot hop it.

2. **Hop the twig**—*escape one's creditors.* After big loans you cannot hop the twig.

3. **On the hop**—*in the act; unawares; at the very moment.* The thief was caught on the hop.

HOPE

Hope against hope—*to continue to hope when all ground is gone.* We are all hoping against hope that one day India will be a land flowing with milk and honey.

HORN

1. **Horn in**—*interpose.* Please don't horn in when I am speaking.

2. **Make a spoon or spoil a horn**—*to attempt something at the risk of failure.* A youth can only make a spoon or spoil a horn in making his career.

3. **On the horns of a dilemma**—*in a difficult situation*. I am on the horns of a dilemma whether to live in the world or to renounce the world.

4. **Put to the horn**—*to outlaw by three blasts of the horn*. Mr. Edward has been put to the horn by his own party.

5. **To blow one's own horn**—*to boast*. Do something solid. No use blowing your own horn every now and then.

6. **To pull or draw in one's horns**—*to decrease one's enthusiasm or claims*. Mr. Jackson can no longer draw in his horns.

7. **To take the bull by the horns**—*to face a problem boldly. One must possess the courage of taking the bull by the horns.*

HORNET

To bring a hornet's nest about one's ears—*to stir up trouble*. His brother is wise enough not to bring a hornet's nest about his ears.

HORSE

1. **Flog a dead horse**—*to try to work up excitement about a dead subject*. When you talk of corruption, you are only flogging a dead horse.

2. **Put the cart before the horse**—*to do things in the reverse order of nature*. By laying more stress on military and less on meals we are putting the cart before the horse.

3. **To ride the high horse**—*to put on airs*. The success lies in seriousness and hard work and not on riding the high horse.

4. **To work like a horse**—*to work hard.* If you want to get first position in your college, you will have to work like a horse.

HOST

1. **Host in himself**—*one with great skill.* Pandit Nehru was a host in himself.

2. **Reckon or count without one's host**—*to fail to take account of an important possibility, as the action of another.* To think that we can depend on Russia or America to pull our chestnuts out of the fire, we are counting without the host.

HOT

1. **Hot air**—*empty talk.* Our plans of socialism are all hot air.

2. **Hot and hot**—*served as soon as cooked.* The service in Standard Restaurant is worth appreciating, you get things hot and hot.

3. **Hot stuff**—*anything remarkable or dangerous.* Indipop is hot stuff now-a-days.

4. **Hot water**—*a state of trouble.* If you spend more than you earn, you will soon find yourself in hot water.

5. **Make a place too hot for one**—*to make one's stay impossible.* George is making Chief Ministership too hot a place for Aziz Ahmed.

7. **To blow hot and cold**—to *contradict oneself.* In today's meeting the speaker was blowing hot and cold.

HOTCH-POTCH

Hotch-potch—*a confused mess.* Life today is all hotch-potch.

HOUR

1. **At all hours**—*at no fixed time.* I return home at all hours.
2. **At the eleventh hour**—*at the last moment.* Nobody will come to your help at the eleventh hour.
3. **In a good hour**—*under a lucky star.* Everybody helps you in a good hour.
4. **In an evil hour**—*in bad luck.* Nobody stands by you in an evil hour.
5. **Keep good hour**—*go to bed early and rise early.* Old people should keep good hours.

HOUSE

1. **Bring down the house**—*to evoke very loud applause.* The great actors bring down the house.
2. **House of ill-fame**—*brothel.* You should stay away from houses of ill-fame.
3. **House to house**—*door to door.* They moved house to house for collecting donations for the temple.
4. **Keep a good house**—*to have plenty to eat.* Rich men keep a good house.
5. **Keep house**—*maintain or manage an establishment.* She keeps house in Bird and Co.
6. **Like a house on fire**—*with great speed.* The news spread like a house on fire.
7. **To keep an open house**—*to provide entertainment to all comers.* Any club is supposed to keep an open house.

HOW

1. **How and how**—*yes, certainly; very much indeed.* I shall meet you at the coffee house how and how.

2. **How now**—*What is this? Why is this so?*

3. **How's that**—*the appeal of the fielding side to the umpire to give the batsman out.*

4. **The how and why**—*the manner and the cause.* Nobody knows the how and why of the economic mess in which the world finds itself today.

5. **How d'ye do, how 'dy do**—*a troublesome state of matters.* Everybody today finds himself in how d'ye-do.

HUE

Hue and cry—*great clamour; great noise.* There is a great hue and cry about corruption now-a-days.

HUM

1. **Hum and haw**—*to make inarticulate sounds when at a loss.* Be at ease. There is no use humming and hawing when you have lost your purse.

2. **Make things hum**—*to set things going briskly.* The new Director has made things hum in the office.

HUMPTY

Humpty-dumpty—*short and squat.* Every successful leader is a humpty-dumpty in India today.

HUNT

1. **Hunt the letter**—*to affect alliteration.* Good poets do not hunt the letter.

2. **Hunt up**—*seek out.* Hunt up one who can help you.

HUP

Neither hup nor wind—*neither do one thing nor the other.* Most of the students today neither hup nor wind.

HURRY

1. **Hurry-scurry**—*confusion and bustle.* You can achieve no peace in hurry-scurry.

2. **Hurry up**—*make haste.* Please hurry up lest you are late.

HUSH

Hush up—*to be silent; to be suppressed; to be stifled.* Please hush up.

Truth cannot be hushed up.

HYDRA

Hydra-headed—*difficult to root out, springing up vigorously again and again.* The troubles of India are hydra-headed.

ICE

1. **Break the ice**—*to make a beginning*. In an atmosphere of pindrop silence, sudden crying of the baby broke the ice.

2. **Cut no ice**—*to count for nothing*. In this city of ministers and millionaires, even a top officer cuts no ice.

ILK

Of that ilk—*of that kind, quality, family, etc.* Son and father are of same ilk.

ILL

1. **Go ill with**—*result in danger or misfortune*. Money goes ill with arrogance.

2. **Take it ill**—*to be offended*. Please don't take it ill if I tell you the truth.

3. **To be ill at ease**—*to be uneasy*. You will always be ill at ease in an immature company.

4. **To be taken ill**—*to fall ill*. My brother has been suddenly taken ill this morning.

284

IMPROVE

Improve the occasion—*to seize an opportunity for edification or other purpose; to draw a moral from what has happened.* When a person misbehaves and receives punishment of misfortune, you can improve the occasion by quoting the Vedas.

IN

1. **In a body**—*together with one feeling.* The decision of appointing Mr. Fisher as the new Secretary was taken at the meeting in a body.

2. **In as far as**—*in so far as.* You can go in as far as you have strength to go.

3. **In as much as**—*considering that.* The Judge let him off with a light punishment in as much as he was a small boy.

4. **In brief**—*in short.* Please tell us the whole matter in brief.

5. **In it**—*in the enjoyment of success; in the running.* When we get success, you will be in it.

6. **In itself**—*intrinsically; apart from relations.* In itself, the work cannot give you your half day's living.

7. **In on**—*participating in.* Labour Party is in on Richard's movement.

8. **In pursuance of**—*while doing it.* He is studying science in pursuance of his desire to become a doctor.

9. **Ins and outs**—*the whole details of the matter. Those who repeatedly enter and leave in a workshop, etc.* It requires a lifetime to know ins and outs of a subject.

10. **In so far as**—*to the extent that.* One can spend in so far as he has money in his pocket.

11. **In time**—*right time*. The train left in time.

12. **Nothing in it**—*no truth, no importance, no difficulty in the matter; no important difference*. Why are you worrying about your work? There is nothing in it.

13. **To be in for a thing**—*determined to get a thing done*. He is in for a job now-a-days.

INCH

1. **An inch of cool iron**—*stab with a dagger*. The old man lost his wife with an inch of cool iron.

2. **At an inch**—*ready at hand*. If you need my help, you will find me at an inch.

3. **By inches; inch by inch**—*by small degrees*. You can achieve great success inch by inch.

4. **Every inch**—*thoroughly*. He is every inch a gentleman.

INCREMENT

Unearned increment—*exceptional increase in the value of land, property, etc., not due to the owner's labour or expense*. In the climate of rising prices all property enjoys unearned increment.

INDIAN

Indian gift—*a gift that is asked back or for which a return gift is expected*. I hope you are not making me an Indian gift by inviting me to the dinner.

INDICTMENT

Find an indictment—*to be satisfied that there is a prima facie case*. The Lok Sabha found an indictment against Shri M.N. Sinha.

INDIRECT

Indirect evidence—*circumstantial or inferential evidence.* The criminal was convicted on the basis of indirect evidence.

INCUMBENT

To be incumbent—*essential.* A general clerk should be incumbent of typing.

INFERIORITY

Inferiority complex—*a feeling of inferiority.* A poor boy in the company of the rich usually suffers from inferiority complex.

INFERNAL

Infernal machine—*a contrivance made to resemble some ordinary harmless object, but charged with a dangerous explosive.* It was an infernal machine that killed David at Liverpool.

INFERNO

To let loose an inferno—*to kill, murder and burn indiscriminately.* During the war many nations let loose an inferno.

INFLUENCE

Back-door influence—*improper approach.* He got the job through back-door influence.

INITIATION

Initiation fee—*entrance fee of a society.* What is the initiation fee of R.O.S.E. ?

INITIATIVE

To take the initiative—*to take the lead.* Unless someone takes the initiative in the matter it is not going to be solved.

INK

Sympathetic ink—*a kind of ink that remains invisible on the paper until it is heated.* Spies write their secret letters in sympathetic ink.

INLAY

Inlay with—*inset; decorate.* Taj Mahal was inlaid with precious stones.

INNATE

Innate ideas—*inborn ideas.* Pandit Nehru's innate ideas made him the leader of our country.

INSIDE

1. **Inside out**—*with the inner side turned outwards.* The police officer studied the criminal inside out.

2. **Inside story**—*behind the scene information.* No one knows the inside story of this big scandal.

3. **Inside track**—*the advantage in position.* In the race of life a minister's son has the inside track.

INSTANCE

1. **At the instance of**—*under the direction of.* At the instance of his uncle he applied for the job and got it.

2. **To give instance of**—*to give an example.* Don't explain things by giving instances, just show us something solid.

INTELLIGENCE

Intelligence test—*a test by questions and tasks to determine a person's mental capacity, or the age at which his capacity would be normal.* Intelligence test indicates the mental age of children who may have an old head on young shoulders.

INTENT

To all intents and purposes—*in every important respect; virtually.* To all intents and purposes she is the queen of the country.

INTEREST

1. **In an interesting condition**—*pregnant.* I do not know yet whether the bride is in an interesting condition.

2. **Make interest for**—*secure favour for.* The ministers make interest for their menials.

INTERVAL

At intervals—*now and then*. He does things at intervals.

INTRUDE

To intrude upon—*to interfere with*. Do not intrude upon my work.

INVINCIBLE

1. **Invincible ignorance**—*ignorance which one cannot help*. Technological progress has led to invincible ignorance in the world.

2. **Invisible green**—green *that is almost black*. She was fond of dressing in invisible green.

IRON

1. **In irons**—*in fetters*. Every thief finds himself in irons one day or the other.

2. **Iron age**—*wicked times*. The world is passing through the Iron age.

3. **Iron will**—*strong mind*. I have an iron will to succeed in my new business.

4. **Man of iron**—*of strong mind*. Sardar Patel was a man of iron.

5. **Rule with a rod of iron**—*to rule with sternness*. The British ruled the Empire on which the sun never set with a rod of iron.

6. **Too many irons in the fire**—*too many things on hand at once*. All the time I have too many irons in the fire.

7. **To strike while the iron is hot**—*to make use of an opportunity in time.* By applying for this job he struck while the iron was hot.

ISSUE

1. **At issue**—*in dispute.* What is the matter at issue ?

2. **Feigned issue**—*an issue made up for trial.* Students fight over feigned issues.

3. **General issue**—*a simple denial of whole charge as,* "Not Guilty". The criminals prefer the general issue.

4. **Join, or take issue**—*to take an opposite position.* The students quite often join issue with the professors.

5. **Material issue**—*one which rightly involves some part of the rights in controversy.* Theft with murder is a material issue.

6. **Side issue**—*a subordinate issue arising from main business.* There are many side issues in this murder.

7. **Special issue**—*an issue taken by denying a particular portion of the whole allegation.* There is always a special issue in court trials.

ITALIANATE

Italianate Englishman—*an Englishman full of Italian learning and vice, proverbially equivalent to a devil incarnate.* Italianate Englishman ruled the British Empire in India.

ITALIAN

Italian garden—*a formal garden with statues.* Mumbai is getting fond of Italian gardens.

ITCHING

Itching palm—*a greed for money.* More and more people of the world today suffer from an itching palm.

ITSELF

1. **By itself**—*along itself; a part.* By itself no man can run a government.

2. **In itself**—*by its own nature.* Gold is not evil in itself.

IVORY

1. **Ivory tower**—*a place of retreat from the world and one's fellows.* A philosopher lives in an ivory tower.

2. **Show one's ivories**—*show one's teeth.* Children are fond of showing their ivories.

★ ★ ★

J-PEN

J-pen—*a pen with a short broad point.* Don't write your flatteries with a J-pen.

JACK

1. **Black jack**—*vessel for liquor.* In yesterday's raid, the police recovered 20 black jacks.

2. **Jack Frost**—*frost personified.* The crop was killed by Jack Frost.

3. **Jack Ketch**—*a public hangman.* Only Jack Ketch can rid the nation of its soaring tide of corruption.

4. **Jack of all trades**—*one who can turn his hand to anything.* A Jack of all trades can always manage to earn his living.

5. **Jack Sprat**—*a diminutive fellow.* Lal Bahadur Shastri was Jack Sprat.

6. **Poor Jack, poor John**—*to poor man.* Nobody cares for poor Jacks and Johns in the world.

JACKAL

1. **Jackal**—*one who would share the spoil without sharing the danger.* Politicians are jackals of the army.

2. **To act as jackal**—*to do preparatory work.* The stenographer acts as jackal for the manager.

3. **To play the jackal**—*to share spoils without sharing dangers*. Business men are always ready to play the jackal.

JACKET

Dust one's jacket—*beat him*. The teachers can teach nothing without dusting their student's jackets.

JACTITION

Jactition of marriage—*pretence of being married to another*. Youth should guard themselves against marriage even by jactition of marriage.

JAIL

Break jail—*force one's way out of jail*. The criminals quite often break jail.

JAM

1. **Money for jam**—*money for nothing*. Don't waste money for jam.
2. **To jam into**—*to thrust violently into something*. His cycle jammed into the bus and he died on the spot.

JAR

1. **To jar upon**—*to irritate*. Do not jar upon your inferiors.
2. **To jar with**—*disagree*. On hearing facts, I jarred with your scheme.

JAW

1. **Hold your jaw**—*stop talking*. Will you please hold your jaw and listen to me ?
2. **To jaw**—*to annoy with words*. The clerk was dismissed because he jawed his manager.

JAY

Jay-walker—*one who walks on road without paying any heed to traffic rules.* Jay-walking is an easy road to hospital.

JEE

Jee one's ginger—*to show perturbation.* If you are mentally upset, don't jee your ginger.

JERRY

Jerry shop—*low beer shop.* The whole town is full of jerry shops.

JEST

In jest—*not seriously.* A person doing things in jest never succeeds in life.

JETSAM

Flotsam and jetsam—*unclaimed, odds and ends.* Life is full of flotsam and jetsam.

JEW

1. **Jew's eye**—*something of very high value.* A job in the Customs is a Jew's eye.
2. **Rich as a Jew**—*very wealthy.* The old man of this city who expired this morning, was rich as a Jew.
3. **Wandering Jew**—*a homeless moneymaker.* Tourists are wandering Jews.
4. **Worth a Jew's eye**—*quite precious.* The ornaments presented by Abdullah are worth a Jew's eye.

JIB

The cut of one's jib—*appearance.* The girl fell in love with the cut of his jib.

JIGGER

1. **Jiggered up**—*exhausted.* When I returned home I was quite jiggered up.
2. **Jiggery-pokery**—*trickery.* People today make money by jiggery-pokery.

JIGSAW

Jigsaw puzzle—*a picture cut up in pieces to be fitted together.* Life today is very much of a jigsaw puzzle.

JIM

1. **Jim Crow**—*Negro.* Jim Crow is coming to power in the U.S.A.
2. **Jim Crow school**—*a school only for Negroes.* No white American child goes to a Jim Crow school.

JITTERBUG

Jitterbug—*one addicted to dancing.* The taste for Jitterbug among young girls is fast spreading in our country.

JOB

1. **A bad job**—*a piece of work ill done.* "Dharna" proved a bad job for J.P.

2. **A good job**—*a piece of work well done.* Indira did a good job in politics.

3. **Job of work**—*a task; hard work.* Fighting an election is a job of work.

4. **Job's comforter**—*one who aggravates the distress of the unfortunate man he has come to comfort.* When you are in trouble, beware of a Job's comforter.

5. **Job's news**—*bad news.* The newspaper is full of Job's news.

6. **Job's post**—*the bearer of a bad news.* Job's post informed me of my brother's death.

7. **Odd jobs**—*occasional pieces of work.* Millions in India survive by doing odd jobs.

8. **On the job**—*at work; in activity.* I am on the job of writing this Dictionary of Idioms and Phrases.

JOCKEY

Jockey—*to deceive; cheat.* It was unfair on his part to have jockeyed his brother in his business.

JOE

1. **Joe Miller**—*an old or stale joke; a jest book.* Joe Miller is not popular anywhere.

2. **Joe Millerism**—*the habit of telling old jokes.* Old men must shake off Joe Millerism.

JOG

1. **Jog away; Jog off**—*get away.* The police ordered the demonstrators to jog away within three minutes.

2. **Jog trot**—*a slow but regular walk.* The police family is in the habit of having jog trot in the morning.

JOHN

John Bull—*a general name for an Englishman or English nation.* John Bull has renounced the world empire in favour of Uncle Sam.

JOIN

1. **Join battle**—*to fight or quarrel.* They joined the battle over a cup of tea.

2. **Join hands**—*clasp hands.* Let us join hands before starting this new venture.

3. **Join issue**—*to begin to dispute.* Danny and Robert have joined issue on leadership of the country.
4. **Join up**—*enlist in the army.* The national emergency necessitates for young men of India to join up defence.

JOINT

1. **During the joint lives**—*when they are all alive.* The children enjoy their best during the joint lives of their parents.
2. **Out of joint**—*dislocated.* The world today is out of joint.
3. **Put one's nose out of joint**—*to supplant in another's love or confidence.* True friends must not put their noses out of joint.

JOKE

1. **Cast jokes at**—*to banter.* Don't cast jokes at your near and dear ones.
2. **No joke**—*a serious or difficult matter.* Living the life successfully is no joke.
3. **Practical joke**—*a harmful joke.* Never play practical jokes on your friends.

JOLLY

1. **A jolly dog**—*a jovial fellow.* A jolly dog is liked in every company.
2. **A jolly good fellow**—*a very social and popular fellow.* Krishna became a jolly good fellow only after joining our club.
3. **Jolly Roger**—*the pirates' black flag with a skull and cross bones.* The ship came flying a Jolly Roger.
4. **The jolly fool**—*happy person.* His brother does not like the company of jolly fools.

JOSEPH

Not for Joseph—*not on any account*. I can forgive you for your fault not for Joseph.

JOY

Joy ride—*reckless pleasure drive in a stolen car.* Our youth have taken to joy rides as ducks take to water.

JUBILEE

1. **Diamond jubilee**—*sixtieth anniversary.* Few couples live to celebrate the diamond jubilee of their marriage.

2. **Golden *jubilee***—*fiftieth anniversary.* We celebrated the golden jubilee of India's Independence in 1997.

3. **Silver jubilee**—*twenty-fifth anniversary*. We have celebrated the silver jubilee of our independence and our Republic.

JUDA

Juda's kiss—*false love*. His wife's love was a Juda's kiss.

JUDGMENT

1. **Judgment reserved**—*decision reserved and delayed after the close of a trial*. Judgment is quite often reserved especially in murder cases.

2. **Judgment respited**—*execution of judgment delayed*. Mr. Andrews got judgment respited in obscenity cases.

JUDICIAL

Judicial separation—*separation of two married persons, by order of the court*. Josephine got judicial separation, from David before marrying Napoleon.

JUGGLE

To juggle with—*deceive*. Never juggle with your friends.

JUICE

Step on the juice—*to speed up a car*. Don't step on the juice when the traffic is jammed.

301

JUMBLE

Jumble sale—*sale of miscellaneous articles*. I bought this purse at a jumble sale.

JUMP

1. **Jump at**—*to accept with eagerness*. Anybody will jump at the opportunity to make easy money.
2. **Jump down**—*come down or fall*. There is hardly any chance of prices of essential commodities to jump down.

3. **Jump down one's throat**—*to attack with violence.* The murderer jumped down on constable's throat.

4. **Jumped on**—*to jump so as to come heavily on; to censure violently.* Dara Singh jumped on King Kong.

5. **Jump one's bail**—*to abscond, forfeiting one's bail.* The professional criminals quite often jump the bail.

6. **Jump to conclusion**—*form judgment quickly.* Let us not jump to the conclusion that the world would end in 2010 A.D.

7. **To jump at an offer**—*to accept it eagerly.* My brother jumped at the offer of Superintendent's post in his office.

8. **To jump to**—*to decide quickly.* Our Manager is in the habit of jumping to wrong conclusions.

9. **To jump to claim**—*to seize somebody else's claim.* Immediately after the death of his father the eldest son jumped a claim on his younger brothers.

10. **To jump together**—*to agree.* Stanley and Susan jumped together.

11. **To jump up**—*to rise.* His honesty is the main cause of his jumping up to this position.

12. **To jump upon**—*to attack.* The Chinese jumped upon Indians in 1962.

JUNK

1. **Junk man**—*a dealer in junk.* My friend, who is a millionniare now, started his life as junk man.

2. **Junk shop**—*a place where junk is sold.* After the kitty party was over, her drawing-room looked like a junk shop.

JUST

Just now—*precisely at this moment.* I am coming to see you just now.

JUSTICE

To do justice to—*to treat fairly.* A student should always do full justice to his studies.

JUSTIFIABLE

Justifiable homicide—*the killing of a person in self-defence or to prevent an atrocious crime.* Every murder is not a justifiable homicide.

JUSTIFICATION

Justification by faith—*the doctrine that men are justified by faith in Christ.* Hindus do not believe in justification by faith.

KAKISTOCRACY

Kakistocracy—*a government by the worst.*
Democracy everywhere has given place to kakistocracy.

KANGAROO

Kangaroo closure—*the method of allowing the chairman to decide which clauses will be discussed and which passed over.* The Speaker of the Lok Sabha seldom applies the kangaroo closure.

KECK

To keck at—*reject.* I cannot keck at my uncle's offer to join him as manager.

KEEN

1. **Keen eye**—*fully alive.* One must have a keen eye to be successful in life.

2. **Keen on**—*devoted to; very much interested in; very desirous of.* The young bridegroom is keen on the bride.

305

3. **Keen prices**—*very low prices*. The days of keen prices are over.

4. **Keen set**—*hungry*. I don't like people keen set at money.

KEEP

1. **For keeps**—*as a permanent possession; for good; permanently*. I can give you this pen for keeps.

2. **Keep an act**—*hold an academic disputation*. They kept an act on Hinduism.

3. **Keep an eye on**—*watch*. Please keep an eye on the child.

4. **Keep body and soul together**—*to maintain life*. It is not easy to keep body and soul together now-a-days.

5. **Keep company**—*to be companion*. Always keep good company. A man is known by the company he keeps.

6. **Keep distance**—*stay away from*. The drivers should always keep distance from other vehicles.

7. **Keep down**—*restrain; repress*. Politicians manage to keep the people down.

8. **Keep from**—*abstain from; remain away from*. Please keep from liquor.

9. **Keep going in**—*a thing; to keep one supplied with*. Please keep the milk supply going in.

10. **Keep house**—*remain indoors*. Many Indians advise their young daughters and sisters to keep house.

11. **Keep in**—*to prevent from escaping; to conceal; to restrain*. Please keep the children in.

12. **Keeping with**—*according to*. Keeping with the traditions of his family the boy got married in a royal family.

13. **Keep in with**—*maintain the confidence of friendship of.* You must keep in with your superiors.

14. **Keep off**—*to hinder from approaching or attacking.* Iran will keep India off Pakistan.

15. **Keep on**—*continue.* Please keep on with your work.

16. **Keep one's balance**—*to remain stable.* It is difficult to keep one's balance due to the high cost of living.

17. **Keep one's breath to cool one's porridge**—*to hold one's peace when further talk is clearly in vain.* In dealing with Pakistan, India should keep her breath to cool her porridge.

18. **Keep one's countenance**—*to avoid showing one's emotions.* In a difficult situation it is best to keep your countenance.

19. **Keep one's hand in**—*to retain one's skill by practice.* I must keep my hand in yoga.

20. **Keep one's powder dry**—*to keep one's energies ready for action; to observe all practical precautions.* D'Souza's followers will have to keep their powder dry till the elections.

21. **Keep open house**—*entertain all comers.* A club must keep open house.

22. **Keep peace**—*remain peaceful.* Pakistan will not keep peace with Afghanistan, for long.

23. **Keep tabs on**—*to keep a check on; to keep account of.* The government must keep tabs on the activities of the smugglers.

24. **Keep time**—*to observe rhythm; to go accurately.* The children keep time in dancing.

    The watch keeps time.

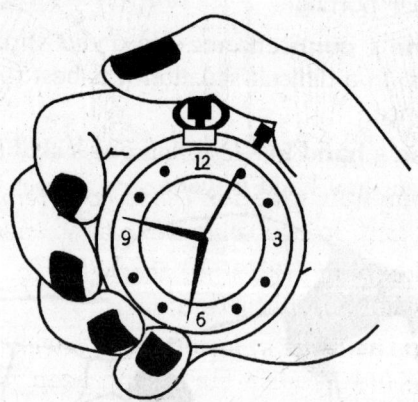

25. **Keep to**—*to stick closely to; to confine oneself to.* The old man keeps to the house.

26. **Keep under**—*to hold his restraint.* The prices must be kept under.

27. **Keep up**—*restrain one's strength or spirit.* You must keep up a long as you live.

    The soldiers keep up on the road.

    The car should be kept up.

28. **Keep wicket**—*to act as wicket keeper.* Will you please keep the wicket ?

29. **Keep your hair on**—*don't lose your temper.* Let us keep our hair on and settle the matter amicably.

30. **Out of keeping with**—*not according to.* It is out of keeping with the principles of life.

31. **To keep at arm's length**—*to check one from becoming too familiar.* He likes to keep her at arm's length.

32. **To keep down**—*to keep expenses low.* His meagre income compels him to keep down his budget.

33. **To keep in touch**—*to remain in contact with.* A pilot has always to keep himself in touch with the nearest airport.

34. **To keep to oneself**—*to refuse to share it.* The amount left with me is so small that I have to keep it to myself.

KEN

Beyond one's ken—*out of one's sight*. Beyond one's ken, beyond one's mind.

KETTLE

1. **Kettle of fish**—*a riverside picnic at which newly caught fish are cooked on the spot*. We had a kettle of fish on the Hindon River, but I did not join the lunch.

2. **Pretty Cattle of fish**—*confusion*. Our office is Pretty Cattle of fish.

KEY

1. **Golden and silver key**—*money used as a bribe*. The habit of offering golden and silver key must be stopped.

2. **Have the key of the street**—*to be locked out; to be homeless*. Tonight it appears I will have the key of the street.

3. **Key**—*that solves some difficulty*. Poison is not necessarily the only key for a distressed man.

4. **Keyed to**—*made to harmonize, or fit exactly with*. The entire Cabinet is keyed to the Prime Minister.

5. **Keyed up**—*raised pitch or standard; stimulated; in a state of nervous tension and excitement*. Bhutto keyed up the political life of Pakistan.

6. **Key industry**—*the main basic industry*. A country has always to subsidise its key industry.

7. **Keynote**—*main idea*. The keynote of the plan is to provide reasonable shelter to poor people.

8. **Power of the keys**—*the power to loose or bind.* A man with money always has the power of the keys for a man without money.

KICK

1. **Kick, or strike, the beam**—*to be of little weight or importance.* A man of merit but without money will kick the beam in any fight of elections.
2. **Kick over the traces**—*to throw off control.* The youth today are trying to kick over the traces.
3. **Kick the bucket**—*to die.* Sooner or later, everyone of us must kick the bucket.
4. **More kicks than half pence**—*more abuse than profit.* The business he has started has more kicks than half pence.
5. **To kick against the pricks**—*to invite trouble.* No wise man will ever kick against the pricks.
6. **To kick up dust**—*to create trouble.* The little kid is kicking up dust for everyone.

KICKIE

Kickie-wickie—*wife.* How is your kickie-wickie?

KICKSY

Kicksy-wicksy—*wife.* I have not met your kicksy-wicksy for quite a long time.

KID

To handle with kid gloves—*to handle with ease.* This matter must be handled with kid gloves.

KILL

1. **Kill by inches**—*by gradual means, as by torture.* The in-laws kill a couple by inches.

2. **Kill off**—*exterminate*. The doctors have failed to kill off the germs of many diseases.

3. **Kill two birds with one stone**—*to do two things with the means needed for one*. By pretending sickness you can kill two birds with one stone, because you can stay away from office and also attend a marriage.

4. **Kill up**—*to exterminate*. The quickest way to remove poverty is to kill up the poor.

5. **To kill**—*in an irresistible manner*. He demanded money to kill.

6. **To kill time**—*to waste time*. Parents must check their children from killing time.

KIN

1. **Kith and kin**—*near and dear ones*. I do not know much about your kith and kin.

2. **Next of kin**—*the nearest relative of a deceased person*. The next of kin were informed about the death of the soldiers.

3. **Of kin**—*of the same kin*. Cat and tiger are of kin.

KIND

1. **Do one's kind**—*act according to one's nature*. In the world, everybody does his kind.

2. **In a kind**—*in a way; to some extent*. The Prime Minister is a king in a kind.

3. **In kind**—*in goods instead of money*. When payment is made in kind, it is called barter.

4. **Take it kind**—*feel it as kindness*. Take it kind that I have come to see you.

KING

1. **King Log**—*a do-nothing king*. Many youth are King Logs.

2. **King mob**—*the vulgar multitude*. King mob rules the nation.

3. **King of beasts**—*the lion*. The king of beasts is now languishing to its death.

4. **King of birds**—*the eagle*. Guru Gobind Singh had a king of birds as his pet.

5. **King of metals**—*gold*. The king of metals is now seldom seen.

6. **King of terrors**—*death*. Why be afraid of the king of terrors ?

7. **King of the forest**—*oak*. The king of the forest is now on its last legs.

8. **King's English or Queen's English**—*correct standard English*. When a King rules the country, it is called King's English, and when a Queen rules the nation, it is called Queen's English.

9. **King stork**—*one who devours his frog subjects*. Democracy is now a government of the King stork.

10. **Turn King's or Queen's evidence**—*to become a witness against an accomplice on the understanding that one would be pardoned*. Police always create a king's evidence in any serious crime to lighten its own work.

KINGDOM

Kingdom come—*the state after death*. He has gone to kingdom come.

KIRK

Make a kirk or a mill of it—*do what you please or can with it*. You cannot make a kirk of a modern boy or a girl but he can make a mill of you.

KISS

1. **Kiss hands**—*accept an office.* Anybody will kiss hand for a big job.

2. **Kiss the book**—*take a legal oath.* You kiss the book for marriage.

3. **Kiss the dust**—*to humble oneself.* Unless one has the quality of kissing the dust, one cannot rise in life.

4. **Kiss the gunner's daughter**—*to get a flagging, tied to the breach of a gun.* If you disobey army rules, you may have to kiss the gunner's daughter.

5. **To kiss one's hand**—*to wish one bon-voyage.* When the train moved, the father kissed his daughter's hand.

KIT

To whole kit of them—*the whole lot of them.* The whole kit of the factory labour is at work.

KITCHEN

Kitchen physic—*substantial fare.* Our hunger calls for kitchen physic.

KITE

To fly a kite—*to test public opinion.* No Government can fly a kite for long.

KNEE

1. **Give or offer a knee**—*to act as a second or bottle-holder in a fight.* I offer you my knee in the wrestling match.

2. **On the knees of the gods**—*awaiting the decision of a fate.* The politician rather than poets wait on the knees of the gods.

3. **To bring to knees**—*to reduce to submission.* The teacher was able to bring to knees his new student.

KNIFE

1. **Have one's knife in**—*to be persistently hostile and vindictive towards.* Please do not have your knife in me.

2. **Under the knife**—*undergoing a surgical operation.* My friend is under the knife now-a-days.

3. **War to the knife**—*unrelenting conflict.* Why should India and Pakistan war to the knife in order to please foreign powers ?

4. **To get a knife into**—*to kill.* The thief got a knife into the old man.

5. **Before you can say knife**—*very quickly.* The man is intelligent enough to do his work before you can say knife.

KNIGHT

1. **Knight of the post**—*a professional false witness and offerer of a bail.* He earns his living as a knight of the post.

2. **Knight of the rainbow**—*flunkey.* Call the knight of the rainbow to ready the horse for the ride.

3. **Knight of the road**—*a highwayman; a tramp; a commercial traveller.* I was robbed by a knight of the road.

4. **Knight of the shears**—*tailor.* The knight of the shears has ruined my suit.

5. **Knight of the stick**—*compositor.* In this press he is a knight of the stick.

6. **Knight of the whip**—*coachman.* The knight of the whip has outlived his days.

KNOCK

1. **Knock about**—*loaf about; saunter; travel.* Many young men are knocking about for jobs these days.

2. **Knock down**—*to fell with a blow; to sell by auction.* The tree was knocked down.

   The table was knocked down for ten rupees.

3. **Knock into a cocked hat**—*to give profound beating.* The police knocks an offender into a cocked hat.

4. **Knock off**—*leave off work; to accomplish hastily; to strike off; to deduct; to steal.* The railwaymen knocked off at lunch.

   His name was knocked off the list of invitees.

5. **Knock out**—*dislodge by a blow; to strike insensible; to overcome; to lose the scent.* A weak man cannot knock out a strong man.

6. **Knock-out auction**—*an auction where the bidders are swindling confederates.* Democracy has become a knock-out auction.

7. **Knock-out drops**—*a drug put in the liquor.* He was rendered unconscious by knock-out drops.

8. **Knock the bottom out of**—*to make or show to be invalid; to make ineffectual; to bring a naught.* Failure knocked the bottom out of his ambition.

9. **Knock together**—*get together or construct hastily.* They knocked together a skyscraper.

10. **Knock together**—*put hastily together.* The thieves were able to knock together jewellery and clothes.

11. **Knock under**—*to give in; to yield.* He knocked under pressure of money and political pull.

12. **Knock up**—*to rouse by knocking; to weary out; to be worn out; to construct or arrange hastily; to score.* He knocked me up at midnight.

    Your work has knocked me up.

    They knocked up a marriage.

    The cricketer knocked up a century.

13. **To knock against**—*to collide.* The car knocked against the tree.

14. **To take the knock**—*be hard hit financially.* I am taking the knock with great difficulty.

15. **Upto the knocker**—*upto the required standard of excellence of fashion.* Nixon was not President up to the knocker.

KNOW

1. **In the know**—*in the possession of private information initiated.* The Prime Minister is in the know of all that happens in the country.

2. **Know better**—*to be too wise; to be well instructed.* The Pakistanis know international diplomacy better.

3. **Know-how**—*knowledge of how to do something.* The technical know-how in our glass factory is very poor.

4. **Knowing to**—*aware; informed.* The Americans are knowing to Indian affairs.

5. **Known as**—*going by the name of.* Gandhiji was popularly known as Bapu.

6. **Know nothing**—*to be ignorant of.* I know nothing about the murder.

7. **Know nothingness**—*ignorance.* Your know nothingness will not solve the problem.

8. **Know the ropes**—*understand the details of procedure.* Only the clerks know the ropes in administration.

9. **Know what is what**—*to be wide awake.* If you read dailies, you know what is what.

10. **Know what's o'clock**—*to be wide awake.* The modern youth must know what's o'clock.

11. **Know which side one's bread is buttered on**—*to be fully alive to one's interests.* Every householder knows which side his bread is buttered on.

12. **To know one's mind**—*to be able to decide within one's oneself.* It is no use talking to a person who does not know his mind.

KNOWLEDGE

To my knowledge—*so far as I know.* To the best of my knowledge he is a good boy.

LABOUR

1. **A lost labour**—*hard work that has resulted in nothing.* All efforts of Rajesh to get through in the examination proved to be a lost labour.

2. **Herculean labour**—*needing enormous labour.* Any industry needs Herculean labour now-a-days.

3. **Labouring heart**—*troubled mind.* A labouring heart cannot do a good job.

4. **Labour of love**—*work undertaken without hope of payment.* True politics is a labour of love.

LACED

Laced mutton—*a prostitute.* You find laced muttons in every city.

LACK

Lack lustre—*dull.* Science is a lack lustre subject for many.

LADY

1. **Ladies man**—*one who is fond of female society*. Michael is a ladies man.

2. **Lady-love**—*sweetheart*. When he failed in getting his lady-love, he committed suicide.

3. **Lady of easy virtue**—*a prostitute*. Every big city has professional ladies of easy virtue.

4. **Your good lady**—*your wife*. Your good lady was with my sister last evening.

LAMB

A wolf in lamb's clothing—*hypocrite*. Many saints are like wolves in lamb's clothing now-a-days.

LAMP

Smell of the lamp—*to show signs of great elaboration and study*. In the work of a thesis there is always a smell of the lamp.

322

LAND

1. **Landed interest**—*the combined interest of the land-owing class in a community.* Politics is seldom free from the landed interest.

2. **Land of the leal**—*heaven.* May God rest the old woman in the land of the leal.

3. **Land of the living**—*present life.* It is difficult to maintain land of the living in our country due to heavy cost of living.

4. **Land-slide**—*a crushing defeat or victory in elections.* Walter got a land-slide in the last elections.

LANGUAGE

1. **Dead language**—*language no longer widely spoken.* Latin and Sanskrit are dead languages of the world.

2. **Living language**—*the language spoken by the people.* The living language of India is neither Hindi nor English, but a mixture of the two.

LANTERN

Lantern of the dead—*a lighted tower in a graveyard.* Religion is no longer a lamp of the living but a lantern of the dead.

LAP

Lapped in luxury—*brought up in luxury.* The whole family of my father-in-law is lapped in luxury.

LARGE

At large—*moving freely.* The thief is at large.

LASH

Lash out—*to kick out; fling out; hit out without restraint.* Mrs. Abraham Lincoln quite often lashed out at her husband.

LAST

1. **At last**—*in the end.* At last India got freedom.

2. **At long last**—*after long delay.* At long last he did make the payment.

3. **Breathe one's last**—*to die.* Sooner or later, everybody must breathe his last.

4. **First and last**—*altogether.* We were fifty men first and last.

5. **Last straw**—*that beyond which there can be no endurance.* This budget may be the last straw that breaks the Indian camel's back.

6. **On one's last legs**—*on the verge of utter failure or exhaustion.* Democracy is on its last legs in the world.

7. **Put the last hand to**—*finish.* The masons have put the last hand to the building.

8. **To the last**—*to the end; till death.* Great soldiers fight to the last.

LATCH

On the latch—*not locked, but to be opened by a latch.* You find everything here on the latch.

LATE

Of late—*recently.* Of late you are not in your mood.

LATIN

Thieves' latin—*thieves' cant.* Don't tell me in thieves' latin that you have not stolen my watch.

LATTER

Latter end—*the final part; the end of life*. The latter end of Mr. Walter was frustrating.

LAUGH

1. **Laugh and lie down**—*attain your objective and relax*. Prime Minister cannot laugh and lie down till after the next elections.

2. **Laugh in one's sleeve**—*laugh inwardly*. When you meet a friend out at the heels, don't laugh in your sleeve.

3. **Laugh on the wrong side of the mouth**—*to feel disappointed or sorry*. The couples after marriage laugh on the wrong side of the mouth.

4. **Laugh to scorn**—*to deride or jeer at*. Don't laugh your mother-in-law to scorn.

LAUREL

1. **To look to one's laurels**—*to be afraid of losing fame*. A film star always looks to his laurels.

2. **To win laurels**—*to win honours*. One must win laurels in life.

325

LAVENDER

To lay lavender—*to set aside something for further use*. The Government is trying to encourage the habit of laying lavender in our country.

LAW

1. **Be a law to oneself**—*to disregard convention*. Let us not be a law to ourselves.

2. **Go to law**—*resort to litigation against*. Avoid going to law against anybody unless you want to get a cat for a cow.

3. **Have the law of**—*enforce the law against*. You must have the law of the peace-breaker.

4. **Law of nations**—*international law*. Law of nations are ethical principles regarded as obligatory on all communities.

   Even at war a country should observe the law of nations.

5. **Law of nature**—*the order of nature*. You cannot violate the law of nature without adequate punishment.

6. **Law of the land**—*the established law of the country.*
Law of the land is a nose of wax in the hands of judges
and lawyers.

7. **To give the law to**—*to impose one's will upon.*
Giving the law in the hands of immature is no wisdom.

8. **To lay down the law**—*to talk authoritatively.* Unless
you are in a position to lay down the law, we are not
willing to listen to you.

9. **To take the law into one's own hands**—*to redress
one's wrong by force.* During war many nations try to
take the law into their own hands.

LAY

1. **Lay about one**—*to deal blows vigorously or on all
sides.* The mother laid about her children.

2. **Lay a course**—*to succeed in sailing to the place
required.* Modern technology has laid the course for
the destruction of civilization.

3. **Lay aside**—*to discard; to put apart for future use.*
He laid aside the old clothes.
He laid aside twenty rupees for tomorrow.

4. **Lay at**—*endeavour to strike.* If you lay at your friends,
they will turn your enemies.

5. **Lay away**—*lay aside.* Lay away some money for the
rainy day.

6. **Lay away**—*lay eggs in out of the way places.* Many
hens do lay away.
Don't lay away your earnings.

7. **Lay bare**—*disclose.* Please lay bare all the pertinent
facts.

8. **Lay before**—*submit to.* You must lay all the facts before the jury.

9. **Lay by**—*to keep for future* use; *to dismiss; to put off.* They laid by one thousand rupees.

   Hundred labourers were laid by.

   Please don't lay by today's meeting.

10. **Lay by the heels**—*to fetter; to put* in *confinement.* They laid the prisoner by the heels.

11. **Lay day**—*day for loading and unloading.* It was a lay day at the railway station.

12. **Lay down**—*to give up; to deposit* as a *pledge; to apply,* as *embroidery; to delineate; to describe; to affirm; to assert; to store; to plant.* They laid down the idea of going abroad.

   He laid down five rupees for tea.

   He laid down good threads.

   Will you lay down the whole plan ?

   Do you lay down what he says ?

   Let us lay down some money for rainy weather.

   They laid down grass in the lawn.

13. **Lay down the law**—*to state authoritatively.* Nobody can lay down the law in this country of complete chaos and confusion.

14. **Lay hands on**—*to arrest; to beat.* Please do not lay hands on the child.

   Police was able to lay hands on the thief.

15. **Lay heads together**—*to confer together.* Let us lay heads together to salvage the ship of state.

16. **Lay hold of or on**—*to seize.* Please lay hold of the pickpocket.

17. **Lay into**—*beat thoroughly*. They laid into the shop-lifter.

18. **Lay it on**—*to charge exorbitantly; to exaggerate; to flatter*. The hotel keeper laid it on us for lunch.

    Don't lay on your old story.

    It pays to lay on your boss.

19. **Lay load on**—*to labour*. Don't lay load on your wife.

20. **Lay off**—*to mark off; to admonish*. They lay off park.

    Please lay off your turban.

21. **Lay on**—*to instal a supply of; to deal blows with vigour*. Please lay on the gas.

    He laid on the servant.

22. **Lay oneself out to**—*to make it one's professed object or practice; take great pains to*. He laid himself out to rid India of corruption,

23. **Lay on the table**—*to put it for all to see*. He laid his cards on the table.

24. **Lay open**—*to make bare; to expose; to cut open*. He laid open his heart.

25. **Lay to heart**—*to grieve; to remember*. He laid to heart the death of his friend.

    I cannot lay to heart when we met last.

26. **Lay under**—*to subject to*. No country should be laid under a military dictator.

27. **Lay up**—*to store, to preserve; to confine in bed or one's room; to put in dock after dismantling*. They laid up food for the coming drought.

She was laid up in bed.

He was laid up with fever.

The ship was laid up.

28. **Lay upon**—*to wager upon.* I cannot lay anything upon the weather.

29. **Lay wait**—*to lie in wait.* They laid wait for the enemy to attack.

30. **Lay waste**—*devastate.* Tamberlaine lay waste the country.

31. **On a lay**—*on shares instead of wages.* It is best to pay your workers on a lay.

32. **To lay out**—*to display.* Our books are being laid out by all the good shopkeepers.

33. **To lay stress upon**—*to impress.* The teacher laid stress upon the students to work hard for their examination.

LEAD

1. **Easier led than driven**—*guide by persuasion.* Even a worker is easier led than driven now-a-days.

2. **Lead apes in hell**—*to have the lot of old maids.* She is destined to lead apes in hell.

3. **Lead astray**—*to draw into a wrong course; to seduce from right conduct.* Money leads a man easily astray.

4. **Lead by the nose**—*to make one follow submissively.* In democracy you cannot lead people by the nose.

5. **Lead in**—*to house the harvest.* They lead in their crop of the season.

6. **Leading business**—*principal role.* The hero.has the leading business in a film.

7. **Leading counsel**—*the lawyer who takes precedence in conducting a case.* Mr. Mathew is the leading counsel in this case.

8. **Leading lady**—*heroine.* Liza was the leading lady of her times.

9. **Leading light**—*very influential member.* The President is the leading light of the ruling party.

10. **Leading man**—*leader; hero.* Michael is the leading man today.

11. **Leading question**—*a question so put as to get the desired answer.* Please don't ask any leading questions from the witnesses.

12. **Lead in prayer**—*to make others pray in assembly.* A priest leads the prayers in assembly.

13. **Lead off**—*to begin something.* Get-rich-quickly led off all kinds of corruption.

14. **Lead on**—*to persuade to go on; to draw on.* He led on the picnic party to the waterfall.

15. **Lead one a dance**—*to chatter; to talk in a roundabout manner.* The politicians lead the people to dance.

16. **Lead out**—*to conduct to execution or a dance.*
Veronica led out the dance.

17. **Lead the way**—*to go first and guide others.* If the
Secretary of our union agrees, I shall be glad to lead the
way.

18. **Lead up to**—*to bring about by degrees.* Corruption
will lead up to the downfall of democracy.

19. **Men of light and leading**—*of great influence.* All
the members of the Labour Party in London are men
of light and leading.

20. **To lead one a life**—*worry one constantly.* She leads
the whole family a life.

LEAF

1. **Take a leaf out of one's book**—*to learn a lesson
from somebody.* Those who dilly-dally should take a
leaf out of the book of those who fail in life.

2. **Turn over a new leaf**—*to begin a new and better course of life*. It is still time for ministers and millionnaires to turn over a new leaf.

LEAK

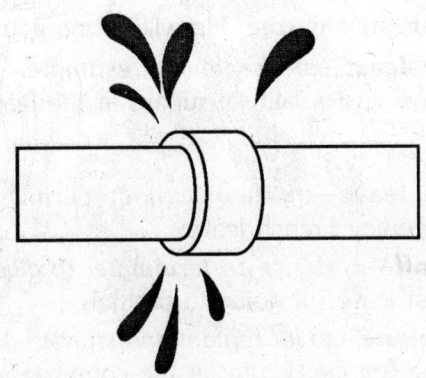

1. **Leak out**—*to find publicity; to get to the public ears*. There is always a great fear of the budget leaking out.
2. **Spring a leak**—*to become leaky*. The ship of state quite often springs a leak.

LEAL

The land of the leal—*the land of the blessed after death*. My brother has gone to the land of the leal.

LEAN

Lean year—*famine*. A lean year generally follows a war.

LEAP

1. **By leaps and bounds**—*very quickly*. The whole country is progressing by leaps and bounds.

2. **Leap in the dark**—*an act of which we cannot foresee the consequence.* A great career is always a leap in the dark.

LEAST

1. **At least**—*at any rate.* He will phone you at least.
2. **At the least**—*at the lowest estimate.* This house must have cost a lakh of rupees at the least.

LEAVE

1. **French leave**—*quitting without permission.* Many students enjoy French leave.
2. **Leave off**—*to desist; to terminate; to give up using.* You must leave off going to brothels.
3. **Leave alone**—*to let remain undisturbed.* Please leave me alone for the day to let me complete my work.
4. **Leave out**—*omit.* Why did you leave out this name from the invitees ?
5. **Take leave**—*take permission to go; say farewell.* In 1960 I took leave of my friends in Delhi.
6. **To take leave of one's senses**—*to go mad.* In anger he murdered his wife and then took leave of his senses.

LED

1. **Led captain**—*a servile attendant; a henchman.* An M.P. has a few led captains at his heels.
2. **Led horse**—*a spare horse led by a servant.* Have you a led horse for my child ?

LEE

1. **Leeward**—*with the wind.* Let us move with leeward.

2. **Make up leeway**—*to make up for lost ground*. If once you have lost the ground, it is not easy to make up leeway.
3. **There are lees to every wine**—*even the best articles have some defects*. He was told by the Publisher that there are lees to every wine.

LEFT

Over the left—*a negative*. The whole job has been done over the left.

LEG

1. **Change the leg**—*change the gait*. To save time and speed up, he made the horse change the leg.
2. **Feed one's legs**—*to begin to support oneself*. The youth must feel his legs sooner rather than later.
3. **Find one's legs**—*to become habituated; to attain ease*. He has found his legs in high society.
4. **In high leg**—*in great excitement*. I found him in high leg.
5. **Not a leg to stand on**—*no case at all*. You have not a leg to stand on in this litigation.
6. **On one's last legs**—*near the end; exhausted*. Our power of expenditure is on its last legs.
7. **On one's legs**—*standing especially to speak*. Mr. Robert was on his legs for two hours in the Parliament the other day.
8. **Show a leg**—*get up; make an appearance*. When the minister was angry, he showed a leg.
   He sometimes shows his leg in our house.
9. **Upon one's legs**—*in an independent position*. My son is upon his legs.

10. **Shake a leg**—*dance.* A person who does not know how to shake his legs is not fit for joining a club.
11. **To pull one's legs**—*to deceive.* Never pull legs of your friends.
12. **Without a leg to stand on**—*with no support.* Without a leg to stand on one cannot win elections.

LEGION

Their name is legion—*they are beyond number.*

LEISURE

At one's leisure—*at one's convenience.* Please meet me at your leisure.

LEND

To lend an ear—*to hear.* Will you please lend me your ear ?

LENGTH

1. **At length**—*in full; fully extended; at last.* We discussed the marriage proposal at length.
He slept at length.
At length he went to see a doctor for cure.
2. **Go all lengths**—*to do everything.* A politician will go all lengths to stay in power.
3. **Go great lengths**—*do a great deal.* He went great lengths to get this job.
4. **Length of days**—*prolonged life.* Nehru was an optimist to the length of his days.

LEOPARD

A leopard in a sheep's clothing—*a dangerous man showing gentleness.* I do not want to warn you against your friends, but beware of the leopard in sheep's clothing.

LESS

Nothing less than—*anything rather than.* A Prime Minister seeks nothing less than his Prime Ministership.

LET

1. **Let be**—*leave undisturbed.* Let peace be in the world.
2. **Let blood**—*bleed.* His nose let blood.
3. **Let down**—*to allow to fall; to lower; to leave*

in the lurch; fail to back up in need. The British let down their Empire.

Don't let down the national flag.

Don't let down a friend.

4. **Let drive**—*to aim a blow.* They let drive at the leader.

5. **Let fly**—*to fling; to discharge; to shoot.* They let fly an arrow.

6. **Let go**—*cease holding; to slacken.* Please let go my arm.

Let agitation go.

7. **Let in**—*to allow to enter; to take in; to swindle; to betray; to insert; to leak inwards.* Let in all sincere men.

The thugs let him in.

The roof is letting in.

8. **Let off**—*drop.* The case against him was let off.

9. **Let one know**—*to inform him.* Let me know if you are going home.

10. **Let oneself loose**—*to have no restraint.* The prince let himself loose in London.

11. **Let out**—*to set free; to become known; to strike out; to widen; to put to hire; to leak outwards.* They let out the prisoner.

Scandal was let out.

The house was let out on Rs. 1000 a month.

The roof is letting out.

12. **Let up**—*to become less.* The wind let up.

13. **Let up on**—*to cease to have to do with.* They let up on the poor man.

14. **Let well alone**—*to let things remain as they are from fear of making them worse.* The politicians should let the people well alone in matters of religion.

LETTER

1. **In letter and spirit**—*in form and in substance.* The Tashkent agreement has been observed in letter and spirit.

2. **Letter perfecting**—*knowing one's part perfectly.* One should always be letter perfecting in one's job.

3. **Man of letters**—*a literary person.* The writer of this book is a man of letters.

4. **To the letter**—*with adherence to every detail.* The company has accepted the manager's proposal to the letter.

LEVEL

1. **Find one's level**—*come to one's natural position or rank.* Every one finds his level in life sooner or later.

2. **Level best**—*one's utmost.* He did his level best to achieve success in life before he came to where he is.

3. **Level down**—*to lower in the level or status.* Death levels down everybody.

4. **Level-headed**—*clever.* Be careful of the level-headed man.

5. **Level up**—*to raise the status.* The students are levelled upto their graduation.

6. **On level with**—*equal with.* In sports, both the brothers are on level with one another.

7. **On the level**—fair; *honestly speaking.* In democracy everything should be on the level.
   On the level, nobody is trustworthy now-a-days.

LEVY

1. **Levy in mass**—*levy of all able-bodied men for military service.* War brings levy in mass.

2. **Levy war**—*to make war.* Leaders levy war to suppress their people at home by external forces of compulsion.

LIBERTY

1. **At liberty**—free; *unoccupied: available.* You are at liberty to go wherever you want.

2. **Liberty Hall**—*a place where one may do what one pleases.* A university is not a Liberty Hall.

3. **Liberty of indifference** — freedom *of the will.* Every youth enjoys the liberty of indifference.

4. **Liberty of the press**—*freedom to print and publish whatever you please.* There is no liberty of the press in communist countries and totalitarian nations.

5. **Take liberties with**—*to treat with undue freedom of familiarity or indecently; to falsify.* Don't take liberties with the ladies, however, you may be related to them.

    Don't take liberties with the original text of the agreement.

6. **Take the liberty**—*presume; venture.* May I take the liberty to speak the truth ?

LICK

1. **A lick and a promise**—*a perfunctory wash.* It was a lick and a promise on cold wintry morning.
2. **Lick into shape**—*to mould into due form.* She-bear licked the young into shape.
3. **Lick one's boots**—*sycophants.* They are your genuine enemies who lick your boots.
4. **Lickpenny**—*that which makes the money go.* Life in a big city is lickpenny now-a-days.
5. **Lick the dust**—*to be slain.* In the battle of Kurukshetra all heroes of India licked the dust.

LID

1. **Put the lid on it**—*end the matter.* If you are bubbling with anger, it is best to put the lid on it.
2. **With the lid off**—*with all its horrors.* I witnessed many deaths with the lid off during the partition.

LIE

1. **Give one the lie in one's throat**—*to charge one to one's face of lying.* You cannot give an officer the lie in his throat.

2. **Give the lie to**—*to charge with lying.* The boy gave his father the lie.

3. **Let seeping dogs lie**—*avoid debatable questions.* Be wise and let sleeping dogs lie.

4. **Lie along**—*to be extended at full length.* The rock lies along the cave.

5. **Lie at one's door**—*to be directly responsible.* The degeneration of India lies at the door of our leaders.

6. **Lie at one's heart**—*to be an object of interest to one.* Eradication of corruption in India lies at my heart.

7. **Lie by**—*to be inactive; to keep out of the way; to lie to.* Why are you lying by in the hostel ?
   Please lie by when the procession passes here.
   Don't lie by me.

8. **Lie by the heels**—*to be in person.* He lay by the heels for seven days.

9. **Lie hard or heavy on, upon, to**—*to oppress; to burden.* The teachers must not lie heavy upon the youth.

10. **Lie in**—*to be in childbed.* The bride *is* lying in.

11. **Lie in one**—*to be in one's power.* It does not lie in me to help you at the moment.

12. **Lie in one's throat**—*to lie shamelessly.* Don't lie in your throat.

13. **Lie in the way**—*to be ready at hand; to be an obstacle.* Money always lies in the way of a Minister.
    Money lies in the way of spiritual progress.

14. **Lie in wait**—*to lie in ambush*. The army lay in wait for the enemy.

15. **Lie in your throat**—*to be suitable*. It does not lie in your throat to accuse your benefactors.

16. **Lie low**—*keep quiet or hidden; to conceal one's actions or intentions*. Truth cannot long lie low.

17. **Lie on one's hands**—*to remain unwanted, unclaimed or unused*. Time lies in the hands of millions of our unemployed youth.

18. **Lie on the oars**—*to relax while on duty*. A nation in trouble such as India cannot lie on the oars.

19. **Lie on, upon**—*to be incumbent on*. It lies on you to help your parents in your days of prosperity as well as adversity.

20. **Lie out of**—*to remain without the good of, without payment of*. This gift lies out of price.

A priest lies out of spirituality.

21. **Lie over**—*to be deferred to a future occasion*. Opportunities cannot lie over.

22. **Lie to**—*to become stationary with head to wind*. When the hurricane blows, the boat lies to.

23. **Lie under**—*to be subject to or oppressed by*. For two centuries India lay under British imperialism.

24. **Lie up**—*to abstain from work; to take to or remain in bed; to go into or be in dock*. More and more workers are lying up.

25. **Lie with**—*to lodge or sleep with*. The man lies with a prostitute.

26. **Take it lying down**—*to endure tamely*. The Prime Minister will not take any insult lying down.

27. **To act a lie**—*to deceive*. Do not act a lie with your friends.

28. **To give the lie**—*to prove one to be wrong*. The students gave their professor the lie.

29. **White lie**—*a clearly false statement*. "Garibi Hatao" is not a white lie.

LIEF

Had as lief—*should like as well to*. I had as lief eat as go hungry.

LIEU

In lieu of—*instead of*. In lieu of his going, I shall myself go there and see what can be done.

LIFE

1. **Bring to life**—*confer life upon.* Oxygen brought the dead man to life.

2. **Come to life**—*to become alive; reanimated.* Frogs come to life during the rains.

3. **For life**—*for the whole period of existence.* Pension is for life.

4. **For the life of him**—*though it were to save his life; do what he might.* He could not find a thousand rupees for the life of him.

5. **High life**—*fashionable society.* High life is an expensive affair.

6. **See life**—*see how other people live.* Every young man wants to see life.

7. **Take one's life**—*kill.* Do not take anyone's life.

8. **To the life**—*very closely like the original.* This is my picture to the life.

LIFT

1. **Lift one's hand**—*to raise it in hostility.* John has lifted his hand against Robert.

2. **Lift the face**—*to perform an operation for smoothening of skin.* Some doctors can lift the face.

LIGHT

1. **According to one's lights**—*as far as one can see.* Everybody is trying to help himself at the cost of others, according to his lights.

2. **Between the lights**—*in the twilight.* Let us meet on the Yamuna River between the lights.

3. **Between two lights**—*under cover of darkness.* We covered the journey between two lights.

4. **Bring to light**—*reveal.* Archaeology has brought great things to light.

5. **Come to light**—*to be revealed.* The murder of Stevenson has not yet come to light.

6. **Floating light**—*a light at the masthead of a light ship.* Mahatma Gandhi was the floating light of India.

7. **Inner light**—*spiritual illumination.* You can get no peace and tranquility without inner light.

8. **In one's light**—*between one and the source of illumination or chance of success, etc.* Go, and pluck the fruit of success in your light.

9. **Light come light go**—*a thing which is easily acquired is easily lost.* Gambling money is always light come light go.

10. **Light literature**—*music, fiction, etc., that requires little mental effort.* Only light literature sells these days.

11. **Lightning strike**—*an industrial strike without warning.* Industry is plagued by lightning strikes.

12. **Light of nature**—*intellectual perception; man's capacity for discovering truth.* Work your way in the light of nature.

13. **Lights out**—*bugle call for extinction of lights.* We are passing through a political lights out.

14. **Light out**—*to make off.* He lighted out with his employer's cash.

15. **Light up**—*to light one's lamp, pipe, etc.; to turn on the light; to make or become light or bright.* Please light up the lamp as it has become dark.

16. **Make light of**—*to treat as of no consequence.* Do not make light of your job when it gives you bread and butter.

17. **See the light**—*to come into being or view.* New plants have come to see the light.

18. **Stand in one's own light**—*to hinder one's own advantage.* To cheat in the examinations is to stand in one's own light.

19. **Throw light upon**—*explain.* Will you please throw light upon your suggestions?

20. **To light upon**—*to find by accident.* Only lucky people get things by light upon.

LIKE

1. **Feel like**—*to be disposed or inclined towards.* The teacher felt like the new student.

2. **Had like**—*was likely; came near; was in danger.* They had like crashed with the locomotive.

3. **Look like**—*show a likelihood of; to appear similar to.* It looked like rain in the morning.

4. **Something like a**—*a fine specimen of; a model of what the thing should be.* The rock looked something like a sculptured statue.

5. **Such like**—*of that kind.* We met sheep, goats and such like on the way.

LIMB

1. **Limb of the devil**—*a mischievous child.* Pinky is a limb of the devil.

2. **Limb of the law**—*one who deals with the law.* Limbs of the law must do justice with their duties.

LIMIT

Limited monarchy—*one in which the monarch shares powers with the people.* Nepal is now a limited monarchy.

LINE

1. **Draw a line**—*fix a limit.* Sooner or later, you have to draw line between your income and expenses.

2. **Give line**—*to allow apparent freedom in order to secure at last.* Law has given line to the whole country.

3. **Hard lines**—*hard luck.* You are a victim of hard lines.

4. **In line**—*in a straight line; in agreement or harmony; in the running.* Practice must be in line with the theory.

5. **Line of**—*some idea or knowledge of*. Can you give me a line of the coming budget?
6. **Line of battle**—*arrangement in line to meet the enemy*. The ruling party and the Opposition have drawn their lines of battle.
7. **Line upon line**—*little by little*. They are doing the work line upon line.
8. **On the line**—*hanging on the level of the eyes*. Let your pictures be on the lines.
9. **Read between the lines**—*infer which is not explicitly stated*. Please read the letter between the lines.

LINEN

1. **Wash one's dirty linen at home**—*to keep family affairs*. It is best to wash dirty linen at home.
2. **Wash one's dirty linen in public**—*to expose sordid family affairs*. It is not good to wash your dirty linen in public.

LINGUA

Lingua franca—*a language understood all over the country or the world*. Hindi is the lingua franca of India. English is the lingua franca of the world.

LINK

Missing link—*any point or fact needed to complete a series or a chain of argument*. There is a missing link between our professions and practice of socialism as well as of our religion.

LINSEY

Linsey-woolsey—*gibberish; neither one thing nor the other*. Politicians talk in linsey-woolsey.

LION

1. **Lion in the way**—*obstacles*. There are many lions in the way for me for getting a suitable job.

2. **Lion's provider**—*jackal; hanger-on*. There are many lion's providers round a successful leader.

3. **Lion's share**—*the greater part*. Lion's share of my income goes to my wife's parents.

4. **To beard a lion in its own den**—*to attack a stronger foe at home*. John is trying to beard the lion in its own den.

5. **To place one's hand in the lion's mouth**—*to expose oneself unnecessarily to a danger*. During the partition many people placed their hand in the lion's mouth to save their kith and kin.

6. **Twist the lion's tail**—*harass a stronger foe*. Kissinger is twisting the lion's tail.

LIP

1. **In Lipsburie pinfold**—*between the teeth*. They talked on the high way in Lipsburie pinfold.

2. **Lip service**—*insincere profession or worship*. People pay lip service to gods in temples and to ministers in their offices.

3. **Keep a stiff upper lip**—*to show a face of resolution*. In the emergency it is best to keep a stiff upper lip.

4. **Make a lip**—*to pour in sullenness*. If you are angry, never make a lip.

5. **To bite one's lip**—*to express annoyance.* When the student was not able to solve the problem in spite of the teacher's explaining thrice, the teacher bit his lips.

6. **To curl the lip**—*to express contempt.* Susan curled her lips while glancing at that scoundrel.

7. **To hand one's lips**—*to be in humiliation.* There is no harm in hanging one's lips sometimes.

LIQUOR

Liquor laws—*laws controlling the sale of intoxicating drinks.* Every country has liquor laws but these are seldom observed.

LIST

1. **Enter the lists**—*come forward to contest.* George and John have entered the lists for the coming electoral fight.

2. **Active list**—*the roll of those liable for active service.* Millions are still on the active list in the U.S.A.

351

LITANY

Lesser litany—*common formula*. Socialism is the lesser litany of Indian political system.

LITTLE

1. **In little**—*on a small scale*. Every village in India is in little.

2. **Little and little**—*by degrees*. You can make money little and little.

3. **Little by little**—*by degrees*. We are dying every day little by little.

4. **Little Mary**—*the stomach*. Little Mary eats up everything.

5. **Little people**—*the fairies*. I have more respect for the little people than for the big guns.

LIVE

1. **Live and let live**—*give and expect toleration*. Let us live and let live, for the alternative is die and let die.

2. **Live down**—*live so as to allow to be forgotten*. My desire is to live down in the world.

3. **Live in**—*dwell in one's place of employment*. Millions today are living in.

4. **Live on**—*live by feeding upon, or with expenditure limited to*. Saint lived on what the people gave him.

5. **Live out**—*live away from one's place of employment*. Millions today are living out.

6. **Live out**—*to survive; to be in domestic service*. Man has lived out millions of years.

The old maid is living out.

7. **Live to**—*live long enough to; come at last to*. She lived to a rich inheritance.

LIVERY

Sue one's livery—*to ask for a writ delivering a freehold into the possession of its heir*. The young heir sued the livery.

LIVING

1. **Living memory**—*the memory of someone still alive*. There is no greater man than Mahatma Gandhi in living memory.

2. **Living rock**—*rock still in its natural position*. Even the living rock is dying, killed by the technological civilization.

3. **Living wage**—*a wage on which it is possible for a workman and his family to live fairly*. The living wage is now becoming the drum din of a distant dream.

LOAD

Load dice—*to make one side heavier than the other so as to influence their fall for purposes of cheating*. The ruling party always loads the dice against the Opposition.

LOAF

1. **Half loaf**—*a load of half the standard weight*. India today is living on half the loaf.

2. **Loaves and fishes**—*temporal benefits*. Truly spiritual men keep aloof from loaves and fishes.

LOCAL

Local colour—*special interest of individual items.* It is the local colour that makes a play spicy and catching.

LOCK

1. **Lock, stock and barrel**—*the whole; altogether.* The British quit India in 1947 lock, stock and barrel.

2. **Lock up**—*confine; lock securely.* All my funds are locked up in the bank due to bankmen's agitation.

LOCO

Locofoco—*a friction match; an equal rights party.* Locofoco in politics does not produce equal rights.

LOFT

1. **Cock of the loft**—*the head or chief of a set.* The leader of the Opposition is cock of the loft.

2. **Lofted house**—*a house of more than one storey.* Few men can afford to live in a lofted house these days.

LOIN

Gird up the loins—*to prepare for energetic action.* The political parties are girding up their loins for election.

LONG

1. **Before long**—*soon.* We will meet before long.

2. **Draw the long bow**—*to exaggerate extravagantly.* Every leader is apt to draw the long bow.

3. **Ere long**—*before long.* Please come here ere long.

4. **In the long run**—*after long struggle.* Truth triumphs in the long run.

5. **Long and the short**—*sum up; the total.* The long and the short is that the modern youth is not only unemployed but also unemployable.

6. **Long figure**—*high price or rate.* Peace can be bought at a long figure.

7. **Long headed**—*clever.* The long headed peon deceived his employer.

8. **Long home**—*the grave.* Let us have our next appointment in the long home.

9. **Long purse**—*abundance of money.* Every politician carries a long purse now-a-days.

10. **Long sheep**—*long wooled sheep.* India needs long sheep.

11. **Make a long arm**—*help oneself freely at the table.* Please make a long arm at the banquet.

12. **Make a long nose**—*to cock a nose or put a thumb on the nose.* The jokers make a long nose.

13. **No longer**—*not now as formerly.* David is no longer the matinee idol of the people.

14. **Not long in the world**—*near death.* Nobody can live long in the world.

15. **So long as**—*provided only that.* You can live here so long as you do not disturb the peace of the house.

16. **The short and the long of it**—*the sum of the matter in a few words.* The short and the long of it is that you are responsible for your distress.

LOOK

1. **Look after**—*take care of.* A mother should look after her children.

2. **Look alive**—*bestir oneself.* Look alive lest you miss the train.

3. **Look down on**—*to despise.* Don't look down on the poor.

4. **Look for**—*search for.* Don't look for a needle in a haystack.

5. **Look here**—*attend to this.* Look here, I say.

6. **Look in**—*make a short call.* Please look in on way to the station.

7. **Look into**—*to inspect closely; to investigate.* Please look into the matter today.

8. **Look on**—*to regard; view; think.* I look on Honey with love.

9. **Look out**—*to be watchful.* Look out lest you slip and fall.

10. **Look over**—*examine cursorily; to overlook or pass over.* Please look over the accounts.

    I cannot look over your faults if I mean business.

11. **Look sharp**—*be quick about it.* Look sharp when the pickpockets are about.

12. **Look through**—*study.* Look through hard and get good marks in your examination.

13. **Look to**—*to take care of; depend on; expect.* Please look to your interest.

14. **Look you**—*observe; take notice of this.*

15. **To look black**—*to be black with anger.* The father looked black on his drunkard son.

16. **To look down upon**—*to hate.* The stage has come when he will look down upon his wife.

17. **To look upto**—*respect*. The students should always look upto their teachers.

LOOSE

1. **At a loose end**—*without anything to do at the moment*. The youth is at loose end.

2. **Break loose**—*escape from confinement*. The prisoners have broken loose from the jail.

3. **Give a loose to**—*to give rein*. Give a loose to your suggestions.

4. **Let loose**—*to set at liberty*. Let loose the goose.

5. **Living on the loose**—*to lead an immoral life*. Many young girls who are kidnapped are forced to live on the loose.

6. **On the loose**—*indulging in a bout of unrestraint*. The youth are on the loose with liquor.

7. **With a loose rein**—*indulgently*. She lives with a loose rein.

LOSE

1. **Lose oneself**—*to lose one' way; to become bewildered or rapt*. Please don't lose yourself in the crowd.

   When he died, I lost myself.

2. **Losing game**—*a game that is going against one*. Selfish life is always a losing game.

3. **Lost to**—*insensible to*. A man of money is lost to the woes of others.

4. **To lose cold**—*get rid of*. Let us try to lose cold from bad company.

5. **To lose patience**—*to become restless*. Never lose patience if you want to rise in life.

LORD

1. **Drunk as a lord**—*extremely drunk*. Stanley was drunk as a lord when we went to meet Michael.

2. **Lord knows**—*Neither I nor anybody else knows*. Lord knows where people go when they die.

3. **My lord**—*used in addressing a judge*. My lord, here are the facts on your table and now you can give judgment and me justice.

LOSS

At a loss—*Off the scent; at fault; nonplussed, perplexed*. I am at a loss to understand what you are saying.

LOT

1. **Across lots**—*by short cuts*. You cannot make progress across lots.

2. **Bad lot**—*a person of bad moral character*. I have to live down with a bad lot.

3. **Cast, or throw in one's lot with**—*share the fortunes of; to draw from a set alike in appearance to reach a decision*. It is best in politics to cast in your lot with the majority.

4. **Lots to blank**—*any odds*. You have to face lots to blanks.

LOTH

Nothing loth—*not at all unwilling*. I am nothing loth to go with you to the end of the road.

Lottery—*chance*; *prize*. He won the Derby Lottery last year.

LOTUS

Lotus-eater—*an eater of lotus*; one given *to indolence*. Life is not for the lotus-eaters.

LOUNGE

Lounge-lizard—*one* who *loafs with women in hotel lounges*. The population of lounge-lizards is growing in India.

LOVE

1. **For love or money**—*in any case whatever.* Please do this for love or money.

2. **In love**—*enamoured.* I am in love with Maria.

3. **Make love to**—*to try to* gain *the affections* of. Make love to the Blue Angel.

4. **Of all loves**—*for any sake; by all means.* I will do your job of all loves.

5. **Play for love**—*play without stakes.* Let us play for love.

6. **There's no love lost between them**—*they have no liking for each other.* There is no love lost between Stanley and Veronica.

LOW

1. **In low water**—*short of money.* I am in low water these days.

2. **Lay low**—*to overthrow; to kill.* A dictator lays low all his enemies and finally his friends lay him low.

3. **Lie low**—*to live unknown to achieve an object.* In politics you often have to lie low.

4. **Low comedy**—*a comedy of farcical situations; slapstick; low life.* Politics is a low comedy.

5. **Low life**—*sordid social circumstances.* There is no more pleasure in high life than in low life.

6. **Low side window**—*a narrow window near the ground.* Education has become a low side window of politics.

7. **Low wines**—*week spirit.* The affluent prefer the low wines; the poor prefer the high.

8. **To lay low**—*to kill.* He tried to lay low his friend but was caught at the spot.

LUBBER

Lubber fiend—*a drudging brownie.* There is hardly any lubber fiend left now.

LUCK

1. **Down on one's luck**—*unfortunate.* The middle class intelligentsia are down on their luck.

2. **He has the luck of the devil**—*everything that he touches turns into gold.* I find, these days, Robert has the luck of the devil.

3. **Not in luck's way**—*in the normal way.* The circumstances are not in luck's way for me.

4. **Worse** *luck*—*more's the pity.* He got little money; worse luck.

LUG

Lug in—*to introduce, without any apparent connection.* Please don't lug in your mother-in-law.

LUMP

1. **A lump of selfishness**—*selfish through and through.* The man with a lump of selfishness is never successful in life.

2. **In the lump**—*in gross.* In the lump I charge you less interest.

3. **Lump**—*if you don't like it, you may lump it, take it as you like but there is no remedy.*

4. **Lump sum**—*a single sum of money in place of many.* This is the lump sum of your dues.

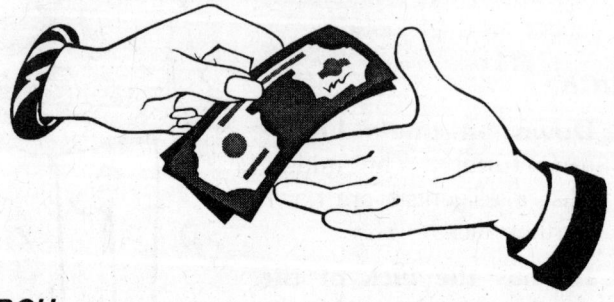

LURCH

Leave in the lurch—*to leave in difficult situation without help.* Please don't leave your friends in the lurch.

LUST

Lust for life—*desire to live and enjoy life.* Lust for life rules supreme in the world of men, mice and mountains.

LUSTRE

Lack lustre—*to be without distinction.* Honesty does not lack lustre.

LYING

Take it lying down—*to make no resistance or protest.* A modern child will not take it lying down if you do not treat him as your equal.

MAD

1. **Go mad**—*to become demented.* Millions go mad these days because of stresses of modern times.

2. **Like mad**—*madly; furiously.* She ran like mad for money.

MADE

1. **Made dish**—*a dish of various ingredients.* Modern men are fond of made dishes.

364

2. **Made ground**—*ground formed by artificial fillings.* Modern youth stand upon the made ground of education.

3. **Made man**—*one whose prosperity is assured.* A minister's son is a made man.

4. **Made road**—*one with deliberately made surface, not merely formed by traffic.* Career is a kind of made road these days.

5. **Made to measure**—*made to individual requirements.* Life and love are not made to measure.

6. **Made to order**—*made as desired.* Career is seldom made to order.

7. **Made up**—*put together; finished; parcelled out; dressed up for a part; disguised; painted and powdered; consumate.* This building has been made up from prefabricated materials.

   This job has been made up.

   Dinner was made up among the diners.

   The girl is made up for a heroine.

   The prince was made up as a pauper.

   Every society girl is made up.

   Modern culture is made up.

MAGIC

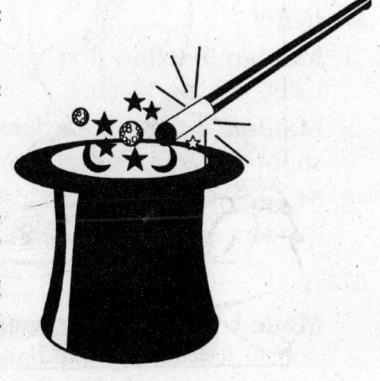

1. **Black magic**—*the black art; magic by evil spirits.* Money making has become a black magic.

2. **Natural magic**—*the art of working wonders by a superior knowledge of the powers of nature; the power of investing a work of art with an atmosphere of imagination.* There is natural magic enlivening science, arts and literature.

3. **Sympathetic magic**—*magic aimed at production of effects by mimicry, as bringing rains by libations; injuring a person by melting his image or sticking pins in it.* There is no scientific denial of the sympathetic magic.

4. **White magic**—*magic without the aid of the devil.* Science is a manifestation of the white magic.

MAID

1. **Maid of all work**—*maid who does general housework.* Science is a maid of all work.

2. **Maid of honour**—*a lady in the service of a Queen or a princess or rich lady generally.* Culture is a maid of honour to science.

3. **Old maid**—*a woman left unmarried.* Mrs. Brown is an old maid in the service of art.

MAIDEN

1. **Maiden battle**—*first contest.* Marriage is a maiden battle for the youth.

2. **Maiden fortress**—*a fortress that has never been captured.* Red Fort is a maiden fortress.

3. **Maiden speech**—*one's first speech.* He made his maiden speech in the college club.

MAIL

Mailed first—*military might.* India had to raise her mailed first during the National Emergency.

MAIN

1. **In the main**—*for the most part*. In the main, I am a writer.

2. **Main chance**—*principal opportunity*. Education is the main chance of your life.

3. **Mainstay**—*main support*. The mainstay for the patient is his regular medicine.

4. **Might and main**—*utmost strength*. She fought with might and main to win the elections.

5. **To splice the mainbrace**—to *indulge freely in strong drinks*. Many young Indians splice the mainbrace now-a-days.

MAINOR

In the mainor—*manner in the act*. He was caught in the mainor of stealing.

MAJOR

Major premise—*that in which major terms occur.*
He has made a major premise to help me in my
difficulties.

MAJORITY

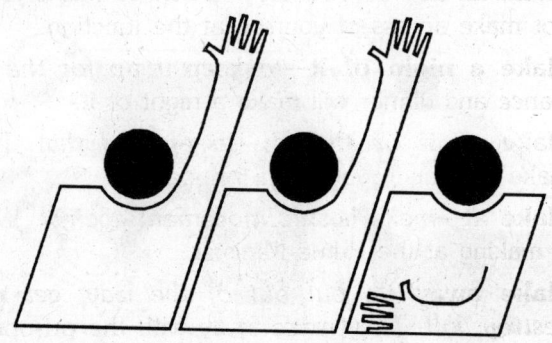

1. **Go over to or join the majority**—*to die.* Our forefathers have joined the majority.
2. **To attain the age of majority**—*to come of age.*
The clerk attains the age of majority only tomorrow.

MAKE

1. **Make account of**—*account for.* You must make
account of your losses.
2. **Make a figure**—*to be conspicuous.* Kim makes a
figure whenever she goes to any party.
3. **Make a fool of**—*befool.* Don't make a fool of your
teacher.
4. **Make after**—*to follow or pursue.* The police made
after the thieves.

5. **Make against**—*to militate against; tell against.* Money makes against spiritual power.

6. **Make amends**—*render compensation.* I will make ample amends for the trouble that I have caused you.

7. **Make an ass of oneself**—*to behave like a fool.* Do not make an ass of yourself at the function.

8. **Make a night of it**—*to keep it up for the night.* Dance and dinner will make a night of it.

9. **Make as if or though**—*to pretend that.* Do not make as though you are a prince.

10. **Make at**—*make hostile movement against.* Williams is making at the Prime Minister.

11. **Make away**—*to put out of the way; get rid of; destroy; kill.* They made away with the prisoners.

12. **Make down**—*to refashion so as to fit a smaller person.* The coat was made down.

13. **Make for**—*set out for; seek to reach; to favour.* After doing their day's work, they made for the airport.

14. **Make free with**—*have freely.* They made free with the food.

15. **Make friends**—*become friendly.* Let us make friends from today.

16. **Make good**—*mend.* I shall make good your loss.

17. **Make head or tail**—*to find any sense in it.* I can make neither head nor tail of your letter.

18. **Make light of**—*to give no importance.* She made light of my troubles.

19. **Make little of**—*to render useless.* He made little of his money.

20. **Make merry**—*to enjoy*. Let us make merry tonight.

21. **Make much of**—*to treat with fondness; to cherish; to foster; to turn to great account; to find much sense in; succeed in understanding.* She made much of her son.

22. **Make no doubt**—*have no doubt; be confident.* Make no doubt, I will always be there to help you.

23. **Make nothing of**—*to think it no great matter; have no hesitation or difficulty; to be totally unable to understand.* He made nothing of his troubles.
    I can make nothing of your letter.

24. **Make off with**—*run away with.* He made off with his friend's watch.

25. **Make on**—*make much of.* He made on his mother.
26. **Make one's way**—*to proceed; succeed.* Make your way to the police station.

    You must make your way in life.
27. **Make out**—*decipher; to prove; to seek; to draw it up.* I am trying to make out what you said yesterday.
28. **Make out**—*understand.* I cannot make out head or tail of your statement.
29. **Make over**—*transfer; to remake; reconstruct.* The thief was made over to the police.
30. **Make sure**—*put beyond doubt or risk.* Make sure that you will come in time.
31. **Make the best of**—*to put to best advantage.* Make the best of your life.
32. **Make the most of**—*to put to best advantage.* Make the most of what you have in hand.
33. **Make up**—*fabricate; to feign; to collect; to put together; to parcel; to put into shape; to arrange; to compose; to repair; to use paint and powder on face; to make good.* The house was made up.

    He made up a saint.
    She made up her face.
34. **Make up one's mind**—*to come to a decision.* I have made up my mind to quit U.K.

35. **Make up to**—*to make friendly approach to; to compensate.* I will make up to her.

36. **Make with**—*to have to do with; interfere with.* You have nothing to make with my pen.

37. **On the make**—*bent on self-advancement or promotion.* She is on the make and will become an actress.

38. **To make or mar**—*to cause success or ruin.* The labour of a man makes or mars his career.

MALT

In meal or malt—*in one way or the other.* I want to settle it in meal or malt.

MAN

1. **Man about town**—*a fashionable idler.* Men about town make the society because they make the town.

2. **Man alive**—*an exclamation of surprise.* Man alive come here quick.

3. **Man Friday**—*a servile attendant.* I will be Man Friday to you.

4. **Man in the moon**—*very rare person.* You have become a man in the moon now-a-days.

5. **Man in the street**—*everyday man.* You and I are men in the street.

6. **Man of God**—*a holy man.* I am no man of God.

7. **Man of his hands**—*a man of prowess.* Napoleon was a man of his hands.

372

8. **Man of law**—*a lawyer*. Mr. Mathew is my man of law.

9. **Man of letters**—*a scholar*. I do no pretend to be a man of letters.

10. **Man of sin**—*the devil*. I have nothing to do with the man of sin.

11. **Man of straw**—*man of no substance*. Men of straw have become M.Ps.

12. **Man of the world**—*a worldly man*. I am no man of the world.

13. **Man to man**—*one man to another; frank and confidential*. Man to man, Napoleon was a superior being.
    Let us talk as man to man.

14. **To a man**—*every man*. They came to the marriage to a man.

MANGER

Dog in the manger—*one who will neither himself use or enjoy something nor let others do so*. Old man sits on his wealth like a dog in the manger.

MANNER

1. **By no manner of means**—*under no circumstances whatsoever*. I can help you by no manner of means.

2. **In a manner**—*in a sense*. In a manner, a writer is a fighter.

3. **Make one's manners**—*to salute a person*. You should make your manners to your friends.

4. **Shark's manners**—*rapacity*. Get rid of your shark's manners.

5. **To the manner born**—*accustomed from birth.* In high society he was to the manner born.

MANY

1. **Many a**—*many.* Many a man came to the meeting.
2. **Many men, many minds**—*as many opinions as there are persons to give them.* Many men, many minds never make a meeting successful.
3. **The many**—*the crowd.* Don't take up your cudgels against the many.

MAP

1. **Map out**—*to plan, divide out and apportion.* The world has been mapped out between Russia and America.
2. **Off the map**—*out of existence.* East Pakistan is off the map.

3. **On the map**—*to be taken into account.* Our African safari is on the map.

MARCH

1. **Forced march**—*a march pressed forward for strategic purposes.* Napoleon conquered Italy by forced marches.

2. **Marching orders**—*orders to march.* I have not yet received my marching orders.

3. **March past**—*the march of a body in front of one who review it.* There is a march past on Republic Day.

4. **On the march**—*foot and journeying.* The army is on the march.

5. **Rogue's march**—*music played in contempt of the person expelled.* After removing the chairman from his post, there was the rogue's march.

6. **To steal a march on**—*to gain an advantage over unperceived.* My brother stole a march on David in this matter.

MARE

The grey mare is the better horse—*the wife rules her husband or is abler.* In my neighbour's house, the grey mare is the better horse.

MARINE

Tell that to the marines—*a phrase expressive of ridicule and disbelief, from the sailor's contempt for the marine's ignorance of seamanship.*

MARK

1. **A man of mark**—*a notable or famous person.* The late Principal of our college was a man of mark.

2. **Below the mark**—*below standard*. The new clerk is below the mark.

3. **Beside the mark**—*not properly referring to the matter in hand*. In the thick of war, courtesy is beside the mark.

4. **God bless or save the mark**—*a phrase expressive of ironical astonishment or scorn, from the usage of archery*.

5. **Make one's mark**—*to make a notable impression; to gain great influence*. The Nehru family has made its mark in the history of India.

6. **Mark down**—*set down in writing; to label at a lower price; to note the position of; to destine for one's own.*
   Let us mark down the agreement.
   Prices were marked down.
   The stars were marked down.
   He marked down the job for himself.

7. **Mark off**—*to lay down the lines of; graduate*. The boundary of the school was marked off.

8. **Mark out**—*to layout the plan or outline of; to destine*. The school building was marked out.
   He marked out his career.

9. **Mark time**—*to keep things going without progressing*. Both David and John are marking time.

10. **Off the mark**—*well away from the start in a race not relevant*. Your remark is off the mark.

11. **Past the mark**—*pass on the badge of demerit to the next offender*. Your offence is now past the mark.

12. **To hit the mark**—*to achieve one's purpose*. He will hit the mark by hook or by crook.

13. **Up to the mark**—*satisfactory*. Your work is not up to the mark.

MARKET

1. **On the market**—*available for buying*. Wheat and sugar are on the market.
2. **To bring one's hog to a bad market**—*fall in prices*. The fruit sellers were able to bring their hogs to a bad market.
3. **To come to the market**—*to be offered for sale*. The grapes have come to the market now-a-days.

MARRY

Marry come up—*an exclamation of defiant protest*.

MASS

1. **In mass**—*as a body; altogether*. The students went to the Principal in mass.

2. **In the mass**—*as a whole; indiscriminately.* In the mass the load weighs a ton.

General Dyer fired in the mass.

3. **The masses**—*the common people.* The masses in our country are ignorant of political implications.

MAST

Before the mast—*as a common soldier.* We met before the mast.

MASTER

1. **A mastermind**—*expert.* My brother is a mastermind in salesmanship.

2. **Be master of**—*to have control over.* Always be master of your children.

3. **Passed master**—*one who has passed as a master.* He is a passed master in gambling.

MAT

On the mat—*under discussion.* Serious matters are on the mat in the House of Common.

MATCH

To match—*in accordance; as in colour.* He wore a blue coat and a turban to match.

MATTER

1. **As a matter of fact**—*really.* As a matter of fact, we have not met in the past.
2. **For that matter**—*as for that; indeed.* I am a man without money. For that matter I am a complete failure in life.
3. **Matter of course**—*a thing occurring in natural order and time.* Seed becomes a plant in a matter of course.
4. **No matter**—*does not matter.* No matter if you do not reach the Yamuna River in time.

MEAL

To make a meal of—*consume.* The city made a meal of the whole available sugar.

MEAN

1. **By all means**—*certainly.* We shall meet tomorrow by all means.
2. **By fair means or foul**—*anyhow.* He will get the job by fair means or foul.

3. **By no means**—*certainly not.* I can see you today by no means.

4. **Golden mean**—*the middle course between two extremes; wise moderation.* Buddha preached the doctrine of the golden means.

MEASURE

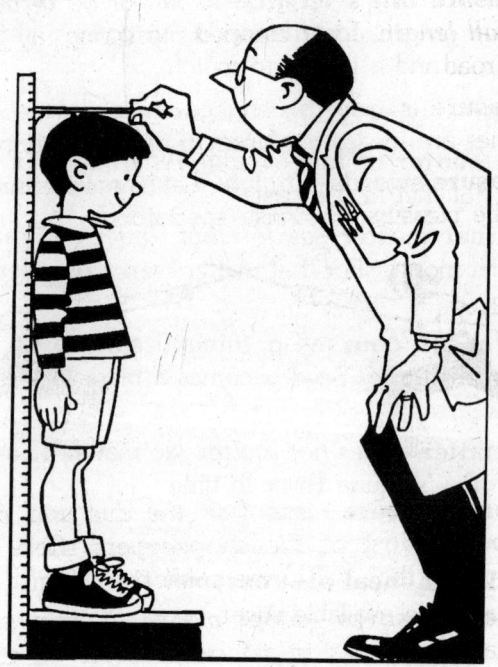

1. **Above, beyond or out of measure**—*to an exceedingly great degree.* The corruption in the country today is beyond measure.

   Your generosity is out of measure.

   God's grace is above measure.

2. **Hard measures**—*harsh treatment.* He received hard measures at the hands of his friends.

3. **In a measure**—*to some degree.* A government servant is a servant of the people in a measure.

4. **In some measure**—*to some degree.* I can help you in some measure.

5. **Measure one's length**—*to fall or be thrown down at full length.* I just escaped measuring my length on the road.

6. **Measure strength**—*engage in a contest.* Political parties are measuring strength in the elections.

7. **Measure swords**—*to fight.* Let us not measure swords to the pleasure of foolish spectators.

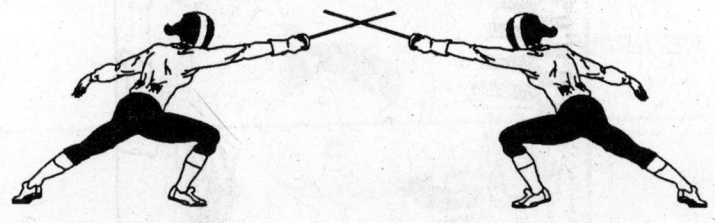

8. **Short measure**—*less than the due and professed amount.* Most of the shopkeepers short measure everything they sell to the public.

9. **Take measures**—*adopt means to gain ends.* Let us take measures to rid ourselves of all colours of corruption.

10. **Take one's measure**—*estimate one's character and abilities.* The Principal will take your measure in an interview before giving you the appointment of a lecturer in his college.

11. **To use hard measure**—*to apply harsh treatment.* The child ran away from the home because his parents were using hard measures constantly.

12. **Tread a measure**—*to go through a dance.* Let us tread a measure tonight.

13. **Within measure**—*moderately.* Your criticism should be within measure.

14. **Without measure**—*immoderately.* Do not do anything without measure lest you may not run into wanton trouble.

MEAT

Meat market—*prostitution.* There is a brisk meat market everywhere in the country and beautiful girls are greatly in demand.

MEDICINE

Bitter medicine—*hard cure.* Every social disease to-day requires a bitter medicine which we are afraid to administer.

MEET

1. **Give the meeting**—*appoint or come to a place for duel or other purpose.* I can give you a meeting at the Coffee House tomorrow afternoon.

2. **Meet half-way**—*give concessions in compromise.* I will gladly meet your needs half-way.

3. **Meet in with**—*to meet with; come across.* Suddenly I met in with him on the road.

4. **Meet the case**—*be adequate.* Milk in the utensil will meet the case of whole family.

5. **Meet the ear or eye**—*to be readily apparent.* Your troubles meet my eye.

   Your request has met the ear of the boss.

6. **Meet with**—*to come unexpectedly; to undergo; chance to experience.* I met with a saint on the hill.

   She met with great trials, troubles and tribulations.

7. **Well met**—*an old complimentary greeting.* Well met my friend, well met.

MELT

Melt one's heart—*cause pity.* Death melts the heart of everybody but the effect does not last long.

MEND

1. **Mend one's pace**—*go quicker.* Mend your pace to catch the train.

2. **Mend one's ways**—*reform one's behaviour.* You ought to mend your ways to be socially popular.

3. **Mend or end**—*improve; finish.* One must mend or end one's life.

4. **On the mend**—*improving; recovering.* The students are on the mend.

MENTAL

1. **Mental age**—*age according to mental development.* The mental age of a child can be higher or lower than his physical age.

2. **Mental case**—*idiocy; madness; craziness.* Susan thinks that Dolly is a mental case.

MENTION

1. **Honourable mention**—*an award of distinction.* Rosie has received many an honourable mention.

2. **Not to mention**—*to say nothing of.* I do not have even five rupees, not to mention five hundred.

MERCHANT

1. **Merchants of death**—*star-war weapons.* The USA should stop selling merchants of death to the people of the world.

2. **Merchant prince**—*a merchant of great wealth, power and consequence.* Gita's father was a merchant prince in Kuwait.

MERCY

1. **At the mercy of**—*wholly in the power of.* We should not be at the mercy of anybody.

2. **For mercy's sake**—*an earnest appeal to pity.* The old woman said to the robber, 'for mercy's sake, let me go', but he did not care and robbed her of her money.

3. **Sisters of mercy**—nurses. Hospitals cannot run without sisters of mercy.

MERIT

1. **Order of merit**—*arrangement in which the best is placed first, the second best next, and so on.* The boys were enlisted for appointment in order of merit.

2. **To make a merit of**—*to look the better side of.* A wise man will always try to make a merit of everything.

MERRY

1. **Make merry**—*to hold festival; indulge in enjoyment; to turn to ridicule.* They made merry throughout the night.

They made merry over my foolishness.

2. **Merry Andrew**—*joker*.
   The last Merry Andrew of
   the circus performed
   wonderfully.

MESS

1. **Mess or mell**—*to
   associate; to have to do.*
   A politician has to mess or
   mell with the rustic people
   for their votes.

2. **Mess of pottage**—*a
   material advantage
   accepted in exchange of
   higher worth.* People are
   losing character and gaining
   wealth for a mess of
   pottage.

   All economic progress today is a mess of pottage.

3. **To get into a mess**—*to
   get into difficulties.* His
   way of work is such that
   everything in the office gets
   into a mess.

4. **To make a mess of**—*to mismanage to utter ruin.*
   Please do not make a mess of everything.

MICKLE

Mickle—*a great quantity.* Many a pickle makes a
mickle.

MID

1. **Midsummer madness**—*madness attributed to the hot sun of summer or the culmination of madness*. Life is getting heated up with agitations and the nation seems to be suffering from midsummer madness.

2. **Midsummer moon**—*a season when madness was supposed to be rife*. Political rivalry suffers from midsummer moon.

MIGHT

1. **Might and main**—*utmost strength*. She fought with might and main against the midnight intruder in her bed-room.

2. **Might-have-been**—*one who, or that which, might have been; or might have come to something*. Indian Coffee House is full of might-have-beens.

   Many might-have-beens who fail in Union Public Service Commission competition flock the offices as clerks.

MILK

1. **Milk and honey**—*abundance; plenty; luxury*. Days are gone when India was a land of milk and honey.

2. **Milk-and-water**—*insipid; wishy-washy*. Indian ideology is a milk-and-water philosophy.

3. **Milk of human kindness**—*natural kindness*. Only a few are gifted with the milk of human kindness.

4. **Milk-sop**—*spiritless youth*. Many Asian countries are still full of milk-sops.

5. **To cry over spilt milk**—*uselessly bewailing over a thing*. No use crying over the spilt milk, it is high time that you should do something.

MILL

1. **Go, put, through the mill**—*to undergo suffering or experience or severe handling.* Everyone goes through the mill before he comes to something.

   Schools and colleges put the boys and girls through the mill.

2. **See through the millstone**—*to see far into or through a difficult situation.* A statesman sees through a millstone to plan adequately for the future requirements of a nation.

MILLION

The millions—*the great body of the people generally.* Robert is today leading the millions against the corrupt government.

MINCE

1. **Mince matters**—*to speak of things with affected delicacy or to soften an account unduly.* You cannot mince matters when the nation is at war.

2. **To make mincemeat of**—*to destroy.* In war every soldier wants to make a mincemeat of the opponent.

MIND

1. **Absence of mind**—*inattention to what is going on owing to the absorption of the mind in other matters.* Due to pressures and pulls of modern stress and strain more and more men are suffering from absence of mind at critical moments.

2. **Bear in mind**—*remember.* Please bear in mind that all men in the world are not your enemies if they are not your friends.

3. **Break one's mind**—*to make known, confide or divulge one's thoughts.* Sooner or later, you have to break your mind about thoughts you are hiding or you will go mad.

4. **Change one's mind**—*to come to a new resolution or opinion.* Politicians quite often change their minds to betray their commitments with the people.

5. **Do you mind**—*would you mind.* Please do this, do you mind.

6. **Have a good or great mind**—*to wish or be inclined strongly.* I have a great mind to run away from this mad, mad, mad world.

7. **Have half a mind**—*to be somewhat inclined.* I have half a mind to turn a reformer for fighting all social and political evils.

8. **If you don't mind**—*if you have no objection.* Please come to my office tomorrow, if you don't mind.

9. **In two minds**—*wavering.* I am in two minds about going to Mumbai or not.

10. **Make up one's mind**—*to come to a decision.* I have made up my mind that Delhi is not a rational place to live and die.

11. **Mind-cure**—*healing a diseased mind of bodily ailments though influence of the mind*. The nation needs a mind-cure for our multifarious ills.

12. **Mind one's p's and q's**—*to be watchfully accurate and punctilious*. You must mind your p's and q's when you are writing an important letter.

13. **Mind's eye**—*visual imagination; mental view; contemplation*. Do only what you see clearly in your mind's eye.

14. **Mind your eye**—*look out*. Mind your eye, lest you fall.

15. **Mind your own business**—*this is none of your affairs*. Please don't meddle with my affairs. Mind your own business.

16. **Month's mind**—*strong desire or inclination*. I have a month's mind to pay you a visit.

17. **Never mind**—*do not concern yourself; it does not matter; you are not to be told*. What is mind? No matter what is matter? Never mind.

18. **Of one mind**—*agreed*. We are of one mind about doing this work immediately.

19. **Of two minds**—*uncertain what to think or do*. I am of two minds about doing this work or not.

20. **On one's mind**—*weighing on one's spirit*. Your commitment is on my mind.

21. **Out of mind**—*forgotten*. The promises I make are never out of my mind.

22. **Put in mind**—*remind*. Please put me in mind if you do not get your work done by tomorrow.

23. **Set one's mind on**—*to fix settle desire* on. I have set my mind on carrying out the will of forces higher than human beings.

24. **Speak one's mind on**—*to say plainly what one thinks*. Please speak your mind if you want anything from me.

25. **Time out of mind**—*from time immemorial*. India has great yogic traditions from time out of mind.

26. **To call to mind**—*to remember*. I don't call to mind having told you that I will give you a job.

27. **To my mind**—*to my thinking; in my opinion; to my liking*. To my mind, you are indeed a great soul come hither to deliver mankind from mess of pottage.

MINERAL

Mineral kingdom—*the department of nature which comprises substance that are neither animal nor vegetable*. Even mineral kingdom is not without sense and feelings.

MINERVA

Minerva—*the Roman goddess of wisdom, identified with the Greek Athena*. Saraswati is the Minerva of India.

MINGLE

Mingle-mangle—*a medley; jumble*. Nauchandi Fair is a mingle-mangle fair.

Marriage is a mingle-mangle affair.

MINIMUM

Minimum wage—*the lowest wage permitted by law.* All my life I have earned only the minimum wage.

MINOR

Minor poet—*a genuine but not great poet.* I don't think I am even a minor poet.

MIRACLE

To a miracle—*surprisingly well.* They have done the whole job to a miracle.

MISPRISON

Misprison of heresy, treason, etc.—*knowledge of and failure to give information about heresy, treason, etc.* When some suffer for treason may pay for misprison of treason.

MISS

1. **Give a miss**—*to allow an opponent to gain by intentionally missing; to leave out, omit, avoid anything.* Indian hockey team has given Pakistan many a miss.

2. **Miss fire**—*to fail to go off or explode.* Pakistan cricket team missed fire in Australia.

3. **Miss Nancy**—*a very effeminate man.* Ashoka is a Miss Nancy.

4. **Miss one's tip**—*to fail in one's plan or attempt.* The U.S.A. missed her tip in Vietnam.

5. **Miss stays**—*to fall in going about from one look to another.* As we grow old, we miss stay.

6. **Miss the bus**—*to lose one's opportunity.* He missed the bus in IAS competition.

MISSIVE

Letter missive—*a letter sent between two parties in which one makes an offer and the other accepts.* Election stunt was a letter missive between the Governor and the President.

MISTAKE

1. **And no mistake**—*assuredly.* Come, and no mistake, I will help you.

2. **Be mistaken**—*to make or have made a mistake; to be misunderstood.* In thinking him as thief I could be mistaken.

3. **Mistake one's man**—*think too lightly of the man one has to deal with.* When the prince comes for help, don't mistake your man.

4. **Mistaken kindness**—*harmful help*. I don't want your mistaken kindness.
5. **Mistake one's way**—take *the wrong road*. We often mistake our way on the map of destiny.

MISTER

Be he prince or mere mister—*everybody*. Be he prince or mere mister, one must die.

MITE

1. **A mite of a child**—*very small child*. He is a mite of a child for going to school at this stage.

2. **Not a mite**—*not at all*. The child had not a mite of milk.

There was not a mite of truth in his statement.

MITTEN

Frozen mitten—*a chilly reception; the cold shoulder*. When the Prince of Wales visited India in 1921, he received a frozen mitten.

MIX

1. **Mixed marriage**—*a marriage between persons of different races, religions, etc.* International weddings are mixed marriages.
2. **Mixy-maxy**—*a confused jumble; in a confused jumble.* Love play is a mixy-maxy.
   They played mixy-maxy.
3. **Mixed sexes**—*promisuous; of both the sexes.* It was a meeting of mixed sexes.

4. **Mixed train**—*a railway train made up partly of passenger carriages and partly of goods wagons.* Mixed trains are also called parcel trains.
5. **Mixter-Maxter**—*a confused jumble; in a confused jumble.* A meeting of mixed sexes is a mixter-maxter.
   When the fire broke out, the people ran mixter-maxter.
6. **Mixtie-maxtie**—*a confused jumble; in a confused jumble.* A library is not a mixtie-maxtie.

7. **Mixty-maxty**—*a confused jumble; in a confused jumble.* Nursery is a mixty-maxty.
   The children ran mixty-maxty.
8. **To be mixed up**—*involved.* Let us not be mixed up in others' affairs.

MOB

Mob it—*to go unobstrusively to an unfashionable part of the theatre.* Quite often the top actors mob it.

MOCK

1. **Mock the pauses**—*throw away the opportunities given by the pauses.* A great actor does not mock the pauses.
2. **Mock turtle soup**—*an imitation turtle soup.* The lunch was a mock turtle soup.

MOLE

1. **Make a mountain out of a molehill**—*to magnify a trifling matter.* It will not help you to make a mountain out of a molehill.

2. **Mole out**—*to seek or elicit bit by bit, as if by borrowing.* The detectives mole out the crime.

MOMENT

1. **Men of moment**—*important people.* Nehru *was* a man of moment.

2. **Of great moment**—*of great importance.* Kashmir is a matter of great moment for both India and Pakistan.

MONEY

1. **For love or money**—*any how.* Everyone must try to succeed in life for love or money.

2. **Hard money**—*coin.* How much hard money do you have in your pocket?

3. **In the money**—*among the prize winners.* Whoever else might be, I am not in the money.

4. **Money down**—*money paid on the spot*. For this book I want money down.
5. **Money for jam**—*profitable return for no labour*. Investment in stocks and shares is a money for jam.
6. **Money-making**—*act of gaining wealth*. The world today is mad after money-making.
7. **Money of account**—*a monetary unit (not represented in current coins) used in keeping accounts*.
8. **Money scrivener**—*one who does financial business for his clients*. I can help you but I am no money scrivener.
9. **Money spider**—*small spider supposed to bring good luck*. In his friendship with the Prime Minister, Peter Rose caught a money spider.
10. **Money spinner**—*successful speculator; any thing which brings much money*. Politics in India is a money spinner.
11. **Money's worth**—*something as a good as money*. A trip to Paris is money's worth.
12. **Pots of money**—*large amount of money*. It requires pots of money to win elections.

13. **Ready money**—*money paid for a thing at the time it is bought.* Please pay the bill in ready money.

MONKEY

1. **Monkey tricks**—*deceitful action.* His monkey tricks brought the whole family into trouble.

2. **Suck the monkey**—*to drink from a cask through an inserted tube; to drink rum, etc. from a coconut.* There is no sucking the monkey here in my house.

3. **To have or get one's monkey up**—*to be angry.* Don't get your monkey up on me.

4. **Young monkey**—*playful contempt.* A boy is a young monkey.

MONSIEUR

Monsieur de Paris—*the public executioner.* If you keep killing, Monsieur de Paris will get you.

MONSOON

Break of the monsoon—*the first onset of the monsoon rain.* Mumbai experiences break of the monsoon usually in May.

MONTH

Month of Sundays—*a tediously long time.* Summer on the hills was a month of Sundays.

MOON

1. **Eggs in moonshine**—*an old dish, fried eggs with onions and various flavourings.* Politics promises you eggs in moonshine.

2. **Minions of the moon**—*thieves who rob by night.* Minions of the moon were able to run away with five thousand rupees last night.

3. **Moonlight flitting**—*a removal by night, with rent unpaid.* Some very aristocratic diners are habituated to moonlight flitting.

4. **Moon madness**—*lunacy, once thought to be connected with the moon's changes.* She suffers from moon madness.

5. **Moonshine**—*visionary*. Moonshine plans are never successful.

6. **Once in a blue moon**—*now and then*. Your visits to our place are once in a blue moon.

MOOT

Moot case—*a hypothetical case for discussion*. Whether the Prime Minister of a country can be dismissed by the Supreme Court can be a moot case.

MOP

1. **Mops and brooms**—*half-drunk; out of sorts*. I found him mops and brooms on the New Year Eve.

2. **Mop the floor with**—*have overwhelming advantage.* The Principal was able to mop the floor with his speech.

3. **Mop up**—*to clear away or clean up with a mop.* The army mopped up the rebels in Iraq.

MORAL

1. **Moral agent**—*one who acts under a knowledge of right and wrong.* Lord Krishna was a moral agent in the Battle of Kurukshetra.

2. **Moral certainty**—*a likelihood great enough to be acted on, although not capable of being certainly proved.* North Vietnam had the moral certainty to win the war against the Americans, and they did

3. **Moral courage**—*power of facing disapprobation and ridicule.* America lacked the moral courage to fight wars in Asia.

4. **Moral defeat**—*a success so qualified as to count as a defeat or to point towards defeat.* One can win a physical war and meet a moral defeat at one and the same time.

5. **Moral faculty**—*moral sense.* Modern man is mostly devoid of moral faculty.

6. **Moral law**—*rules of life on what is right.* There is a moral law that rules the world.

7. **Moral sense**—*power of the mind that knows or judges actions to be right or wrong, and determines conduct accordingly.* Many men do not have any moral sense in their public dealings.

8. **Moral support**—*help afforded by approbation.* India has extended moral support to all countries in their struggle for national emancipation.

9. **Moral victory**—*a defeat in appearance but in important sense a real victory.*

MORE

1. **More and more**—*continually increasing.* T.V. influence is more and more on young generation.

2. **More by token**—*in proof of this; besides.* I promise to pay all your dues; more by token, here's a tenner.

3. **More or less**—*about; in round numbers.* Every politician is more or less a social worker.

4. **No more**—*nothing in addition; never again; no longer in existence; dead.* I can give you just now no more.

The thief was seen no more.
The British Empire is no more.
My brother Tara Singh is no more.

MORNING

Morning sickness—nausea *and vomiting in the morning, common in the early stages of pregnancy.* She is suffering from morning sickness.

MORTAL

1. **In mortal hurry**—*in great hurry.* Please give me ticket, I am in mortal hurry to see the beginning of the film.
2. **Mortal agony**—death. Mortal agony is knocking the door of the patient.
3. **Mortal-staring**—*deadly visage.* Morarji Desai was mortal-staring during the fast to expedite elections in Gujarat.

MORTMAIN

Statutes of mortmain—*acts of parliament restricting or forbidding the giving of property to religious houses.* The Indian Parliament should pass statutes of mortmain.

MOSS

A rolling stone gathers no moss—*one who is constantly changing his profession is never successful in life.* I suggested to him to stick to his job as a rolling stone gathers no moss.

MOST

1. **At the most**—*at the utmost computation.* At the most, I can offer you a cup of tea.

2. **For the most part**—*chiefly; in the main.* For the most part, India is a land of villages.

3. **Make the most of**—*to avail of; to put to best use.* In famine we must make the most of available food and water.

MOTE

So mote I thee—*so may I prosper.*

MOTHER

1. **Every mother's son**—*everybody.* Every mother's son in this meeting must listen to me.

2. **Mother earth**—*earth as mother of its inhabitants.* We must worship the mother earth.

3. **Mother tongue**—*one's native tongue.* His mother tongue is Spanish.

4. **Mother wit**—*common sense.* Mother wit lacks in many young people.

MOTION

1. **In motion**—*moving.* Do not get down from the bus while it is in motion.

2. **To put in motion**—*to set moving.* Put in motion the machine and let us see how it works.

MOUNTAIN

1. **Mountain high**—*high as a mountain.* Her gratitude was mountain high.

2. **Mountain sickness**—*sickness brought about by rarefied air*. People going to the high hills suffer from mountain sickness.

MOURN

In mourning—*wearing black*. I found the woman in mourning, as her husband has died recently.

MOUSTACHE

Old moustache—*an old soldier*. I meet many an old moustache at the milk booth.

MOUTH

1. **By word of mouth**—*orally*. Vedas were handed down from man to man by word of mouth.
2. **Hold your mouth**—*hold your tongue*. Will you please hold your mouth and listen to us now?
3. **Make a poor mouth**—*to profess poverty*. Many well-off folk make a poor mouth.
4. **Mouth waters**—*tempts*. His mouth waters when he sees sweets.

5. **Put words in his mouth**—*tell him what to say.* Please put some words in your brother's mouth.

6. **Stop the mouth of**—*to silence.* Bribe is the best bait to stop the mouth of many disgruntled elements.

MOVE

1. **Get a move on**—*hurry up; make progress.* If you are patient and keep on working, you will surely one day get a move on.

2. **Know a move or two**—*to be sharp or knowing.* I know a move or two about politics.

3. **Make a move**—*to go.* Will you please make a move from here now?

4. **Move on**—*a policeman's warning to those who obstruct traffic by standing still.* "Please move on" ordered the police Inspector.

5. **On the move**—*changing or about to change one's place; going.* Edward is always on the move.

6. **To move heaven and earth**—*to make strenuous efforts.* The boy moved heaven and earth but he failed in the examination.

MUCH

1. **Make much of**—*to put to best use; to give importance to.* You should make much of your time.

2. **Much about it**—*something like what it usually is.* There is not much about your position as an officer.

3. **Much of a muchness**—*just about the same value or amount.* There is not much of a muchness in political glory.

4. **Too much for**—*more than a match for.* The struggle of life is too much for many an artist.

MUD

To throw mud at—*to make unworthy charges.* Those who stay in mud houses should not throw mud at others.

MUDDLE

1. **Muddle away**—*to squander or fritter away confusedly.* Don't muddle away small opportunities in life vainly crying for the moon.

2. **Muddle on**—*get on in a haphazard way.* It is high time that you should improve and leave the habit of muddling on with your work.

3. **Muddle through**—*to get through difficulties blunderingly.* You will have to muddle through your job somehow.

MULTIPLE

1. **Common multiple**—*a number or quantity that can be divided by each of several others, without a remainder.* The Prime Minister is the common multiple of political leadership.

2. **Multiple fruit**—*a single fruit formed from several flowers in a combination, as pineapple, fig, mulberry, etc.* Spiritual tranquility is the multiple fruit of life.

3. **Multiplying glass**—*a many faceted glass for multiplying reflexions.* Politics is a multiplying glass of social merry-go-round.

MUM

Mum's the word—*not a word.*

MUMBO

Mumbo-jumbo—*useless tamasha; vain spectacle.* Conspicuous living is a mumbo-jumbo.

MURAL

Mural crown—*an embattled crown given among the ancient Romans to him who first mounted the wall of a besieged city.* Mahatma Gandhi got the mural crown for the independence of India.

MURDER

Murder will out—*murder cannot remain hidden.*

MUSIC

1. **Face the music**—*face the consequences of.* If you break discipline, you must face the music.
2. **Musical chairs**—*the game of prancing round a diminishing row of chairs and securing one when the music stops.* Political leadership is a game of musical chairs.
3. **Rough music**—*uproar.* There is much rough music in a drinking spree.

MUSTARD

1. **Grain of mustard seed**—*small thing capable of vast development*. Agriculture is fast becoming a grain of mustard seed.

2. **Mustard plaster**—*zestful person*. Mustard plasters are always successful in life.

MUSTER

1. **Muster in**—*to enrom,mmmml; receive as recruits*. The army mustered in thousands for war.

2. **Muster out**—*to discharge from service*. Many soldiers are mustered out after the war.

3. **Pass muster**—*to bear examination; to be well enough*. I hope you will pass muster in the I.A.S. competition.

MUTE

Mute of malice—*refusing to plead*. Many great criminals are mute of malice in court.

MUTTON

1. **Dead as mutton**—*absolutely dead*. The topic is now as dead as mutton.

2. **Lace mutton**—*a loose woman*. Nobody wants a laced mutton in the house.

3. **Return to one's mutton**—*return to the subject of one's discussion*. When we return from office, we shall return to our mutton in politics.

NABS

As his nabs—*himself*. I am confident that he will do your work as his nabs.

NADIR

At the Nadir—*the lowest point of anything*. Susan's relations with her husband are at the nadir.

NAIL

1. **Hard as nails**—*in fine training*. Soldiers are hard as nails.

2. **Hit the nail on the head**—*to touch the exact point*. If you want to get high marks in the competitive examination, you must hit the nail on the head.

3. **Nail a lie to the counter**—*to expose it and put it out of circulation*. If you want to get back your goodwill, you must nail the lie to the counter that you are a corrupt man.

4. **Nail up**—*close*. The matter is nailed up once for all.

5. **On the nail**—*on the spot*. The police arrested the pick-pocket on the nail.

6. **To nail to the counter**—*to expose a falsehood*. Unless you nail to the counter, nobody will know the truth.

NAKED

1. **In its naked absurdity**—*undisguised*. He was falsehood in naked absurdity.

2. **Stark naked**—*entirely nude*. When he returned home, he found his wife stark naked.

3. **The naked truth**—*truth without trimmings*. The naked truth is before you.

NAMBY

Namby pamby—*feeble; wishy-washy; sentimental; childish*. Namby pamby youth do not go far in life.

NAME

1. **Call names**—*to bestow abuse upon*. Please don't call anybody names.

2. **In name**—*fictitiouly as an empty title*. He is a minister in name.

3. **In the name of**—*on behalf of*. Our house is mortgaged in the name of the President of India.

4. **Name a day**—*fix a day, especially for marriage*. November 2, 1986, was named for the marriage of my son.

5. **Name after a person**—*give the name of.* Dr. Luther named his dog after my friend Timmy.

6. **Take a name in vain**—use *a name lightly or profanely.* Don't take the name of Lord Krishna in vain.

7. **To put one's name down for**—*to apply as a candidate.* Michael has also put his name down for the post of clerk.

NANCY

Nancy—*an effeminate young man.* I meet a Miss Nancy.

He is a Nancy boy.

NAP

1. **Go nap**—*to risk all.* He went nap to win elections.

413

2. **Nap hand**—*taking risk for something success of which is almost certain.* 'Lucky' horse has a nap hand on the racing bets.

3. **To catch one napping**—*to come upon when one is unprepared.* Chinese caught Indians napping in 1962.

NARROW

1. **Narrow circumstances**—*poverty.* He is passing through narrow circumstances now-a-days.

2. **Narrow escape**—*to escape with extremely slight margin.* He had a narrow escape.

3. **Narrow-minded**—*mean.* Narrow-minded people are never successful in life.

4. **Within narrow bounds**—in *limit.* I am within narrow bounds of my financial circumstances.

NATURE

1. **By nature**—*inherently.* He is rich by nature.

2. **Debt of nature**—*death.* My brother has paid the debt of nature.

3. **Ease/relieve nature**—*to evacuate the bowels.* We go to the cloak room to ease nature.

4. **In a state of nature**—*nude or naked.* When I returned home, I found the child in a state of nature.

5. **In nature**—*existing everywhere.* Love is in nature.

6. **Natural law**—*the sense of right and wrong which arises from the constitution of the mind of man.* Natural law over rules all laws in the last run.

7. **Natural religion**—*religion derived from reason.* Natural religion is the real religion.

8. **Natural selection**—*evolution by the survival of the fittest with inheritance of their fitness by next generation.* There is no natural selection in politics is it not.

NAUGHT

1. **Be naught**—*keep out of the way; efface yourself; go to the mischief.* When the Governor is here, be naught.
2. **Come to naught**—*to come to nothing.* When death overtakes us, all our dreams come to naught.
3. **Naughty pack**—*a person, especially a woman, of loose life; a "bad lot".* A film actress is usually a naughty pack.
4. **Set at naught**—*to treat as of no account.* Don't set your friends at naught when you achieve wealth or victory.

NAVAL

Naval crown—*a garland awarded to a Roman who had distinguished himself in a sea fight.* Lord Nelson wore the naval crown in the Battle of Trafalgar.

NAY

1. **Cannot say one nay**—*cannot contradict one.* Unless he has guts he cannot say nay to you.
2. **Nay say**—*a refusal.* His answer to my request was nay say.
3. **Will not take nay**—*disregards; refusals.* He will not take nay.

NEAP

Neap tide—*low tide at sea.* Napoleon reached the neap tide of his career at St. Helena.

NEAR

1. **Far and near**—*everywhere*. God exists far and near.

2. **Nearby**—*close by*. His house is nearby to that school.
3. **Nearest to one's heart**—*quite dear*. Susan is nearest to my heart.
4. **Near miss**—*a miss that is nearly a hit*. A near miss may be a matter of life and death.
5. **Near point**—*the nearest point an eye can focus*. Self-aggrandisement is the near point of a political career.

NEAT

Neat and clean—*tidy*. Few leaders lead a neat and clean life now-a-days.

NECESSITY

1. **Logical necessity**—*need according to intelligence*. Education is a logical necessity.

416

2. **Moral necessity**—*need according to moral law.* Religion is a moral necessity.

3. **Natural necessity**—*the condition of being necessary according to the law of nature.* The Government must assure the people their natural necessities.

4. **Necessity knows no law**—*when a thing is necessarily required in a country, it will try to acquire the same by all means.* The thief told the judge that necessity knows no law.

5. **Of necessity**—*necessarily.* He became a thief of necessity.

6. **To make a virtue of necessity**—*to laugh through what is inheritable.* He always tries to make a virtue of necessity.

NECK

1. **Get it in the neck**—*to be severely dealt with; hard hit.* If you do not do your duty to the employer, you will get it in the neck.

2. **Harden the neck**—*to grow more obstinate.* When you are rebuffed, don't harden the neck.

3. **Neck and crop**—*completely; bodily; in a heap; summarily and unceremoniously.* He was down and out neck and crop.

4. **Neck and neck**—*side by side.* It was a neck and neck race to invent the aeroplane.

5. **Necking party**—*pecking party.* The youth often enjoy necking parties where sex blooms and love blossoms forth.

6. **Neck or nothing**—*risking everything.* For Napoleon every battle was neck or nothing.

417

7. **Talk through the back of one's neck**—*to talk wildly or absurdly wide of the truth.* Please stop talking through the back of your neck, if you want me to believe what you tell us.

8. **To save one's neck**—*to escape hanging.* The thief must not save his neck.

9. **Tread on the neck of**—*to oppress or tyrannize over.* Changez Khan rode over the heads of his subjects.

NEED

1. **Need and necessity**—*vitally important.* Education is need and necessity of life.

2. **The needful**—*ready money.* Have you the needful to buy a ticket for Dubai.

NEEDLE

1. **Get the needle**—*to be irritated.* If someone cracks a joke, don't get the needle.

2. **The needle**—*fit of nervousness*. He suffered the needle.

3. **To hit the needle**—*to make a perfect hit*. Unless you hit the needle in getting a job, Mary's father is not going to marry her to you.

4. **To look for a needle in a haystack**—*to engage in a hopeless search*. If you seek peace in technological civilization, you are looking for a needle in a haystack.

NE'ER

Ne'er-do-well—*good for nothing*. Ne'er-do-wells have invaded the universities.

NEGATIVE

Negative causes of dissatisfaction—*sins of omission*. Negative causes of dissatisfaction are really worse.

NEIGHBOUR

1. **Good neighbours**—*fairies*. We must depend on the good neighbours to sustain us through thick and thin.

2. **In the neighbourhood of**—*somewhere near or about*. The Principal lives in the neighbourhood of the college.

NERVE

1. **A fit of nerves**—*a nervous state*. Many soldiers suffer a fit of nerves in war.

2. **Get on one's nerves**—*to become oppressively irritating*. When a person misbehaves, he gets on your nerves.

3. **To possess nerves of steel**—*to be unperturbable*. Great men possess nerves of steel.

NEST

1. **Feather one's own nest**—*to seek one's own benefits.* Every politician is trying to feather his own nest.

2. **Hornet's nest**—*dangerous place.* Few take the courage of going to a hornet's nest.

3. **Nest egg**—*money laid by.* A wise businessman always maintains a nest egg.

NET

Dance in a net—*to act in imagined concealment.* The saboteurs quite often dance in a net laid by the detectives.

NETHER

Nether world—*hell.* He is living in a nether world now-a-days.

NEVER

1. **Better late than never**—*it is better to do something good however late, than not to do it* at all. Start with your studies right now; it is better late than never.

2. **It is never too late to mend**—*one* can *improve matters* at any *stage.* Pandit Nehru had the quality of doing anything at the stage when it was never too late to mend.

3. **Never-was**—*one who never was of any account.* I and you are never-were.

NEW

1. **New poor**—*those who have come to think themselves poor by the loss of advantage.* The retired officials soon become the new poor.

2. **New rich**—*the recently enriched.* Business executives and I.A.S. recruits are the new rich.

3. **New-fangled**—newly *achieved.* New-fangled things do not live long.

4. **Of new**—*anew; of late.* We met of new after a long time.

5. **To turn over a new leaf**—*to lead* a new *life.* After marriage every person has to turn over a new leaf.

NEWSY

Newsy-viewsy—*gossipy.* The journals are full of newsy-viewsy stories.

NEXT

1. **Next door to**—*in the neighbourhood*. She stays next door to ours.

2. **Next of kin**—*nearest relative*. He is my next of kin.

3. **Next to nothing**—*almost nothing at all*. His arguments command a respect which is next to nothing.

NIB

His nibs—*himself; his mightiness*. He his nibs will come to your assistance.

NICE

Nice and—*commendably; pleasantly*. Your lady friend is nice and.

NICETY

To a nicety—*with great exactness*. You must work to a nicety for success.

NICK

1. **Nick stick**—*tally*. Check your accounts with a nick stick.

2. **Out of all nick**—*out of all reckoning*. Black money in India is out of all nick.

3. **Old nick**—*the devil*. The old nick will kick you to death.

4. **In the nick of time**—*at the last moment*. I caught the train in the nick of time.

5. **To nick the nick**—*to win or accomplish*. He nicked the nick by getting first prize in his examination.

NIDDLE-NODDLE

Niddle-noddle—*with nodding head.* The Principal was niddle-noddle.

The niddle-noddle man fails in life.

NIFF

1. **Niff-naff**—*a trifle; a diminutive person.* Lal Bahadur Shastri was giant of a niff-naff.

2. **Niffy-naffy**—*fastidious.* The young girls are niffy-naffy about their clothing.

NIGGER

1. **Nigger in the wood pile**—*a hidden motive.* When a minister or a millionnaire curries favour, you must look for the nigger in the wood pile.

2. **Work like a nigger**—*to toil hard; like a slave.* How long can an artist work like a nigger ?

NIGHT

1. **Day and night**—*all the hours.* Many chemists' shops remain open day and night.

2. **Nightmare**—*dreadful scene.* When I am reminded of the nightmare of partition of our country, I find a nightmare before me.

3. **Night of ignorance**—*barbarous times.* Many countries of the world are still under the night of ignorance.

4. **Night sight**—*power of vision by night.* Cats and owls have night sight and so have you. I wonder if you are a cat or an owl.

5. **Night air**—*a peculiarly unwholesome gas imagined by some to circulate by night.*

Beware of the night air, which is everywhere.

6. **Night out**—*a domestic servant's night of freedom to be absent; a night away from home, work or restrictions.* Everybody appreciates a night out.

7. **Of a night**—*in the course of a night.* You get dreams of a night.

NILLY

Willy-nilly—*Will he; nill he, whether he will or not; by hook or by crook; willingly or unwillingly.* Willy-nilly everyone must die sooner or later.

NIMINY

Niminy-piminy—*affectedly fine and delicate.* Most of the young girls today are niminy-piminy.

NINE

1. **Nine days' wonder**—*short-lived sensation.* Every great event of contemporary politics is a nine days' wonder.

2. **Nineteen to the dozen**—*with great volubility.* The politicians sell nineteen to the dozen their credentials to the voters.

3. **Nine points of the law**—*worth nine-tenths of all the points that could be raised.* Possession is nine points of the law.

4. **Nine times out of ten**—*chances are far greater.* Nine times out of ten, my son is going to get a job in a government office.

5. **To the nines**—*to perfection; fully: elaborately.* Nehru did every work to the nines.

NINTH

Ninth part of a man—*tailor.* Your brother is at the shop of a ninth part of a man.

NIP

1. **Just a nip**—*little wine or beer*. Let us just have a nip.

2. **Nip and tuck**—*full speed; neck and neck*. They ran nip and tuck to reach the destination.

3. **Nip in**—*to cut in*. When parents are speaking, children should not nip in.

4. **Nip in the bud**—*cut off in the earliest stage*. Evil must be nipped in the bud.

NO

1. **No doubt**—*surely*. No doubt, I shall stand by you in any danger.

2. **No joke**—*no trifling matter*. To earn one's living today is no joke.

3. **No man's land**—*a waste region on which no one has a recognised claim; a debatable land between entrenched hostile forces*. I was born in the no man's land between Pakistan and Afghanistan.

4. **No one**—*nobody*. No one can save you from the clutches of death.

5. **No time**—*very short time*. I shall see you in no time.

NOB

One for the nob—*blow on the head*. David was killed by the police with one for his nob.

NOBLE

Noble metal—*one that does not readily tarnish on exposure to air, as gold, silver, platinum*. A public man should be made of noble metal.

NOD

1. **Land of nod**—*sleep*. It requires no passport to visit land of nod.

2. **Nodding acquaintance**—*slight acquaintance as with a person one nods but does not speak to*. Walter and I are no longer of nodding acquaintance.

3. **On the nod**—*on tick.* You will always find me on the nod.

NOISE

1. **A big noise**—*a person of great importance.* President Nixon was a great noise.

2. **Make a noise in the world**—*to achieve great notoriety.* President makes a noise in the world.

NOM DE PLUME

Nom de plume—*writer's assumed or borrowed name.* My nom de plume is 'Razia'.

NONCE

Nonce word—*a word coined for use at the moment.* My writings bristle with many nonce words.

NONE

None the less—*nevertheless.* I was poor and ill. None the less the professor in Mumbai welcomed me and gave me meal and medicine.

NOOK

Nook and corner—*everywhere.* I looked for him in every nook and corner.

NORTH

Northern lights—*the aurora borealis.* After the fall of Vietnam, U.S.A. closed its eyes to northern lights from China.

NOSE

1. **Cut off one's nose to spite one's face**—*to injure oneself when you fail injure other person.* When you

427

meet a stronger foe, do not cut off your nose to spite your face.

2. **Follow one's nose**—*to go straight forward.* It is best to follow your nose in life and not squander your energy on crooked ways which lead nowhere but drive you dead in a vicious circle.

3. **Lead by the nose**—*diotate; dominate.* Hitler led Germany by the nose.s

   No mother can lead a modern girl by the nose; rather the reverse is true.

4. **Make a long nose**—*to put one's thumb to one's nose in defiance or derision.* When a mother gives an advice to a modern boy, he makes a long nose.

5. **Plain as the nose in your face**—*easily seen.* His face is plain as the nose in the face.

6. **Snap off one's nose**—*to speak snappily.* When Prime Minister speaks, he snaps off the Opposition's nose.

7. **Through the nose**—*exorbitantly.* In these days of high prices even for the rations you have to pay through the nose.

8. **Thrust one's nose into**—*to meddle officiously with.* Please do not thrust your nose into my affairs.

9. **To count noses**—*to count supporters.* In elections every candidate is confined to counting noses.

10. **To put one's nose to the grindstone**—*to do a difficult job; to receive punishment stoically.* The Americans put their nose to the grindstone in Vietnam.

11. **Turn up one's nose at**—*to refuse or receive contemptuously.* When I offered her a rose, she turned up her nose.

12. **Under one's nose**—*before one's eyes.* Great corruption is corroding the country under the nose of the politicians.

13. **Under one's very nose**—*in full view; close at hand.* You cannot challenge corruption under your very nose.

NOT

1. **Not-I**—*that which is not the conscious ego.* Not-I is more powerful than I.

2. *Not-out*—*still in.* After being in the Cabinet for thirty years, he is still not-out.

NOTABLE

A notable quantity—*perceptible.* A notable quantity of milk is lying at home.

NOTE

1. **Note a bill**—*to record a refusal of acceptance as a ground of protest.* When the majority in Parliament was against him, he alone noted the bill.

2. **To make a note of**—*to record.* Make a note of this letter.

NOTHING

1. **Come to nothing**—*to have little or no result; to turn out a failure.* When death is at hand, all our achievements of life come to nothing.

2. **Make nothing of**—*fail to utilize properly, to give no importance.* He made nothing of the gift I gave him. They made nothing of the Queen.

3. **Next to nothing**—*almost nothing.* I inherited from my parents next to nothing.

4. **Nothing gift**—*a gift of no value.* The watch that Mary gave to Walter was a nothing gift.

5. **To be nothing**—*to be untrue.* I find nothing in his statement.

6. **To have nothing of**—*to be without individuality.* We have nothing with us.

NOTICE

1. **Give notice**—*to warn beforehand; to inform; to intimate, especially the termination of an agreement.* The Arabs have given notice to Jews to quit Palestine.

2. **To come into notice**—*to attract attention.* She was the cause of coming into notice.

NOUGHT

1. **Noughts and crosses**—*a game in which one tries to make three noughts, the other three crosses, in a row in the space of crossed parallel lines.* U.S.A. and Russia. are making noughts and crosses in the world.

2. **Set at nought**—*despise; disregard; flout.* Do not set at nought the orders of your superiors.

NOW

1. **Now and again**—*sometimes; from time to time.* I go to Sweden now and again.

2. **Now and then**—*sometimes; from time to time.* He sees me now and then.

3. **Now of late**—*lately.* Now of late Tom is losing his head.

4. **The now**—*at present; presently; very lately.* The now is the time to make good our promises.

NOWHERE

Nowhere near—*not nearby.* You will find water nowhere near in desert.

NUMBER

1. **Have or get one's number**—*to size him up.* The tailor has your number.

The politician will get your number in no time.

2. **Number is up**—*is doomed; has not long to live.* Long before my brother died on June 19th, 1985, it was clear that his number was up.

3. **Number one**—*the first in the series; most important.* Prime Minister A.B. Vajpayee is Number one in the Union Cabinet.

He always thinks of number one.

NURSE

Put to nurse—*to commit to a nurse; usually away from home; to put an estate under trustees.* She put her old father to nurse.

I put my house in U.K. to nurse.

NUT

1. **A hard nut to crack**—*a difficult problem.* Inflation is a hard nut to crack for any government

2. **In nutshell**—*in brief.* In a nutshell, life is secure for nobody now-a-days.

3. **Not for nuts**—*not on any account.* I can lend you money not for nuts.

Not for nuts I can accompany you today.

4. **To be nuts on**—*to be very fond of.* The woman was nuts on her grandson.

O.K.

O.K.—*all correct.* Everything is O.K. with me.

O'S

O's advent—*seven anthems, each beginning with O, sung on the days before Christmas eve.* Let us sing O's of advent for the new government.

OAK

Sport one's oak—*keep one's outer door shut when one does not want visitors.* When I come to see you, do not sport your oak.

OAR

1. **Put in one's oars**—*to interpose when not asked.* Please do not put in your oars when the wise old men are talking.

2. **Rest on one's oars**—*to take things easily; to cease from work.* When you have taken your examination, it is time to rest on your oars.
   In the battle of life none can afford to rest on his oars.

3. **To pull a good oar**—*to be a good man.* You should pull a good oar.

433

4. **To put your oar into my boat**—*to unnecessarily interfere in my affairs.* Please do not put your oar into my boat.

OATS

1. **Feel one's oats**—*to be frisky or assertive.* You can feel your oats when you are called upon to speak out your mind.

2. **Sow one's wild oats**—*to indulge in youthful excesses.* Old men stop sowing wild oats any more.

OATH

1. **On oath**
2. **Under oath** }—*sworn to speak the truth*
3. **Upon oath**

He stated on oath that he was not present in the meeting of rebels against the government, although others said under oath that he was.

One can say anything on oath, because it costs nothing.

4. **To take an oath**—*to swear.* The new minister has taken an oath to serve the country faithfully.

OBEDIENCE

Passive obedience—*unresisting and unquestioning obedience to authority.* A government servant learns quickly enough the value of passive obedience.

OBJECT

Money, salary, etc. no object—*not being reckoned worthy of.* When I yearn to live in Mumbai and Mumbai only, money, salary etc. no object.

OBLIQUE

1. **Oblique motion**—*upward or downward motion of one part while another remains stationary.* Moneymaking calls for oblique motions.

2. **Oblique narration or speech**—*indirect speech.* Stop this oblique narration and call spade a spade.

3. **Obliquity of the ecliptic**—*the angle between the plane of the earth's orbit and that of the earth's equator.* There is an obliquity of the ecliptic in the political spheres as well as motions of the earth.

OBSERVE

1. **Observation car**—*a railway carriage designed to allow passangers to view scenery.* The party travelled to Simla in an observation car.

2. **The observed of all observers**—*person on whom all attention is concentrated.* The Queen was the observed of all observers in America.

OCCASION

1. **Occasional table**—*a small portable ornamental table.* Bring the occasional table for the breakfast.

2. **Occasioned by**—*owing to.* He went to Mumbai occasioned by his employment.

3. **On occasion**—*in case of need; as opportunity offers; from time to time.* You can rely on me for help on occasion.

   You should save money on occasion.

   Please see me on occasion.

4. **Take occasion**—*take advantage of an opportunity.* When you get a job, take the occasion to save something against a rainy day.

5. **To take occasion by the forelock**—*to make an immediate use of opportunity.* Hadn't he taken occasion by the forelock, he wouldn't have been abroad now.

OCCUPATION

1. **Army of occupation**—*army life in a country to hold the occupied region till a regular government is set up.* Russia had an army of occupation.

2. **Occupational disease**—*a disease among common workers engaged in a particular occupation.* T.B. is an occupational disease for sweepers.

3. **Occupational therapy**—*treatment of a disease or an injury by a regulated course of suitable work.* Occupational therapy can cure neurosis.

4. **To occupy oneself with**—*to keep oneself busy.* He is occupying himself in painting.

OCEAN

Oceanic islands—*islands far from the mainland.* Art and authorship are oceanic islands in the ocean of commerce and industry.

1. **Od**—*a minced form of God.*

2. **Od's bobs**—*God's body.* Who has seen Od's bobs?

3. **Od's bodkins**—*God's body.* Creation and the creatures are Od's bodkins.

4. **Od's life**—*God's life.* Who can measure Od's life?

5. **Od's nouns**—*God's wounds.* Jesus Christ suffered Od's nouns.

6. **Od's pitikins**—*God's pity.* Od's pitikins on you, lady!

ODD

1. **At odds**—*at variance.* Your theory and practice of religion are at odds.

2. **By long odds**—*by a great difference.* Michael got distinction by long odds.

3. **Make no odds**—*make no significant difference.* My life in Delhi or Mumbai makes no odds.

4. **Odd and even**—*game of chance.* In odd and even he won five thousand rupees.

5. **Odd-come-short**—*a short remnant.* Your life is an odd-come-short of your father.

6. **Odd-come-shortly**—*an early day; any time.* You can meet me odd-come-shortly.

7. **Odd-even**—*apparently neither one thing nor another.* Midnight is odd-even time.

   Your chances of success are odd-even.

8. **Odd fellow**—*member of a secret benevolent society.* Certainly you are an odd fellow.

9. **Odd-man-out**—*a man who is left out when numbers are made up.* He is an odd-man-out of the last cabinet.

10. **Odd means**—*wrong means.* I do not want to earn any money by odd means.

11. **Odds and ends**—*remnants.* You can make novelties with odds and ends of wood and furniture.

12. **Take odds**—*accept the advantage.* I want to take odds of going to London.

ODOUR

1. **In bad odour**—*in bad repute.* Politics is in bad odour.

2. **Odour of sanctity**—*fragrance after death alleged to be evidence of saintship.* He died rich in the odour of sanctity.

OEDIPUS

Oedipus complex—*a boy's unconscious rivalry and hostility towards his father.* Many a modern youth suffers oedipus complex.

OF

1. **Of new**—*anew.* Read this book of new.
2. **Of purpose**—*intentionally.* He came of purpose to meet you.

OFF

1. **Be off**—*go away.* Don't stand here. Be off !
2. **Come off**—*happen.* Diwali comes off in November.
3. **From off**—*from a position on.* He shouted from off the coat.
4. **Go off**—*go quickly away.* Soon they went off to the hills.
5. **Ill off**—*poor or ill provided.* Many families are ill of now-a-days.
6. **Off and on**—*now and then.* He comes to see me off and on.
7. **Off one's reed**—*without appetite.* I am off my feed today.
8. **Off one's head**—*crazy.* Are you off your head to say so ?
9. **Off with**—*take off at once.* Off with you.
10. **Show off**—*to be showy.* Please don't show off here.
11. **Take off**—*remove.* Please take off your coat.
12. **Tell off**—*count; assign; chide.* He was told off to bombard the enemy positions.

13. **Well off**—*prosperous*. Only the dishonest and corrupt are well off.

OFFENCE

1. **Give offence**—*to cause displeasure*. Please don't give offence to anybody.

2. **Take offence**—*to feel displeasure*. Please do not take offence if I point out your faults and foibles.

OFFICE

1. **Good office**—*used for a third party in a dispute*. We have requested his father to use his good offices in settling the dispute between Robert brothers.

2. **Ill-office**—*disservice*. Avoid ill-office habit.

OIL

1. **Oil one's hand**—*to bribe*. Even oiling one's hand is common in many public sector offices.

2. **Oil one's palms**—*to bribe*. It is impossible to get anything done unless you oil someone's palms in the office.

3. **Oil the wheels**—*make things go smoothly by courtesy*. For success in life, learn the art of oiling the wheels.

4. **Smell or oil**—*bears marks of study*. Krishna's last story published in paper smells of oil.

5. **Strike oil**—*find oil in soil*. Our scientists are striking oil in the ocean.

6. **To pour oil on the waters**—*Smooth matters over*. Only a few leaders can pour oil on the international waters.

1. **Old and young**—*every body.* Old and young of India are going to contribute something towards the Prime Minister Relief Fund.

2. **Old boy**—*one's father; husband; an oldish man in authority; old man with air of youthfulness; a former pupil.* The old boy can give you lot of help.

   It was an old boys' meeting.

3. **Old country**—*the mother country.* Indians abroad never forget the old country.

4. **Old hand**—*an experienced performer.* Old hands are usually indispensable.

5. **Old head on young shoulders**—*wisdom beyond years.* Don't try to have your old head on young shoulders.

6. **Old maid**—*spinster.* Old maids find love in each others' company.

7. **Old man**—*unregenerated human nature; one's father, husband, employer, etc., a friendly term of address.* They invited the old man to eats and drinks.

8. **Old man's beard**—*a kind of moss.* You can't find anything here except old man's beard.

9. **Old salt**—*an experienced sailor.* Old salt is welcome in a ship.

10. **Old school tie**—*emblem of minor loyalties.* The students of Government College, Ludhiana wear the old school tie.

11. **Old song**—*a trifle; a very small price.* He got the job for an old song.

12. **Old story**—*something that has happened long ago.* Defections are an old story in Indian politics.

13. **Old wife**—*old woman.* You will meet the old wife in the market.

14. **Old woman**—*one's mother, wife, old womanish person.* You will find the old woman in the kitchen.

OLIVE

1. **Olive branch**—*a symbol of peace.* Pakistanis held the olive branch in Dacca.

2. **To hold out the olive branch**—*to make overtures for peace.* It was after a long war the Americans were able to hold out the olive branch.

OMNIBUS

1. **Omnibus box**—*a theatre box for many persons*. The Duke hired an omnibus box.

2. **Omnibus clauses**—*one that covers many different cases*. There are many omnibus clauses in the constitution of India.

3. **Omnibus train**—*a train that stops on every station*. An omnibus train runs slower than express trains.

4. **An omnibus bill**—*a bill covering various aspects of questions*. The Sales Tax Bill introduced in Parliament was an omnibus bill in the beginning.

ON

1. **On to**—*to a position on; forward to*. They went on to Simla from Delhi.

2. **On and on**—*quickly without stopping*. I read that novel on and on.

3. **On dit**—*rumour*. It is merely an on dit that all banks in India will be privatised soon.

ONCE

1. **At once**—*without delay*. Please see me at once.

2. **For once**—*for one occasion only*. For once do come to my house.

3. **Once and again**—*now and then*. We meet once and again.

4. **Once for all**—*once for ever*. Let us come to terms once for all.

5. **Once in a way**—*occasionally*. I can see you only once in a way.

6. **Once or twice**—*a few times*. We did meet once or twice.

7. **Once upon a time**—*at a certain time in the past*. Once upon a time there lived fairies in the world.

ONE

1. **All one**—*just the same*. It is all one to me whether you come or not.

2. **At one**—*of one mind*. They are at one to help you.

3. **One another, each other**—*for more than two persons*. They lived happily by helping one another.

4. **One by one**—*singly in order*. I want to meet the boys one by one.

5. **One day**—*on a certain day; at an indefinite time*. One must die one day.

ONER

A oner at—*expert in*. He is oner at driving.

ONLY

Only and lonely—*only*. Maria is my only and lonely daughter.

OPEN

1. **Keep open doors**—*be hospitable*. Major White's whole family keeps open doors.

2. **Open access**—*public access to the shelves of a library.* U.S. libraries in India have an open access.

3. **Open book**—*anything that can be interpreted without difficulty.* Thc life of Mahatma Gandhi was an open book.

4. **Open door**—*free and equal opportunity of trading for all.* No country today has an open door for international trade.

5. **Open fire**—*to begin to shoot.* The army opened fire on the robbers.

6. **Open heart**—*frankness.* Will you please open your heart ?

7. **Open house**—*hospitality to all comers.* It is my ambition to run an open house.

8. **Open letter**—*a letter addressed to a person but intended for public reading.* I want to write open letters to Prime Minister, because no closed letter ever gets through to him.

9. **Open mind**—*an unprejudiced mind.* He had got an open mind.

10. **Open out**—*to make or become more widely open; to expand; to disclose; to unpack; to develop; to bring into view; to open the throttle; to accelerate.* Many opportunities are opening out for the youth of the country in these critical times because every challenge is an opportunity.

11. **Open question**—*a matter undecided.* India's next General Election is still an open question.

12. **Open sea**—*unenclosed sea, clear of headlands.* The youth must row in the open sea for his survival. He must swim or sink.

13. **Open secret**—*a matter known to many.* Corruption in the highest political and official circles is an open secret.

14. **Open shop**—*a factory not confined to union labour.* There is hardly an open shop in the industrial world of India today.

15. **Open town**—*a city immune from hostile attacks during war.* Paris became an open town during the Second World War.

16. **Open up**—*to open thoroughly; to lay open; to disclose; to make available for traffic colonization, etc.* Indo-Pakistan borders are not yet opened up.

17. **Open verdict**—*a verdict that crime has been committed without specifying the criminal.* There is an open verdict on the crimes of Yahya Khan in Bangladesh.

OPERATE

To operate—*to affect.* Try your best, your plans are not going to operate on me.

OPERATION

1. **Combined operation**—*an army campaign in which land, air and naval force jointly participate.* War is a combined operation.

2. **To come into operation**—*to become effective.* The medicine given by the doctor is coming in operation now.

OPERATIVE

Operative words—*the words in a deed legally effecting the transaction.* The operative words of Simla Agreement are being honoured more in breach than the observance.

OPINION

To act upon one's opinion—*to put into practice.* He always acts upon his father's opinion.

OPPOSITE

1. **Be opposite with**—*to be perverse and contradictory in dealing with.* Edward and Stanley are opposite with each other.

2. **Opposite number**—*one who has a corresponding place in the other set.* The Indian Volleyball Association wrote to the opposite number in Australia for playing the next series in India.

OPPOSITION

Opposition of the thumb—*persistent opposition.* Every candidate has to face opposition of the thumb in election.

OPTION

To have an option—*to have a choice.* You have an option to stay here or go.

ORACLE

Work the oracle—to *achieve the desired result by manipulation, intrigue, wire-pulling, favour, etc., to raise money.* The enemies of Danny worked the oracle before his assassination.

ORDER

1. **Full orders**—*priesthood.* Church is under full orders.
2. **In short order**—*promptly.* The Americans evacuated Kabul in short order.
3. **In order**—*kept/arranged properly.* Everything is lying in order.

4. **Low order**—*poor quality.* The fruits purchased by the servant are of low order.

5. **Of high order**—*of great quality.* The fruits purchased by the servant are of high order.

6. **Orderly bin**—*a street receptacle for refuse.* There are orderly bins in New Delhi but few people use them.

7. **Orderly officer**—*officer on duty for the day.* If you have anything urgent, meet the orderly officer.

8. **Order of battle**—*order of troops, ships, aeroplanes, etc. in readiness of war.* Alan and Richard are chalking out order of battle for the coming elections.

9. **Order paper**—*paper showing order of deliberative business,* Where is the order paper ?

10. **Out of order**—*improper; not working.* The car is out of order.

11. **Sailing orders**—*written instructions given to the commander of a vessel before sailing.* No ship can leave the port without sailing orders.

12. **Sealed orders**—*instructions not to be opened until a specified time.* Ships at war are often issued sealed orders to be opened later at fixed times.

13. **Standing orders**—*regulations for procedure.* Every assembly has its standing orders.

14. **Take order**—*take measures.* You should take orders for restoring peace in the camp.

15. **Take orders**—*to become a priest.* If you are afraid of fighting, take orders.

16. **To order**—*according to, and in fulfilment of, an order.* You should set the house to order.

17. **To order one's life**—*to discipline oneself.* Stanley has ordered his life beautifully.

ORDINARY

In ordinary—*in regular customary attendance.* You find police always in ordinary.

ORGANIC

1. **Organic disease**—*a disease accompanied by changes in the structures involved.* The world today is full of organic diseases.

2. **Organic sensation**—*sensation from internal organs, as hunger.*

Sex and hunger are organic sensations and the world today is both food hungry and sex hungry.

ORIGINAL

Original sin—*the sin of Adam*. World today is obsessed with sex which is the original sin.

OSAGE

Osage orange—*an orange like inedible fruit*. Prosperity today is an osage orange.

OSTRICH

1. **Have the digestion of an ostrich**—*strong stomach*. I have the digestion of an ostrich.
2. **Ostrich belief**—*wrong belief*. He has an ostrich belief in luck.

OTHER

1. **Every other**—*each alternate*. He comes to my house every other day.
2. **One or the other**—*any one out of the two*. Here are two books you can have one or the other.
3. **Rather than otherwise**—*rather than not*. I will rather leave Delhi than otherwise.
4. **The other day**—*an unspecified day, not long past*. The Prime Minister disappeared in U.S.A. the other day.

OUST

Oust from—*turn out*. The captain has been ousted from the club.

OUT

1. **At outs**—*at odds*. I found Peter and Robert at outs.
2. **Murder will out**—*murder cannot be hidden*. Please remember, murder will be out.

3. **Out and about**—*able to go about; convalescent.* Jane is now out and about.

4. **Out and away**—*by far; beyond competition.* Tony is out and away the best boy at the Milk Booth.

5. **Out and out**—*completely.* He is out and out involved in debts now-a-days.

6. **Out at elbow, heel, knee**—*showing poverty.* You will find him out at elbow.

   Tom manages not to be out at heel.

   The Governor was deliberately out at knee when he visited us in our city.

7. **Outed**—*expelled.* The Principal outed Walter from college on account of his misbehaviour.

8. **Out for**—*abroad in quest for; expressly aiming at; dismissed from batting with a score of.*

   Dr. Paul is out for clinical success.

   David is out for success in authorship.

   He was out for twenty runs.

9. **Out for**—*out to be.* His financial circumstances compelled him to be out for his misbehaviour.

10. **Out of character**—*not in keeping with character.* Mary is out of character now-a-days.

11. **Out of common**—*unusual.* Mahatma Gandhi was a man out of the common.

12. **Out of course**—*out of order.* You cannot do pretty little out of course in an office.

13. **Out of doors**—*in or into open air.* You should do your exercise out of doors.

14. **Out of favour**—*disliked*. It is easy to be out of favour with the boss if you do not flatter him.

15. **Out of hand**—*instantly beyond control*. He paid cash out of hand.

    The riot in Muslim area was soon out of hand and army was called to restore peace.

16. **Out of it**—*excluded from participation; without a chance*. When election comes, many Congressmen will be out of it.

17. **Out of joint**—*dislocated*. "Times are out of joint" said Shakespeare. And so indeed are.

18. **Out of one's mind**—*mad*. Many prosperous men today are out of their mind.

19. **Out of print**—*no longer to be had from the publisher.* Many books written by me are now out of print.

20. **Out of temper**—*cross; annoyed.* Little trifles make modern men out of temper.

21. **Out of the wood**—*free from confusion.* I am not yet out of the wood.

22. **Out of time**—*too soon or too late; not keeping time in music.* Both the old and the young are out of time with the technological music.

23. **Out of tune**—*not true in pitch.* Democracy is out of tune in India.

24. **Outs and ins**—*secrets.* I do not know outs and ins of even a little mouse.

25. **Out to out**—*in measurement from outside to outside; overall.* Our house is out to out 29 feet long and 27 feet broad.

26. **Out upon**—*shame upon.* Out upon you !

27. **To be out**—*on strike.* The staff of Paul Company is out today.

OVER

1. **All over**—*at an end; everywhere; at the most characteristic; covered with; besmeared or bespattered with.*
   It is all over in Vietnam.
   Communism is all over Asia.
   I am all over with mud.

2. **All over**—*finished; dead;* It's all over now.

3. **Over again**—*afresh; a new.* Democracy must be tried over again.

455

4. **Over against**—*opposite*. He stands over against you.

5. **Over and above**—*in addition*. I have a DVD over and above a CD.

6. **Over and over**—*many times; repeatedly*. You should read this book over and over.

7. **Over and over again**—*very many times*. Practice over and over again makes a man perfect.

8. **Over head and ears**—*completely submerged*. I am over head and ears in commitments.

9. **Overseas**—*in foreign lands*. I wonder if my friend, Mr. John is now overseas.

OWING

Owing one a grudge—*cherish resentment against*. No use owing a grudge now.

OWL

Owl train—*a night train*. Many people prefer to travel by owl train.

OWN

1. **Get one's own back**—*retaliate; get even*. Danny is afraid lest Stanley gets his own back on him.

2. **Hold one's own**—*face up*. You must hold your own against a sea of troubles.

3. **On one's own**—*on one's own account; on one's own initiative; by one's own initiative or resources; independently; set up in independence*. John does everything on his own.

Alan wants to fight on his own.

4. **Own up**—*confess freely*. When the police torture the offenders, they own up even what they have not committed.

OX

1. **An ox in one's tongue**—*bribed to keep mum*. He has been given an ox in his tongue on Susan's affairs.
2. **Black ox**—*misfortune*. Black ox has spoiled his whole career.
3. **Have the black ox tread on one's foot**—*to experience sorrow or misfortune*. If you go wrong mentally, you will have the black ox tread on your foot.

P'S

Mind one's P's and Q's—*to be watchfully careful in language and behaviour.* For a top success in Indian Administrative Services, it is best to mind your P's and Q's.

PACE

1. **Go the pace**—*to go at a great speed; to live a fast life.* Let us go the pace to catch the train.

   Modern man lives to go the pace.

2. **Keep, hold, pace with**—*go as fast as.* Russia is holding pace in science with U.S.A.

   We must keep pace with modern trends.

3. **Make or set the pace**—*to regulate the speed of others by example.* Professor Raman has set the pace for the country.

4. **Put one through one's paces**—*to set him to show what he can do.* The teacher should put the students through their paces.

458

PACK

1. **A pack of fools**—*a group of idiots.* Michael comes from the company of a pack of fools.

2. **Pack a jury, meeting, etc.**—*fill up with persons of one's own choice.* The Prime Minister had packed the Supreme Court with committed comrades.

3. **Pack off**—*to send off quickly.* Pack off your dishonest peon.

4. **Send one packing**—*dismiss summarily.* The Prime Minister sent William Nelson packing.

5. **To pack up**—*to go out of action.* The cycle is packed up.

PAD

1. **Pad the hoof**—*to walk; trudge.* Please pad the hoof to my house.

2. **Stand pad**—*to beg by the roadside.* Quite well-off people are willing to stand pad.

PAGE

1. **Page of honour**—*officer of the royal house.* The President of Yugoslavia has many pages of honour. For all his pains he earned Rs. 25.

2. **To fill a page in history**—*to be remembered in history.* The life of Nehru will fill a page in history.

PAIN

1. **For one's pains**—*as a reward or result of one's troubles.* He lost his mother for all his pains.

2. **Take pains**—*to be very careful.* Please take pains to do the work punctually.

3. **To be at pains**—*to put oneself to trouble.* Don't be at pains to please the boss, because he will never be pleased.

4. **To be at the pains of**—*doing.* He is at the pains *of* writing an essay.

PAINT

1. **Painted lady**—*a butterfly.* A painted lady is sitting on the floor.

2. **Paint the lily**—*to attempt to beautify that* which is *already beautiful.* In Kashmir the Government often paints the lily.

3. **Paint the town red**—to *break out* in a *boisterous spree; to enjoy much.* In Kabul the victorious alliance painted the town red.

   When he got first class all his family members painted the town red.

4. **To paint one black**—*to criticise a person malignantly.* Many a saint is subject of painting them black now-a-days.

PAINTER

1. **Cut the painter**—*to sever ties.* Peter has cut the painter with Dolly.

2. **Lazy painter**—*a rope for fastening a boat for use in fine weather only.* Lazy painter cannot anchor a ship at sea.

PAIR

1. **Pair of colours**—*two flags* carried *by a regiment, the national flag as also the regimental colour.* The battalion is marching with a pair of colours in their hand.

2. **Pair off**—*arrange; set against each other; set* aside *in pairs; to become associated in pairs.* Husband and wife are paired off by nature.
Nations quite often pair off in war.
India and Bangladesh have been paired off.

PALAIS

Palais de danse—*dancing hall.* The United Nations is a palais de danse of international politics.

PALE

1. **Pale-hearted**—*dispirited.* After failing to get a job for two years, he has now become pale-hearted.

2. **To look pale before**—*to be nothing as compared with.* Honey looks pale before Dolly.

PALM

1. **Palm off**—*to pass something counterfeit as* genuine. Mediocres are being palmed off as big leaders.

2. **Palmy days**—*prosperous days.* Palmy days do come in everyone's life.

3. **To bear away the palm**—*to* win laurels *of victory.* India bore away the palm in the Afro-Asian Games Hockey Competition.

4. **To grease one's palm**—*bribe.* You can get nothing done in this office unless you grease someone's palm.

PAN

Flash in the pan—*a fitful show of beginning without accomplishing anything.* Indian Five-Year Plans are a flash in the pan.

PANEL

Panel working—*a method of working a coalmine by dividing it into two compartments,* Production of coal can be stepped up through panel working.

PANTABLE

On one's pantables—*on one's dignity; high horse; lofty in manner.* Many men fail because they choose to stand on their pantables rather than soil their reputation.

PAPER

1. **On paper**—*planned; decreed; existing theoretically only.* Our agreement is on paper.

   The constitution of India is on paper.

   The spirit of religion is on paper only.

2. **Paper profits**—*hypothetical gains.* The profits shown by the company are merely paper profits.

3. **Paper *tiger***—*propaganda war by press; weakling.* China has launched paper tiger against America.

America is a paper tiger, said Mao Tse-tung.

4. **Papery plan**—*a plan on paper only.* Many Indian plans are papery plans only.

PAR

1. **Above par**—*at a premium; at more than nominal price.* Reliance shares are marketed above par.

2. **At par**—*at exactly the nominal price.* The Government of India has floated a new loan at par.

3. **Below par**—*at a discount; below the nominal price; out of sorts.* When a company goes down, its shares sell below par.

   I feel below par this morning.

4. **Nominal par**—*value with which a bill or share is marked or by what it is known.* The nominal par of a Tata share is Rs. 100.

5. **No par value**—*with no stated nominal price.* Shares with no par value find their own level in market.

6. **Par of exchange**—*the value of currency of one country expressed in that of another.* The par of exchange for £100 is Rs. 7200 only.

7. **Par value**—*value at par.* The par value of a Tata share is Rs. 100.

PARADISE

1. **Fool's paradise**—*foolish ideas.* I don't agree with you, you simply live in a fool's paradise.
2. **Paradise on earth**—*a living heaven.* The rich family of our village is living in a paradise on earth.

PARALLEL

1. **Parallel bars**—*a pair of fixed bars used for gymnastics.* N.P. and R.N. are on parallel bars in the political gymnasium.
2. **Parallel rulers**—*rulers joined by two pivoted strips for ruling parallel lines.* Get me a pair of parallel rulers to draw the map.
3. **To draw a parallel**—*to compare.* One cannot draw a parallel between those two friends.

PARAMOUNT

Of paramount importance—*very important.* A child is always of paramount importance to his parents.

PARDON

Pardon—*I beg your pardon; What did you say?*

Pardon me—*excuse me; used in apology and to soften a contradiction.*

PARISH

Parish pump—*the symbol of petty local interests.* The parish pump in Delhi is strongly behind Congress.

PARROT

Parrot coal—*cannel coal; possibly from chattering as it burns.* If we have nothing to talk, let us have some parrot coal.

PART

1. **For my part**—*as far as concerns me.* For my part I am ready to do my best for you.

2. **For the most part**—*commonly.* For the most part, ladies take no interest in politics.

3. **In bad or ill part**—un*favourable*. Please do not take in ill part the harsh words I spoke to you.

4. **In good part**—*favourably*. People will take in good part what leaders say if they are only honest to the people.

5. **In part**—*partly*. I make your payment in part today.

6. **On the part of**—*so far as concerns*. It is not good on the part of a minister to criticize the Prime Minister.

7. **Part and parcel**—*essentially a part*. Sikkim is a part and parcel of India.

8. **Part company**—*separate*. Let us part company gracefully.

9. **Parthian shot**—*a parting shot, from the parthian habit of turning round in the saddle to discharge an arrow at a pursuer*. There will be a parthian shot before the dictator quits the office.

10. **Parting of the ways**—*a point at which a fateful decision may be made*. India and Pakistan stood at the parting of the ways in 1947.

11. **Part of speech**—*one of the various classes of words*. Noun is a part of speech.

12. **Take part with**—*take the side of*. I take no part in politics.

Maria takes part with Grace against Michael.

PARTICULAR

In particular—*specially*. He poisnted out John's statement in particular.

PARTY

Party-spirited—*with zeal for the party.* Many members of our club are party-spirited.

PAS

Have the pas of one—*to take precedence of him.* The wife should have the pas of husband.

PASS

1. **Bring to pass**—*bring about; cause to happen.* Vajpayee has brought great events to pass in India.
2. **Come to pass**—*happen.* Death will come to pass whether you like it or not.
3. **Make a pass at**—*to aim a short blow at; to make an amorous advance.* The French lancer made a pass at the enemy.
   Don't make passes at street girls.
4. **Pass away**—to *come to an end; go off; die.* "Even this will pass away", wrote a king on the portal of his palace. My mother passed away on December 2, 1987.

467

5. **Pass off**—*to impose fraudulently; to palm off.* He passed off for a minister.
He passed off the spurious coin.

6. **Pass on**—*to go forward; to proceed, to die; to transmit, hand on.*
Work and pass on to greatness and glory.
The property passed on from father to son.

7. **Pass out**—*to distribute; to die; to faint; dead drunk.*
Please pass out the sweets to the beggars.
The patient passed out in hospital.
The woman passed out in frenzy.
Heavily drunk, he passed out.

8. **Pass over**—*to overlook; to ignore.* The ministers pass over cases of corruption.

9. **Pass the time of day**—*to exchange any ordinary greeting of civility.* The old men pass the time of day in a garden.

10. **Pass through**—*experience; undergo.* My brother passed through many hardships.

11. **Pass up**—*renounce; have nothing to do with.* Let us pass up this world of money and illusion.

PASSAGE

1. **Bird of passage**—*migratory bird.* A true saint is a bird of passage.

2. **Passage of arms**—*quarrel of words.* A passage of arms is very common in every Parliament.

PASSIVE

1. **Passive resistance**—*deliberate refusal, from scruples of conscience, to do what law or regulation orders, and submission to consequent penalties.* Mahatma Gandhi pioneered passive resistance in South Africa.

468

2. **Passive resister**—*one who offers passive resistance.* Mahatma Gandhi was a passive resister.

PAST

1. **A past master**—*an expert.* He is a past master in repairing TVs.
2. **Pastrycook**—*maker of pastry.* The Professor of Botany is a pastrycook.

PAT

1. **Pat on the back**—*a mark of encouragement or approbation.* The professor gave John Paul a pat on the back.
2. **Stand pat**—*to decide to play one's hand as it is; refuse to change.* The U.S.A. stood pat in Vietnam and lost everything.

PATCH

1. **Not a patch on**—*not fit to be compared with.* Honey is not a patch on Grace.
2. **To patch up quarrel**—*to arrange to compromise.* A good mediator can always patch up a quarrel.

PATIENCE

Have no patience with—*irritated.* I have no patience with your silly argument.

PATIENT

Patient of—*complete.* The manager is patient of bringing a settlement to the dispute of workers.

PAVE

1. **Crazy pavement**—*irregular.* The old cities in India are still full of crazy pavements.

2. **On the pavement**—*without a lodging.* Millions in Mumbai are on the pavement.

3. **Pave the way for**—*to prepare the way for; make easier; help to bring on.* Your presence during the examination paved the way for my success.

PAY

1. **In the pay of**—*hired by.* This car is in the pay of the American Ambassador.

2. **Pay back**—*to pay in return; to give tit for tat.* I shall pay back your loan soon.

   He paid back the joker by cracking a joke at his cost.

3. **Pay down**—*pay in cash on the spot.* Please pay down for the car.

4. **Pay for**—*make amends for; to suffer for.* You will pay for your crime.

5. **Pay in**—*to contribute to a fund.* Please pay in something for the refugees.

6. **Pay off**—*pay in full; to take revenge.* The servant was paid off on dismissal.

   He paid off the murderer by killing him.

7. **Pay one's way**—*meet one's expenses.* It is getting more and more difficult to pay one's way.

8. **Pay out**—*cause to run out, as a rope.* When the chain paid out, he pulled it back.

9. **Pay round**—*turn the ship's head.* The captain paid the ship round.

10. **Pay through the nose**—*pay dearly.* If you borrow money at high interest, you shall have to pay it through the nose.

11. **Pay up**—*pay in full.* The dismissed employees must be paid up immediately.
12. **To pay for one's whistle**—*to be punished for one's deeds.* All human beings are paid for their whistles.
13. **To pay off**—*to pay in full.* My employers have paid off my arrears.
14. **To pay one back in one's own coin**—*tit for tat.* The attitude of paying one back in one's own coin is not always good.

PEACE

1. **At peace**—*in a state of peace; not at war.* India and Pakistan are at peace.
2. **Hold one's peace**—*remain silent.* When somebody is speaking, hold your peace.
3. **In peace**—*in enjoyment of peace.* We live in peace here.
4. **Keep the peace**—*refrain from disturbing the public peace.* Good citizens keep the peace.

5. **Make one's peace with**—*to reconcile or be reconciled with.* You should make peace with your family.
6. **Make peace**—*end a war.* Delhi and Islamabad have made peace.
7. **Peace at all costs**—*to pay heavy price for peace.* A wise nation will not keep peace at all costs but will fight when necessary.
8. **Peace establishment**—*the reduced military strength maintained in time of peace.* Indian Defence Services are a peace establishment.
9. **Swear the peace**—*to take oath before a magistrate that a certain person ought to be put under bond to keep peace.* He swore the peace against his enemy.

PEACOCK

Peacock throne—*the throne of the Kings of Delhi carried off to Persia in 1739.* Democracy in India still sits on the peacock throne and hesitates to come down to the gutters.

PEDAL

Pedal softly—*persuade gently.* You must pedal your proposed marriage softly in the family.

PEDESTAL

To put on the pedestal—*to worship.* Pandit Nehru has been put on the pedestal.

PEEL

1. **Pack and peel**—*to have any dealings.* I don't pack and peel with dishonest folk.
2. **Peel and eat**—*self help in eating potatoes.* Democracy means peel and eat potatoes.

PEG

1. **Off the peg**—*ready-made*. I want to buy some goods off the peg.
2. **Peg away**—*work on assiduously*. He pegged away a book.
3. **Peg too low**—*tipsy*. In the evening he is a peg too low.
4. **Round peg in a square hole**—*one who is unsuited to the particular position one occupies*. At college as a professor I was a round peg in a square hole.
5. **Take down a peg**—*humble; snub*. The Prime Minister quite often takes his ministers down a peg.
6. **To peg out**—*to die*. The low temperature will peg out the patient soon.

PEGASUS

Pegasus—*winged horse of poetry*. Politics does not ride on pegasus.
Maria often rides on pegasus.

PELICAN

Pelican in her piety—*a pelican with wings indorsed, feeding her young with her blood.* True democracy is pelican in her piety.

PELT

To pelt one with roses—*honour one.* The Prime Minister was pelted with roses.

PEN

1. **Pen and ink**—*in writing.* Unless you give me your statement in pen and ink I cannot take any action.

2. **Talk like a pen-gun**—*to chatter volubly.* The little lady talked like a pen-gun.

PENALTY

Under or on penalty of—*with liability of.* They left the worship under penalty of being arrested and jailed.

PENNY

1. **A penny for your thoughts**—*your thoughts are worthless.* Here's penny for your thoughts.

2. **Not a penny the worse**—*never a while the worse.* He was never a penny the worse for resigning from the Parliament.

3. **Penny wedding**—*wedding at which guests contribute money to set up bride and bridegroom.* Penny weddings need to become popular in India.

4. **Penny wisdom**—*prudence in petty matters*. Traders show much penny wisdom.

5. **Penny wise pound foolish**—*to serve a low cost thing at the cost of very costly thing*. Lucy is penny wise pound foolish.

6. **Pretty penny**—*considerable sum of money*. It requires pretty penny to build a house.

7. **Turn an honest penny**—*to earn some money honestly*. Everybody should turn an honest penny.

PEPPER

Pepper-and-salt—*mingled black and white*. My bread is pepper-and-salt.

PERCH

1. **Hope the perch**—*die*. The child has hoped the perch.

2. **Perched block**—*a block of rock transported by ice and left aloft, often in an unstable position, when the ice retires*. A bureaucrat in a village is like a perched block, appointed by the power of the government, but surrounded by hostile folk who just don't like him.

PERFECTION

To perfection—*perfectly*. Jane does everything to perfection.

PERIL

1. **At your peril**—*at your risk*. I am informing you again, all you are doing is at your peril.

2. **In peril of**—*in danger of*. In peril of his life, the fireman went up to save the child.

PERIOD

Period wind—*wind which blows at or for certain periods, e.g., a trade wind, monsoon, a land breeze, a sea-breeze.* Politics is a period wind that brings the election fever and occasionally plagues the nation.

PERSEVERANCE

Perseverance of saints—*the Calvinistic doctrine that those who are called by God cannot fall away so as to be finally lost.* Those who push and pull for the political salvation of the world finally acquire the perseverance of saints, such as Mahatma Gandhi and Mother Teresa.

PERSPECTIVE

In perspective—*in prospect.* In perspective the future of India appears to be dark unless our leaders acquire the perseverance of saints.

PESTER

To pester with—*trouble.* He is pestered with family affairs.

PET

1. **Pet aversion**—*chief object of dislike.* Flattery is not the pet aversion of politicians, but it should be so.
2. **Petting party**—*a gathering for the purpose of caressing as an organized sport.* Petting parties are acquiring popularity in India too.

PETARD

Hoist with one's own petard—*to be punished with one's own weapon of defence.* Science is hoisting civilization with its own petard.

PETER

To peter out—*to give out.* The whole problem is petering out soon.

PETIT

Petit point—*work in tent stitch.* She did her embroidery in petit point.

PETTICOAT

1. **In petticoats**—*small child.* Peter and Robert have played together since they were in petticoats.

2. **In petticoat government**—*predominance of women in the home or politics.* Petticoat governments are rarely successful.

PETTY

Petty cash—*small sums of money received or paid.* It is a job of the housewife to keep account of the petty cash.

PHILOSOPHER

Philosopher's stone—*an imaginary stone or mineral compound long sought after by alchemists as a means of transforming other metals into gold.* Mr. Andrews died in his search for the philosopher's stone. I don't believe in it, but he did, and he was certainly no crazy fellow.

PHOTO

Photo-finish—*a race finish in which a special type of photography is used to show the winner, etc.; a neck-to-neck finish of any contest.* There is a photo-finish race between the forces of vice and virtue in the world. Vice is leading but virtue will survive.

PHRASE

1. **Enough of phrases**—*mere words*. I have enough of phrases from you, will you please give something practicable?

2. **In simple phrase**—*in simple expression*. Always try to put your ideas in simple phrases.

PHRASY

Phrasy fellow—*one inclined to emptiness and verbosity of phrase*. Most of the modern scholars and journalists are phrasy fellows. They are shallow thinkers without depth of thought or action.

PHYSIC

1. **A dose of physic**—*medicine*. A dose of physic will cure the child.

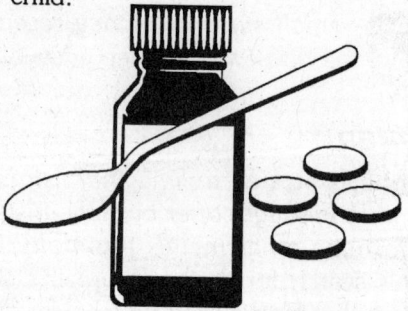

2. **Physical force**—*force applied outwardly to the body, as distinguished from persuasion, etc*. The cult of the physical force is gaining popularity in international politics.

3. **Physic garden**—*a garden of medicinal plants*. Human body is a physic garden. All medicines grow inside the man but unfortunately we have no science to study and utilize them.

PHYSICAL

1. **Physical explanation**—*tangible proof.* I want to have a physical explanation of your statement.
2. **Physical impossibility**—*absolutely impossible.* The economic theory introduced by Dev is a physical impossibility.

PIA

Pia mater—*brain.* I hope nothing is wrong with your pia mater.

PIANO

Piano player—*a piano with a piano player.* Do you want a piano player or a player piano ?

PICCALILLI

Piccalilli—*a pickle of various vegetable substances with mustard and spices.* T.V. is a piccalilli and a hot favourite of the children.

PICK

1. **Pick a hole in one's coat**—*to find fault with*. Do not pick holes in the coats of others.

2. **Pick and choose**—*select fastidiously*. Our manager is an expert at picking and choosing the right man for the right job.

3. **Pick-me-up**—*a stimulating drink*. For some fruit juice is a pick-me-up; others must have beer or whisky to stimulate them. I prefer aqua pura.

4. **Pick off**—*to select from a number and shoot*. The hunter picked off a pigeon.

5. **Pick on**—*to single out, especially for anything unpleasant; to nag at; to carp at*. Please do not pick on your friends whose help you need.

6. **Pick one's way**—*to choose carefully where to put one's feet, as on dirty ground*. In the rain you must pick your way carefully.

7. **Pick out**—*to make out, distinguish; to pick out; to select from a number; to mark with spots of colour, etc*. Pick out the good from evil and hang on to it

8. **Pick over**—*to go over and select*. Pick over a suitable pen from a shop.

9. **Pick purse**—*one who steals the purse or from the purse of another*. There is a pick purse in every running bus today.

10. **Pick thank**—*one who seeks to ingratiate himself by officious favours or by tale-bearing*. High society is plagued with pick thanks.

11. **Pick to pieces**—*to pull as under; to criticize adversely in detail.* They picked the import licence scandal to pieces in parliament.

12. **Pick up**—*to lift from the ground, floor, etc; to improve gradually; to gain strength bit by bit; to take into vehicle or company; to scrape acquaintance informally with; to acquire as occasion demands; to gain; to come upon; make out; distinguish.* They picked the child up.
They picked up the lady in their car.
The patient is picking up.
They picked up a friendship.

13. **To pick a quarrel**—*to seek fight.* Avoid picking a quarrel with anyone.

14. **To pick holes in**—*to criticize.* Do not pick holes in other's affairs.

15. **To pick one's pockets**—*to steal from one's pocket.* The thief made an unsuccessful attempt to pick my pocket.

PICKLE

To have a rod in pickle—*to have a punishment ready.* When the child returned home, his parents were having a rod in pickle.

PICTURE

1. **In the picture**—*having a share of attention; adequately briefed.* When he did the dirty deed, I was nowhere in the picture.

I will gladly help you so long as I am not in the picture. Dr. Paul would like me to help him but he does not like to be in the picture.

2. **The very picture**—*perfect.* The patient looks the very picture of health now.

PIE

By cook and pie—*by God and the pie.* By cook and pie, I shall stand by you through thick and thin.

PIECE

1. **All to pieces**—*into a state of disintegration or collapse.* Democracy in India is going all to pieces.

2. **A piece**—*each.* The price of these books is five rupees a piece.

3. **A piece of**—*an instance of.* Bribery in high places is a piece of corruption.

4. **A piece of one's mind**—*a frank outspoken rating.* If you misbehave, I shall have to give you a piece of my mind.

5. **In pieces**—*in or to a broken-up state.* I will buy the merchandise in pieces.

6. **Of a piece**—*as of the same piece, the same in nature; homogeneous; uniform; in keeping; consistent.* The politician, the bureaucrat and the black-marketeer are of a piece.

7. **Piece by piece**—*little by little.* I don't mind if you do things piece by piece but please do them right.

8. **Piece of goods**—*a woman.* He met a fascinating piece of goods at a bus stand.

9. **Piece of work**—*a task; a fuss; ado.* There is a piece of work in marriage.

Let there be no piece of work about it.

10. **Piece together**—*put together bit by bit.* The detectives piece together small bits of evidence to find out the truth.

11. **Piece up**—*patch up.* Let us piece up our difference.

12. **To pieces**—*in a state of disruption*. Joint family system has gone to pieces.

PIG

1. **Pig-headed**—*stupid*. Do not talk to that man; he is simply pig-headed.

2. **Pig in a poke**—*buy undesirable things without examining them*. While getting your rations, see that you don't buy pig in a poke.

3. **Pigs and whistles**—*wreck and ruin*. Civilization today is all pigs and whistles.

4. **Pigs might fly**—*wonder might happen*. He can get through only if some pigs fly.

5. **To buy a pig in the poke**—*to buy something without seeing it*. A wise man will never buy a pig in the poke.

PIGEON

1. **Pigeon English**—*broken English*. Many Indians speak pigeon English.

2. **Pigeon's milk**—*an imaginary liquid for which children are sent out on 1st April*. Let us order for supply of pigeon's milk on 1st April.

PILE

1. **Pile on**—*exaggerate*. Please do not pile on the statement.

2. **Pile on the agony**—*to overdo painful effects by accumulation, etc*. If you are full of sorrow, weep and relieve yourself, don't pile on the agony.

3. **To make one's pile**—*to earn as much as one needs*. The circumstances are such now-a-days that everyone must try to make his pile.

PILGRIM

Pilgrim's sign—*a badge worn by a pilgrim*. Our old leaders do not wear yet a pilgrim's sign.

PILL

1. **A bitter pill to swallow**—*an insult*. His words are just a bitter pill to swallow which I cannot tolerate.

2. **To swallow the bitter pill**—*to do an unpleasant task*. I have no money for cinema tickets but I must swallow the bitter pill.

PILLAR

1. **From pillar to post**—*from one state of difficulty to another; hither and thither.* Many a youth is going from pillar to post in search of a job.

2. **Pillar of hope**—*faith.* Keep pillar of hope in God and you will succeed.

PILLOW

Pillow-fight—*the sport of thumping one another with pillows.* Politics is no pillow-fight. It is a gun battle.

PIN

1. **A merry pin**—*a merry mood.* Meet her for a favour when she is in a merry pin.
2. **A pin**—*not at all.* I care a pin for money.
3. **On one's pins**—*on one's legs.* After three years of struggle my son is now able to stand on his pins.
4. **Pinhole photography**—*the taking of photographs by the use of a pinhole rather than a lens.* Literary criticism is a sort of pinhole photography.
5. **Pin one down**—*keep one strictly to.* Pin him down to the terms of his agreement.
6. **Pin one's faith on**—*to put entire trust in.* Pin your faith on God and no lesser luminary.
7. **Pin on one's sleeve**—*to make entirely dependent on oneself or at one's disposal.* I cannot afford to pin Alan on my sleeve.
8. **Pin point**—*minute.* Threading the needle is a pin point job.
9. **Pins and needles**—*a tingling feeling as numbness passes off.* I am feeling pins and needles in my foot. Politics will bequeath you pins and needles.

PINCER

Pincer movement—*a twofold advance that threatens to isolate a part of the enemy's force.* The General of terrestrial army trapped the enemy in a pincer movement.

PINCH

1. **At a pinch**—*in a difficulty,* You can ring me up at a pinch.

487

2. **Know where the shoe pinches**—*to know what the rear trouble is.* Every man knows where the shoe pinches.

3. **Pinch of salt**—*with some caution.* Drive your car with a pinch of salt.

PINE

Done to pine—*starved to death.* The famine did to pine many in our country in 1987.

PINK

Pink of perfection—*the acme.* In 1947, Nehru was in the pink of perfection.

PIOUS

Pious opinion—*a belief widely held but not made a matter of faith.* There is a pious opinion about politics being a sacrilegious profession.

PIPE

1. **Drunk as a piper**—*very drunk.* I found him drunk as a piper.

2. **Pay the piper**—*bear the expenses.* One who pays the piper, calls for the tune.

3. **Pipe and tabor**—*pipe and drum.* You can win elections by pipe and tabor provided you serve drinks with music.

4. **Pipe down**—*subside into silence.* All critics inside a political party are piped down.

5. **Pipe off**—*to watch a house or person for purposes of theft.* The house of every minister is piped off.

6. **Pipe of peace**—*desire for peace.* There is a pipe of peace every where in the country.

7. **Pipe one's eye**—*to weep.* Please don't pipe your eye here.

8. **Piping hot**—*hissing hot.* Nehru was fond of coffee piping hot.

9. **The time of piping peace**—*great peace.* The time of piping peace has almost vanished from world's history now.

10. **Tune one's pipes**—*weep.* Children get their demands by tuning their pipes.

PIRN

Wind one a bonny pirn—*set a fire problem for one; involve one in difficulties.* Mr. Edward winds me a fine pirn.

PISS

Piss pot—*chamber pot for urine.* Ocean has become the piss pot of world pollution.

PIT

1. **Pit and gallows**—*a feudal baron's right to drown female and hang male felons.* There are people who pit and gallow in the villages.

Rich landlords exercise pit and gallows.

PITCH

1. **Pitch and pay**—*pay ready money.* Pitch and pay your expenses.

2. **Pitched battle**—*well-entrenched fight between two parties.* The English and the French fought a pitched battle at Waterloo.

3. **Pitchers have long ears**—*children tell tales. There may be listeners.*

4. **Pitch in**—*set to work briskly.* Please pitch in for examination.

5. **Pitch into**—*to assail vigorously.* The French pitched into the English.

6. **Pitch on**—*to let one's choice fall upon.* The Principal pitched on Rosy for the Head Girl.

PITFALL

Pitfall—*unexpected danger.* The Chinese invasion was a pitfall for India.

PITTER

Pitter patter—*with light pattering sound.* Rain fell pitter patter on the window sill.

PITY

It pitieth me, you, them, etc.—*it caused pity in me you, them, etc.*

PLACE

1. **Give place**—*to make room; to be superseded.* Major Mathew gave place to Major Brown.

2. **Have place**—*have existence.* All religions have place in India.

3. **Out of place**—*out of due place; inappropriate; unreasonable.* Your remark is out of place here.

4. **Take place**—*to come to pass.* The Indo-Pak wars took place in 1965 and 1971.

PLAGUE

Plague pit—*a common grave for plague victims.* The world will come to end as a plague pit.

PLAIN

1. **Plain as a pikestaff**—*quite clear.* The road to success in our firm is plain as a pikestaff.

2. **Plain sailing**—*easy work or going.* There is no plain sailing in life.

PLANET

Planet-struck—*affected* by *the influence of the planets.* Superstitious folk are easily planet-struck.

PLANK

Walk the plank—*walk compulsorily along a plank projecting over the ship's side into the sea.* To get through the gauntlet of life you have to walk the plank.

PLANT

Plant out—*to transplant to open ground.* The flowering tree must be planted out.

491

PLASTIC

1. **Plastic force**—*the power of growth in animals and plants*. I hope you have not lost the plastic force yet to overcome political whirlwinds.
2. **Plastic surgery**—*surgery for beautification*. More and more women are undergoing plastic surgery.

PLAY

1. **Hold in play**—*keep occupied*. The army held the enemy in play to gain time.
2. **In, out of, play**—*in, out of, such a position that it may be played*. J. P. is no longer out of play in politics. Sonia is in play again.
3. **Make play**—*keep things going; push on with a game*. Let us make play through the night.
4. **Play at**—*engage in the game of; make a pretence of; to practise without seriousness*. They are playing at yoga.

   The soldiers are playing at war.

   The children are playing at judges and robbers.
5. **Play fast and loose**—*to act in a shifty, inconsistent and reckless fashion*. David is playing fast and loose with his life.
6. **Play fine**—*play well*. He is playing fine in politics.
7. **Play full**—*to play thoroughly well*. Let us play full in life.
8. **Play off**—*to manipulate so as to counteract*. India played off Dacca against Islamabad.
9. **Play on**—*work on*. The speaker played on sentiments of patriotism.

10. **Play the game**—*to act honourably.* Whether you win or lose, you must play the game in life.

11. **Play up**—*strike up; begin music; to redouble one's efforts; play more vigorously; to show up well in a crisis or emergency; to give prominence to; to boost.* The band played up.

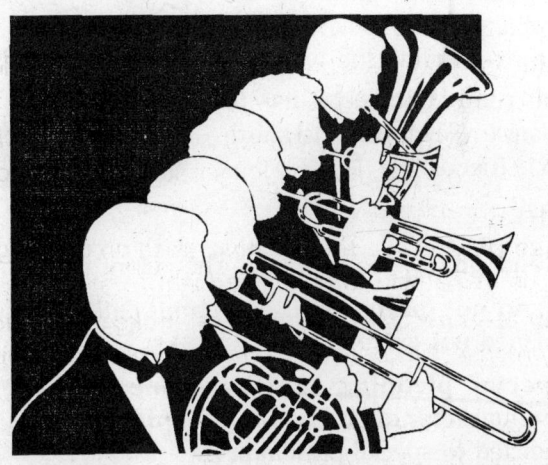

Play up ! play up ! play up the game !

U.S.A. must play up after withdrawal from Asia.

Don't play up religious sentiments.

12. **Play upon**—*practise upon; work upon.* Rosy plays upon harmonium.

13. **Play upon words**—*pun.* "My dear, deer is very dear" is a play upon words.

Another play upon words is "I saw a saw which could not saw."

14. **Play up to**—*to act so as to afford opportunities to.* The police plays up to the ministers.

15. **Play with**—*dally with*. Pakistan is playing with India.

16. **To play one's card well**—*make a good use of opportunities*. A wife is one who plays her cards well.

17. **To play the fool**—*to act like a fool*. He played the fool in today's meeting.

18. **To play the man**—*to act bravely*. Many soldiers play the man during the war.

19. **To play trick**—*to try to deceive*. Never play tricks with your friends.

PLEAD

1. **Plead guilty**—*admit guilt*. The culprit pleaded guilty.

2. **Plead not guilty**—*refuse to admit guilt*. The students pleaded not guilty of theft.

3. **Special pleading**—*unfair or one-sided argument aiming rather at victory than at truth*. The lawyers are addicted to special pleading.

PLEASURE

1. **At pleasure**—*when, if and as one pleases*. I will meet at your pleasure.

2. **Pleasure-pain principle**—*principle dominating instinctual life in which activities are directed towards seeking pleasure and avoiding pain*. Pleasure-pain principle is supreme in the world.

PLEASE

1. **If you please**—*if you can*. We can discuss the matter if you please.

2. **May it please you**—*a polite formula of request*. May it please you to attend the marriage of my son.
3. **Please it you**—*old form of address*. Please it you to grace my house.
4. **Please you**—*may it please you*. Please you, to stand by me.
5. **Please yourself**—*do as you like*. If you don't listen to me, please yourself.
6. **So please you**—*polite request*. So please you, to help me.

PLEDGE

1. **Sign the pledge**—*to give a written promise*. They have signed a pledge to abstain from liquor.
2. **Take a pledge**—*make a promise*. We took a pledge to fight for freedom.

PLENTY

Horn of plenty—*cornucopia*. India has lost the horn of plenty when rivers flowed with milk and honey.

PLOT

Plot-proof—*safe from any plots*. No government in the world is plot-proof now-a-days.

PLOUGH

1. **Plough lonely furrow**—*to be separated from one's friends and go one's own way*. Near his end Napoleon as well as Nehru ploughed a lonely furrow.

495

2. **Plough in**—*to cover with earth by ploughing.* Dead bodies were ploughed in the field of battle.
3. **Plough the sands**—*work in vain.* For forty years I have been ploughing the sands.
4. **Put one's hand to the plough**—*to begin an undertaking.* When you have committed to do something, you must put your hand to the plough.
5. **To turn swords into ploughshares**—*to turn from ways of war to professions of peace.* Now that the war is over in Iraq, Americans should turn their swords into ploughshares.

PLUCK

1. **Pluck off**—*to remove; to take by force.* Roots were plucked off.
   They plucked off a great victory.
2. **Pluck up**—*to summon courage; to gather strength.* They plucked up to fight to the bitter end.
3. **Pluck out**—*to draw out suddenly.* He had hardly spoken a word when his brother plucked out his tongue.
4. **Pluck down**—*to demolish suddenly.* The whole city was plucked down by earthquake, just in three minutes.

PLUNGE

To take the plunge—*to take the risk.* Come what may, you must take the plunge and appear in your examination.

PLUS

Plus fours—*baggy knickerbokers.* Mahatma Gandhi said to the British, "You wear plus fours, I wear minus fours."

POCK

Pock pudding—*a Scottish contemptuous name for a mere Englishman.* The Scot laughed at the pock pudding.

POCKET

1. **In pocket**—*with money.* Peter is in pocket now-a-days.

2. **Out of pocket**—*without money.* Robert is out of pocket now-a-days.

3. **Pick a person's pocket**—*to steal from his pocket.* Take care lest the gentleman on your right picks your pocket.

4. **Pocket an insult, affront, etc.**—*to submit to insult, etc. and put up without protest.* No youth is inclined to pocket insult now-a-days.

POET

Poetic justice—*ideal administration of reward and punishment.* There is no poetic justice in the world.

POINT

1. **At all points**—*completely; in all respects.* You will find him a gentleman at all points.

2. **At a point**—*in readiness.* I found him at the point of leaving his house.

3. **At the point of**—*on the verge of.* The economic world is at the point of bankruptcy.

4. **Carry one's point**—*to obtain what one wants.* With love, rather than with violence, you can carry your point.

5. **From point to point**—*from one particular to another.* General Fisher conquered Iraq from point to point.

6. **Give points to**—*to give an advantage*. India has given many points to Pakistan.

7. **In point**—*opposite*. Your remark is in point here.

8. **In point of fact**—*as a matter of fact*. In point of fact, Pakistan does not want to be closer to India.

9. **Make a point of**—*treat as essential*. Pakistan made a point of India's nuclear test for peace as an act of hostility to her.

10. **On the point of**—*close upon; very near*. Every nation is on the point of bankruptcy.

11. **Point for point**—*exactly in all particulars*. The U.S.A. and Russia are equal point for point.

12. **Point of honour**—*question of dignity*. The only point in the conflict of two professors was a point of honour.

13. **Point of order**—*a question of rules*. Many points of order come up in the House of Common.

14. **Point of view**—*the position from which one looks at anything*. There is a great difference in our points of view.

15. **Potatoes and points**—*a feigned Irish dish, potatoes alone and herring etc. to point at*. When you do get what you long for, it is all potatoes and points.

16. **Put upon points**—*to ration by points*. Delhi has been put upon points.

17. **Stand upon points**—*to be punctilious*. Don't stand upon points when you deal with the mob.

18. **Stretch a point**—*expand a point of view*. If you seek compromise, don't stretch a point.

19. **To point**—*to the smallest detail.* You must get ready to point.

20. **To point out**—*to find out.* The stitching of the shirt is so nice that you cannot point out any defect in it.

21. **To the point**—*opposite.* Your remark is not to the point.

POISON

To poison one's ears against—*to set one against.* Never poison anyone's ears against your friends.

POKE

1. **Poke fun at**—*banter.* Please don't poke fun at me.

2. **Poke one's head**—*hold the head forward.* In judo never poke your head.

3. **Poke one's nose**—*pry.* Don't poke your nose into my affairs.

POLAR

1. **Polar forces**—*forces that act in pairs and in different directions as in magnetism.* There are polar forces at work in international diplomacy.

2. Polar *lights*—*aurora borealis or australis.* When there is no sun, there are polar lights.

POLE

1. **Pole star**—*guide or director.* A guru acts as a pole star on the road to godhead.

2. **Under bare poles**—*with all poles furled.* The ship sails under bare poles.

3. **Up the pole**—*in a predicament; drunk; crazy; in favour.* When he asked for money, I was up the pole. Mr. Mathew was up the pole on New Year Eve.

POLICE

Police trap—*a police method to detect offenders against law.* The criminals running away from town often run into police traps at crossing points.

POLISH

Polish off—*finish off; dispose of finally.* One day I hope to polish off this world of money, mice and madness.

POLITICAL

Political science—*study of Government.* You need to study political science to promote your career.

POLL

1. **At the head of a poll**—*having the greatest number of votes in an election.* Mrs. Indira Gandhi was at the head of the poll in 1980.

2. **Poll parrot**—*to parrot.* Don't poll parrot your ideas in elections.

3. **Poll tax**—*a tax of so much a head.* There was poll tax in India in Muslim rule.

PONY

Pony engine—*shunting engine.* There is a pony engine in politics. They call him "whip".

POOR

Poor man of mutton—*cold mutton broiled, especially the shoulder.* For dinner, we have poor man of mutton.

POP

1. **Pop off**—*to make of; to die; to fall asleep.* While I was working, he popped off.

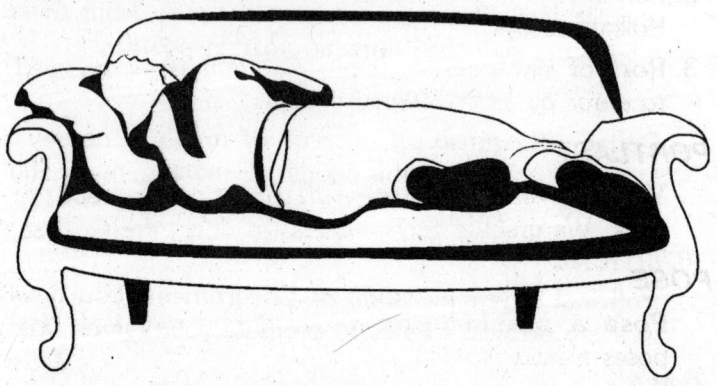

Timmy popped off last year.

2. **Pop the question**—to *make an offer of marriage.* David popped the question of his marriage.

POPE

1. **Pope's eye**—*the gland surrounded with fat in the middle of the high of an ox or sheep.* Don't eat the Pope's eye, my friend!

2. **Pope's head**—*a long-handled brush.* Clean the room with the Pope's head.

3. **Pope's nose**—*the fleshy part of a cooked bird's tail.* Let him eat the Pope's nose.

POPSY

Popsy-wopsy—*a term of endearment for a girl.* Susan is a popsy-wopsy.

PORT

1. **Port the helm**—*turn the ship to port.* They ported the helm when they sighted Bali.

2. Port of call—*where ships can call for stores and repair.* Kolkata is a port of call.

3. **Port of entry**—*port where merchandise is allowed to enter by law.* Chennai is a port of entry.

PORTLAST

Yards down a portlast—*with yards down or near the neck.* We greeted each other yards down the portlast.

POSE

Pose a problem—*set a question.* Every new day poses a new problem.

POSITIVE

Positive philosophy—*that man can have no knowledge of anything but phenomenon and that the* *knowledge of phenomena is relative, not absolute.* Science follows a positive philosophy.

POSSESS

What possess him ?—*What malign influence causes him ?*

POSSESSION

Writ of possession—*a process directing a sheriff to put a person in possession of property recovered in ejectment.* Mr. Brown obtained a writ of possession against Mr. Fisher.

POSSUM

Play possum—*play death.* The saint reported that when two beggars were playing possum, one actually died while feigning death.

POST

1. **Between you and me and the bedpost or lamppost**—in *confidence.* Between you and me and the bed-post, he is a cheat, a thug and a murderer.

2. **Poste restante**—*where letters are kept till called for.* Send my mail c/o Poste Restante, G.P.O., Mumbai.

3. **Postman's knock**—*a parlour kissing game.* Let's play postman's knock.

4. **Post-mortem examination**—*examination after death.* Murder cases are subjected to post-mortem examination.

5. **To run your head against a post**—*to go to work as if you had no eyes.* While in office, be alert and do not run your head against a post.

POT

1. **A pot or money**—*a large amount of money*. A pot of money is required for doing this job.

2. **Big pot**—*important person*. Indira Gandhi was a big pot.

3. **Go to pot**—*go to ruin*. It appears Mother India is going to pot.

4. **Keep the pot boiling**—*procure necessaries of life; keep going briskly without stop*. It is quite a big job to keep the pot boiling.

   If you want to reach office in item, keep the pot boiling.

5. **Pot belly**—*fat man*. Get away from my sight, I don't want to see your pot belly.

POTATO

1. **Small potatoes**—*anything of no great worth*. What I own are small potatoes.

2. **The clean potato**—*the right thing*. What you *said* was the clean potato.

POTENTIAL

Potential energy—the *power of doing work possessed by a body in virtue of its position*. Liza has a great potential energy.

POTTER

Potter—*to be busy in a desultory way.* What are you pottering about here?

POUND

Pound foolish—*neglecting the care of large sums in attending to little ones.* Don't be pennywise and pound foolish.

POUR

1. **It never rains but pours**—*things never happen singly.* Misfortune never rains but pours.
2. **Pouring wet**—*raining hard.* It was pouring wet the whole day.

POVERTY

Poverty-stricken—*suffering from poverty.* Poverty-stricken people don't know that poverty is power.

POWER

1. **In one's power**—*at one's mercy; within the limits of what one can do.* Pakistan is in the power of China. Your problem is not in my power.
2. **In power**—*in office.* Mr. Jackson Paul is in power.
3. **Out of power**—*out of office.* Some ministers are out of power.
4. **Power politics**—*world politics based on balance of power.* India and Pakistan are in the claws of power politics.
5. **Power that be**—*the existing ruling authorities.* The powers that be have little sympathy for the have-not sections of society.

POWWOW

Powwow—*to confer.* They powwowed at midnight.

PRACTICAL

1. **Practical joke**—*a joke that consists in action, not words usually an annoying trick.* The boys played a practical joke on their teacher by informing him that his wife had suddenly died and so declaring the school was closed on 1st April.

2. **Practical politics**—*proposals or measures that must be carried out in the near future.* India should practise practical politics.

PRAGMATIC

Pragmatic sanction—*practical decision.* Mrs. Indira Gandhi gave a pragmatic sanction to save Morarji Desai when he fasted to death.

PRAY

1. **Pray in aid**—*to call for help.* Veronica prayed in aid but her brother failed to rise to the occasion.

2. **Praying insect**—*mantis etc.* The temple swarms with praying insects.

PREACH

1. **Preach down**— *decry.* Don't preach down democracy.

2. **Preach up**—*extol.* Don't preach up dictatorship.

3. **Preaching with a view**—*preaching for elections.* In gurdwaras and mosques, temples and churches there is no preaching with a view.

PRECEDENCE

Take precedence of—*to precede in ceremonial order.*
The President takes precedence of the Prime Minister.

PREJUDICE

Without prejudice—*without bias.* Please consider the case without prejudice.

PRESENCE

Presence of mind—*power of keeping one's wits about coolness and readiness in emergency.* A nation requires great presence of mind to face an invasion from a superior power.

PRESENT

1. **At present**—*at the moment.* I can do nothing for you at present.

2. **For the present**—*for the moment; for the time being.* This money should suffice for the present.

PRESS

1. **At press**—*in the course of printing.* The book is at press.

2. **In the press**—*at press.* The paper is in the press.

3. **Go to press**—*to begin to print.* We go to press tomorrow. Our journal goes to press tomorrow.

4. **Liberty of the press**—*the right to publish books. etc. without permission of the authorities.* India enjoys liberty of the press de jure.

5. **The press**—*newspapers, journals, etc.* Government of India no longer heeds the press.

PRETTY

1. **Only pretty Fanny's way**—*only what must be expected and accepted of a person.* Coming late is only pretty Fanny's way.

2. **Pretty much**—*very nearly.* He survived death pretty much.

3. **Pretty penny**—*a large sum of money.* Marriage costs a pretty penny.

4. **Pretty-pretty**—*a knick-knack, namby-pamby.* She is a pretty-pretty lady.

5. **Sitting pretty**—*in any advantageous position.* The ruling party always sits pretty on power.

PREY

1. **Beast, bird of prey**—*hunting bird, animal.* Vulture is a bird of prey.

   Lion is a beast of prey.

2. **To fall prey to**—*become victim of.* My friend has fallen prey to liquor.

PRICE

1. **Above, beyond, price**—*so valuable that no price can be quoted.* Old documents are above price.

   Truth is beyond price.

2. **At a price**—*somewhat at a high price.* You can have your rations at a price.

3. **Every man has his price**—*every man can be won by inducements.*

4. **In great price**—*in great estimation.* Honesty is no longer in great price.

5. **Of price**—*of value.* This is a book of price.

6. **Price of money**—*rate of discounting in leading or borrowing capital.* Inflation has raised the price of money.

7. **Price of one's head**—*a reward offered for one's capture or killing.* There is a price on the head of the gang who killed Mr. Hardy.

8. **To set a price on one's head**—*to offer reward for capture.* A few years back the police had set a very heavy price on a dacoit's head.

9. **What price ?**—*What about this or that now ? What do you think of?*

10. **Without price**—*priceless; without anything to pay.* Truth is without price.

    Water here is without price.

PRICK

Prick up one's ears—*to begin to listen intently.* When I am talking to friends, don't prick up your ears, my dear wife.

PRIDE

Take a pride in—*be proud of*. A worker should take a pride in his work.

PRIG

Prig down—*to seek to beat down a price or seller*. Nobody is interested in prigging down the prices but only in prigging them up.

PRIMA

Prima donna—*the leading lady in opera*. The housewife is prima donna of the kitchen.

PRIMROSE

Primrose path—*the life of pleasure*. The upper classes follow the primrose path.

PRINCE

1. **Prince of darkness**—*Satan*. The prince of darkness rules the world today.

2. **Prince of peace**—*Christ*. The prince of peace has failed to bring peace.

PRINCIPLE

1. **First principles**—*fundamental rules*. Truth and honesty are first principles of life.

511

2. **In principle**—*so far as theory is concerned*. In principle, a man can live without food.

3. **On principle**—*on grounds of principle; for the sake of obeying principles*. On principle, you cannot go even to take a cup of tea.

4. **Principle of contradiction**—*the logical principle that a thing cannot both be and not be*. It is hard to steer clear of the principle of contradiction in politics.

5. **Principle of excluded middle**—*the principle that a thing must be one thing or its contradiction*. Capitalism and Communism follow the principle of the excluded middle.

6. **Principle of sufficient reason**—*with reasonableness*. Life is moulded on the principle of sufficient reason.

PRINTER

Printer's devil—*mistakes in printing*. You generally find the printer's devil in everything printed.

PRISCIAN

1. Priscian—*grammarian*.

2. **Break Priscian's head**—*to commit false grammar*. You can break Priscian's head but save yours.

PRIVATE

Private wrong—*an injury done to an individual in his private capacity*. The Government of India pays no compensation for private wrong.

PRIZE

Play one's prize—*engage in a match; sustain one's part*. Everybody must play his prize in life.

PRO

1. **Pro and con**—*for* and *against.* Let us discuss the pros and cons of the subject.
2. **Proing and coning**—*discussion.* The subject requires much proing and coning.
3. **Pro'd and conned**—*discussed.* The subject was pro'd and conned.

PROBLEM

1. **Problem child**—*a child different from others* and *difficult to manage.* There should be a separate school for problem children.
2. **Problem play**—*one presenting a social or moral problem.* Poll is a problem play.

PROMOTION

Be on one's promotion—*likeness in the colour of animals to their natural surroundings tending to prevent them from being seen by their enemies.* The Defence Services often use protective colouration in war.

PROTECTIVE

Protective colouration—*to have right or hope of promotion; to be on good behaviour with a view to promotion.* Every government servant is on protective colouration.

PROUD

1. **Do one proud**—*treat one sumptuously.* The Prime Minister of India did the King of Nepal proud.
2. **Proud as a peacock**—*very much proud.* The head of the department of this institution is as proud as a peacock.

3. **Proud-pied**—*gorgeously variegated*. Dussehra procession is proud-pied.

PROVE

Exception proves the rule—*the making of an exception proves that the rule holds good.*

PROXIMATE

1. **Proximate cause**—*a cause which immediately precedes the effect.* A hand-grenade was the proximate cause of L.N. Mishra's death.
2. **Proximate object**—*immediate object.* Money is the proximate object for the modern man.

PRUNES

Prunes and prism—*part of a formula for setting the lips "serviceable in the formation of a demeanour".*

PSYCHIC

Psychic force—*a power not physical or mechanical, causing spiritualistic phenomena.* There is a psychic force which determines human destiny before and after death.

PSYCHOLOGICAL

Psychological moment—*when the mind can be best worked upon; the nick of time.* He asked for money at the psychological moment when he saw my purse.

PUBLIC

In public—*in open view; among people; in society.* Political trials must be conducted in public.

PUDDING

Pudding time—*dinner time*. We will discuss it at the pudding time.

PUFF

1. **Puffed out**—*quite out of breath*. When I met him, he was quite puffed out.

2. **Puffed up**—*swollen with pride*. If we have won a tournament, let us not be puffed up.

3. *Puff-puff*—*railway engine or train*. We shall travel by puff-puff.

PULL

1. **Pull a face**—*to grimace*. If you have lost a purse, don't pull a face.

2. **Pull apart**—*bring as under by pulling*. The bridge was pulled apart.

3. **Pull caps**—*scuffle*. Let us not pull caps in public.

4. **Pull devil pull baker**—*do your best, both ways*. Pull devil pull baker, you won't get me down to agree with you.

5. **Pull down**—*demolish; reduce in health*. The building was pulled down.

6. **Pull for**—*row for*. Let us pull for the Royal Garden.

7. **Pull off**—*carry through successfully*. Engineering college pulled off a war with Science college.

8. **Pull oneself together**—*collect one's faculties*. Pull yourself together and face the foe.

9. **Pull one's leg**—*flatter*. Please don't pull my leg for a petty favour.

10. **Pull one's weight**—*do one's full share of work*. In the family everyone must pull his weight.

11. **Pull round**—*bring or come round to health or consciousness*. She pulled round after long illness.
The doctor pulled her round after frenzy.

12. **Pull the long bow**—*boast*. Don't pull the long bow when dealing with an honest man.

13. **Pull through**—*manage to overcome a difficulty*. Somehow we pull through this period of acute shortages.

14. **Pull up**—*stop; reprimand; tighten reins; gain ground*. The horse pulled up at my door.
The President pulled up the Secretary for negligence.

15. **Pull up stakes**—*prepare to leave a place*. I am pulling up my stakes in Delhi.

16. **To pull about**—*to treat roughly*. Will you please stop pulling about that child's leg?

17. **To pull on**—*to live*. It is difficult to pull on with this meagre amount, now-a-days.

PULSE

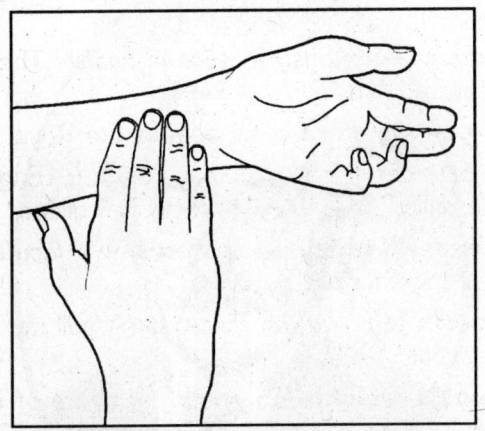

To feel one's pulse—*to measure heart-beat, feelings, etc.* The rich people cannot feel the pulse of the poor.

PUNCH

Punch-drunk—*stupefied by blows*. The pickpocket was punch-drunk.

PUP

1. **In pup**—*pregnant*. The woman is in pup.
2. **Sell a pup**—*swindle*. He sold his father a pup.

PURE

1. **Pure reason**—*reason without any mixture or sensibility*. The world is not run by pure reason.

517

2. **Pure science**—*science apart from practical applications.* Einstein devoted himself to pure science. Pure science is the mother of all scientific applications.

PURPLE

Purple emperor—*a large British butterfly, most richly coloured.* Let us have a purple emperor than a dictator in our country.

PURPOSE

1. **Of purpose**—*of use.* This is of no purpose to me.
2. **Of set purpose**—*intentionally.* He pushed you of set purpose.

3. **To good purpose**—*with good effect*. He did the job to good purpose.

4. **To the purpose**—*to the point*. Please speak to the purpose.

PURSE

1. **Privy purse**—*royal private expenses*. India has stopped paying privy purses to princes.

2. **Public purse**—*nation's finances*. The ministers must not dip their hands deep in the public purse.

3. **Purse-proud**—*puffed up with money*. Do not be a purse-proud fellow.

4. **To put up a purse**—*to give a purse as prize*. Albert has put up a purse in his school on getting first position in the class.

PUSH

1. **At a push**—*when circumstances urgently require*. He gave me money at a push.

2. **Push off**—*row off the shore*. They pushed off in a boat.

3. **Push one's fortune**—*busy oneself in seeking a fortune*. The youth pushes his fortune.

4. **Push out**—*row towards open sea*. They pushed out at night.

5. **Push the bottle**—*take one's liquor and pass the bottle round*. No business can be conducted today without pushing the bottle.

6. **To give one the push**—*to dismiss from service*. The manager of your company has given the push to the new clerk.

7. **To make a push**—*to try*. There is no harm in making a push in the examination.

8. **To push through**—*to bring to confusion*. Please do not push through your statement.

9. **To push up**—*to give promotion*. John has not been pushed up in his seven years of service.

PUT

1. **Put across**—*to carry out successfully*. The Prime Minister put across the bill for the abolition of privy purses.

2. **Put an end to or a stop to**—*to cause to discontinue*. We should put an end to corruption in high places.

   We should put a stop to thuggery everywhere.

3. **Put away**—*renounce; kill; set aside; imprison; eat*. The king put away the throne.

   The rebel was put away.

   He put away Rs, 50,000 for the wedding.

   Let us put away ice cream.

4. **Put back**—*push backward; delay; repulse*. Inflation has put back all planning.

   Windstorm put back my departure.

5. **Put by**—*set aside*. Put by something for a rainy day.

6. **Put down**—crush; *killed*. The rebellion was put down.
7. **Put for**—*make an attempt to gain*. He put for the first position in the examination.
8. **Put forth**—*extend; propose; to publish*. He put forth a new proposal for work.
9. **Put in an appearance**—*appear*. Mathews put in an appearance at the marriage.
10. **Put in mind**—*remind*. Please put me in mind about our promise.
11. **Put off**—*postpone*. Do not put off till tomorrow what you can do today.
12. **Put on**—*wear*. You look very beautiful when you put on this green saree.

13. **Put out**—*to expel; to extinguish; place at interest; expand; publish; offend; exert; dislocate; produce; go out to sea; leave port.* Please put out the fire.

14. **Put over**—*carry through successfully; impress an audience; impose; pass off.* He put over the job beautifully.

15. **Put through**—*bring to an end.* The campaign was put through successfully.

16. **Put to death**—*kill.* The murderer was put to death.

17. **Put to sea**—*begin a voyage.* The ship was put to sea.

18. **Put two and two together**—*draw a conclusion from various factors.* The detectives put two and two together.

19. **Put up**—*reside; put aside.* Where are you putting up ?

20. **Put upon**—*take undue advantage of.* Please don't put upon your father.

21. **Stay put**—*remain passively in the position assigned.* Please stay put till the wind of inflation blows over.

22. **To put up with**—*to bear.* I can not put up with your silly arguments.

PYRRHIC

Pyrrhic victory—*victory gained at too great a cost.* Britain won a Pyrrhic victory in the Second World War. It lost the empire.

Q-BOAT

Q-boat—*a naval vessel disguised as a merchant ship or fishing boat to deceive and destroy submarines.* India has yet no Q-boat. Or has she not?

QUAGMIRE

In a quagmire—*in a slippery and dangerous position.* Indian economy is in a quagmire.

QUAIL

Quail-pipe—*a whistle for alluring quails into a trap.* Indira won 1980 elections with the quail-pipe of "Stable Government."

QUALITY

1. **People of quality**—*upper classes.* You must learn to move with people of quality.
2. **Quality test**—*test applied to industrial and consumer products.* Quality test will increase our exports.
3. **The quality of a defect**—*good mixed with evil.* His rude speech with a good heart is the quality of a defect.

QUALMS

Qualms of conscience—*uneasy conscience.* Corrupt people suffer from qualms of conscience which they ignore.

QUANTIFICATION

Quantification of the predicate—*the attachment of a sign of quantity of the predicate*. Your demand of money requires quantification of the predicate.

QUANTITY

Pure quantity—*numbers*. The pure quantity of man was very poor in the whole gathering.

QUARREL

1. **Quarrel with one's bread and butter**—*to act in a way prejudicial to one's means of subsistence*. Quite often I have quarrelled with my bread and butter.
2. **To pick up a quarrel**—*to seek occasion for fighting*. Robert and Michael are always on the look-out for picking up a quarrel with their class-mates.
3. **To take up a quarrel**—*to settle a dispute*. Even the U.N. is unable to take up a quarrel of India and Pakistan over the "Kashmir issue".
4. **Find quarrel in a straw**—*be captious*. Your habit of finding quarrel in a straw is no good.

QUART

Quart and pierce—*practise between fencers*. The fencers practise quart and pierce.

QUARTER

1. **At close quarters**—*in very near proximity; hand to hand*. In the battle of Waterloo they fought at close quarters.
2. **From all quarters**—*from all sides*. He is deprived of a service from all quarters.
3. **Keep a bad quarter**—*make a disturbance*. Please don't make a bad quarter here.

4. **Keep good quarter**—*keep good watch or good order.* The student should keep good quarter.
5. **To take one's quarter**—*to lodge.* We are going to take up our quarter in Sydney.

QUEECHY

Queechy-squeachy—*boggy, sickly.* Politics is queechy-squeachy.

QUEANY

Queany (quinie)—*a saucy girl.* Queany quinie makes the modern world go topsy-turvy.

QUEEN

1. **Queen Anne's dead**—*that is old news.* When I told him about yesterday's accident, he replied, "Queen Anne is dead."
2. **Queen mother**—*mother of ruler.* The queen mother should always guide the ruler on proper lines.
3. **Queen of grace**—*Virgin Mary.* Worship the queen of grace and she will bless you to succeed in your mission.
4. **Queen of heaven**—*Virgin Mary.* Jesus Christ was born of the queen of heaven.

5. **Queen of the May**—*May Queen*. Yuvette was chosen queen of the May.

6. **Queen of the meadow**—*meadow sweet*. Let us look for queen of the meadow.

7. **Queen's tobacco pipe**—*a kiln in London for bringing contraband goods (till 1891)*. Why don't we have Queen's tobacco pipe in India ? This alone will end smuggling.

QUEER

1. **In queer street**—in *debt*. Throughout his life, his father lived in queer street.

2. **Queer street**—*the feigned abode of persons in debt or other difficulties*. Johnson is a resident of the queer street.

3. **Queer the pitch**—*make the place of performance unavailable; to spoil one's chances*. Dr. Paul queered the pitch for David.

4. **Shove the queer**—*pass bad money*. Children are employed to shove the queer.

QUENCH

Quench the thirst—*drink water or liquor.* He needs money to quench his thirst.

QUERY

To suppress query—*to hide facts*. Please make us known of the true statement and not suppress query.

QUEST

1. **In quest of**—*in search of.* In quest of his son, he met with a car accident and died on the spot.

2. **To quest about**—*to go in search.* What have you done to quest about ?

QUESTION

1. **In question**—*under consideration.* The entire set-up is in question.

2. **Make question**—*demur.* If he steals money, why don't you make question ?

3. **Oblique question**—*indirect question.* India

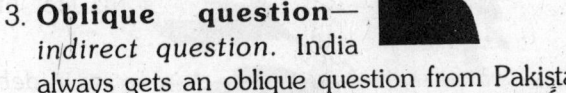

always gets an oblique question from Pakistan.

4. **Out of question**—*doubtless.* Out of question, everyday who can steal is stealing in the government.

5. **Out of the question**—*not to be thought of.* That I should beg food is out of the question, I can very well live without it.

6. **Question mark**—*doubt; suspicion.* The new rich class raises a question mark.

7. **To call in question**—*to challenge.* Can you accept the call in question given by him.

8. **To put a question to**—*to ask something.* Every student is at liberty to put a question to his teacher.

QUICK

1. **Quick trick**—*a card that would win a trick.* Money-making is a quick trick.

2. **Quick witted**—*intelligent.* The quick witted man of the class has died.

3. **The quick and the dead**—*the living and the dead*. The quick and the dead have no uniformity.

4. **To cut to the quick**—*to hurt bitterly*. Your taunts are cutting to the quick, please stop speaking.

5. **To the quick**—*to the heart*. I am touched to the quick by your misbehaviour.

QUICKLE

Quickle-quackle—*the sound of a cock*. If you fail to do your duty, don't quickle-quackle.

QUIET

1. **On the quiet**—*clandestinely; unobtrusively*. Many men have entered the U.S.A. on the quiet.

2. **To have a quiet dig**—*to taunt gently*. The wise is one who has a quiet dig in society.

QUIFF

Quiff-quaff—*cosmetics and liquor*. Modern sophistication is quiff-quaff.

QUILL

1. **Drive a quill**—*write; be a clerk*. He drives a quill.
2. **Quill driver**—*writer*. I am a quill driver.

QUIP

To make quips—*utter sarcastic remarks*. Will you please stop making quips now?

QUIT

1. **Cry quits**—*declare oneself even with another, and so satisfied*. Pakistan does not cry quits with India.
2. **Double or quits**—*the alternative; left to chance, of doubling or cancelling payment*. They played double or quits on cards.

3. **To quit oneself well**—*to behave well*. He did not quit himself well in yesterday's party.

QUITS

To be on quits with—*on equal terms*. They are both on quits with one another.

QUIXOTIC

Quixotic—*extravagantly romantic*. Politics is no longer quixotic but rather pragmatic.

RABBLE

Rabble rout—*the mob.* Democracy is the rule of the rabble rout.

RABEL

Rabelaisian—extravagantly *humorous; robustly outspoken.* There are Rabelaisian remarks in Parliament.

RABID

1. **Rabid democrat**—*unreasoning democrat.* No one likes the rabid democrats.
2. **Rabid hate**—*great hate.* He has of late developed a rabid hate for his wife.

RACE

Race hatred—*animosity accompanying difference of race.* Race hatred is one of the greatest causes of quarrel in the world.

RACK

1. **On the rack**—*in distress.* His failing business has resulted in going whole of his family on the rack.
2. **Rack and ruin**—*a stage of neglect and collapse.* If you let out a house for rent, you must be ready for rack and ruin.

3. **Rack one's brains**—*strain one's memory.* If you don't remember my name, please don't rack your brains.

4. **To go to rack and ruins**—*complete destruction.* In war many nations go to rack and ruins.

RACKET

Stand the racket—*endure the strain; take the consequences or the responsibility; pay expenses.* If you enter the rat race, you must stand the racket.

It you organize a picnic, who will stand the racket?

RADICAL

1. **Radical change, reform or cure**—*fundamental; right from the root.* Unless a radical change takes place in the country, the Government will not improve.

2. **Radical error**—*fundamental mistake.* Such radical error will ruin your career one day.

3. **Radical idea**—*basic principles.* Mahatma Gandhi preached the radical idea of non-violence.

RAFF

Riff-Raff—*vagabond; common unreliable person.* Keep clear of the riff-raff in organizing this fun fair.

RAG

1. **In rags**—*in torn clothes.* When Rajesh returned home, he was all in rags.

2. **Lose one's rag**—*lose one's temper.* If you have lost your coat, still don't lose your rag.

3. **Rag bag**—*a dirty untidy woman.* Your housemaid is a rag bag.

4. **Rag money**—People have less faith in God than paper money in rag money.

5. **Rag tag and bobtail**—*riff-raff*. Every political gathering is stuffed with rag tag and bobtail.

RAGE

All the rage—*all the fashion*. Mini skirts are all the rage now-a-days.

RAID

Raid the market—*derange prices artificially for future gain*. Blackmarketeers quite often raid the market through monopoly purchases.

RAIL

Off the rail—*disorganised*. Do not disturb me, my mind is off the rail now-a-days.

RAILWAY

Railway stitch—*a name for various quickly worked stitches*. You can't mend a mini skirt with a railway stitch.

1. **It never rains but pours**—*events usually happen together*. When misfortune comes, it never rains but pours.
2. **Rainbow dressing**—*a gaudy display of flags*. When an important person comes to Delhi, there is a rainbow dressing in Connaught Place.
3 **Rainbow-tinted**—*many-coloured*. Youth live in rainbow-tinted castles.

4. **Rain doctor**—*rain maker.* In case of famine, call a rain doctor.

5. **Rain or shine**—*in small weathers.* He is very strict on his promise; don't worry, he will come here rain or shine.

6. **Rain print**—*a small pit made by a rain drop.* A rain print may be preserved in a rock.

7. **Rainy day**—*a possible future time of need; bad days.* You must put something by against a rainy day.

   We should always have something for the rainy day.

8. **Right as rain**—*perfectly in order.* Everything here is right as rain.

9. **To rain cats and dogs**—*to rain very heavily.* It is raining cats and dogs for the last four days.

RAISE

1. **Raise a siege**—*put an end to a siege.* If General Aurora had not raised the siege, the people in the city would have starved.

2. **Raised pastry pie**—*pastry, pie with the support of a dish at the side.* Let us have a bit of this raised pastry. Let us have a bit of this raised pie.

3. **Raise money**—*to get money by pawning.* He raised money by pawning his gold ring.

4. **Raise one's hat**—*to salute*. Let us raise our hat to martyrs.

5. **Raise the market upon**—*to bring about a rise in prices to the disadvantage of*. The industrialists raise the market upon the common purchasers.

6. **Raise the roof**—*make a prodigious din*. If you take any action against the students, they will raise the roof.

7. **Raise the wind**—*get together the necessary money by any shift; to procure money for some purpose*. The Government is raising the wind to meet its budget.

   The Government is raising the wind for the 'Jawahar Lal Nehru Memorial Fund'.

8. **To raise from the dead**—*to restore to life*. The doctor was able to raise the baby from the dead.

9. **To raise hell**—*to create confusion*. You are always raising a hell for us.

10. **To raise the banner**—*to lead*. Who will raise the banner ?

RAKE

Rake up—*revive*. Please do not rake up old troubles.

RAM

To ram into—*to make and learn by force*. You cannot ram education into your children.

RANGE

Range oneself—*take side*. Don't range yourself against the Prime Minister.

RANK

1. **Rank and file**—*common soldier; ordinary people*. Rank and file does not care who wins the war.

2. **Rank with**—*be of the same standard*. Pandit Nehru ranked with the top dignitaries of the world.

3. **Take rank of**—*take precedence of*. The President takes rank of the Prime Minister.

RANSOM

1. **Hold to ransom**—*to retain until a ransom shall be paid; to hold up to gain a concession*. The dacoits held his son to ransom for Rs. 20,000 only.

2. **Put to ransom**—*to offer to release for ransom*. Pakistan put the spies to ransom.

The hijackers put the aeroplane to ransom.

RAP

1. **Not worth a rap**—*not worth even a half penny; useless*. The old man is not worth a rap.

2. **Rap on the knuckles**—*a nice beating*. The chief was given a rap on the knuckles by the police but to no avail.

RAPTURE

To go into raptures—*to drive to extreme delight*. After seeing the film all the spectators went into raptures.

RARE

Rare earth—*elements difficult to separate*. Greatness is made of rare earth.

RAT

1. **Rat rhyme**—*a bit of doggerel*. The youth is fond of singing a rat rhyme.

2. **Smell a rat**—*have a suspicion of something afoot*. When something is amiss, you can smell a rat.

RATE

1. **At any rate**—*any how*. I must get this job done at any rate.
2. **At the rate of**—*at the speed of*. The car is running at the rate of 30 km per hour.

RATHER

Rather better than—*somewhat in excess*. He is earning rather better than his labour.

RAW

1. **Raw deal**—*harsh inequitable treatment*. The labourers received a raw deal after the strike was called off.
2. **Raw material**—*that out of which something is made*. The youth are the raw material for future leadership.
3. **Raw-spirits**—*strong drinks*. Do not indulge in raw-spirits.
4. **Raw youth**—*inexperienced*. Do not appoint a raw youth in your company; he will not be of much use to you.
5. **Touch one in raw**—*wound one's feeling*. Today's speech of the Principal has touched every student in raw.

RAY

Ray of hope—*slight hope*. If you have even a ray of hope, you should sit for the examination.

RAZOR

Razor-edge—*a dangerous position*. Our country is passing through a razor-edge these days.

RAZZLE

Razzle-dazzle—*a rowdy frolic or spree*. Nauchandi fair is a razzle-dazzle.

REACH

Reach-me-down—*readymade*. Get me a pair of reach-me-down suits.

READ

1. **Read a riddle**—*to solve it*. Can you read this riddle?
2. **Read between the lines**—*to detect a meaning not expressed*. To get at the truth, read this letter between the lines.

3. **Read off**—*to take a reading from an instrument.* Please read off the thermometer.

4. **Read one's meaning**—*comprehend.* Please read the meaning of this book.

5. **Read up**—*amass knowledge by reading.* He read up all the Vedas.

READY

1. ***Ready-to-eat***—*cooked.* Let us have ready-to-eat food for picnic.

2. **Ready-to-wear**—*readymade.* Ready-to-wear clothes are getting popular day by day.

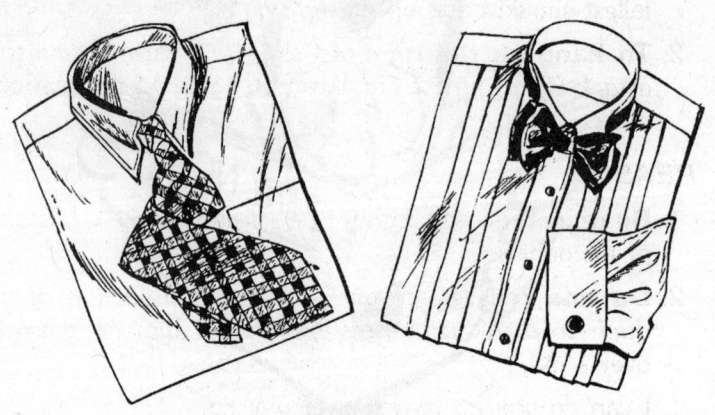

REAL

1. **Real image**—*one through which rays actually pass capable of being projected on a screen.* A film is made of real images.

2. **Really and truly**—*positively.* Really and truly, we shall be able to complete the job by evening.

REAP

1. **To reap the fruit of**—*to enjoy the consequences of*. You will have to reap the fruits of your doings.

2. **To reap where one has not sown**—*to profit by others' toil*. In politics, many became lucky of reaping where they have not sown.

3. **To sow wind and reap whirlwind**—*the result of bad actions is necessarily bad*. When you are sowing wind you will naturally reap whirlwind only.

REAR

1. **Bring up the rear**—*to come last*. In a march the tallest should bring up the rear.

2. **To hang on the rear of**—*to follow with a view to attack*. The Chinese are always hanging on the rear of India.

REASON

1. **By reason of**—*on account of*. He succeeded by reason of his genius.

2. **Do one reason**—*to give one the satisfaction of a duel; to drink without shirking*. Do him no reason over a girl.

   I can do you no reason over whisky.

3. **No reason but**—*no reason for being otherwise*. There is no reason but you have to do it.

4. **Principle of sufficient reason**—that *nothing happens without a sufficient reason, why it should be as it is and not otherwise*. The principle of sufficient reason must be applied to life on all occasions.

5. **Pure reason**—*reason absolutely independent of experience*. Pure food and pure reason are unavailable now-a-days.

RECEDE

Recede from—*withdraw*. The stand taken by us is such that if we recede from it, we shall be insulted very much.

RECK

What reck? —*What does it matter?*

RECKON

1. **Reckon with**—*to call to account*. It is high time that you should reckon with your manager or else he will deceive you one day.
2. **The day of reckoning**—*the day of judgment*. The criminal absented himself from the court on the day of reckoning.
3. **To reckon on**—*to depend*. You can easily reckon on his work.

RECOLLECT

Recollected terms—*variously explained as known by heart, picked, studied, wanting spontaneity*. Science is full of recollected terms.

RECORD

1. **Beat or break the record**—*to outdo the highest achievement yet recorded*. She has broken the high jump record.
2. **Matter of record**—*established as a fact*. You cannot deny this matter of record.
3. **Off the record**—*not for publication*. The greatest bit of news is off the record.

4. **Recording angel**—*an angel supposed to record every good and bad deed committed by a man.* Think of the recording angel before you kill your conscience.

RECOVER

1. **Recover the wind of**—*to gain an advantage over.* A professor cannot recover the wind of a politician.

2. **To recover one's senses**—*to regain consciousness.* He has recovered his senses after three days.

RED

1. **Don't care a red cent**—*don't care at all.* I don't care a red cent for you.

2. **In the red**—*overdrawn at the bank; in debt.* Robert is in the red.

3. **Red cent**—*a cent.* I have not got a red cent in my pocket.

4. **Red-handed**—*at the spot.* The manager was caught red-handed while being bribed.

5. **Red light**—*a danger signal; a brothel.* Beware of the red light over there.

6. **Red rag**—*the tongue; a cause of infuriation.* Keep your red rag under control.

   Hunger is quite often a red rag.

7. **Red tape**—*official formality.* It is high time that red tapism should disappear at higher levels.

8. **See red**—*to become furious; to thirst for blood.* When the mother called him home, the boy saw red.

REED

A broken reed—*an unreliable person.* You cannot depend upon him, he is simply a broken reed.

REEL

1. **Off the reel**—*in uninterrupted course of succession; without stop or hesitation.* Prime Minister Vajpayee delivered a dozen speeches off the reel.

2. **Reel off**—*to give out with rapidity or fluency.* He reeled off a great oration.

REFERENCE

With reference to—*apropos; in connection with.* With reference to your postcard of today, we have despatched the goods by rail.

REFLECT

To reflect upon—*to affect.* Your laziness reflects upon your health.

REFUGE

To take refuge—*to find shelter.* Till you get a suitable accommodation, you can take refuge at our place.

REGARD

1. **In regard of**—*in view of; with respect to; in comparison with.* He stopped work in regard of his falling health.

2. **In this regard**—*in this respect.* If you need money, in this regard I can do a bit for you.

REIN

1. **Reinforced concrete**—*concrete strengthened by embedded steel bars.* You need a character of reinforced concrete to face current economic difficulties.

2. **Take the reins**—*take the control.* John took the reins of the factory after the death of his father.

3. **To give rein**—*to allow free play; to apply no check to.* Please give free rein to your emotions here.

4. **To rein one's anger**—*to control one's anger.* Please rein your anger if you want to work here.

RELATION

In relation to—*as compared with.* In relation to Tom, Alan is quite weak in his studies.

RELATIVITY

Relativity of knowledge—*the doctrine that the nature and extent of our knowledge is determined not merely by the qualities of the objects known, but necessarily by the conditions of our cognitive powers.* Relativity of knowledge creates political differences in the world.

RELEGATE

To relegate to the past—*forget*. We can never relegate to the past the partition of our country.

RELIEVE

To relieve one of—*to deprive one*. The thief relieved him of his watch.

RELY

To rely upon—*to depend*. One can never rely upon the faithfulness of his wife.

REMEDY

1. **No remedy**—*of necessity*. No remedy, you have to eat.
2. **What remedy**—*what help is there for it?*

RENDER

1. **Render into**—*translate*. The foreign ambassador's whole speech was rendered into Hindustani afterwards.
2. **Render to**—*give in return*. Can you render this book for two rupees?

For rent—*to let*. This house is not for rent.

REPUTED

Reputed owner—*a person who has to all appearances the title of property*. I am the reputed owner of the house I live in.

RESERVATION

Mental reservation—*the holding back of some word or phrase which is necessary to convey fully the meaning really intended by a speaker*. Our editors write political speeches with mental reservations.

RESPECT

To pay one's respects—*to compliment*. Please pay my respects to your elders.

RESPONSIBILITY

1. **Sense of responsibility**—*to feel that one has to perform any duty assigned to him*. Sense of responsibility is realized by a very few in our country.

2. **To shoulder the responsibility**—*to be responsible for*. I am prepared to shoulder the responsibility *of* educating you.

REST

1. **For the rest**—*as regards other matters*. Give me money today, for the rest, we will discuss later.

2. **Set up one's rest**—*make one's final stake; take a resolution; take up abode*. We set up our rest on fighting it out.

I will set up my rest here.

RETAIN

Retaining wall—*a wall to prevent a bank from slipping down*. America has failed to act as retaining wall of democracy in the world.

RETARD

To retard the progress of—*to check*. The death of his father was responsible for retarding his progress of studies.

RETRACT

To retract one's promise—*to go back on one's word*. Come what may, one must not retract from one's promise.

RETRUN

By return of post—*by the next post leaving in the opposite direction*. Please reply to this letter by the return of post.

REVERSE

Reverse the charges—*charge a telephone call to the one who receives it instead of the caller*. Please reverse the charges on this call.

RHYME

1. **Rhyme to death**—*to pester with rhymes*. Please don't rhyme me to death.

2. **Without rhyme or reason**—*without either sound or sense*. The servant attacked the master without rhyme or reason.

RID

1. **Get rid of**—*to save oneself from*. You cannot get rid of beggars.

2. **Rid way**—*make progress; cover ground*. You cannot rid way fast in life.

RIDDLE

To be riddled with—*full of*. The whole house was riddled with nice men.

RIDE

1. **Ride and tie**—*to ride and go on foot alternately; each tying up a horse or leaving the bicycle on the roadside and walking on*. Four of us rode and tied a hundred miles in ten hours.

2. **Ride down**—*to overtake by riding*. The constable rode down the pickpocket.

3. **Ride for a fall**—*to court disaster*. Stanley went to Sweden to ride for a fall.

4. **Ride to hounds**—*to take part in fox-hunting*. Our princes no longer ride to hounds.

5. **Ride up**—*to work up out of position*. He was rode up by his rivals.

6. **Riding the fair**—*the ceremony of opening a fair by procession*. I look part in riding the Royal Fair.

7. **To ride a whirlwind**—*to direct a mighty force*. The Chief Minister is riding a whirlwind for establishing a new factory for his sons.

8. **To ride on the shoulder of**—*to use the power and influence of*. If you ride on the shoulder of your brother, you can get this job at any moment.

RIGHT

1. **By rights**—*rightfully; if all were right.* We can live in the world only by rights.

2. **Do one right**—*to do one justice; to keep pace with in drinking; to drink the health of.* I hope judge will do you right.

3. **Have a right**—*to be entitled to.* You have a right in this property.

4. **In one's own right**—*by absolute and personal rights.* He is a minister in his own right.

5. **In one's own right mind**—*sane.* I hope you were in your right mind when you gave away your money in charity.

6. **In right of**—*in virtue of.* He was honoured in right of reward he won.

7. **In the right**—*right.* A man of truth and justice is always in the right.

8. **Put, set, to rights**—*to set in order.* Shivaji set the country to rights.

9. **Right away**—*straight-away; without delay.* I need some money right away to reach Mumbai.

10. **Right down**—*plainly.* Please let me know your mind right down.

11. **Right of entry**—*legal right to enter a place.* You have no right of entry here.

12. **Right off**—*without delay*. Please go home right off.

13. **Right of way**—*right of public to cross a place*. Right of way is restricted here.

14. **Right out**—*outright*. He bought the house right out.

15. **Send to the right-about**—*to dismiss summarily, or force to retreat*. The Minister sent the Secretary right-about.

RING

1. **Hold, keep, the ring**—*to watch a fight and keep others from interfering*. While wrestlers combat, someone must hold the ring.

2. **Ring a bell**—*to begin to arouse a memory*. This picture rings a bell in my brain.

3. **Ring in, out, year**—Ring in the new year.

4. **Ring-leader**—*the chief, used in bad sense.* Who is the ring-leader of this gang ?

5. **Ring the bell**—*achieve a great success.* Rosie rang the bell in her school ?

6. **Ring true**—*sound genuine.* Your statement rings true.

7. **Ring up**—*summon by bell or telephone.* If you are in any trouble, please ring me up.

8. **To make rings round one**—*to defeat a person completely in a competition, etc.* Mr. Fisher made rings round Mr. Hardy during the last election.

RIOT

To run riot—*to lose all control.* The Principal has run riot on his teachers in the school.

RISE

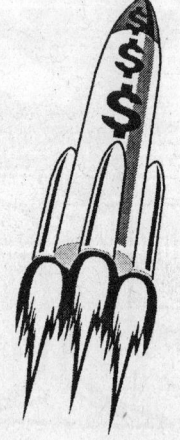

1. **Give rise to**—*to cause to happen.* Dishonesty gives rise to corruption.

2. **One's soul to rise against**—*to find it intolerable.* Your statement is merely your soul's rise against mine.

3. **On the rise**—*in the process of increasing.* Prices are on the rise.

4. **Rise from the ranks**—*to work one's way up from a low position in life.* Abraham Lincoln rose from the ranks.

5. **Rise to the occasion**—*prove equal to an emergency.* Mrs. Indira Gandhi rose to the occasion during the 1980 mid-term elections.

6. **Take a rise out of**—*make a sport of.* They took a rise out of the boy.

7. **Take rise**—*originate.* Mathematics took rise in India.

8. **The rise of**—*more than.* What we say is the rise of what we do.

9. **The rising generation**—*the young people.* The rising generation of our country must be prepared to work hard.

10. **To get a rise**—*to get promotion.* He is likely to get a rise in office.

ROACH

As sound as a roach—*perfectly sound.* Your son, madam, is as sound as a roach in the hostel here.

ROAD

1. **In or out of one's road**—*in or out of one's way.* Please don't stand in my road to progress.
I am positively out of your road.

2. **On the road**—*travelling.* Guru Nanak, even in those very old times, was always on the road in and out of India.

3. **Take the road**—*set off; depart.* Mr. Edward has taken the road to Mumbai.

4. **Take to the road**—*become a highway man.* If you cannot take a road, don't take to the road.

5. **The rules of the road**—*etiquette.* If you want to rise in life, you must learn the rules of the road.

ROCK

1. **Off one's rocker**—*out of one's mind.* Dr. Paul appears out of his rocker.

2. **On the rocks**—*no money.* A clerk is generally on the rocks during the last days of the month.

ROD

1. **Rod in pickle**—*punishment in reserve.* For erring politicians, there is the rod in pickle.

2. **Kiss the rod**—*accept punishment with submission.* The members of society are kissing the rod for their folly of having voted undeserving people to executive committee.

3. **Make something a rod for one's back**—*to prepare trouble for oneself.* By going there, you made something a rod for your back.

ROLL

1. **Rolled gold**—*metal coated with gold and rolled very thin.* Many rich ladies wear ornaments of rolled gold.

2. **Rolling stone gathers no moss**—*a man wandering from place to place cannot grow rich.*

3. **Roll of honour**—*list of those who have died for the country.* The complete Roll of Honour during the Kargil war is yet to be published by the Government.

4. **Roll up**—to *assemble; arrive.* They rolled up at dawn.

5. **To strike off the rolls**—*to debar from practising on account of dishonesty.* The Chartered Accountants Association has struck off the rolls Messrs. A.B. & Co.

ROLY

Roly-poly—*a round podgy-person.* Nobody likes a roly-poly in the house.

ROMAN

Roman candle—*a firework discharging a succession of white, or coloured stars.* The children burn Roman candles on Diwali night.

ROME

1. **Do in Rome as the Romans do**—*adopt yourself to your surrounding.*

2. **Rome was not built in a day**—*encouragement to the faint hearted.*

ROOM

Room-ridden—*confined to one's room.* The old man is room-ridden.

ROOST

1. **Come home to roost**—*recoil on oneself.* Our sins always come home to roost.

2. **Go to roost**—*retire for the night.* I am in the habit of going to roost early.

3. **To rule the roost**—*be master.* The old man rules the roost in our home.

ROOT

1. **Root and branch**—*the whole of it without any omission or exception.* Will you please do the job root and branch ?

2. **Strike, take, a root**—*to become established.* If you pursue an idea diligently, it will take a root.

3. **The root of the matter**—*its base.* Unless we are convinced of the facts of the root of the matter, we cannot proceed further.

4. **To strike roots**—*to get established.* Now we have struck roots of our business fully.

ROPE

1. **Give one rope (to hang himself)**—*to allow a person full freedom to defeat his own ideas.* Michael is giving James rope.

2. **On the high ropes**—*elated; arrogant.* Stanley was on the high ropes when he was elected as the President of the club.

3. **Rope in**—*bring in, enlist.* The politician has roped in many big guns to fight for his election.

4. **Ropes of sand**—*a bond with no cohesion.* The Arab nations are bound with ropes of sand.

557

5. **To know the rope**—*to become familiar with all tricks.* It is very difficult to understand the ropes of the British policy.

ROSE

1. **A bed of roses**—*a pleasant experience.* Life is not a bed of roses.

2. **Path strewn with roses**—*life of delight.* Path strewn with roses is available for the very rich only.

3. **To be not all roses**—*not to be pure enjoyment.* Everything in the world is not all roses.

4. **To gather roses**—*to seek pleasure.* Please stop the habit of gathering roses and do something solid.

5. **Under the rose**—in *confidence.* Can you please tell me the whole scandal under the rose ?

ROT

Left to rot—*left to suffer.* By his going to Dubai, his whole family has been left to rot.

ROTTEN

Rotten (Bad) egg—*a useless person.* The manager has been instructed to check out all the rotten eggs from the office.

ROUGH

1. **Cut up rough**—*ride rough-shod over; set at nought; domineer without consideration.* The Ministers must not cut up the people rough.

2. **Rough in**—*to sketch in roughly.* Rough in the whole story.

3. **Rough on**—*hard luck for; pressing hard upon.* Don't rough on the lad.

4. **Rough out**—*shape out roughly.* Please rough out the news story.

ROUND

1. **A good round sum**—*a large sum of money.* The Government is spending a good round sum on planning only.

2. **In round numbers**—*roughly; approximately.* There are billion stars in round numbers.

3. **Round dance**—*dance in a ring; a dance in which couple revolve round each other.* They had a round dance in Rosy's marriage.

4. **Round dealing**—*honest and straightforward.* A businessman with round dealings is always successful in life.

5. **Round off**—*finish off neatly.* The wedding was rounded off with a hearty tea.

6. **Round on**—*to turn on, assail in speech.* Jaiprakash rounded on the Prime Minister at the Boat Club.

7. **Round robin**—*a paper with signature in a circle so that no one may seem to be a ringleader.* They sent a round robin to the government for higher wages.

8. **Round to**—*to turn the head of a ship to wind.* The ship was rounded to at last.

9. **Round up**—*ride round and collect.* All the bad characters were rounded up by the police.

ROWDY

Rowdy-dowdy—*uproarious.* It was a rowdy-dowdy meeting.

RUB

1. **Rub-a-dub**—*the sound of a drum.* They danced rub-a-dub.

2. **Rub down**—*rub from head to foot; to search by passing the hands over the body.* The Customs people rubbed down the passengers.

3. **Rub into**—*force into pores by friction; to be unpleasantly inconsistent in emphasizing.* Oil was rubbed in.

   The police rubbed in evidence.

4. **Rub out**—*erase.* The name of Stalin has been rubbed out in Russia.

5. **Rub shoulders**—*come into social contact.* In democracy the rich and the poor rub shoulders.

6. **Rub the wrong way**—*to irritate by wrong handling.* Elders should not rub the youth the wrong way.

7. **Rub up**—*to polish; to freshen one's memory.* Let us rub up our days of love and romance.

8. **To rub one's hand**—*to show satisfaction.* When he learnt that his son got second division in the Matriculation examination, he rubbed his hands.

9. **Without rub or interruption**—*without any obstruction,* I was able to get this good post without rub or interruption.

RUIN

To bring to ruin—*to cause destruction.* The Nagas are bent upon bringing to ruin the Indian borders.

RULE

1. **As a rule**—*usually.* As a rule, the youth are restless.

2. **Be ruled**—*take advice.* Please be ruled and go home.

3. **Rule of thumb**—*any rough and ready practical method.* Governments are run by the rule of thumb.

4. **Rule out**—*exclude.* Defeatism must be ruled out.

RUN

1. **In out, of the running**—*competing with, without, a fair chance of success.* In this rat race I am out of the running.

2. **In the long run**—*in the end or final result.* In the end truth always triumphs.

3. **Make, take up, the running of**—*take the lead; to set the pace.* The Principal makes the running of a college.

4. **On the run**—*moving from place to place as a fugitive.* Since losing his job he is on the run for the last six months.

5. **Run across**—*to come upon by accident.* I ran across a friend in the Super Bazar.

6. **Run down**—*to pursue to exhaustion.* The rabbit was run down by captors.

7. **Run hard**—*to press hard from behind.* Life is running us hard now-a-days.

8. **Run in**—*to go in; to arrest and jail; to insert.* Please run in for breakfast.

   The police ran in the culprit.

   Please run in this word in the para.

9. **Run in the blood, family**—*to be hereditary character.* Defiance to insult runs in our family.

10. **Run into debt**—*to get into debt.* I ran into debt because of Alan.

11. **Run it fine**—*allow a very narrow margin.* Please run the passage fine.

12. **Run off**—*to cause to flow out; to print; to repeat.* Don't run off the tap.

    A new edition of the book was run off.

    Please run off the story.

13. **Run on**—*continue in the same line, and not in a new para.* The sentence must be run on.

14. **Run out**—*to run short; to terminate; to leak.* We ran out of petrol.

    My service has run out.

    Water is running out.

15. **Run over**—*overflow; overthrow; to read rapidly.* Water ran over the river.

    Please run over this letter.

16. **Run short**—*to lack.* We are running short of food in India.

17. **Run through**—*exhaust; read.* The boy ran through his pocket money.

    Please run through this book by tomorrow.

18. **Run together**—*to mingle or blend.* Oil and water do not run together.

19. **Run to seed**—*to go to waste.* The youthful energy of India is running to seed.

20. **Run up**—*build hastily.* They ran up a skyscraper in two years.

21. **To run the show**—*to be successfully managing some establishment.* Our proprietor runs the show of office himself.

RUSH

Not worth a rush—*useless.* I don't know how he has been appointed as Secretary; he is not worth a rush.

SABRE

Sabre-toothed tiger—*an extremely ferocious man.*
A ruthless dictator is a sabre-toothed tiger.

SACK

1. **Sack-cloth and ashes**—*repentance.* You never meet a politician in sack-cloth and ashes.
2. **To be sacked**—*dismissed.* The new clerk has been sacked because of his dishonesty.

SACRED

Sacred ape—*Hanuman.* May the sacred ape come to your aid.

SAD

In sad earnest—*seriously.* Please do not laugh. I am telling you everything in sad earnest.

SADDLE

1. **In the saddle**—*in control.* Prime Minister Vajpayee is in the saddle of India today.

2. **In the saddle**—*in office.* One must perform his duties properly in the saddle.

3. **Put the saddle on the right horse**—*to put blame where it is deserved.* In controlling corruption we must put the saddle on the right horse.

4. **Saddle up**—*to saddle a horse; mount.* When are you going to saddle up in power?

SAFE

1. **Err on the safe side**—*to choose the safer alternative.* In a social experiment, it is best to err on the safe side.

2. **Safe and sound**—*secure and healthy.* I am quite safe and sound here, I hope you are the same there.

SAIL

1. **Full sail**—*full speed.* The ship sailed full sail.

2. **Set sail**—*set forth on a journey.* They set sail for U.K.

3. **Take in sail**—*moderate one's ambition.* It is right time that you should take in sail if you want to rise in life.

4. **To sail close to the wind**—*to break a moral principle.* If your leaders sail close to the wind, what will the public do?

SAKE

1. **For old sake's sake**—*for the sake of old times; for aulalangsyne.* Let us drink milk for old sake's sake.
2. **For one's namesake**—*out of consideration for one's good name.* You should not indulge in such habits for your namesake at least.

SALE

Forced sale—*a sale compelled by a creditor.* Bankruptcy leads to forced sale.

Forced sale leads to bankruptcy.

SALT

1. **Above, below, the salt**—*of high or low status.* You are above the salt.

   I prefer to be below the salt.
2. **Lay, put, cast salt on one's tail**—*to catch someone.* When he joins the crowd in the funfare, you can't put salt on his tail.
3. **Salt down**—*preserve; lay by; store up.* Let us salt down a thousand rupees against a rainy day.
4. **Salt of the earth**—*the choice few of the highest excellence.* The salt of the earth is not found on political tables.
5. **Salt out**—*shift.* You cannot salt out truth from falsehood.
6. **Take with a grain of salt**—*to believe with some reserve.* Whatever Mr. Brown tells me, I take it with a grain of salt.

7. **To take with a pinch of salt**—*to be incredulous.* The company is taking up the union's matter with a pinch of salt.

8. **To eat one's salt**—*to be one's guest.* He is eating our salt now-a-days.

9. **True to his salt**—*faithful to his boss.* It is difficult to get a servant who is true to his salt.

10. **Worth one's salt**—*loyal; good; true.* There are few folk worth their salt today.

SAND

1. **A rope of sand**—*something nominally effective and strong.* The government laws regarding corruption seem to be a rope of sand in our country.

2. **Sands are running out**—*time is nearly at an end.* Sands are running out for the Matric examination.

SAME

1. **All the same**—*for all that.* John has not been up to my expectations.

All the same, I cannot help helping him.

2. **All the same time**—*still; nevertheless.* He was rich; at the same time, he mixed freely with the poor.

3. **The same**—*the same thing or person; the aforesaid; in the same way.* I received your letter and thank you for the same.

SAM

To stand Sam—*to pay.* Every parent has to stand Sam for his children.

SANDWICH

A sandwich of good and bad—*mixture of good and evil.* The notorious dacoit Robert was a sandwich of good and bad.

SAP

Sap the energy—*exhaust.* Hunger saps the energy of a man.

SA ! SA !

Sa ! Sa ! —*interjection of excitement.* The spectators of the match cried, sa ! sa !

SATIRE

To be satire upon—*to contradict.* People like you are merely a satire upon our society.

SAUCE

Without the sauce of—*without the interest of.* Without the sauce of promotions and ambitions one can never be successful in life.

SAVE

1. **Save appearances**—*keep up an appearance of wealth, comfort, consistency, harmony, etc.* Middle

class people are always trying to keep up their appearances.

2. **Save one's face**—*save one's honour.* Don't try to save your face if it is not worth saving.

3. **To save the situation**—*to provide a way out of difficulty.* He saved the situation by reaching there in time.

SAVING

Saving game—*a policy to avoid loss rather than to make a game.* At Trade Fair, Sunil Khanna Agriculture Co. was playing a saving game.

SAY

1. **To say a good word for**—*recommend.* If you just say a good word for me, I am sure to get this job.

2. **To say one nay**—*refuse anything.* The parents are so disgusted that they will say nay to Danny now.

SCALE

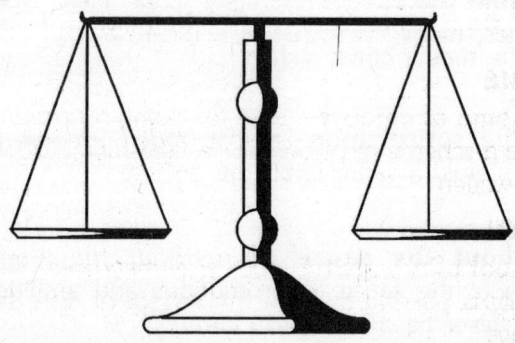

1. **Hold the scales even**—*impartial.* Our government is holding the scales even for all the communities in the country.

2. **To turn the scales**—*to outweigh the other side.* Pandit Nehru's speech always turned the scales of other parties.

SCANDAL

A scandalous state of affairs—most *shocking circumstances.* A scandalous state of affairs exists in many ministries.

SCAPEGOAT

To make a scapegoat of—*to make one bear the mistakes of another.* Bhutto made Yahya Khan scapegoat of debacle in Bangladesh, while he himself was equally responsible.

SCARCE

To make himself scarce—*to retire.* He has made himself scarce from the service now.

SCENE

Behind the scenes—*outside public view.* Behind the scenes, money is responsible for all evils.

SCHEME

Scheme of colours—*plan for doing something.* They have a scheme of colours for establishing a new factory in Sweden.

SCHOOL

School of adversity—*poor circumstances.* The whole family is passing through the school of adversity now-a-days.

SCISSORS

Scissors-and-paste—*compilation work.* Mr. Fisher is an expert in scissors-and-paste.

SCORE

1. **Go off at a score**—*to make a spirited start.* The soldiers went off at a score to restore law and order in the town.

2. **Payoff old score**—*repay old grudges.* Pathans often payoff old scores in blood feuds lasting over generations.

3. **Run up a score**—*run up a debt.* I am always mortally afraid of running up a score.

4. **Score off**—*achieve a success against; get the better of.* Pakistan must get rid of the dreams of scoring off a "Crush India War".

SCOT

Scot-free—*quite free.* A child after school is scot-free to play as he likes.

SCRAP

On the scrap-heap—*thrown aside as worn out.* Prohibition rules in many cities are now on the scrap-heap.

SCRAPE

1. **Scrape acquaintance with**—*to contrive somehow to get on terms of acquaintance.* Dr. Paul scrapes acquaintance with M.P.s'.

2. **Scrape through**—*carry out a task somehow.* I must scrape through this book to begin another.

SCRATCH

1. **Scratch of the pen**—*signature of written order.* Rich people do a lot just by the scratch of their pen.
2. **To scratch one's face**—*to attack directly.* The Chinese have no guts to scratch their face.

SCREAM

Screaming face—*highly ludicrous.* One must avoid a screaming face at a funeral.

SCREW

1. **His head is screwed on the right way**—*he is quite an intelligent person and knows what he is after.*
2. **There is a screw loose somewhere**—*all is not right.* There is a screw loose in every society.
3. **To press on the screw**—*to press for payment.* Let us first press on the screw and then see what he has to say.
4. **To screw up one's courage**—*to gather resolution.* The coming generation has to screw up its courage to face the coming hard days.

SCRUB

To want a good scrub—*thorough cleaning.* Every government wants a good scrub at regular intervals.

SEA

1. **All at sea**—*completely confused.* I am all at sea to do this work.

2. **At full sea**—*at full tide.* The ship entered the port at full sea.

3. **At sea**—*away from land; astray.* Most of the youth today are at sea.

4. **To be at sea**—*confused.* You must be firm-minded; it's no use being at sea always.

5. **To go to sea**—*to become a sailor.* Youth don't want to go to sea.

574

SEAL

1. **Give under my hand and seal**—*under my signature.* This new plan has been introduced under my hand and seal.

2. **Seal of love**—*kiss.* He has never put a seal of love on his wife.

3. **Set one's seal to**—*give one's authority.* Don't set your seal to a document without having read it.

SEAMY

Seamy side of things—*sordid affairs.* Today we are witnessing the seamy side of things in democracy.

SEASON

1. **In season**—*ripe, fit and ready for use; allowed to be killed; fit to be eaten.* India is in season for dictatorship.

2. **In season and out of season**—*at all times.* Don't bother me in season and out of season.

3. **Out of season**—*inopportune.* Religion is out of season now-a-days in politics.

SEAT

Take a seat—*sit down.* Please take a seat.

SECOND

1. **Second childhood**—*mental weakness in extreme old age.* Many old people suffer from second childhood.

2. **Second nature**—*a deeply ingrained habit.* Yoga is my second nature.

3. **Second thoughts**—*reconsideration.* On second thoughts she refused to accept his invitation to dinner.

SECRET

1. **In the secret**—*having knowledge of secret.* A secretary is usually in the secret of the minister.

2. **Of secret**—*of secret character.* It was a meeting of secret.

3. **Secret agent**—*one employed in the secret service.* The secretary of a minister may be a secret agent.

   He may be a secret agent of the enemy.

SECULAR

Secular fame—*enduring reputation.* Very few leaders enjoy a secular fame.

SEE

1. **Have seen one's best days**—*to be now on decline.* I have not yet seen my best days.

2. **Please see to it**—*please look well to it.*

3. **See about**—*consider; attend to; do whatever is to be done.* I will see about your application tomorrow.

4. **See off**—*to bid farewell.* They saw me off at the railway station.

5. **See out**—*to conduct to the door; to see to the end; to outlast.* I will see you out.

6. **See over**—*to be conducted all over.* Let us see over the whole story.

7. **See through**—*to participate in to the end; to back up till difficulties end; to understand the hidden nature of.* I will see you through your ordeals.

8. **See to**—*to look after; to make sure about.* I will see to your interest.

9. **See what I can do**—*I will do what I can*. I will see what I can do about your problem.

10. **To see off**—*to go to bid off*. We went to see off our Manager at the railway station.

11. **To see the light**—*to be published*. Our book on idioms will see the light next month.

12. **To see through**—*to help*. Can you see through me anything ?

SEEK

1. **Seek after**—*go in quest of*. Few people today seek after God.

2. **Seek for**—*look for*. I am seeking for a good friend.

3. **Seek out**—*to look for and find to bring out from a hidden place*. Good workers must be sought out.

4. **Sought after**—*in demand*. Money is much sought after.

5. **To seek**—*not to be found; wanting; at a loss to know*. I am still to seek where he is now.

6. **To seek one's fortune**—*to advance position in life; to try luck*. He is bent upon seeking his fortune these days.

SELF

To be beside one's self—*to be out of control*. The teachers should always see that the students are never beside themselves.

SELL

1. **Sell one's life dearly**—*to cause a great loss to the enemy before one is killed*. A soldier should sell his life dearly.

577

2. **Sell out**—*to dispose entirely of; to sell one's commission*. She has sold out her interests in this firm.

3. **Sell up**—*to sell off the goods for debt*. He sold up his shop to pay his creditors.

SEND

1. **Send down**—*rusticate or expel*. Many students are sent down for copying in examinations.

2. **Send for**—*to call*. I will send for you when I need your help.

3. **To send one to the right about**—*to dismiss unceremoniously*. The peon has been sent to the right about for his misbehaviour.

4. **To send word**—*to send a message*. The manager sent a word through peon to his wife.

5. **A warm send-off**—On Stanley's transfer to Delhi, the whole staff of our office gave him a warm send-off.

SENSES

1. **Bring one to one's senses**—*to make one recognise the facts*. Even two severe beatings have not brought our neighbour to his senses.

2. **Out of senses**—*mad*. Do not talk to that person; he is always out of senses.

3. **Sensual pleasure**—*joys of the flesh*. Those who live for the sensual pleasures are never successful in life.

SENSIBLE

Sensible horizon—*visible horizon*. There is little future for the youth in the sensible horizon.

SERPENT

The old serpent—*Satan*. Beware of the old serpent in whatever you do.

SERVE

1. **Serve one a trick**—*to play trick on one*. Please don't serve me a trick when serious business is on.

2. **Serve one right**—*to give due punishment*. If you come late, it serves you right to miss dinner.

3. **Serve one's time**—*to pass through apprenticeship*. You must serve your time before you can become a leader.

4. **Serve one's turn**—*to suffice for immediate* need. This food will serve my turn.

5. **Serve time**—*to undergo a term of imprisonment*. He is serving time for smuggling.

6. **To serve one out**—*to distribute*. Serve out the sweets among the children.

SERVICE

1. **Active service**—*service of a soldier.* Many Punjabis are on active service.

2. **At your service**—*at your disposal.* I am always at your service to do any job.

3. **Have seen service**—*to have fought in war.* Old soldiers have seen service in the Indo-China war.

SET

1. **Set about**—*to begin; to take in hand.* Please set about this work at once.

2. **Set afoot**—*to get going.* The government has set the project afoot.

3. **Set against**—*oppose; pitted.* Pakistan team is set against West Indies.

4. **Set agoing**—*set in motion.* Please set the plan agoing.

5. **Set apart**—*set aside.* Please set apart some money for emergency.

6. **Set by**—*lay up.* Let us set by some food for monsoon.

7. **Set down**—*to put in writing.* Let us set down this agreement.

8. **Set eyes on**—*see.* She recognised him as soon as she set eyes on him.

9. **Set fire to**—*burn.* The ruffians set fire to the house.

10. **Set forth**—*to start; to exhibit.* They set forth on a journey.

11. **Set free**—*release.* The prisoner was set free.

12. **Set hand to**—*to set to work; to begin to work on.* Do well whatever you set your hand to.

13. **Set in**—*begin*. Summer has set in.

14. **Set in hand**—*to undertake*. He has set a great work in hand.

15. **Set little, much by**—*regard, esteem, little, much*. He set much by his father.

    You set little by your friends.

16. **Set off**—*start off*. They set off for home at sunset.

17. **Set on**—*move on*; *attack on*. They set the people on him.

18. **Set oneself against**—*to oppose*. The opposition has set itself against the government.

19. **Set oneself to**—*bend one's energies*. He set himself to liberate the country.

20. **Set one's face against**—*oppose*. The Americans have set their face against Communism.

21. **Set one's heart on**—*desire very much*. Rosie has set her heart on a car.

581

22. **Set one's teeth**—*clench the teeth, in strong resolution*. He set his teeth to do the work in time.

23. **Set one up**—*enable one to begin*. She set him up in business.

24. **Set out**—*to mark off; to begin*. They set out on a long journey.

25. **Set purpose**—*great determination*. Sardar Patel was a man of set purpose.

26. **Set to**—*affix; apply to*. Set yourself to work here.

27. **Set up**—*erect; establish*. They set up a shop.

28. **Set upon**—*to make to attack*. She set her dog upon him.

29. **To set oneself against**—*oppose*. I have no guts to set myself against his arguments.

SEVEN

At sixes and sevens—*at loggerheads*. The members of this club are always at sixes and sevens.

SHADOW

1. **Shadow factory**—*a factory built for* emergency. Many shadow factories were built during the World Wars.

2. **Shadow of death**—*threatening approach of death*. Everybody today is under the shadow of death.

SHAKE

1. **Of no great shakes**—*of no great account*. Her performance is of no great shakes.

2. **Shake down**—*to cheat of* one's *money at one stroke.* He shook him down completely.

3. **Shake hands**—*to salute by grasping* hands. Let us shake hands and forget the past.

4. **Shake the dust off one's feet**—*to renounce and forget.* He shook the dust of his motherland off his feet.

5. **Shake up**—*loosen by shaking.* Shake up the bottle.

SHAPE

1. **In any shape or form**—*at all.* This agreement will not do in any shape or form.

2. **In the shape of**—*in the guise of.* One may meet an enemy in the shape of a friend.

3. **Shape one's course**—*direct one's way.* You must shape your course to business.

4. **Take shape**—*assume form.* By and by the project will take shape.

SHARE

1. **Go shares**—*divide.* Let us go shares.

2. **Share and share alike**—*in equal shares.* Let us share and share alike.

3. **To share one's last crust**—*to give away everything.* Acharya Vinoba Bhave shared his last crust.

SHARP

1. **Look sharp**—*be quick.* Look sharp lest you may not miss the train.

2. **Sharp practices**—*knavish ways.* People today make money through sharp practices.

3. **Sharp's the word**—*be brisk.* Please remember, sharp's the word, if you wish to reach the station in time.

SHED

Shed crocodile tears—*pretend sorrow.* There is no use shedding crocodile tears over your dead enemy.

SHEEP

1. **Black sheep**—*disreputable member of a family or group.* There is a black sheep in all communities.

2. **Sheep and goats**—*good and bad.* Sheep and goats always go together.

3. **Sheep's eye**—*a living, wishful glance.* He gave a sheep's eye to his wife.

4. **Sheep that have no shepherd**—*helpless crowd.* Pakistani people are sheep that have no shepherd.

SHELL

1. **Shell out**—*pay*. Please shell out a hundred rupees.
2. **To come out of one's shell**—*to throw off reserve*. Robert was at last able to come out of his shell.

SHIFT

1. **Shift about**—*to vacillate*. Please don't shift about if you want to accomplish anything meaningful.
2. **Shift for oneself**—*depend on one's own resources*. If you want to live here, you must shift for yourself.

SHILLY

Shilly-shally—in *silly hesitation*. If you want to achieve anything in life, don't shilly-shally.

SHINE

1. **Put a good shine on**—*to make a good show*. Let us put a good shine on the stage.
2. **Take the shine out of**—*outshine*. Michael is taking the shirt out of Stanley.

SHIP

Take ship—*embark*. They took ship for home.

SHIRT

1. **In one's shirt**—*wearing nothing but a shirt or nothing over the shirt*. I travel in any shirt.
2. **In one's shirt sleeves**—*with the coat off*. You work best in your shirt sleeves.
3. **Keep one's shirt on**—*Keep calm*. Despite all irritations keep your shirt on.
4. **To give one a wet shirt**—*to work one till he sweats*. The labourers in our country are being given a wet shirt by their employers.

SHOE

1. **Another pair of shoes**—*quite another matter.* I can give you food but lending money is quite another pair of shoes.

2. **Be in, step into, one's or dead man's shoes**—*to be in or succeed to one's place.* You are now stepping into the shoes of your father.

3. **Dead man's shoes**—*dead man's property.* The dead man's shoes are being auctioned in the market.

4. **Die in one's shoes**—*die by violence, especially hanging.* The criminals die in their shoes.

5. **To know where the shoe pinches**—*to know the cause of the trouble.* Only wearer knows where the shoe pinches.

SHOOT

A **shooting pain**—*a quick, sharp pain.* I have a shooting pain in my back.

SHOP

1. **To come to the wrong shop**—*to apply to the wrong person.* By calling Mr. Jackson to this place, you have come to the wrong shop.

2. **To talk shop**—*to talk business.* If you are free, we can talk shop now.

SHORT

1. **In short**—*in a few words.* In short, I am ready to help you.

2. **Make short work of**—*settle promptly.* Let us make a short work of this dispute.

3. **Short of**—*less than.* He will accept nothing short of victory.

4. **Stop short**—*to come to a sudden standstill.* India stopped short of taking over the whole of Kashmir.

5. **Take up short**—*take by surprise; interrupt curtly.* He took up the enemy short.

6. **The short and the long or the long and the short**—*in brief.* Death is the long and the short of life.

7. **To go short**—*to be less than expected.* The fruits purchased for the party have gone short.

8. **To run short**—*to get used up prematurely.* The city is running short of sugar now-a-days.

SHOT

1. **Big shot**—*a person of importance.* We are no big shots here.

2. **Shot in the locker**—*something in reserve.* You must have shot in the locker for an emergency.

3. **Stand short**—*pay the bill.* If you order coffee, you must stand short.

SHOULDER

Put one's shoulder to the wheel—*set to work in the earnest.* You must put your shoulder to the wheel immediately.

SHOW

1. **Show a leg**—*get out of bed.* When are you going to show a leg ?

2. **Show fight**—*show readiness to resist.* If somebody attacks you, you must show fight.

3. **Show forth**—*manifest; proclaim.* He showed forth his determination to achieve his objective.

4. **Show off**—*display ostentatiously.* The youth loves to show off.

5. **Show of hands**—*vote indicated by showing hands.* Many important decisions are made by show of hands.

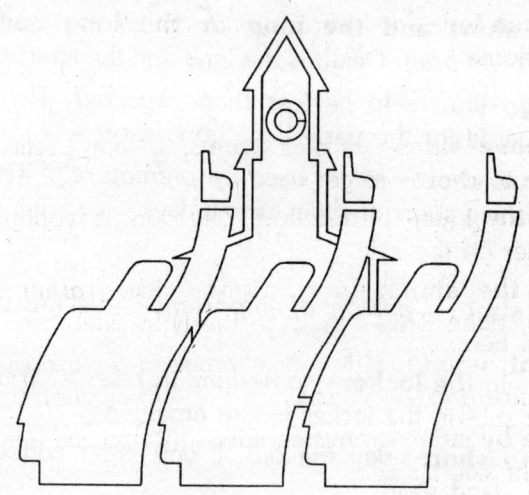

6. **Show up**—*expose; to show clearly by contrast.* He showed up the sordid deal.

He showed up in marriage.

SHUT

1. **Shut down**—*stop working.* Many factories have shut down.

2. **Shut off**—*exclude; switch off.* He was shut off from the meeting.

Current was shut off.

3. **Shut out**—*prevent from entering.* Please shut out all rowdies.
4. **Shut up**—*confine; cease talking.* He was shut in the house.
   The boy was told to shut up.

SICK

Sicken for—*show early symptoms for.* He is sickening for home.

SIDE

1. **Choose sides**—*to pick teams.* In any conflict you have to choose sides.
2. **On the side**—*in addition.* The clerk is working as a soldier on the side.
3. **On the short, long, tight, side**—*rather short, long, tight.* This shirt is on the tight side.
4. **Right, wrong, side**—*side intended to turn outward or inward.* Your short is on the wrong side.
5. **Side by side**—*alongside.* Once Indians and Pakistanis fought side by side.
6. **Take sides**—*range oneself with one party or another.* I do not take sides in politics.

SIGHT

1. **At sight**—*without previous view or study; as soon as seen; on presentation.* Please pay the bill at sight.
2. **Catch sight of**—*to get a glimpse of; begin to see.* I caught sight of Mary's sister, rosy with golden hair, whizzing and whirling about in Rosy's marriage.
3. **Out of sight**—*not in a position to be seen.* The land was soon out of sight.

4. **Put out of sight**—*remove from view*. Please put this statue out of sight.

5. **Sight for sore eyes**—*a most unwelcome sight*. Robert's brother was a sight for sore eyes.

6. **To lose sight of**—*to overlook*. Do not lose sight of minor events; sometimes they are very important in one's life.

SIGN

1. **Sign away**—*transfer by signing*. The British signed away an empire on which the sun never set.

2. **Sign in, out**—*sign one's name on coming in or going out*. Please sign your name in when you enter the office and sign your name out when you leave it.

3. **Sign on**—*engage by signature*. Twenty men were signed on the job.

SILENCE

1. **To pass into silence**—*to die*. The old man has passed into silence.

2. **To put to silence**—*to refuse an argument*. The students put the professor to silence.

SING

1. **Sing another song or tune**—*change to a humbler tune*. When his mother came, he sang another tune.

2. **Sing small**—*assume a humble tone*. It pays to sing small among the tycoons.

SIT

1. **Sit down**—*take a seat.* Please sit down.
2. **Sit on or upon**—*to hold an official enquiry.* They sat on corruption in office.
3. **Sit out**—*to sit to the end of; to outstay.* He sat out the whole function.
4. **Sit tight**—*to maintain one's position.* The ministers sit tight on their chairs.
5. **Sit under**—*to be in the habit of hearing* He sits under political orations.
6. **Sit up**—*to become alert.* When he heard the news, he sat up.

SIX

At sixes and sevens—*in disorder.* The nation today is at sixes and sevens.

SIZE

Size up—*take mental measure of.* The boss sizes up every employee.

SKELETON

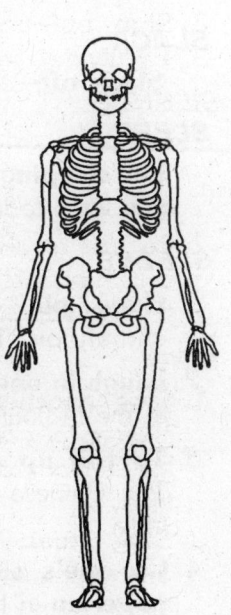

Skeleton in the cupboard, closet, house—*a hidden domestic secret, sorrow or shame.* There is a skeleton in the cupboard of every house.

SKIM

To skim the cream off—*to take the best part.* She skimmed the cream off the whole show.

SKIN

1. **By or with the skin of one's teeth**—*very narrowly.*
He escaped by the skin of his teeth.

2. **Change one's skin**—*to undergo impossible changes.*
He talks all nonsense; he cannot change his skin.

3. **Escape with the skin of one's teeth**—*narrowly.*
Many of us escaped with the skin of our teeth during
the partition of the country.

4. **Save one's skin**—*to escape without injury.* During
the partition all the persons of our street were able to
save their skins.

5. **To the skin**—*completely.* When doctor arrived he was
wet in blood to the skin.

SLACK

Slack off—*ease off.* Please slack off.

SLEEP

Let sleeping dogs lie—*avoid stirring up trouble.* If
you want to lead peaceful life, let sleeping dogs lie.

SLEEVE

1. **Hang, pin, on one's sleeves**—*to depend or rely
entirely on.* Tom hangs on my sleeves.

2. **Laugh in one's sleeves**—*laugh privately.* Don't laugh
at me in your sleeves.

3. **To roll up one's sleeves**—*to get ready to fight.*
The Chinese rolled up their sleeves in 1962 against
India.

4. **Up one's sleeve**—*in secret reserve.* He has some
power up in his sleeve.

SLIP

Slip of the tongue—*slight mistake in speaking.* Be very careful in your speech; a slip of the tongue can cause enormous harm.

SOLID

To be solid with—*to have a firm footing with.* He is solid with his service.

SMALL

1. **In small**—*in miniature.* This is my story in small.
2. **In the smallest**—*in the least.* He did not help me in the smallest.

SMOKE

1. **To end in smoke**—*to be in vain.* All my efforts ended in smoke.
2. **Like smoke**—*very quickly.* The news spread like smoke.
3. **Sell smoke**—*swindle.* Please don't sell me smoke.
4. **Smoke-room story**—*one unsuitable for telling elsewhere.* A sex scandal is a smoke-room story.
5. **Somehow or the other**—*anyhow.* I will get this job somehow or the other.

SNAIL

At a snail's pace—*very slowly.* Things in India move at a snail's pace.

SNAKE

Snake in the grass—*lurking danger.* Disease is a snake in the grass.

SNAP

Snap one's head, nose off—*to answer irritably and rudely.* If you argue with a youth, he will snap your head off.

SNEEZE

Not to be sneezed at—*not to be despised.* People spend lavishly on marriage, not to be sneezed at.

SNOW

Snowed up—*blocked or isolated by snow.* Mountain villages are snowed up in winter.

SOFT

Soft thing—*an easy job; a snug task.* His career was a soft thing.

SORRY

1. **A sorry fellow**—*mean fellow.* I hate talking to such sorry fellows.
2. **To cut a sorry figure**—*to be subjected to shame.* When he found the Principal coming to his room, he had to cut a sorry figure.

SORT

1. **A good sort**—*a decent fellow.* Jane was a good sort.
2. **In a sort**—*in a manner.* In a sort, Maria is the queen of our club.
3. **In sort**—*in a body.* They met the minister in sort.
4. **Of a sort, of sorts**—*inferior.* It was food of a sort.
5. **Out of sort**—*out of order; unwell.* He is out of sorts today.
6. **That's your sort**—*that is right; well done; go ahead.*

SOUL

Soul sick—*morally diseased.* Modern man is soul sick.

SOUP

In the soup—*in difficulty.* The whole family is in the soup now-a-days.

SPACIOUS

Spacious times—*days of expansion.* India had spacious times under Ashoka, the Great.

SPEAK

1. **Speak for**—*speak on behalf of.* Who is speaking for the teachers?
2. **Speak out**—*speak boldly.* The students often speak out their sex adventures.
3. **Speak to**—*reprove.* Mother spoke to the boy.

4. **Speak up**—*speak so as to be easily heard.* Please speak up.

5. **To speak of**—*worth mentioning.* To speak of Ram Singh, he was absent.

SPEED

Speed up—*quicken the pace of working.* We must speed up production.

SPIN

To spin a yarn—*to tell a story.* Please stop spinning a yarn and tell us something which is true.

SPINE

To the spine—*fully.* He is a sissy to the spine.

SPLIT

Split one's sides—*to laugh and laugh.* His joke split our sides.

SPONGE

To throw up the sponge—*to acknowledge defeat.* Pakistanis threw up the sponge in Dacca.

SPOON

Spoons on—*is silly in romance.* The boy spoons on his girl friend.

SPOT

Spot cash—*money down.* A car costs Rs. 85,000 spot cash.

SPRING

Spring a leak—*begin to leak.* The bucket has sprung a leak.

SPUR

1. **On the spur of the moment**—*without thinking.* He slapped the youth on the spur of the moment.
2. **Set spurs to**—*ride off quickly.* He set spurs to his horse.
3. **Win one's spurs**—*to gain distinction.* Mr. Andrews has yet to win his spurs.

SQUARE

1. **How squares go ?**—*what is doing ? How things are going ?*
2. **On the square**—*honestly.* Let us serve our motherland on the square.
3. **Square up to**—*face up to and tackle.* You must square up to your troubles.

STAIRS

Below stairs—*among the servants.* He lives below stairs.

STAMP

Stamp out—*put out by tramping.* Fire was stamped out.

STAND

1. **Make a stand**—*resist*. Bengalis made a stand against Biharis.
2. **Stand against**—*resist*. You should stand against evil.
3. **Stand by**—*support*. You should stand by your friends.
4. **Stand down**—*withdraw from contest*. How can you stand down in boxing ?
5. **Stand fast**—*to be unmoved*. You must stand fast on your promise.
6. **Stand fire**—*to face enemy*. The soldiers stood fire.
7. **Stand for**—*to be a candidate for*. He is standing for the House of Common.
8. **Stand one's ground**—*maintain one's position*. The soldiers must stand their ground.

STEAM

1. **Full steam ahead**—*at greatest possible speed*. The ship sailed full steam ahead.

2. **Under one's own steam**—*by one's own efforts.* You must work under your own steam.

STEP
Step up—*increase.* Production should be stepped up.

STILL
1. **Still and anon**—*from time to time.* He comes to my house still and anon.
2. **Still and on**—*nevertheless.* He was ill; still and on he attended the function.

STOCK
1. **Take stock in**—*to trust; to attach importance to.* I take no stock in your ability.
2. **Take stock of**—*to make a list; to estimate.* You should take stock of inimical forces.

STONE
1. **Make with a white stone**—*to mark as particularly fortunate.* Destiny has marked your career with a white stone.
2. **To leave no stone unturned**—*to do everything possible.* He left no stone unturned to help you.

STOP
1. **Stop over**—*break one's journey.* He stopped over at London.
2. **Stop thief**—*to cry for help to nab thief.* They stopped the thief.

599

STRAIN

Strain courtesy—*be discourteous to.* They showed him strained courtesy.

STRIKE

Strike root—*take root.* Trees strike roots quickly in rains.

STRING

1. **On a string**—*under complete control.* Mother has the family on a string.
2. **Pull the strings**—*use influence behind scenes.* Ministers pull the strings everywhere.

SUDDEN

Of a sudden—*all at once.* He left of a sudden.

SUM

Sum and substance—*gist.* Give me sum and substance of the story.

SUN

1. **Have the sun in one's eyes**—*to be drunk.* Don't have the sun in your eyes.
2. **Sun and sun**—*from sunrise to sunset.* He talked sun and sun.

☆ ☆ ☆

T

1. **Marked with a T**—*branded as a thief.* When were you marked with a T?
2. **To a T**—*with perfect exactness.* He did everything nicely to a T.

TABLE

1. **At table**—*at a meal.* I found the whole family at table.

2. **Lay on the table**—*lay aside for future discussion.* The House of Common laid the bill on the table for want of time.
3. **Turn the tables**—*bring out a complete reversal of circumstances.* Lord Wellington, who said, "I won the Battle of Waterloo on the cricket field of Eton," turned tables on Napoleon.

4. **Under the table**—*in a position lower than.* When we returned home, we found him under the table.

TADPOLE

Tadpole and taper—*political hacks.* There are many Tadpoles and tapers in Parliament.

TAIL

1. **Tail of the eye**—*outer corner of the eye.* He gave me tail of the eye.

2. **Turn tail**—*run away.* The enemy turned tail from the scene of the battle.

3. **Twist the lion's tail**—*irritate a stronger foe.* It is sometimes good politics to turn the lion's tail.

4. **With the tail between the legs**—*like a beaten dog.* He ran with the tail between the legs.

TAILOR

Tailor makes the man—*a man is judged by his clothes.*

TAKE

1. **Take after**—*resemble*. Rosie takes after her grandmother.

2. **Take down**—pull *down, report, write down*. Please take down the report.

3. **Take effect**—*to come into force*. New railway time-table takes effect from 1st October.

4. **Take for**—*suppose to be, especially wrong*. Whom do you take me for.

5. **Take heed**—*be careful*. Take heed lest you fall.

6. **Take in**—*comprise; enclose; to annex; to conduct to the dining table; to cheat; to accept as true*. He has taken in some of my land.

Even the cleverest man is sometimes taken in.

7. **Take in hand**—*to undertake*. Please finish the work you have taken in hand.

8. **Take into one's head**—*to be seized with a notion*. Susan has taken into her head that she is a moving T.V.

9. **Take it out of**—*to extract the outmost from; to exhaust strength or energy of*. She takes it out of her husband.

10. **Take me with you**—*let me understand what you mean*. Speak slowly and take me with you.

11. **Take notice**—*observe*. Please take notice that you have to quit this shop.

12. **Take off**—*remove; swallow*. Please take off your shoes here.

    Please take off this sandwich.

13. **Take on**—*to receive aboard; to undertake*. Don't take on more responsibilities than you can reasonably handle.

14. **Take out**—*to remove from within; extract; to go out with*. They took out a procession.

15. **Take over**—*receive by transfer*. He took over the responsibility.

16. **Take thought**—*grieve*. He took thought after his mother's death.

17. **Take to**—*become fond of*. I took to Timmy.

18. **Take to pieces**—*to separate into component parts*. Please take the machine to pieces.

19. **Take to task**—*to call to account; reprove*. Mother took the boy to task.

20. **Take to wife**—*marry*. It is dear to take to wife, for wife is dear.

21. **Take upon oneself**—*to assume; to presume.* He took upon himself to help the poor.
22. **Take up with**—*to begin to associate with; form a connection with.* He took up with his friend's wife.
23. **To take off**—*to put off.* Please take off your wet coat.
24. **To take to heels**—*to run away.* On seeing the policeman, the thief took to his heels.

TALE

1. **Be in a tale**—*to be in full accord.*
2. **Old wives' tale**—*a marvellous story for the credulous.* Religion is an old wives' tale.

TALK

1. **Talk against time**—*to keep on talking merely to fill time*. Back benchers quite often talk against time in the class-room.
2. **Talk big**—*to talk boastfully*. If your uncle is a minister, don't talk big.
3. **Talk down**—*to argue; to talk as to an inferior*. Let us talk down the differences.
   Please don't talk him down.
4. **Talking of**—*having mentioned before*. Talking of Sarojini, she was a unique lady.
5. **Talk over**—*discuss; convince*. Let us talk over the subject.
6. **Talk round**—*to persuade; to beat about a bush*. He talked me round to help him.
   Please don't talk round and round.

TALL

1. **Tall copy**—*a book with ample margin above and below*.

2. **Tall hat**—*top hat*. I don't need a tall hat to talk through the hat.

3. **Tall man of his hands**—*a deft worker; a steady fighter*. Brown is a tall man of his hands.

4. **Tall men**—*loaded dice*. He is playing with tall men.

5. **Tall talk**—*only words and no actions*. He is simply a man of tall talk; he cannot be anything in reality.

TANGENT

At a tangent—*off the course*. Your practice runs at a tangent with your precept.

TAP

1. **On tap**—*ready to be drawn upon*. I keep my money on tap.

2. **Take one's tap on one's lap**—*to bundle up and go home*. Mr. Andrews always takes his tap on his lap.

607

TAPIS

On the tapis—*under consideration*. Your case is on the tapis.

TAR

1. **Tar and feather**—*to besmear with tar and then cover with feather*. The crowned clown was tarred and feathered.

2. **Tarred with the same brush or stick**—*with the same defects*. Ram and Sham are tarred with the same brush.

3. **Touch of the tar-brush**—*an infusion of Indian, Negro and coloured blood*. Cleopatra had the touch of the tar-brush.

TASTE

1. **Good taste**—*intuitive feeling for what is aesthetically or socially right*. The school girls have good taste.

2. **To one's taste**—*to one's liking*. "To one's taste", said the old woman, and kissed the cow.

TATOO

The devil's tatoo—*drumming with finger on a table, etc. in absence of mind or impatience*. While waiting for the Governor, don't busy yourself with the devil's tatoo.

608

TEA

1. **Another cup of tea**—*a very different thing.* Going abroad is another cup of tea.

2. **A tea fight**—*a tea party.* On his success in the examination he is arranging a tea fight this evening.

3. **High tea**—*tea with snacks.* I don't want high tea.

4. **One's cup of tea**—*what appeals to one.* Money is everyone's cup of tea.

TEACH

Teach school—*to be teacher in a school.* David teaches school.

609

TEAR

1. **Tear a cat**—*to rant.* Don't tear a cat in my house.
2. **Tear off a strip**—*reprimand.* Don't tear children off a strip.
3. **Tear oneself away**—*to go away with great unwilling-ness:* She had to tear herself away from her children.
4. **Tear one's hair**—*to be in frenzy.* Don't tear your hair when someone dies.
5. **Tear up**—*to pull to pieces.* They tore up the whole show.
6. **To tear up by the roots**—*to destroy completely.* The earthquake has torn up the whole city by the roots.

TEE

1. **Tee up or off**—*to start (play).* They teed up the play.
2. **To a tee**—*exactly.* He copied the letter to a tee.

TEENY

Teeny-weeny—*very small.* His teeny-weeny son has been over-run by a car.

TEETH

In the teeth of opposition—*in the face of.* In the teeth of opposition from his class-mates, he lost the chance of senatorship.

TELL

1. **Take a telling**—*to do as one is bid without having to be told again.* Few workers today can take a telling.

2. **Tell off**—*count off; chide.* Twenty men were told off for work.

3. **Tell one's own tale**—*speak for oneself.* Please tell your own tale.

4. **Tell tales**—*to play the informer.* It does not pay to tell tales.

5. **Tell tales out of school**—*reveal confidential matters.* Please do not tell tales out of school.

6. **To tell upon**—*to affect.* His hard labour has told upon his health.

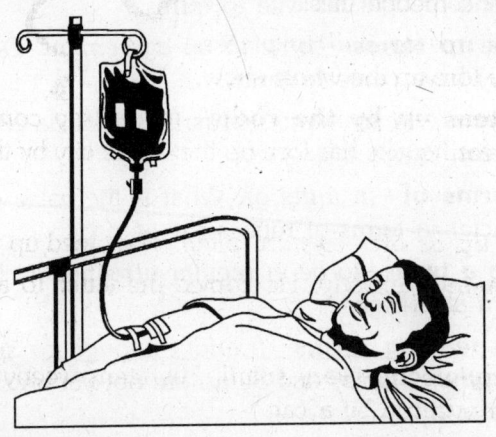

TEMPER

1. **Bad temper**—*angry mood.* I found him in bad temper.

2. **Good temper**—*good nature.* He is a boy of good temper.

3. **Lose one's temper**—*break into anger.* Please do not lose your temper.

611

TEN

Ten to one—*chances are quite high.* Ten to one are the chance of your success so you must appear in your examination.

TENOR

The tenor of one's life—*direction.* You have absolutely no right to interfere in the tenor of her life.

TERM

1. **Bring to terms**—*persuade acceptance of terms.* The husband brought his wife to terms.

2. **Come to terms**—*come to an agreement.* Dolly and Honey have come to terms.

3. **In terms**—*in so many words.* I cannot describe God in terms.

4. **In terms of**—*in units of.* What is the value of good character in terms of rupees?

5. **Keep a term**—*to be in regular attendance.* He kept a term at college.

6. **On speaking terms**—*friendly enough to speak to each other.* Stanley and Susan are not yet on speaking terms.

7. **On terms**—*on an equal footing.* Let us discuss on terms.

8. **Stand upon terms**—*insist upon conditions.* She will stand on terms before meeting her husband.

TEST

1. **To give a test**—*to appear in the examination.* I shall be taking my final test by the end of this month.

2. **To give a test**—*to examine.* The college is giving a test to all the new entrants.

THANKS

1. **No thanks to**—*not owing to.* He got his job, no thanks to his uncle.

2. **Thanks to**—*owing to.* Thanks to you doctor, I am better now.

THAT

1. **And all that**—*and all the rest of that sort of thing.* I know authorship, journalism and all that.

2. **And that's that**—*and that is the end of the matter; no more of that.* Dr. Paul was killed for leaking out the information, and that's that.

3. **This and that**—*odds and ends.* Do not waste your time in this and that.

THEN

Then and there—*at the very place and time.* The thieves caught hold of my friend and robbed him then and there.

THICK

1. **A bit thick**—*more than one can be reasonably expected to put with.* Your argument is a bit thick.

2. **Lay it on thick**—*to flatter extravagantly.* They lay it on thick in official circles.

3. **Thick-headed**—*stupid.* It is no use talking to that thick-headed fellow.

4. **Through thick and thin**—*inspite of all obstacles.* They teamed up through thick and thin.

THING

1. **Do the handsome thing by**—*treat generously.* They did the handsome thing by the rebel.

2. **Know a thing or two**—*be shrewd.* Dr. Paul knows a thing or two.

3. **Make a good thing of it**—*reap a good advantage from.* When he resigned, he made a good thing of it.

THINK

1. **Think aloud**—*utter one's thoughts in public.* Mr. Nehru was fond of thinking aloud.

2. **Think little of**—*have poor opinion of.* They think little of my dress.

3. **Think much of**—*have high opinion about.* People think much of your genius.

4. **Think out**—*devise.* Let us think out a way of peace.

5. **Think over**—*consider.* I will think over the whole matter.

6. **Think shame**—*to be ashamed.* Robert thinks shame of his failure in his class.

7. **Think up**—*find out.* Think up a plan to feed yourself.

8. **To give something a thing**—*to think about.* Develop the habit of giving something a thing among your children.

THORN

1. **Thorn in the flesh**—*a constant source of irritation.* Maria is a thorn in the flesh of her mother.

2. **To sit on the thorns**—*to be continuously in trouble.* Ever since I left that job I am sitting on the thorns.

THOROUGH

Thorough paced—*complete.* He is a good worker and you can always expect a thorough paced work from him.

THOUGHT

1. **On second thoughts**—*on reconsideration.* On second thoughts I feel he cheated me.

2. **Take thought**—*bethink oneself.* Take thought and return home.

3. **Upon, with, a thought**—*with the speed of thought.* He helped me upon a thought.

THOUSAND

1. **One in a thousand**—*rare.* The diamond offered for sale at this counter is one in a thousand.

2. **Thousand and one**—*numberless.* Thousand and one are the animals in our country but only a few are good.

THRASH

1. **To thrash a matter out**—*to discuss a subject from all angles*. Let us all sit together and thrash the matter out.

2. **To thrash a point home**—*to make one understand*. Our new Principal is not intelligent enough to thrash a point home.

THRAW

1. **Dead thraw**—*agony of death*. I found him in dead thraw.

2. **Heads and thraw**—*side by side*. They slept heads and thraw.

THREAD

1. **Lost the thread**—*lost the link*. In listening to him I just lost the thread of your speech; please repeat what you said.

2. **Thread and thrum**—*good and bad together*. You have to take thread and thrum in life.

3. **Threadbare**—*completely*. When he returned home, we discussed the problem threadbare.

4. **To hand by a thread**—*to be in a precarious state*. The patient's life is hanging by a thread.

THREE

1. **Three times three**—*three cheers thrice repeated*. We gave them three times three.

2. **Three-went ways**—*a meeting place of three roads*. You find three-went ways before my house.

THROAT

1. **Cut one's throat**—*pursue some course ruinous to one's interest.* Economic competition cuts one's throat.
2. **Give one the lie in his throat**—*accuse someone to his face.* Gandhi gave Jinnah the lie in his throat.
3. **Ram down one's throat**—*hammer home a point without listening to the other party.* He rammed his point of view down my throat.

THROUGH

1. **Be through**—*have done with.* Let us be through this work.
2. **Through and through**—*completely.* He is through and through an honest man.

THROW

1. **At a stone's throw**—*quite near.* When we were discussing about his marriage, he was standing only at a stone's throw.
2. **Those who live in glass houses should not throw stones at others**—do *not find fault with others when you have faults yourself.*
3. **Throw a fit**—*to have a fit; behave wildly.* When everybody was fit, he threw a fit.
4. **Throw a party**—*give a party.* He threw a party to celebrate the birthday of his son.
5. **Throw away**—*reject; toss aside.* He threw away all opportunities in life.
6. **Throw down**—*demolish.* They threw down the house.
7. **Throw off**—*get rid of.* They threw off slavery.
8. **Throw on**—*put on hastily.* He threw on his clothes.

9. **Throw oneself into**—*engage heartily*. They threw themselves into the battle.
10. **Throw open**—*swing open*. They threw open all doors.
11. **Throw up**—*erect hastily*. They threw up a skyscraper.

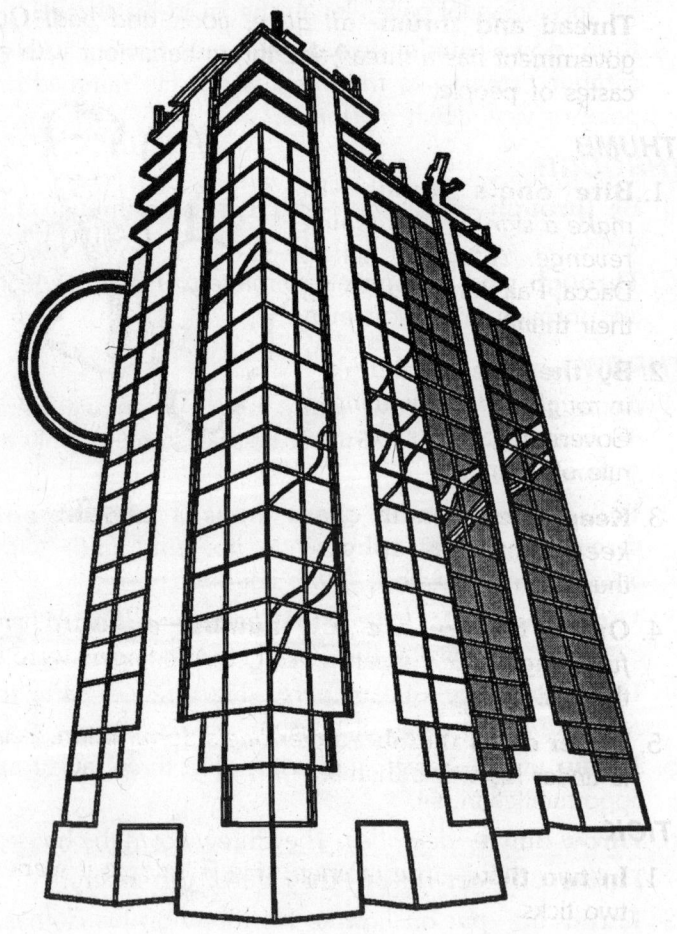

12. **To throw out**—*to remove by force.* The manager ordered the peon to throw out the new clerk on account of his misbehaviour.

THRUM

Thread and thrum—*all alike; good and bad.* Our government has a thread and thrum behaviour with all castes of people.

THUMB

1. **Bite one's thumb**—*to make a sign of threatening revenge.* After the fall of Dacca, Pakistanis were biting their thumb.

2. **By the rule of thumb**—*in rough and ready manner.* Government is run by the rule of thumb.

3. **Keep one's thumb on**—*keep secret.* Keep your thumb on his death.

4. **One's fingers are all thumbs**—*awkward and fumbling.* After Vietnam's fall, U.S.A.'s fingers were all thumbs.

5. **Under one's thumb**—*under one's domination.* Peter is under his wife's thumb.

TICK

1. **In two ticks**—*in a moment.* He will do your work in two ticks.

2. **On the tick**—*with exact punctuality*. He is always on the tick in office.

3. **Tick off**—*reprimand*. Don't tick off the maidservant.

TIDE

1. **Time and tide**—*opportunities*. Once in life the time and tide knocks the door of everyone.

2. **To go with the tide**—*to follow the masses*. One should always think and not simply go with the tide.

3. **To take at a tide**—*to take at the best possible moment*. Be wise and take everything at the tide.

4. **To tide over difficulty**—*to surmount it by sheer circumstances, and not any personal hard endeavours.*

TIDY

Neat and tidy—*absolutely clean*. In honour of the foreign Prime Minister the whole city has been made neat and tidy.

TIE

1. **Tie of blood**—*blood relationship*. Just a little misunderstanding lost the tie of blood among them.

2. **Tie up**—*parcel up*. The U.S.A. and Russia have tied up the globe.

TIGHT

1. **Tight-fisted**—*stingy*. A tight-fisted fellow is not liked by anyone.

2. **To be in a tight corner**—*to be in a difficult situation*. Since I lost that job, our whole family is in a tight corner.

TILT

Full tilt—*full speed*. He raced home full tilt.

TIME

1. **At the same time**—*simultaneously*. He wrote me a letter. At the same time, he telephoned me.
2. **At times**—*at distant intervals*. We do meet at times.

3. **Behind the times**—*not abreast of changes.* Children think their parents are behind the times.

4. **Between times**—*in the intervals.* We meet between the times we go home and return to office.

5. **Do time**—*serve a term of imprisonment.* He is doing time for forgery.

6. **For a time**—*temporarily.* I can help you only for a time.

7. **For the time being**—*at the present moment.* You can stay with me for the time being.

8. **From time to time**—*now and then.* You can ring me up from time to time.

9. **In good time**—*early enough.* Please meet me in good time before you catch the bus.

10. **Lost time**—*fall behind in time.* My watch loses time.

11. **Make time**—*to regain the advantage of lost time; find an opportunity.* Please make time to reach the top.

TIP

1. **Tip and run raid**—*sudden attack and instantaneous disappearance with the booty.* Tip and run raids are increasing all over the world day by day.

2. **Tip the scale**—*to depress one end of the scale.* He tipped the scale against me.

3. **Tip-top**—*first rate.* Our office always maintains tip-top cleanliness.

4. **To have at one's finger tips**—*to remember thoroughly.* He has mathematics at his finger tips.

TIRE

Tire down—*hunt to exhaustion.* The deer was tired down.

TITTLE

Tittle-tattle—*gossip*. Everybody is not fond of tittle-tattle.

TO

To and fro—*here and there; coming and going*. To and fro fare to London is Rs. 40,000 only.

TOKEN

By the same token—*merely by the way*. He helped me by the same token; he gave a cup of tea to everybody.

TOLL

To take in the toll—*to ensure*. The government is planning to take all the candidates in the toll.

TOMORROW

Today and tomorrow—*present and future*. Earn sufficient to spend today and tomorrow.

TONGUE

1. **To be on the tongues of men**—*much talked of*. Pandit Nehru is on the tongues of men.

2. **To hold one's tongue**—*to keep silent*. Unless somebody asks you to give your suggestion, you must hold your tongue.

TOO

1. **It is never too late to mend**—*improvement is always possible*. Start it now, it is never too late to mend.

2. **It is too good to be true**—*this is such a good news that I can't believe it is true*.

TOOTH

1. **Armed to the teeth**—*armed completely*. Pakistan is armed to the teeth.

2. **A sweet tooth**—*a taste for sweet things*. I have a sweet tooth.

3. **By the skin of one's teeth**—*narrowly*. He escaped death by the skin of his teeth.

4. **Cast, throw, in one's teeth**—*taunt*. He cast hard words in his teeth.

5. **In one's teeth**—*in one's face.* He told the truth in his teeth.
6. **In the teeth of**—*in direct opposition.* He raced in the teeth of wind.
7. **Long in the tooth**—*elderly.* She is a lady long in the tooth.
8. **To fight tooth and nail**—*with great determination or violence.* Every army has to fight tooth and nail in war.
9. **Tooth and nail**—*with full fury.* She contested elections tooth and nail.
10. **To show one's teeth**—*to adopt a threatening attitude.* Since that happening our manager always shows his teeth in the office.

TOP

1. **At the top of one's voice**—*at one's loudest.* He shouted for you at the top of his voice.

2. **Top dog**—*winner or dominant person.* For many years P.T. Usha was the top dog.
3. **Top one's part**—*to surpass oneself* in *playing it.* He has topped his part in cricket.

TORCH

To hand on the torch—*to keep knowledge alive.* Let us join hands together and make efforts to hand on the torch.

TOTAL

1. **Total abstainer**—one *who abstains from all forms of alcohol.* Gandhi was a total abstainer.
2. **Total war**—*war with all kinds of weapons.* Iraq war was a total war.

TOUCH

1. **In, out of touch**—*in or out of direct relation.* Rosy is in touch with her Principal.
   He is out of touch with his master.
2. **Touch up**—*improve by light touches.* The painter touched up the whole building.

3. **Touch upon**—*say something about.* Please touch upon nuclear energy for peace.

TRAIL

1. **Trail a pike**—*serve as a soldier.* He trailed a pike in war.

2. **Trail one's coat**—*invite a quarrel.* Don't trail your coat.

TREAD

1. **Tread in the footsteps of**—*to follow the examples of.* Let us tread in the footsteps of Pandit Nehru.
2. **Tread on one's heels**—*follow close behind.* Son treads on the heels of the father.

TREE

Up a tree—*in a fix.* He was up a tree when he lost his purse.

TROT

Trot out—*produce for show.* Please trot out the horse for sale.

TRUST

In trust—*in charge for safe keeping.* This temple is in trust.

TRUTH

1. **God's truth**—*a thing or statement absolutely true.* "Truth triumphs" is God's truth.
2. **In truth**—*truly.* In truth, man himself is God.
3. **Of a truth**—*truly.* He spoke of a truth.

TUMBLE

1. **Tumble over**—*to upset.* My plans have tumbled over.
2. **Tumble up**—*get out of bed.* Please tumble up quick.

TUNE

1. **Change one's tune**—*alter one's attitude.* An opportunist is quick to change his tune.

2. **To the tune of**—*to the amount of.* He cheated the government to the tune of a crore of rupees.

TURN

1. **By turns**—*one after the other.* The students came in by turns.
2. **Not to turn a hair**—*to be undisturbed.* The lady spoke not to turn a hair when her husband died.
3. **On the turn**—*on the turning point.* Indian politics is on the turn.
4. **Serve the turn**—*do well enough.* This book will serve the turn.
5. **Take one's turn**—*participate.* He took his turn in the freedom struggle.
6. **To a turn**—*exactly.* Please copy this letter to a turn.
7. **To have turn for**—*fitness.* My brother has turn for cricket only.
8. **To turn one's coat**—*to change to the opposite side.* Many political leaders are clever enough to turn their coats at times.

9. **Turn about**—*spin, rotate.* He turned about to face the enemy.

10. **Turn a deaf ear to**—*ignore.* He turned a deaf ear to whatever I told him.

11. **Turn against**—*rebel against.* Many Congressmen had turned against the Prime Minister.

12. **Turn around one's little finger**—*to be able to persuade to anything.* She turned the Minister around her little finger.

13. **Turn aside**—*deviate.* He has turned aside from his resolution.

14. **Turn away**—*dismiss from service.* He was turned away from his factory.

15. **Turn back**—*return.* He turned back home late at night.

16. **Turn down**—*reject.* He turned down an offer of help.

17. **Turn loose**—*set at liberty.* The horse was turned loose.

18. **Turn on**—*set running.* Please turn on the tap.

19. **Turn one's hand to**—*apply.* I will turn my hand to farming.

20. **Turn one's head**—*make proud.* Money has turned his head.

21. **Turn turtle**—*turn bottom up.* The car turned turtle.

22. **Turn up**—*to happen.* It is no use waiting for him; he will never turn up.

TWO

Two or three—*a few.* Two or three men came to me.

629

UGLY

1. **An ugly situation**—*in an awkward position.* Your today's speech in the college has put the whole class in an ugly situation.

2. **Ugly customer**—*a dangerous antagonist.* In Communism the U.S.A. has an ugly customer.

3. **Ugly duckling**—*a despised member, of a family or a group who later proves the most successful.* China is ugly duckling of the Communist family.

4. **Ugly man**—*an actual hangman.* Every criminal in jail fears the ugly man.

UMBRELLA

Nuclear umbrella—*protection against nuclear attack.* The U.S.A. has provided nuclear umbrella to NATO allies.

UMPTEENTH

Umpteenth times—*unlimited number of times.* The Mughal invaders attacked India umpteenth times until they won after many defeats.

UNACCOUNTED

Unaccounted for—*without counting.* India's losses in the Second World War are yet unaccounted for.

UNATTENDED

Unmourned and unattended—*without proper mourning ceremony.* Hitler and Mussolini died unmourned and unattended.

UNBEARABLE

Unbearably hard—*very hard.* Life today is getting unbearably hard.

UNBESOUGHT

Unbesought—*without asking for.* True fame comes unbesought. It is the fruit of great deeds.

UNCALLED

Uncalled for—*without reason; irresponsible.* Your taunting remarks are uncalled for.

UNCANNY

Uncanny and eerie—*ghostly and ghastly.* The atmosphere in a graveyard at night is uncanny and eerie.

UNCARED

Uncared for—*unprotected.* Children of the poor are uncared for.

UNCLE

1. **Uncle Sam**—*the United States or its people.* Uncle Sam is a prosperous businessman.

2. **Uncle Sham**—*(U.S.A.) in a bad sense.* Uncle Sham is unpopular everywhere in the world.

UNCLOUDED

Unclouded unconsciousness—*clear subconsciousness.* You can see God on the screen of unclouded unconsciousness. Patanjali calls this "spectator without the spectacle".

UNCROWNED

Uncrowned king—*popular hero.* Mahatma Gandhi was the uncrowned king of India.

UNCONVERTIBLE

Unconvertible fact—*undeniable thing.* Power politics is an unconvertible fact of modern world.

UNCULTURED

Uncultured and uncouth—*rough and tough.* Industry is a heaven for the uncultured and uncouth.

UNENCUMBERED

Unencumbered wedding—*a marriage in which there is no burden of in-laws and children from previous divorces.* Divorcees prefer an unencumbered second wedding.

UNDERSTANDING

To come to an understanding—*to agree.* Let us come to an understanding and end the matter once and for all.

UNDER

1. **Under cloud**—*under suspicion.* Old discredited leaders are under a cloud.

2. **Under lock and key**—*in safe custody*. We have kept all our cash and ornaments under lock and key.

3. **Under the mark**—*inferior*. People under the mark find hard to live in modern society.
4. **Under the sun**—*anywhere*. Even a beggar has some place under the sun to live.

UNFAILING

Unfailing companion—*one who accompanies you everywhere*. Your dog, money and wife are unfailing companions.

UNFOUNDED

Unfounded fears—*fears without reason*. Pakistan harbours many unfounded fears.

UNITY

1. **To be at unity with**—*to be in harmony with*. The husband and wife are at unity with each other.
2. **Unity of idea**—*coherence of thought*. Unity of my ideas is affected by your silly argument.

UPSIDE

Upside-down—*topsy-turvy*. We live in an upside-down world.

UNTIL

Until and unless—*under condition*. Until and unless you come, we will not go.

UP

1. **On one's uppers**—*very short of money*. I am on my uppers now-a-days.
2. **On the up and up**—*improving*. Since taking that medicine the patient is up and up every moment.
3. **Up and doing**—*progressive*. The youth is very much up and doing.
4. **Up and down**—*here and there*. The servants have searched the child up and down in the house but he is nowhere.
5. **Upper crust**—*aristocracy*. The upper crust rules democracy everywhere.
6. **Upper hand**—*mastery*. My wife has the upper hand in our house.
7. **Up-putting**—*lodging and entertainment*. Up-putting costs a tidy sum now-a-days.
8. **Ups and downs**—*misfortunes*. Ups and downs are always there in one's life.

634

9. **Up-to-date**—*complete.* His accounts are never up-to-date.

UPSIDE

Upside down—*in total disorder.* The new secretary has put all my files and other office papers upside down.

USE

1. **Have no use for**—*have no liking for.* I have no use for this maid.

2. **In use**—*in employment.* Machines are in use everywhere.

3. **Make use of**—*employ.* You can make use of my pen for your work.

4. **Of no use**—*useless.* This pencil is of no use to me.

5. **Of use**—*useful.* You will find pen and paper of use.

6. **Out of use**—*out of fashion, etc.* Hat is out of use now-a-days.

7. **Use and wont**—*customary practice.* It is use and wont for the trader to fleece the customer.

8. **Use up**—*consume.* Arabs are afraid that all their oil will be used up by 2050 A.D.

USUAL

As usual—*as is usual*. I go to buy milk as usual in the morning.

UTILITY

1. **Of no utility**—*of no use*. A watch is of no real utility to man.

2. **Public utility**—*of great use to public*. Electricity is a great public utility.

UTMOST

To do one's utmost—*to do one's best*. Unless you do your utmost, you will not succeed in this examination.

UTTER

1. **Utter disgust**—*extreme displeasure*. Your marksheet is an utter disgust for the whole family.

2. **Utter failure**—*extreme failure*. He is an utter failure in hockey.

UTTERANCE

To give utterance to—*express*. Please give utterance to your view.

V

V for Victory—Lord Churchill made V for victory famous with his two raised fingers during the Second World War.

VACANT

Vacant frivolities—*useless enjoyment.* Stop indulging in vacant frivolities, if you want to rise in life.

VAIN

In vain—*useless.* When a man dies, all his victories are in vain.

VALUE

1. **Good value**—*full worth in exchange.* Gold has good value.

2. **Valuable consideration**—*having monetary or material value.* Property has valuable consideration.

3. **Value in exchange**—*exchange value.* What is the value in exchange of a rupee?
4. **Value received**—*accepting a bill.* We write value received on a bill.

VAMP

To vamp up an old story—*to refurbish an old story.* Some newspapers just vamp up old stories.

VAN

In the van of—*at the head of.* In the van of this institution is its president.

VANITY

Vanity bag—*a bag containing mirror and cosmetics.* Every fashionable woman carries along a vanity bag.

VARNISH

1. **Varnishing day**—*a day before the opening of an exhibition when exhibits are varnished.* There is a varnishing day before marriage.

2. **Varnish the story**—*make it more interesting*. Every writer varnishes the story.

VARIANCE

1. **At ·variance**—*in disagreement*. Your statement is at variance with facts.

2. **To be at variance with**—*different from*. Pakistan is generally at variance with India's suggestions regarding settlement of the Kashmir problem.

VEIL

1. **Beyond the veil**—*in the unknown state after death*. Nobody knows what happens beyond the veil.

2. **To draw a veil over**—*to avoid discussing*. Let us draw a veil over the old matter and start afresh.

3. **To raise the veil**—*uncover*. He has raised the veil and the truth is known to everyone.

VEIN

1. **In one's vein**—*in one's blood*. Heroism runs in his vein.

2. **In the same vein**—*in the same style*. He talked of money and God in the same vein.

VELVET

1. **On velvet**—*in a safe and advantageous position*. The children of the rich are on velvet.

2. **Velvet glove**—*gentleness concealing strength*. He has an iron hand in a velvet glove.

VENGEANCE

1. **What a vengeance**—*What a mischief*.

2. **With a vengeance**—with *a curse; violently; exceedingly*. After long starvation he took his dinner with a vengeance.

VENT

Give vent to—*express*. The weeping woman gave vent to her feelings.

VENUE

Change of venue—*change of place*. There is a change of venue for the meetings.

VERGE

On the verge of—*on the point of*. His brother is on the verge of death.

VERY

In very need—*of a truth*. You are a great man in very need.

VEST

1. **To vest with**—*furnish*. Many Asian countries' interest is vested with each other.
2. **Vested interests**—*rich classes*. Vested interests are making a mockery of democracy.

VESTIGE

The vestige—*evidence of*. The vestige of the fact exists in the criminal's statement.

VIAL

Pore out vials of wrath—*inflict punishment*. God is pouring out vials of wrath on our sinful world.

VICE

1. **Vice versa**—*the other way round.* You may go there vice versa I shall come.
2. **Vice of the constitution**—*physical defect.* Every human being has some vice of the constitution.

VIE

Vie with—*compete.* Wealth vies with youth in romance.

VIEW

1. **Beyond the view**—*which cannot be seen.* Just within five minutes the train went beyond the view from the railway station.
2. **In view**—*in sight.* Peace in the world is not yet in view.
3. **In view of**—*because of.* The judge punished the culprit lightly in view of his youth.

4. **On view**—*open for public inspection*. God is not on view.
5. **Point of view**—*opinion*. His point of view differs much from ours.
6. **To come to view**—*to be seen*. The ship has now come to view.
7. **With a view to**—*having in mind*. I got a passport with a view to going abroad.

VINE

Dwell under one's vine and fig tree—*to live at peace on one's own land*. Nobody today wants to dwell under his own vine and fig tree.

VIOLENT

To lay violent hands on—*to kill*. The thief laid violent hands on the Seth and ran away with five thousand rupees.

VIRTUE

1. **By virtue of**—*because of*. He got success by virtue of hard work.
2. **Make a virtue of necessity**—*do as a sense of duty what one has to*. If you cannot make a necessity of virtue, at least make a virtue of necessity.

VISIBLE

Visible means—*means which are clear to others*. Everybody has visible and invisible means of income to tide over social requirements.

VISIT

1. **To pay a visit**—*to go and meet*. During my sickness, he paid me a visit daily.

2. **Visit with**—*to be a guest with.* He visited with a friend.

VISTA

To open a new vista—*to show new prospects.* The government has opened many vistas for young men of our country.

VOGUE

In vogue—*in fashion.* Waist-coat is no longer in vogue.

VITAL

1. **Vital air**—*oxygen.* Nobody can live without vital air.
2. **Vital spark**—*principle of life in man.* There is a vital spark in the universe.

VOICE

1. **To give voice to**—*express.* All the members of the club have equal right to give voice to their feelings.

2. **With one voice**—*unanimously.* The new president was elected with one voice by the Congress party.

WADE

1. **Wade in**—*make a very vigorous attack*. The Taliban waded in war against the Americans.
2. **Wade into**—*tackle a job energetically*. India should wade into food and population problem.
3. **Wade through book**—*read it despite dullness*. I cannot wade through this book.

WAGER

Wager of battle—*trial by combat*. The ancients decided their differences by wager of battle.

WAGON

Hitch your wagon to a star—*have big ambitions in life*. If you can't hitch your wagon to earth, don't hitch your wagon to star.

WAIF

Waifs and strays—*homeless, destitute people*. India is full of waifs and strays.

WAIT

1. **Lie in wait**—*hunt*. People today lie in wait for money-making.
2. **Play a waiting game**—*to avoid action to take maximum advantage later*. Many businessmen and black-market operators play a waiting game.

3. **Wait attendance on**—*attend*. Many men wait attendance on a minister.

4. **Wait up**—*stay out of bed waiting*. She waited up till morning.

5. **Wait upon**—*attend*. Two servants waited upon him.

WAKE

1. **In the wake of**—*close behind*. Son follows in the wake of father.

2. **Wake a night**—*awake all night*. Wake a night to concentrate your mind on higher things.

3. **Wake upto**—*become conscious of*. Wake upto your responsibilities in life.

WALK

1. **Walk into**—*to beat; to storm at; to eat heavily of*. He walked into her.

    They walked into marriage meal.

2. **Walk off**—*depart; leave*. He walked off from the meeting.

3. **Walk out**—*to leave as a gesture of disapproval*. They walked out of the Parliament.

4. **Walk out on**—*leave in lurch*. He walked out on his wife.

5. **Walk over**—*cross over*. The leader walked over to the opposition.

6. **Walk the chalk**—*keep a correct course in manners and morals.* Few people walk the chalk today.

WALL

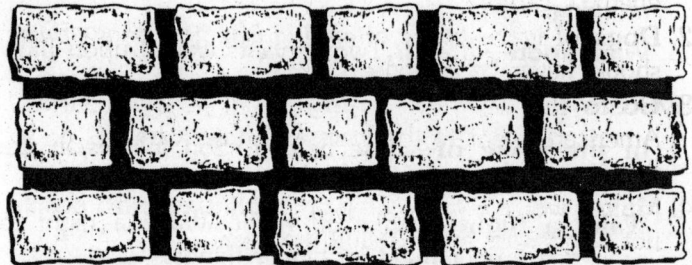

1. **Drive to the wall**—*to push to the extremes.* The government must not drive the people to the wall.
2. **Go to the wall**—*to be hard pressed.* American forces went to the wall in Iraq.
3. **Hang by the wall**—*to remain unused.* Don't hang by the wall when there are things to be done.
4. **Push to the wall**—*to force to give place.* Please don't push me to the wall.
5. **To run one's head against the wall**—*attempt impossibilities.* If you just leave the habit of running your head against the wall, I am sure you can rise to a good position in life.
6. **Wall up**—*to block with a wall; to entomb in a wall.* The sons of Guru Gobind Singh were walled up.
7. **With one's back to the wall**—*in desperate straits.* The American troops fought with their back to the wall.

WANE

On the wane—*in decline.* Popularity of America is on the wane.

WAR

1. **Carry the war into the enemy's camp**—to *take the offensive boldly.* Iraqis carried the war into the enemy's camp.
2. **Dogs of war**—*havoc attending war.* The dogs of war should never be let loose.
3. **Go to the wars**—*to go to fight in foreign country.* Americans went to the wars and now wars will go to the Americans.
4. **Make, wage, war**—*carry on hostilities.* India should not wage wars and disband the army.
5. **War baby**—*a baby born during the war, especially a soldier's illegitimate child.* War babies had been flown to America from Vietnam.
6. **Warm reception**—*vigorous resistance.* The Americans received a warm reception in Afghanistan.
7. **War of nerves**—*threats of war.* Pakistan is always waging a war of nerves on India.
8. **War to the knife**—*struggle to the bitter end.* Dara Singh is strong enough to war to the knife.

WARM

1. **A warm corner**—*a hot part of battle.* The days have gone when Japan was a warm corner of Asia.

2. **Keep a place warm**—*hold place for someone else.* The Congress is keeping the place warm for the Communists.

3. **To give warm reception**—*to welcome enthusiastically.* Wherever Pandit Nehru went, he was given a warm reception.

4. **To make things warm for one**—*to create strong feelings against one.* Never make things warm for your friends.

5. **Warm up**—*to become animated.* When I talked of Lahore, my friend warmed up.

6. **Warm up to**—*become enthusiastic about.* Pakistan warmed up to India's nuclear test for peace.

WASH

1. **To wash one's hands off**—*to give up altogether.* I have washed my hands off my hope for getting through in the examination.

2. **Wash dirty linen in public**—*to expose private affairs.* Let us not wash dirty linen in public.

3. **Wash down**—*eat hard food with drinks.* Wash down your food with tea or coffee.

4. **Wash one's brain**—*to drink copiously.* Don't wash your brain here.

5. **Wash up**—*wash face and hands; wash dishes; wash rooms, etc.* Please wash up for dinner.

WASTE

1. **In waste**—*in vain.* All my work is in waste.

2. **Run to waste**—*to be waste.* India's rivers are running to waste.

3. **To go to waste**—*to be wasted*. Sincere efforts never go to waste.

WATCH

1. **On the watch**—*waiting*. Please hurry up, the taxi is on the watch outside.
2. **To be on the watch**—*to be on the look out*. I am on the watch for a good servant.
3. **To pass as a watch in the night**—*to be forgotton soon*. Rest assured, our friendship will never be passed as a watch in the night.
4. **Watch in**—*keep awake to welcome*. Watch in the New Year.
5. **Watch one's steps**—*to step with care*. Watch your steps as you enter life.
6. **Watch out**—*be careful*. Watch out for the serpent in the grass.

7. **Watch up**—*sit up at night.* I have watched up many nights.

WATER

1. **Above water**—*out of difficulties.* Thank God! I am above water.
2. **Blood is thicker than water**—*there is always a greater sympathy for relatives than for anyone else.*
3. **Deep waters**—*difficulty or distress.* She is in deep waters.

4. **Hold water**—*to be correct*. Your theory does not hold water.

5. **In smooth waters**—*going easily*. They are passing a life in smooth waters.

6. **Keep one's head above water**—*to keep free from debt*. It is in your interest to keep your head above water.

7. **Like water**—*copiously*. Don't waste money like water.

8. **Make a hole in water**—*down oneself*. Shame on you; Make a hole in water.

9. **Make the mouth water**—*tempt*. Your pudding makes my mouth water.

10. **Make water**—*urinate*. Don't make water here.

11. **Still waters run deep**—*Quiet exterior hides deep emotions.*

12. **Throw oil on troubled waters**—*restore peace*. If there is a quarrel in the family, it is best to throw oil on troubled waters.

13. **To be, go, on the water wagon**—*to abstain from alcoholic liquors*. I am always on the water wagon.

14. **To throw cold water on**—*to discourage*. Please do not throw cold water on your son or else he will become a coward.

15. **Under water**—*below the surface*. There is much under water.

16. **Water of life**—*spiritual refreshment*. Yoga promises water of life.

WAX

Wax and wane—*increase and decrease*. I have guts enough to stand in wax and wane.

WAY

1. **By the way**—*incidentally.* By the way, do you want lunch ?
2. **Come one's way**—*come in the same direction.* Money has never come my way.
3. **Go the way of all earth**—*die.* Timmy has gone the way of all earth.
4. **Have one's way**—*carry one's point.* You cannot have your way in everything.

WEAR

1. **To wear a principle in one's heart**—*be devoted to.* Vinobaji wore the principle of sympathy for poor in his heart.
2. **To wear well**—*to maintain youthful strength.* Even at the age of fifty he wears well.
3. **Wear and tear**—*loss by way of use.* Everything undergoes wear and tear.
4. **Wear away**—*impair.* Don't wear away your health by over-work.

WEATHER

1. **Keep one's weather eye open**—*to be alert.* While you live here, keep your weather eye open.
2. **Make fair weather**—*flatter.* People make fair weather with ministers.
3. **Under the weather**—*indisposed; drunk.* The man is under the weather.

WEIGH

Weigh up—*consider the quality of a man.* Weigh up your friends.

WELL

Well up in—*well versed in*. He is well up in mathematics.

WEND

Wend one's way—*make one's way*. You must wend your way in life.

WET

Wet out—*wet thoroughly*. Wet out the cloth to clean it.

WHEEL

1. **Go on wheels**—*move swiftly*. Please go on wheels to your house; don't loiter here.
2. **To break a butterfly upon the wheel**—*to inflict punishment out of all proportion to the crime*. If a child plays tricks, don't break a butterfly upon the wheel.
3. **To break on the wheel**—*to kill*. The thief broke on the wheel of the old man and ran away with five hundred rupees.
4. **Turn of wheel**—*change of fortune*. Just a little turn of wheel has made him a millionnaire in two years.

5. **Wheel of life**—*vital processes*. One dies without the wheel of life.

6. **Wheels within wheels**—*complicated influences at work*. There are wheels within wheels in the political world.

WHIP

1. **To have the whip- hand of**—*in a position to control*. The new teacher is having a whip-hand over the naughty students.

2. **Whip and spur**—*with great haste*. They went whip and spur.

3. **Whip the cat**—*practise small economies*. Every housewife whips the cat.

WHIRL

In a whirl—*confusion*. Try to get out of a whirl.

WHISTLE

1. **Let one go whistle**—*disregard one's wishes*. Unless you let her go whistle you cannot do anything good for her.

2. **Wet one's whistle**—*to take a drink of liquor*. Don't wet your whistle too often.

3. **Whistle down the wind**—*abandon*. In view of foreign exchange difficulties, the government had to whistle down the wind of imports in the country.

4. **Whistle for**—*summon by whistling*. Don't whistle for a girl here.

5. **Worth the whistle**— *worth the trouble of calling for*. Is your girl friend worth the whistle ?

WHITE

1. **White night**—a *sleepless night*. We passed a white night.

2. **White slave**—*prostitute*. There are white slaves in every city.

WIG

Wigs on the green—*fray*. Don't enter wigs on the green.

WILL

1. **Have one' will**—*obtain what one desires*. The children have their will.
2. **Willy-nilly**—*willingly or unwillingly*. Willy-nilly I have to go out of Delhi.
3. **Work one's will**—*do exactly what one chooses*. Only God can work His will in the world.

WIN

1. **Win by a short head**—*to win narrowly*. He won the race by a short head.
2. **Win in a canter**—*to win easily*. They won the race in a canter.
3. **Win one's spurs**—gain *reputation by merit*. Suchita has won her spurs.

WIND

1. **Find out how the wind blows**—*what developments are likely*. Let us go and find out how the wind is blowing regarding the election of president.
2. **Get the wind of**—*secure an advantage over*. She will never get the wind of him.
3. **Go like the wind**—*swiftly*. An aeroplane always goes like the wind.
4. **In the teeth of the wind**—*right against the wind*. He cycled in the teeth of the wind.
5. **Sow the wind and reap a whirlwind**—*act wrongly and receive crushing punishment*. Modern youth sows the wind and reaps the whirlwind.
6. **To come from the four winds**—*to come from all sides*. We were caught in heavy rain when it came from the four winds last night.

WIPE

1. **To wipe one's eyes**—*to comfort*. Money wipes everybody's eyes.

2. **Wipe out**—*destroy utterly*. The whole city has been wiped out by the earthquake.

WISE

Wise woman—*witch*. Beware of the wise woman in politics.

WISH

1. **If wishes were horses then beggars would ride**—*wishes alone cannot fulfil desires*.

2. **Wishful thinking**—*belief founded on wishes rather than facts*. To migrate to Canada is my wishful thinking.

WIT

1. **At one's wit's end**—*utterly perplexed*. I was at my wit's end for a few rupees.
2. **Have one's wits about one**—*to be alert and resourceful*. You must have your wits about you if you seek a good career.

WOE

In weal and woe—*in prosperity and sorrow*. I shall stand by you in weal and woe.

WOLF

1. **Cry wolf**—*give false alarm*. Please don't cry wolf here.
2. **Have a wolf by the ears**—*to be in a difficult situation*. Vajpayee has the wolf by the ears.
3. **Have a wolf in the stomach**—*to be very hungry*. Just now I have a wolf in the stomach.
4. **Keep the wolf from the door**—*keep away poverty or hunger*. It is not easy to keep the wolf from the door.
5. **See a wolf**—*to be tongue-tied*. When he met his boss, he saw a wolf.
6. **A wolf in sheep's clothing**—*hypocrite*. A diplomat is a wolf in sheep's clothing.

WOMAN

1. **Kept woman**—*mistress*. She is a kept woman.
2. **Woman of the world**—*woman of fashion*. She is a woman of the world.

WOOD

Cannot see the wood from the tree—*cannot grasp the whole because of too much of details.* A modern man cannot see the wood from the trees.

WOOL

Pull, draw, the wool over the eyes—*hoodwink.* The leaders are drawing the wool over the people's eyes.

WORD

1. **A man of word**—*who keeps promise.* He is a man of word.
2. **A good word**—*recommendation.* I will put in a good word for you.
3. **At a word**—*at once.* He does everything at a word.
4. **Break one's word**—*fail to fulfil one's promise.* Please never break your word.
5. **By word of mouth**—*orally.* Wisdom travels best by word of mouth.
6. **Fair words**—*flattery.* You can get anything done by fair words.
7. **Have a word with**—*converse.* I will have a word with you before you go.
8. **In a word**—*in short.* In a word, I cannot help you.
9. **In so many words**—*explicitly.* Tell him everything in so many words.
10. **In word**—*in speech only.* Convey the message in word.

WORK

1. **Have one's work cut out**—*have one's work proscribed.* His work was cut out in films.

2. **Out of work**—*unemployed*. Million are out of work today.

3. **Shoot the works**—*make maximum effort*. He shot the works for success.

4. **Work for, against**—*exert oneself for or against*. He is working for prohibition.

5. **Work off**—*get rid of*. Work off all worries.

WORLD

The other world—*the non-material sphere, the spiritual world*. I, who belong to the other world, strayed here by error.

WORM

To worm himself into another's favour—*to get into a person's good graces through underhand means*. He wormed himself into her favour.

WORST

If worst comes to worst—*even under the worst circumstances*. If worst comes to worst I will lose only five hundred rupees.

WORTH

For all one is worth—*with all one's might*. He worked for all he was worth.

WRITE

1. **To write oneself out**—*to exhaust one's capacity to write*. He has now written himself out for the last few months.
2. **Writing on the wall**—*a happening foreshadowing disaster*. Famine and overpopulation is a writing on the wall.

★ ★ ★

661

X-RAY

X-ray scrutiny—*careful examination*. The whole controversy must be submitted to X-ray scrutiny to arrive at the truth.

XANTHIC

Xanthic flowers—*persons of everlasting beauty*. Her daughter is a xanthic flower.

XANTHIPPE

Xanthippe of Socrates—*a quarrelsome woman.*
Don't have Xanthippe of Socrates as your wife.

XANTHOUS

Xanthous eye—*prejudice; jaundiced eye.* Don't see
the world with a xanthous *eye.*

XENOMANIA

Xenomania—*an inordinate attachment to thing
foreign.* The upper crust of society suffers from
xenomania.

XENOPHOBY

Xenophoby—*fear of things foreign.* Common people
suffer from xenophoby.

YANKEE

Yankee—*an American citizen.* Yankees have invaded the world.

YARD

1. **By the yard**—in *large quantities.* We bought cloth by the yard.
2. **Yard of ale**—*a tall slender glass of wine or its contents.* He had a yard of ale before he set to work.

YARN

To spin a yarn—*to tell tales.* Would you give up the habit of spinning a yarn?

YAWN

Yawning gap—*big difference*. There is a yawning gap between the rich and the poor.

YEAR

1. **Year by year**—*yearly*. We are making progress in our business year by year.

2 **Young for one's years**—*bearing age lightly*. Your father looks young for his years.

YELLOW

1. **Yellow flag**—*yellow-coloured people*. The ship flew a yellow flag.

2. **Yellow jack**—*yellow fever*. He suffered from yellow jack.

3. **Yellow press**—*newspapers giving sensational news*. There is yellow press everywhere.

4. **Yellow streak**—*a tendency to cowardice*. There was yellow streak even in Napoleon.

YEOMAN

Yeoman's service—*powerful aid*. They did me a yeoman's service during my sickness.

YOKE

1. **Put a yoke on**—*join together*. The students should put a yoke on themselves.

2. **Yoke of opinion**—*force of public opinion*. The Prime Minister was left with no choice except to accept the yoke of opinion.

YON

Hither and yon—*hither and thither*. Why are you wandering hither and yon?

YOU

1. **You and Yours**—*you and your family and property*. You need peace for you and yours.

2. **You are another**—*you are different from what you used to be*. After your marriage, you have become another.

YOUNG

1. **With a young**—*pregnant*. The woman is with a young.

2. **Young blood**—*young people*. Young blood is in revolt.

3. **Young things**—*young persons*. Young things should realize their responsibilities.

★ ★ ★

ZEAL

With zest and zeal—*with great fervour.* The main quality in him is that he does everything with zest and zeal.

ZEND

Zend Avesta—*ancient sacred Parsi scripture.* There is spiritual light and life in Zend Avesta.

ZENITH

To be at one's zenith—*to be at the highest point of fame, glory, wealth, etc.* Elizabeth was at her zenith in her last days.

ZERO

1. **To become zero**—*to become useless.* Because of shortage of money all your plans have become zero.

2. **Zero hour**—*exact time fixed for launching, etc.* Zero hour is approaching for our inauguration ceremony.

ZEST

1. **To add zest to**—*to make interesting.* Unless the writer adds zest to his writing the readers will not buy his books.

2. **Zest and zeal**—*with fervour.* Near the exams students study books with zest and zeal.

ZIGZAG

1. **Zigzag**—*short, sharp turning.* Life is full of zigzags.
2. **Zigzaggery**—*angular crookedness.* There is much zigzaggery in the world today.

ZOOT

Zoot suit—*a flashy type of man's suit, baggy at the knees.* He was dressed in zoot suit.